Change in Communist Systems

396 - 1
72

Contributors

JEREMY R. AZRAEL

GEORGE W. BRESLAUER

R. V. BURKS

PAUL COCKS

ALEXANDER DALLIN

ZVI Y. GITELMAN

CHALMERS JOHNSON

RICHARD LOWENTHAL

ALFRED G. MEYER

JOHN MICHAEL MONTIAS

DANKWART A. RUSTOW

H. GORDON SKILLING

Change in Communist Systems

Edited by
CHALMERS JOHNSON

Stanford University Press
Stanford, California

Stanford University Press
Stanford, California
© 1970 by the Board of Trustees of the
Leland Stanford Junior University
Printed in the United States of America
Cloth ISBN 0-8047-0723-5
Paper ISBN 0-8047-0828-2
Original edition 1970
Last figure below indicates year of this printing:
82 81 80 79 78 77

Preface

According to one of the latest samples of Poland's most endearing exports—jokes about Communist societies—a high-ranking Soviet dialectician recently addressed an assembly of Marxist-Leninist theoreticians in Warsaw. There he reported the most up-to-the-minute discovery of Moscow's hard-working social scientists: "Only the future is certain; the past is always changing."

Whatever the future may hold, our dialectician's comment applies equally well to the current state of Western attempts to understand Communist societies. Our theoretical pictures of Communist systems and our interpretation of the meaning of their dramatic histories range from an undiluted totalitarianism to theories of "nation-building" and "modernization," including some theoretical positions that view Communism as epiphenomenal, the proper conceptual entity being "Russia" or "China" as unique systems. At the conference from which the present volume grew one opinion or another was not favored, but there was an attempt to mitigate the confusion brought about by Communism's changing past. Under the sponsorship of the American Council of Learned Societies, the conferees met for two months of seminars, lectures, study, and informal discussions before they even selected the particular topics that were to be studied and written about by individual participants. This procedure explains in part why two years passed before this volume was published; hopefully the procedure has also fostered a greater awareness and appreciation in each participant, and perhaps in the reader, of just how difficult it is to capture the core of commonality shared by the fourteen nations calling themselves Communist.

The twenty-three scholars who participated in the conference that preceded the writing of this book are:

Jeremy R. Azrael	Political Science	Chicago
Joseph S. Berliner	Economics	Brandeis
Severyn Bialer	Political Science	Columbia
George Breslauer	Political Science	Michigan
R. V. Burks	History	Wayne State
Paul M. Cocks	Political Science	Harvard
Alexander Dallin	Political Science	Columbia
Alexander Eckstein	Economics	Michigan
Zvi Y. Gitelman	Political Science	Michigan
Chalmers Johnson	Political Science	Berkeley
Kenneth Jowitt	Political Science	Berkeley
Kenneth Lieberthal	Political Science	Columbia
Richard Lowenthal	Political Science	Berlin
Maurice Meisner	History	Wisconsin
Alfred G. Meyer	Political Science	Michigan
John Michael Montias	Economics	Yale
Michel Oksenberg	Political Science	Stanford
Dankwart Rustow	Political Science	Columbia
H. Gordon Skilling	Political Science	Toronto
Robert C. Tucker	Political Science	Princeton
Ezra F. Vogel	Sociology	Harvard
Benjamin S. Ward	Economics	Berkeley
Martin Whyte	Sociology	Harvard

The editor made the selection of papers to be included in this volume in consultation with other members of the ACLS Planning Committee for Comparative Communist Studies. Alexander Dallin and George Breslauer collaborated on what ultimately proved to be a book-length study of *Political Terror in Communist Systems,* which is being published by Stanford University Press simultaneously with this volume. A modified chapter from the Dallin-Breslauer volume particularly relevant to the theme of change is included here. For further information on the Workshop on the Comparative Study of Communism, 1968, readers should consult the account of the seminars themselves written by R. V. Burks and published in the *Newsletter on Comparative Studies of Communism,* II: 2 (June 1969), 2–11.

I would like to thank Gordon B. Turner, Vice-President of the American Council of Learned Societies, for his assistance and support of the Planning Group's activities, and to acknowledge my gratitude to Anne Firth Murray and J. G. Bell of Stanford University Press for their expert editorial assistance. Josephine Pearson of the Center for Chinese Studies, University of California, Berkeley, was of constant assistance to me in corresponding with and reproducing the work of many authors.

Finally, I would like to thank the authors and seminar participants themselves. Their commitment to the project of comparing Communist nations and to seeking serious answers to baffling problems of change made possible that all-too-rare but most exciting of scholarly activities—the exchange of views on problems about which the best informed will differ.

Berkeley, California
December 1969

CHALMERS JOHNSON

Contents

Contributors

JEREMY R. AZRAEL received his doctorate from Harvard University in 1961. He is presently a Professor of Political Science and Chairman of the Committee on Slavic Area Studies at the University of Chicago. He is the author of *Managerial Power and Soviet Politics* (1968) and of a forthcoming book on education and political development in the Soviet Union, as well as of numerous essays and articles.

GEORGE W. BRESLAUER received a B.A. and a Certificate in Russian Studies from the University of Michigan in 1966 and 1968 and is currently working on a doctoral dissertation in political science at that university on the subject of "Bureaucracy and Policy in the USSR." He is the co-author, with Alexander Dallin, of *Political Terror in Communist Systems* (1970).

R. V. BURKS is a Professor of History at Wayne State University, Detroit. He is the author of *The Dynamics of Communism in Eastern Europe* (1961) and the editor of *The Future of Communism in Europe* (1969). From 1961 to 1965 he was policy director of Radio Free Europe in Munich. He currently serves as a consultant to the RAND Corporation, Santa Monica, California.

PAUL COCKS received his B.A. from Stanford in 1961. He then spent eight years in graduate work at Harvard, where he received master's degrees in Soviet studies (1963) and East Asian studies (1966) and a doctorate in political science in 1968. He is now a Research Fellow of the Russian Research Center and an Assistant Professor of Government at Harvard.

ALEXANDER DALLIN is Adlai E. Stevenson Professor of International Relations at Columbia University. He was Director of the Russian Institute at Columbia (1962–67) and served as chairman of the Planning Group on Comparative Communist Studies of the American Council of Learned Societies (1966–69). He is the author of *German Rule in Russia, 1941–45* (1957), *The Soviet Union at the United Nations* (1962), and *The Soviet Union, Arms Control and Disarmament* (1964), among other books; he has edited *The Soviet Union in World Affairs* (1960), *Diversity in International Communism* (1963), *Soviet Politics: Seven Cases* (1966), and *Soviet Politics since Khrushchev* (1968).

ZVI GITELMAN received his undergraduate and graduate training at Columbia University, where he also taught in the Department of Government and was a Fellow of the Research Institute on Communist Affairs. He is now an Assistant Professor of Political Science at the University of Michigan. He is the author of articles on Soviet nationality policy in *Survey, Problems of Communism*, and other scholarly publications; his study of the Jewish sections of the Soviet Communist party will be published by Princeton University Press. He is now conducting research on political change in Eastern Europe, focusing on attitude formation and institutional development.

CHALMERS JOHNSON received his B.A. in economics and his doctorate in political science from the University of California, Berkeley, where he is presently a Professor of Political Science and Chairman of the Center for Chinese Studies. His major works are *Peasant Nationalism and Communist Power* (1962), *An Instance of Treason* (1964), and *Revolutionary Change* (1966). He has visited Asia numerous times, doing research in Hong Kong and Japan, and has received research fellowships from the Ford Foundation and the Social Science Research Council. He is a member of the Joint Committee on Contemporary China of the Social Science Research Council and the American Council of Learned Societies.

RICHARD LOWENTHAL is Professor of International Relations at the Free University, West Berlin. He has long specialized in the comparative study of totalitarian movements and particularly in the study of relations between Communist governments and parties. He is the author of *World Communism: The Disintegration of a Secular Faith* (1964).

ALFRED G. MEYER, who received his graduate training at Harvard University, has taught at the University of Washington and Michigan State University and is now a Professor of Political Science and Director of the Center for Russian and East European Studies at the University of Michigan. His books, which deal with Soviet foreign policy, Marxist and Leninist theory, and Soviet politics, include *Leninism* (1957) and *The Soviet Political System* (1966). At the present time he is interested primarily in problems of political philosophy.

JOHN MICHAEL MONTIAS received his doctorate from Columbia in 1958 and is now a Professor of Economics and Chairman of the Russian and East European Council at Yale University. He is the author of *Central Planning in Poland* (1962), *Economic Development in Communist Rumania* (1967), and a number of articles on economic systems, foreign trade, and economic development in Eastern Europe. His major interest at present is the methodology of system comparisons.

DANKWART A. RUSTOW received his early education in his native Germany and in Turkey. He received his B.A. from Queens College and his doctorate from Yale. He taught Near Eastern politics at Princeton (1952–59) and since then has been teaching at Columbia, where he is Professor of International Social Forces. His publications include *The Politics of Compromise: A Study of Parties and Cabinet Government in Sweden* (1955), *Politics and Westernization in the Near East* (1956), *A World of Nations* (1967), and contributions to scholarly journals here and abroad. He also has edited *Political Modernization in Japan and Turkey* (with R. E. Ward, 1964) and *Philosophers and Kings: Studies in Leadership* (1970).

H. GORDON SKILLING graduated from the University of Toronto in 1934, studied at Oxford as a Rhodes scholar, and received his doctorate from the School of Slavonic Studies at the University of London, England, in 1940. He is now Professor of Political Science and Director of the Centre for Russian and East European Studies at the University of Toronto. He is the author of *Canadian Representation Abroad* (1945), *Communism National and International* (1964), and *The Governments of Communist East Europe* (1966). He is the co-author with Franklyn Griffiths of *Interest Groups in Soviet Politics* (1970) and with Peter Brock of *The Czech Renascence of the 19th Century* (1970). He is at present engaged in a study of Czechoslovakia's "interrupted revolution of 1968."

Change in Communist Systems

Comparing Communist Nations

CHALMERS JOHNSON

On August 21, 1968, the armed forces of the Soviet Union and its satellite and client states in Eastern Europe occupied Czechoslovakia. That this act had profound political and moral consequences was apparent to all; it also had far-reaching intellectual implications for students of Communist systems. The events of August 1968 reenergized in the most dramatic manner possible the continuing debate over the direction, tempo, and form of change in the Communist world, and indeed in the entire international system. Some argued that the Czech invasion showed how little the Soviet dictatorship had changed in any fundamental respect. Others, citing Czechoslovakia as an example of how greatly things had changed, attributed the invasion to political "backlash," to a last desperate effort by the old order to reverse the prevailing socioeconomic trends. At the very least, the experience of Czechoslovakia, by showing that change in the Communist world is neither easy nor automatic, made several simple theories of the inevitability of "liberalization" appear jejune. Intellectually and academically, the Czech crisis of 1968 illuminated the need for a new understanding of the social, political, and economic forces shaping the Communist world.

Even before the Czech crisis, many had come to realize that our understanding of totalitarian systems was being outpaced by events, and that scholarship on the various Communist systems was not adequately exploiting new social science concepts of change, development, and "modernization." In 1966, the American Council of Learned Societies appointed a committee of scholars, the Planning Committee for Comparative Communist Studies, to review existing concepts of change in Communist systems and develop new ones.[1] During 1967 this committee sponsored a week-long conference to survey the problems of comparing Communist nations, and during 1968 some twenty scholars met for two months under the committee's auspices at the Center for Advanced Study in the Behavioral Sciences, located on the Stanford University campus, to confer on these issues and to write this volume. The 1968 group considered two basic questions: how do Communist systems change, and why do they change?

These questions were not commonly asked in the past by scholars specializing in the analysis of Communist political systems, thanks in good part to the model that has guided most prior research on Communist systems. Within the confines of the so-called "totalitarian model," it is hard enough to conceptualize "development" and its consequences—that is, to say at what rate a Communist regime is moving toward achieving some or all of its self-proclaimed, ideologically circumscribed socioeconomic investment goals. It is even harder to conceptualize the resulting unintended changes in the social structure and the consequences of those changes.

The models that guide a social scientist in his inquiries directly influence the types of questions he is able to ask about a particular social system. As Alex Inkeles has observed:

Most social scientists approach the subject they are studying with some kind of conceptual scheme which we may call a model. These models play an enormously important role in deciding what is taken into consideration and what is left out, what weight is assigned to one factor as against another, which sets of interrelationships are assumed to exist and which will go largely unnoticed. There is a great deal of debate about models, most of which deals with the question of whether or not a particular model is right or wrong. In my opinion there is no such thing as a right or wrong sociological model. There are richer and poorer ones.[2]

A social scientist who relies on the totalitarian model, for example, will find it hard to formulate the question "How do totalitarian systems develop and change?" because the answer is an axiom of the model: they don't, at least not in their Nazi and Stalinist manifestations. Yet contemporary Communist systems differ widely both in their choice of organizational strategies for revolutionary develop-

[1] This Planning Committee consisted of Alexander Dallin, Chairman (Columbia University), R. V. Burks (Wayne State University), Alexander Eckstein (University of Michigan), Chalmers Johnson (University of California, Berkeley), Joseph LaPalombara (Yale University), Gordon B. Turner (American Council of Learned Societies), and Ezra F. Vogel (Harvard University). See *Newsletter on Comparative Studies of Communism*, I: 1 (Feb. 1968).

[2] "Models and Issues in the Analysis of Soviet Society," *Survey*, 60 (July 1966), 3.

ment and in the forms of structural strain they exhibit (e.g., "revisionism"). For the analysis of such systems the prevailing totalitarian model seems clearly poorer rather than richer. It is therefore time to review and amend that model, or perhaps to replace it with one better attuned to what is basic and what is secondary in the functioning of Communist systems.[3]

The totalitarian model does not, of course, rule out all kinds of change. Rather, it restricts itself to changes of certain types, namely those that the regime seeks to achieve (e.g., mobilization for defense or war) or to prevent (e.g., development of extra-elite bases of power). Its weakness is that it does not allow for certain far more fundamental kinds of change that are occurring or seem about to occur in the Communist world. These are: (1) changes in the structure of the political system, generally from a one-party system with an autonomous dictator to collective leadership and toward a party-dominated national front; (2) changes in the reliance on terror to elicit elite-approved social behavior, generally from a high reliance on terror to a medium and toward a low reliance; (3) changes in the structure of the economic system, generally from a centralized command economy to a semi-centralized managerial system and toward market socialism; and (4) in the case of externally imposed Communist regimes, changes from the status of satellite to that of client state and toward independence as a national Communist state.

These four classes of change are by no means mutually dependent either analytically or in terms of the intentions of a given regime. Analytically, for example, it is possible to conceive of a centralized command economy operated by some political structure other than a single-party dictatorship.[4] As for intentions, some advanced Communist regimes have been willing to introduce a measure of market socialism because of its alleged greater efficiency, but not at the cost of a drastic change in the political structure. At the same time, these classes of change do have two things in common. One is a sort of domino effect: historically, change in one of these classes has tended to arouse

---

[3] Students of Communist systems are not the only social scientists who employ the totalitarian model; it is also used by specialists concerned with categorizing basic types of political systems, often with misleading implications. See, for example, Gabriel Almond and G. Bingham Powell, *Comparative Politics: A Developmental Approach* (Boston, 1966), pp. 271 *et seq.* In general typologies, the totalitarian social system is commonly portrayed as a stable, institutionalized type, whereas to the specialist the institutionalization of totalitarianism is one of its most problematic characteristics.

[4] See, for example, Benjamin N. Ward, *The Socialist Economy: A Study of Organizational Alternatives* (New York, 1967).

popular demands and expectations for change in one or more of the others. The other is that they all seem to have come about as a result of policies adopted in an earlier, highly radical phase of Communist revolutionary innovation.

What about this earlier phase? Is it possible to characterize the policies adopted by radical Communist regimes in their first years in power, and to generalize about the kinds of problems or consequences that are implicit in such policies? Any effort at generalization immediately runs up against the fact that each of the various self-styled Communist regimes, from China and North Korea to Czechoslovakia and the Soviet Union, not to mention Cuba and Albania, appears to have less in common with many of the others than with certain non-Communist states. Is it not more fruitful to consider Communist states primarily in terms of cultural area or level of economic development or degree of autonomy, rather than to lump them together as Communist? Albania may have more in common with Nepal or Haiti than with any other Communist state, Yugoslavia with India, Czechoslovakia with Italy, the Soviet Union with the United States. Does the term "Communist" denote any truly distinguishing characteristics?

Yes, it does. In the first place, although political characteristics can properly be reduced to social or economic characteristics for some purposes, such a procedure would dissolve rather than elucidate the peculiarly political problems of Communist policy-making. A Communist world does exist, not simply in terms of self-identification but more importantly as a set of reference groups, a source of moral and intellectual support for authority, and a source of economic and technological support—and increasingly as a group whose members compete among themselves and may even fight each other in the name of truth versus heresy. It is possible, as this volume shows, to develop concepts that allow for a meaningful comparison between such nations as Bulgaria and North Vietnam, to explain with these concepts why there is such marked diversity among the nations of the Communist world, and to show with some precision where the limits of the term "Communist" lie—where, in short, it becomes meaningless to speak of a Communist regime, regardless of what the regime calls itself.

Several papers in this volume elaborate on the distinctiveness of Marxist-Leninist values and Leninist strategies of nation-building. Other papers report on the distinctive structural characteristics of authentic and derivative Communist systems. Our concern in this paper is to suggest a research strategy for dealing with the problems of change and diversity in the Communist world—a strategy that was thoroughly discussed in the seminars that preceded this volume and that may be presumed to have influenced, if not necessarily guided, the papers that follow. We shall begin by trying to identify specifically Communist orientations toward the development problems that confront a revolutionary regime after seizing power. We shall then hold this set of orientations as a parameter while introducing a range of operative variables in an effort to account for the manifest diversity in the practices of ruling Communist parties.[5]

The Revolutionary Configuration: Communist Political Systems as Totalitarian Mobilization Regimes

Robert Tucker has written that "Communism . . . is not inherently a local phenomenon but a form of society or civilization that can spread and take root in virtually every part of the globe where circumstances are propitious."[6] This is undoubtedly true, but what exactly are these propitious circumstances? One thing is certain: they are not necessarily the circumstances identified as propitious in Marxist ideology. Historically, Communist parties have come to power in societies plagued by incoherence in their basic values and institutions—incoherence resulting from backwardness and the disruptions of initial industrialization (Russia), from colonial rule and the demise of colonial power (Vietnam and Korea), from semicolonial rule following abortive nationalist movements (China and Cuba), and from other harrowing conditions, including catastrophic defeat and military occupation (Eastern Europe).[7] Not a single Communist party has come to power under circumstances of the sort that Marx identified as propitious for revolutions—for example, those of Japan in the 1920's, a maturing industrial society with a large, exploited

---

[5] Parameters, be it noted, are conditions that are known or suspected to influence the outcome under investigation but that are assumed not to vary for the purposes of the investigation. Operative variables are conditions that are known or suspected to influence the outcome under investigation and that are made or allowed to vary in the investigation in such a way as to permit the analyst to assess this influence. See Neil J. Smelser's important article "Notes on the Methodology of Comparative Analysis of Economic Activity," *Social Science Information* (UNESCO), VI: 2–3 (Apr.-June 1967), 7–21, esp. p. 15.

[6] "On the Comparative Study of Communism," *World Politics*, XIX: 2 (Jan. 1967), 242.

[7] For a theoretical treatment of the relationship between incoherence in values and institutions and the occurrence of revolution, see Chalmers Johnson, *Revolutionary Change* (Boston, 1966).

proletariat.[8] In concrete historical terms, Communist ideology has adapted itself to revolutions immensely more complicated and often of an entirely different nature than the revolutions for which it claims to be an analysis and a guide. However, in making this adaptation, Communist ideology has affected the revolutionary movement it captured as much as the ideology itself has been distorted or tended to deteriorate in the process.

It has often been said that Communist revolutions and the subsequent innovations engineered by ruling Communist parties can be understood and evaluated without reference to Communism as such. Thus we speak of the Chinese Communists' contributions to the Chinese revolution, now better than a century old, or of the Russian Communists' acceleration of Russia's economic development, even though Communism itself is not a theory of economic development. According to John Kautsky:

> The revolutions that brought Communist parties to power took place in traditional societies disrupted by the impact of early industrialization.... Obviously, this makes Communist revolutions far from unique. They share these characteristics and many others that accompany them with the general upheaval throughout the underdeveloped world in our time. I would suggest, then, that Communist revolutions, including the Russian revolution, be placed, for analytical purposes, in the context of revolutions in underdeveloped countries.[9]

This view is important. By giving a broader meaning to Communist revolutions than they are given in Communist ideology itself, it enables us to distinguish Communist movements from structurally similar fascist or reactionary movements, and to judge certain basically "progressive" results of Communist activities by universal criteria. There is no denying the greater economic justice, security, life expectancy, and social integration that many—even most—Chinese, Cubans, Czechs, and Yugoslavs have enjoyed under varying periods of Communist rule. But there is also no denying the opposite point: namely, that Communist ideology has shaped and influenced the revolutionary process in its own specific ways.

The progress made by Communist regimes in economic development, increased national autonomy, and the training of skilled workers is an intermediate and often unintended outcome of policies adopted in the service of an ideological "transfer culture." We follow

---

8 See Robert A. Scalapino, *The Japanese Communist Movement, 1920–1966* (Berkeley, Calif., 1967), pp. 328–34.

9 "Communism and the Comparative Study of Development," *Slavic Review*, XXVI: 1 (Mar. 1967), 14.

Anthony Wallace in identifying two components of any revolutionary ideology as its "goal culture" and its "transfer culture."[10] An ideology's goal culture is its image of the ultimate utopia, its idealized contrast to the present, which elicits purposive revolutionary behavior and sacrifice from a significant part of the revolutionary party and which may be used to justify the party's resort to coercion and violence against the noncompliant. An ideology's transfer culture, on the other hand, provides the norms that guide policy formation: it specifies what steps the revolutionary leadership must take (or is invoked to justify the steps the leadership does take) to move toward the goal culture. Since without a goal culture there would be no transfer culture, when and if the goal culture comes to perform only symbolic functions (i.e., becomes only a final end, one without influence over routine decisions), it is no longer appropriate to speak of a transfer culture. Other things being equal, the policies of a regime without a goal culture are addressed solely to the functional requisites of the social system.

Communist regimes are the product of revolutionary movements, not rebellious ones. They seek not merely to correct certain wrongs or to restore an older, betrayed society, but to build a new society. Such a goal calls for massive social renovation and a recasting of the division of labor. This is so even when the revolutionary impulse has been imported, as in Tibet by Chinese Communist agents or in Rumania by Soviet agents. Communists do not merely rule, or dominate, or suppress; they institute a process of change. The chief difference between authentically revolutionary and derivatively revolutionary Communist-dominated regimes lies in the expectations of the mass of the population—a factor, as we shall see later, that may be more troublesome to the authentic than to the derivative regime.

Soon after the revolution, the Communist revolutionary directorate is confronted by growing pressure from the society either to establish a new equilibrium—one reflecting the elimination by revolutionary violence of the most hated social groups or conditions—or to conform to the main goals of the non-Marxist social movement with which the Communist party associated itself before taking power. This pressure is not necessarily "counterrevolutionary"; rather, it reflects the normal inertia that characterizes transrevolutionary social customs and norms and the fact that Communist leadership of revolutions has been based on more or less substantive united fronts for

[10] *Culture and Personality* (New York, 1961), p. 148.

the alleviation of specific non-Marxist social problems rather than on Marxist ideology.

In the face of this growing inertia, the revolutionary directorate must make a choice. Either it acquiesces in an ideologically unacceptable suboptimal equilibrium, albeit with Communists occupying key positions of the system (Albania and Mongolia have done something like this), or it engineers a forced-draft movement of the society toward its ideologically defined goals. Communist parties characteristically choose the latter course. Precisely because the ruling Communist party has a goal culture, it will develop or borrow a transfer culture for attaining that goal. It does not matter whether or not the intermediate goals specified by the transfer culture are in fact rational steps toward the goal culture—e.g., whether forced industrialization actually has anything to do with achieving a classless society. What matters is that these intermediate goals are justified and vigorously pursued without regard to public opinion, and that they are pursued in the name of a utopia that serves at once as a challenge, an excuse, and a potent source of identity in both domestic and international politics. Not all the leaders need personally believe in the goal culture for it to function effectively in this manner. So long as it is the guiding principle of the culture they share, serving the ideology and serving one's personal ambition coincide.

The actual definition of transfer-culture goals comes from a subtle interaction between what the leadership sees as the requirements of the goal culture (e.g., the elimination of classes) and what it sees as the requirements for the persistence and maintenance of the social system (e.g., industrialization), although such goals will always be justified, and sometimes even understood, as steps toward the goal culture. Generally speaking, any goal dictated by ideology will give way if it is known to contradict a functional requisite or if it tends to weaken the ruling position of the Communist party, although this rule will never of course be openly acknowledged. In such cases a process of ideological innovation is undertaken in order to bring the ideology into line with the recalcitrant social reality.

The historical experience of the Soviet Union is important here; as the first Communist nation, it inevitably serves as a reference group for all others. In the Soviet Union some of the main transfer-culture goals were the preservation of the power monopoly of the Communist party and its leader, the building up of heavy industry for national defense purposes, agricultural collectivization, nationalization of the means of production, the elimination of "consumer sovereignty" and hence of markets, and the training of a technologically competent labor force. All these goals have been copied to a greater or lesser extent by later Communist regimes.

Most Communist transfer-culture goals require sacrifices of the population; commonly such goals are unpopular or entail means that are not popularly supported. They are accordingly imposed by a "revolution from above," with profound consequences for the potentialities of the total system, the social structure, and the revolutionary party itself. "Revolution from above" is very like what Amitai Etzioni calls "societal mobilization" and what happens in the situation David Apter describes as "the mobilization system." In Etzioni's words:

Mobilization is the process by which energy that is latent from the viewpoint of the acting unit is made available for collective action. . . . The concept of mobilization was first used to refer to the shifting of the control of resources from private-civilian to public-military purposes. More recently, it has been applied to a society's (or collectivity's) deliberate increase in the control of a variety of assets, such as new nations' mobilization of economic resources for development or a civil rights movement's mobilization of the attention of previously less attentive and inattentive citizens. The characteristic which these processes share with military mobilization is that they all entail an increase in the assets the unit under study controls collectively.[11]

Etzioni further points out that "when the *direction* of mobilization (the unit(s) which gain in control), its *scope* (the sectors encompassed), and its *intensity* (the extent of the change in each sector) do not coincide with what is legitimate for and supported by the evolving consensus, mobilization generates alienation in the same way as other exercises of power."[12]

Thus it is with the transfer culture of a newly installed ruling Communist party. In the service of its ideology, the survival of the social system it dominates, and its own position, the ruling party draws power over virtually all assets to the center; it takes as its scope all subunits of the society; and it brings about changes that were unprecedented, unforeseen, and undesired, even in the authentically revolutionary but non-Marxist-Leninist society. Apter generalizes about the resulting political system:

Possessing an ideology of the future with an emphasis on the urgency of action turns the mobilization system toward direct planning and the drastic

---

[11] *The Active Society: A Theory of Societal and Political Processes* (New York, 1968), pp. 388–90.
[12] *Ibid.*, p. 389.

restratification of society. The atmosphere of mobilization is one of crisis and attack. Normalcy or passivity can even be regarded as dangerous. Individuals are called upon to declare themselves even in the most humble activities. There is no legitimate sphere of personal privacy, nor is privacy a recognized value. All social life becomes politicized. In the most extreme forms of mobilization system, having children is even endowed with supreme national importance. In the end, the state exerts its primacy over everything.[13]

The key to the totalitarian configuration of the Communist transfer culture is, as Etzioni observed, a lack of congruence between the regime's mobilization program and "what is legitimate for and supported by the evolving consensus." This lack of congruence exists precisely because Communist goals (as distinct from other revolutionary goals, e.g., national prestige) have never been legitimized among the mass of the population. As we have seen, the population is not necessarily counterrevolutionary; but even when it accepts the desirability of revolutionary change under Communist leadership, its goals are not Communist goals.

In some authentically revolutionary systems, there occurs a process of translation between Communist goals and popular goals. For example, however much the Communists may portray China's atomic bomb as "a victory for the thought of Mao Tse-tung," the average Chinese may see it more as a triumph or vindication of the Chinese nation as such, one of the authentic goals of the Chinese revolution. Similarly, Vietnamese Communist struggles against foreign domination or intervention can be made to coincide with the objectives of Vietnamese nationalism, whereas Vietnamese Communist mobilization efforts to collectivize agriculture generate alienation. During 1960, citizens of Havana applauded Fidel Castro the anti-American Cuban nationalist, but after 1962 many of them went into exile to escape Fidel Castro the ideological Communist innovator. Even in Czechoslovakia, many of the Communist mobilization policies of 1948–68 could be accepted as the price of achieving the authentic postwar goal of alliance with Russia for defense against Germany. When the alleged threat of Germany became less credible, the cost of the alliance in its original form became too high for both the Czech people and the Czech party;[14] nevertheless, the transfer-culture goals of the Soviet Union continued to be forced on the Czechoslovak population. Precisely because Communist parties continue to work toward a Communist goal culture, their programs of mobilization,

13 *The Politics of Modernization* (Chicago, 1965), p. 360.
14 This point was developed by R. V. Burks in the seminars that preceded the writing of this volume.

even if softened by the process of translation, ultimately generate alienation—not only in nonrevolutionary systems where Communist rule has been imported (e.g., Tibet), but also in authentically revolutionary systems.

At the outset of the mobilization phase in an authentically revolutionary context, i.e., one in which there is a recognized gap between values and institutions, the mass of the population may approve a proposed development program or it may be wavering. On the one hand, the population may accept or be persuaded to accept the revolutionary leadership's ideologically determined priorities and be willing to forgo the alternative rewards of a reconciliation system, in which priorities are determined by competition among many political forces. On the other hand, the symbols of developmental progress inevitably and fairly rapidly suffer some decay as a result of the different time perspectives of the elite and the masses in "revolutions from above," and the population also comes to disvalue the unintended consequences that attend the pursuit of the ideologically set priorities. As Alec Nove has written with regard to Russia:

A situation which requires many bureaucrats, or which gives exceptional power to many policemen, may bring into action certain forces, certain behavioral tendencies, which are typical of bureaucrats or policemen and which, though not needed or desired as such, cannot in the circumstances be avoided.... The aims of the bulk of the people were bound to be in conflict with the aims of the party. It should be added that this conflict is probably bound to arise in some form wherever *the state* is responsible for financing rapid industrialization; the sacrifices are then imposed by political authority, and the masses of "small" people do not and cannot provide voluntarily the necessary savings, since in the nature of things their present abstinence cannot be linked with a future return which they as individuals can identify.[15]

The dynamics of this situation—the forcing of quasi-popular goals on a population by a determined leadership—lead to the characteristic pattern articulated in the totalitarian model: the state tends to dominate, even to displace, the society; information is controlled by censorship and artificial isolation; "politics" are suppressed; the "party" is transformed into an instrumental or bureaucratic organization (i.e., one that serves to execute policies it does not make); and a single dictatorial figure, often with manufactured claims to charisma, emerges. The effects of the mobilization regime on the party itself and on the potentialities of its future leadership are particularly profound. Nove, again, is suggestive on this matter:

---

[15] *Economic Rationality and Soviet Politics* (New York, 1964), pp. 20, 24.

In this situation, the party was the one body capable of carrying out enormous changes and resisting social and economic pressures in a hostile environment; this was bound to affect its structure. For a number of years it had already been in process of transformation from a political into a power machine. The problems involved in the "revolution from above" intensified the process of turning it into an obedient instrument for changing, suppressing, controlling. This, in turn, required hierarchical subordination, and suppression of discussion; therefore there had to be an unquestioned commander-in-chief. Below him, toughness in executing unpopular orders became the highest qualification for party office.[16]

Totalitarian mobilization generates alienation, but to the extent that it genuinely mobilizes it may also generate the benefits of modernization. As Etzioni has observed, mobilization is not the same thing as modernization, but the two processes are closely related.[17] Totalitarian mobilization helps bring about modernization by transferring the control of assets from subsystemic collectivities (families, rural communities, ethnic groups) to national institutions. The Communist goal culture does not aim at a "modernized society," but overcoming the conditions of backwardness becomes the main task of the transfer culture as it seeks both to prepare the society for the goal culture and to maintain the society in the here and now. Part of the modernization that accompanies totalitarian mobilization is intended; it is a goal of the transfer culture. The rest is a by-product of the direction, scope, and intensity of totalitarian mobilization. The economic development of Soviet Central Asia, for example, was due almost exclusively to the unintended effects of national wage scales, a national tax system, and the financing of economic development out of a national budget.[18]

Yet however much totalitarian mobilization may contribute to modernization, it can never *complete* the modernization process. One of the characteristics of totalitarian mobilization is its extreme imbalance, its stress on achieving one overriding transfer-culture goal to the exclusion of all others. Herbert J. Spiro isolates this as the defining feature of totalitarianism:

Ruthless pursuit of a single, positively formulated goal is the most distinctive common denominator of totalitarianism. Nontotalitarian systems, to the extent that they articulate their goals at all, are either committed to a plurality of goals, such as those listed in the preamble to the Constitution of

---

16 *Ibid.*, p. 25.
17 *The Active Society*, pp. 418–21.
18 This point was developed by Benjamin N. Ward in the seminars that preceded the writing of this volume. See Alec Nove and J. A. Newth, *The Soviet Middle East: A Communist Model for Development* (New York, 1967).

the United States, or concentrate on such procedural [reconciliation] goals as the settlement of conflicts, or state their substantive goals negatively, for example, the prevention of foreign domination. . . . On the other hand, the single-minded pursuit of a positive substantive goal, such as racial hegemony, the dictatorship of the proletariat, or the rapid industrialization of a backward economy, in utter disregard of all other possible goals, is characteristic of totalitarianism. All the resources of the system are ruthlessly harnessed to the attainment of the one great goal. . . . Whatever is considered distracting from this single-mindedness of purpose is condemned and eliminated. As a result, no procedures are worked out for the resolution of disagreements. All disagreement within the system is identified as evil. Internal politics is therefore banned.[19]

It is precisely this monomania or lack of balance that gives totalitarianism both its innovative and its repressive features. For the sake of analysis, we may reduce the sectors of development inherent in any process of modernization to three: economic development, political development, and social development. Economic development refers to increases in per capita productivity. Political development refers to increases in per capita representation in the political processes by which legitimate priorities binding on all are established. Social development refers to per capita increases in level of living and in ease of access to the means of self-fulfillment (e.g., educational opportunities).

As we know from the experience of the so-called developing nations, mobilization policies designed to advance development in one sector often conflict with policies in other sectors. Policies of economic development, for example, may give rise to a new stratum of possessors or managers whose political power may conflict with efforts at political development. Conversely, mobilization of the population for economic development may produce unexpected pressures for political and social development, e.g., demands for the organization of trade unions or for a more equitable distribution of national income. Policies of political development (such as the creation of Workers' Councils in Yugoslavia or Mao Tse-tung's attempt to increase the representation of workers and peasants during the Cultural Revolution) may well conflict with the efficient use of labor in the industrial development program, and at the same time increase the demand for greater economic output. Policies of social development are possible only after relatively high levels of economic and political development have been attained, to judge from Third World experience

[19] "Totalitarianism," *International Encyclopedia of the Social Sciences* (New York, 1968), XVI, 111.

with such policies. Otherwise health programs produce soaring birth rates that wipe out economic gains; educational programs produce an unemployable and thus politically alienated intellectual proletariat; and, as in the early Chinese communes, new consumption patterns destroy incentives to work.

The Communist totalitarian model (as distinct from the reality) calls for mobilization to be directed exclusively toward development in one sector, usually industrial development, while totalitarian instruments of control and repression are used to demobilize the other sectors, i.e., to inhibit popular demands for development in those sectors. The result is that if we compare a mature totalitarian mobilization system with a system undertaking balanced development (e.g., India), we find that the balanced system looks like a gray slab and the totalitarian system looks like a black-and-white checkerboard.[20] Herein lies the dilemma of the totalitarian regime that has successfully mobilized its system's assets to attain a single developmental objective. What is it to do? Its very success has led to mounting pressures to bring the system into balance, to allow development in the hitherto unauthorized areas; yet if it does so, it will be sanctioning the end of the revolution from above, the end of the movement toward the goal culture. All the changes currently taking place in mature Communist systems tend toward righting the developmental imbalance in those systems. As the slow rate of change and the "backlash" of 1968 reveal, however, this is an extremely difficult and delicate undertaking.

The pressures for dismantling a successful Communist mobilization system, as well as the obstacles to doing so, arise from the very successes of the regime in attaining its intermediate, transfer-culture goals. These pressures and obstacles are inevitable, partly because of the fundamental imbalance of such systems, partly because the totalitarian policy of controlled underdevelopment in unauthorized sectors is never total. It is not merely that there are residual uncontrolled areas; it is rather that the very effort to control the side effects of the main mobilization effort gives rise to bureaucracies, institutions, and loyalties with dynamics of their own. A group or class of people that the regime has created for purely instrumental purposes develops independent interests and policies designed either to preserve the basic imbalance or to make adjustments in its own favor. To appreciate just how difficult it is to dismantle a totalitarian mo-

[20] This metaphor, in which development is conceived as a series of stages in a continuum from black to white, is from Robert T. Holt and John E. Turner, *The Political Basis of Economic Development* (Princeton, N.J., 1966), p. 17.

bilization regime, even when there is a general desire to do so and when the goal culture has receded further and further into the future (like the "pursuit of happiness"), it is necessary to look in greater detail at the actual side effects of totalitarian mobilization as distinct from those feared by the elite.

Mobilization, Bureaucratization, and Institutional Innovation

"What characterizes every ideology," writes George Lichtheim, "is discordance between the actual state of affairs and the socially determined pressure to rearrange reality in the light of certain overriding concepts which may be altogether at variance with what the individuals know to be the case within the limits of their own experience."[21] In the Communist mobilization regime, this pressure to rearrange reality is determined politically, whether or not there is also social pressure for change. In order to move the system toward the ideologically desired configuration, as well as to keep the social system going during the transition period, the mobilization regime leadership must create new organizations that bridge the gap between ideology and reality.[22]

If the regime does not collapse during the transition period, the interaction between its ideological goals and the requirements of the social system (i.e., the limits of the possible) will generate a process that in time modifies both the ideology and the reality. To the extent that the ideology lays down unrealistic criteria of social control, for example, it will have to be modified, since not to modify it would ultimately destroy the social system. Conversely, to the extent that the social system's potentialities are realized as various ideological goals are achieved, the constraints on political choice will be relaxed and the reality will move closer to the ideology. This process ends when the ideology has been transformed into a system of values—one that identifies the roles, coordinates the actions, and legitimizes the institutions of socialized actors in a stable social system.

This is what eventually happens in societies mobilized for change by a small ideological elite.[23] The more difficult questions are why

---

[21] *Marxism: An Historical and Critical Study* (London, 1961), pp. 377–78.

[22] See Franz Schurmann, *Ideology and Organization in Communist China* (Berkeley, Calif., 1966), pp. 7–8.

[23] See the extensive literature on the "end of ideology." For a guide to this literature and also an important statement on its validity, see M. Rejai, W. L. Mason, and D. C. Beller, "Political Ideology: Empirical Relevance of the Hypothesis of Decline," *Ethics*, LXXVIII: 4 (July 1968), 303–12. On the distinction between "ideology" and "value" and their differing functions in social systems, see Johnson, *Revolutionary Change*, pp. 81–87.

this process occurs and particularly *how* it occurs. How, for example, do organizations set up by the mobilization regime for purely instrumental purposes become infused with value, i.e., become legitimate institutions? The answer to this question lies in the nature and interests of such organizations.

Political life, according to Bernard Crick, involves the reconciliation of diverse interests through a relatively free choice among competing alternatives, yielding a legitimate set of priorities for all persons who participate in politics.[24] Totalitarian organization, by contrast, seeks to resolve "the ancient dilemma of how to combine personal with public interest in such ways as to put an end to politics."[25] In practice, totalitarian organization eliminates politics by defining personal interests as identical to the public interest, which in turn is defined however the regime chooses to define it.

Eliminating the category of private interests makes it impossible for a mobilization regime to use the market mechanism as a way of coordinating behavior. Bureaucracy thus becomes the logical form of mobilization regime organization. As Anthony Downs argues:

Individual productive and distributive units in socialist and communist societies are expected to take explicit account of many external as well as internal costs and benefits in conducting their operations [i.e., growth or national need rather than profit]. Since external costs and benefits generally cannot be dealt with through markets, this means that these economic enterprises must be operated primarily as non-market-oriented organizations. Furthermore, such societies usually eschew the principle of consumer sovereignty regarding certain important economic functions (such as determining the overall rate of investment). Therefore, in these societies, bureaucratic forms of organization are the only ones suitable for carrying out significant economic functions that are performed by market-oriented firms in primarily free-enterprise systems.[26]

"Totalitarianism," says Tucker, "carries the process of bureaucratization to its farthest extreme in modern society."[27]

Even the extremes of bureaucratization, however, never completely eliminate politics. The politics of a totalitarian bureaucracy are very different from the politics of a reconciliation regime, but there is no eliminating the need to reconcile conflicting bureaucratic interests

24 *In Defence of Politics* (Chicago, 1962), pp. 16–17. See also ch. 2, "A Defence of Politics Against Ideology," pp. 29–50.

25 Allen Kassof, "The Administered Society: Totalitarianism Without Terror," *World Politics*, XVI: 4 (July 1964), 573.

26 *Inside Bureaucracy* (Boston, 1967), p. 36.

27 Robert Tucker, "The Dictator and Totalitarianism," *World Politics*, XVII: 4 (July 1965), 560.

and points of view by essentially political means. In short, bureau-cratization inevitably has unintended consequences that the leaders of a totalitarian mobilization regime can never fully control or eli-minate. As Downs has observed:

> No one can fully control the behavior of a large organization; any attempt to control one large organization tends to generate another; each official tends to distort the information he passes upward in the hierarchy, exag-gerating those data favorable to himself and minimizing those unfavorable to himself; each official is biased in favor of those policies or actions that advance his own interests or the programs he advocates, and against those that injure or simply fail to advance those interests or programs.[28]

To escape from the rigidities of extreme bureaucratization, the top leadership will on occasion resort to massive campaigns or shake-ups to achieve particular goals, or it will implement schemes of decen-tralization or recentralization in response to the competing criteria of efficiency and control. Such campaigns are a prominent feature of the cyclical, or convulsive, pattern of development displayed by Communist mobilization regimes. Rarely, however, do they lead to fundamental changes. As Downs remarks, "large bureaucratic sys-tems in totalitarian societies will attempt periodic 'reforms' in or-ganizational structure aimed at 'shaking up' the whole system, but these reforms will not greatly affect day-to-day procedures at the low-est level of each bureau."[29]

Ultimately, perhaps after the single-dictator phase has given way to collective leadership, the main bureaucracies come to have their organizational interests represented within the top leadership of the party, where they are taken into account along with national and party interests. In short, despite the fact that Communist transfer-culture doctrine rejects the right of autonomous groups to develop or articulate interests distinct from those of the party, the Communist mobilization regime slowly generates autonomous groups within the party leadership.

The bureaucracies in question are of two broad types, occupational and territorial. The first type consists of functionally specific (usually ministerial) agencies with a vertical, system-wide jurisdiction—the police, the military, the economic chiefs, the diplomats, as well as opinion groups, or wings, within these groups. The second type con-sists of multi-level, multi-functional party committees with a terri-torial jurisdiction. These two types of bureaucracy correspond

[28] *Inside Bureaucracy*, pp. 262, 266.
[29] *Ibid.*, p. 272.

roughly to the two faces of totalitarian mobilization: the functionally specific ministries and commissions carry out the regime's positive mobilizing tasks in the authorized developmental sector, while the territorially based, lower-level party committees and units under their jurisdiction are responsible for social control, i.e., demobilization in the unauthorized developmental sectors.

Generally speaking, and oversimplifying slightly, once true mobilization has been launched, the single-function units having national jurisdiction are most concerned with what the transfer culture requires the population to do, and the multiple-function units having territorial jurisdiction are most concerned with what the transfer culture prohibits the population from doing. (It goes without saying that both types of units are staffed by Communist party members.) However, the transfer culture commits the territorial units to carrying out their tasks both positively and negatively. They are under pressure not only to help fulfill the authorized priorities by preventing the articulation of competing priorities, but also to help produce "new men," people committed to working and making sacrifices for the regime's ideological objectives.

The determination to build "new men" produces two interacting processes: a modification of reality by ideology, and a modification of ideology by reality. The state apparatus of the mobilization regime penetrates deeply into the nonpoliticized society, altering the performance of some roles in accordance with its ideology and suppressing other, competing roles; at the same time, given the inability of the state to replace the society totally (totalitarianism in this respect is always a matter of degree), innovations are made in the ideology in order to prevent the gap between ideology and reality from growing to unmanageable proportions. If this latter process goes on long enough, the ideology will be transformed, either by reinterpretation or by a reduction in scope, into a stable postrevolutionary structure of values for real men interacting in an equilibrium system.

Changing Soviet views of crime and juvenile delinquency provide a good example of the modifying of ideology in the interests of social control. Soviet legal theory during the 1920's stressed that crime was a matter of defects in the social system, not of individual "guilt." By the late 1930's, however, as Raymond Bauer observes, this view was no longer put forth:

The social system could be blamed for the antisocial behavior of children only when the Communist Party itself was not clearly responsible for the system as it existed. If crime is a product of the contradictions of a class society, then the elimination of the contradictions by the liquidation of classes should eliminate the social basis of crime. Soviet theorists were quick to point out that Stalin's declaration of the achievement of socialism in 1936 meant that the social basis for crime had been eliminated, and that any subsequent deviations from the moral norm are an evidence of "capitalist remnants in the consciousness of man" and must be eliminated. Thus, when the system had generated more problems than could be conveniently explained away, the responsibility for them was shifted by blaming them on a previous system. Since that system no longer obtained, the individual carrier of the influence of that system was held responsible.[30]

This is a typical example of the slow, incremental process of transforming a revolutionary ideology into a value structure. Another example is the development of the Chinese Communist distinction between antagonistic and nonantagonistic contradictions. In the Russian case the ideology was reinterpreted; in the Chinese case it was reduced in scope to place certain intractable realities beyond the bounds of ideological concern. In both cases the change was made to preserve the ideology from a damaging "contradiction."

Totalitarian socialization and social control have positive, ideological goals—the molding of new men—but they can and should also be conceived instrumentally as helping to fulfill the regime's priorities and to prevent the articulation of competing priorities. Lewis Coser finds in the Soviet regime's policies in 1951 an almost purely instrumental approach to family planning. The medals for high-breeding mothers—the "Motherhood Medal" (5–6 children), the "Order of Motherhood Glory" (7–9 children), and the "Heroine Mother" medal (10 children)—were to stimulate the production of a resource needed by the regime, not to reward ideologically perfect Soviet women.[31]

A useful concept for analyzing both the ideological and instrumental aspects of totalitarian socialization and social control is that of "preemptive organization." Preemptive organization refers to the practice of setting up official organizations for youth, women, occupation groups, ethnic groups, etc., with a view both to serving the regime's mobilization goals and to inhibiting the formation of private loyalties. The inhibition function appears to have the greater long-term significance. Allen Kassof offers an example:

Backed by the full power and authority of the party, it [the Komsomol organization] effectively blocks the formation of independent youth groups that might challenge the official outlook. Indeed, the entire history of the

---

[30] *The New Man in Soviet Psychology* (Cambridge, Mass., 1959), pp. 38, 42–43.
[31] "The Case of the Soviet Family," in Rose L. Coser, ed., *The Family: Its Structure and Functions* (New York, 1964), p. 528.

youth program can be viewed as a series of attempts to deprive new generations of self-expression, while creating the appearance of enthusiastic support for the system and its leaders. Thus does the regime forestall the potentially explosive issues that would arise if young persons could speak in their own voices and act on their own behalf.[32]

Other examples of preemptive organizations include nationalized churches (in China, for example), state-sponsored ethnic organizations, "democratic parties," trade unions (in at least part of their activities), intellectuals' groups, and, generally, the organizations of the "united front" in power.[33]

The various official bureaucracies, territorial party units, and preemptive organizations are all part of the structure that must be dismantled when the regime's unbalanced mobilization effort begins to produce diminishing returns; they also happen to be the groups that must make the decision to undertake the dismantling. In addition to vertical bureaucracies and territorial control organizations, each of which will have to modify if not abandon its role when the crisis of imbalance is reached, the Communist mobilization regime also produces its share of professionals, or "experts." As Downs observes:

Professionals develop their own quality standards and media of expression. In fact, some analysts of bureaus consider professionals as a separate bureaucratic type because each is more strongly influenced by his occupation than his organization.... Such personnel are heavily influenced by ideas generated within their professions and therefore outside the control of the bureau. When they base their intra-bureau behavior upon those ideas, they may act as radical innovators ... or as rigid conservatives.[34]

These key men must also be taken into account in any decision to dismantle the mobilization structure.

The fact that mobilization produces competing interests within the governing elite does not itself generate a mobilization regime crisis; rather, it encourages mobilization regime politics, as within the Presidium after Khrushchev's fall. The competing groups reconcile their divergent interests by bargaining and other means, and they continue to present a united front toward the society and external systems. The boundaries of intra-elite, bureaucratic politics are established by three norms of party life: (1) the quasi-ethical training and commitment of those who are granted entry to the restricted "commu-

[32] *The Soviet Youth Program* (Cambridge, Mass., 1965), pp. 18–19.

[33] See, for example, Lyman P. Van Slyke, *Enemies and Friends: The United Front in Chinese Communist History* (Stanford, Calif., 1967).

[34] *Inside Bureaucracy*, pp. 95–96, 203.

nity" of revolutionary leaders; (2) the use of political criteria in determining advancement to the top of any hierarchy, including technical and professional hierarchies; and (3) the use of terror to inhibit stable expectations and suppress deviants. As Jeremy Azrael remarks with regard to factory managers:

For purposes of political analysis it is of decisive significance that the group activities of the Soviet managerial elite have never been accorded political legitimacy, that members of the group have occupied bureaucratic positions within a centralized state system, that recruitment into the managerial elite has been governed in large part by political criteria, and that collective action on the part of the managers has been a high-risk enterprise likely to evoke a terroristic response from the political leadership.[35]

The leadership of a mature mobilization regime typically responds to the pressures of intra-elite politics by introducing some kind of temporary decentralization, on the understanding that if the move breeds organized interests, it will be reversed.

Communist mobilization regimes thus do possess homeostatic, or self-correcting, processes for maintaining the structure, continuity, and effectiveness of their elite corps. It is not the bureaucratic structure of the elite as such that leads to demands for political reform, but the pressures generated by the regime's very success in mobilizing the system in an unbalanced manner. These pressures, typically to reform or replace institutions that are no longer appropriate to society's needs, may be seen as threatening by the elite groups associated with the institutions in question, who may accordingly be moved to put their particular group interests ahead of their society's interest in reform. What are some of these pressures?

Any regime using coercion to elicit compliance with its policies encounters problems of information and communication, problems that Apter sees as bound to create a crisis of continuity for the regime. He observes: "Different polities employ different mixtures of coercion and information in trying to maintain authority, achieve stability, and increase efficiency. . . . [There is] an inverse relationship between information and coercion in a system: that is, high coercion systems are low information systems."[36]

There is some analytical and empirical evidence to suggest that such a principle does influence mobilization regimes. As we have seen, Downs regards information problems as implicit in large-scale bureaucratization (which is itself a consequence of the resort to coercion);

[35] *Managerial Power and Soviet Politics* (Cambridge, Mass., 1966), pp. 9–10.
[36] *The Politics of Modernization*, p. 40.

and Harold Wilensky sees the same kind of problem in the hierarchical structure of mobilization regime organizations. He writes:

Insofar as the problem of control—coordinating specialists, getting work done, securing compliance—is solved by rewards of status, power, and promotion, the problem of obtaining accurate, critical intelligence is intensified. For information is a resource that symbolizes status, enhances authority, and shapes careers. In reporting at every level, hierarchy is conducive to concealment and misrepresentation. Subordinates are asked to transmit information that can be used to evaluate their performance. Their motive for "making it look good," for "playing it safe," is obvious.[37]

Historically, Communist mobilization regimes have sometimes had to insulate various key sectors, notably science and the military, from the pattern of coercion in order to maintain their efficiency at an acceptable level.

And yet it does not seem empirically true that information problems create a crisis for the Communist mobilization regime. Alfred Meyer acknowledges that Soviet bureaucratic communications display "typical pathological symptoms," but he also shows how the system homeostatically generates "out-of-channel communications" in order to maintain its effectiveness.[38] Moreover, Apter's principle does not explain the deep-seated crisis of the mature mobilization regime, a crisis characterized by the need for fundamental reform and the possibility of internal explosion. If information problems are one symptom of this crisis, they would seem to be attributable not so much to the regime's reliance on coercion as to the unintended side effects of its partial success in mobilizing and modernizing the system.

An inescapable concomitant of economic modernization—what might be called a "built-in boomerang"—is increased functional differentiation and societal complexity. At the outset of the "revolution from above," it is relatively easy to mobilize the resources and control the reverberations of this mobilization in order to manufacture tractors or rifles, or even locomotives. The role structure associated with this level of technology is more complex than that of a traditional economy, but it does not pose insuperable problems of control for a determined mobilization regime. However, by the time the modernized sector of the mobilization regime is manufacturing jet aircraft, computers, and nuclear reactors, its role structure has become extraordinarily specialized and complex. At this point the regime is forced to relax some of its clearly dysfunctional controls (such as the

[37] *Organizational Intelligence: Knowledge and Policy in Government and Industry* (New York, 1967), pp. 42–43.
[38] *The Soviet Political System: An Interpretation* (New York, 1965), pp. 223–24.

use of terror), thereby opening the door to the possibility of rising demands that the basic developmental imbalance be corrected.

Why do functional differentiation and complexity force the leadership to relax controls? There are many reasons, and we shall cite only a few. One is that the efficient manufacture of advanced technical products, which have a long gestation period from prototype to production model, requires a certain degree of tranquility in the economy. This requirement in itself restricts the exercise of political intervention for ideological purposes.

Another is the necessity of engaging in foreign trade as the modernized sector becomes more complex. Autarky of sorts may be possible at the outset of mobilization, but no social system has all the raw materials required by an advanced economy. To purchase these materials abroad, a Communist regime must earn foreign exchange by selling some of its products on the international market. This means meeting international standards of price and quality; poor workmanship and bureaucratic indifference to costs can no longer be tolerated. It also means developing new specialties such as industrial design and marketing. All these accommodations to the international system are possible only with a relaxation of the regime's basic controls, which in turn accelerates pressures for modernization in the unauthorized sectors.

A third consideration making for the relaxation of controls is the problem of lagging domestic innovation. During the early mobilization phase, industrialization is often seen as a matter of "catching up" with one or another advanced external system that serves as a reference group—commonly the industrialized West or Japan. This early process of catching up does not require indigenous technological innovation: what advanced technology it uses can be bought, borrowed, or stolen from abroad. A catching-up policy, however, is not viable indefinitely, because the mobilizing regime is trying to overtake a moving target. Moreover, as the semi-modernized mobilization regime moves into the international market to acquire the materials it increasingly needs, it must compete in innovation, not just in emulation. Innovators may not be ideologically pure—no matter. The regime has no choice but to indulge them at the expense of ideology, a process that calls into question the very raison d'être of the mobilization regime.[39]

All these pressures induce the leadership to consider dismantling

[39] These points on the impact of functional differentiation were developed by Joseph S. Berliner, Alexander Eckstein, and J. Michael Montias in the seminars that preceded the writing of this volume.

certain controls that appear to be no longer desirable and to begin experimenting with market mechanisms. This is not to say that markets are an inherently more efficient means for organizing a complex economy; in fact, neither the market system nor Communist command economies have proved particularly efficient in managing today's unprecedentedly complex economies.[40] It is rather that the specific pressures on the regime dictate reforms in the direction of the external reference groups—i.e., toward a market system.

The obstacle to such economic reforms is not any distaste for market mechanisms as such; as the crisis of success in unbalanced modernization deepens, the regime silently jettisons its goal culture and becomes, in Tucker's phrase, an "extinct movement regime."[41] The obstacle to economic reform, even when its necessity and desirability in the abstract are acknowledged by the entire elite, is fear of unleashing the artificially bottled-up demand for political and social reform. Here is the dilemma. Demands for greater political representation and participation, probably leading to revised priorities favoring social development, can be silenced only at the cost of stunting economic growth; yet any policy that responds favorably to such demands must have survival consequences for the regime and its leaders.

Any attempt to resolve this dilemma moves the focus of attention from political sociology to political leadership—in Machiavelli's vocabulary, from *necessità* to *virtù*. The most farsighted Communist leaders may not necessarily be hostile to reform or averse to bringing the stunted sectors of society into line with the system's economic achievements, but they are properly skeptical about the possibility of undertaking such sweeping reforms in a rational and controlled fashion. The less enlightened, by contrast, concerned above all with preserving their own and their organization's positions, may recommend policies of retrenchment rather than reform. These will be the majority: men raised to high party office, in Nove's terms, for their "toughness in executing unpopular orders." Such men may be proficient in emulative, bureaucratic skills, but typically lack the necessary creativity and vision to solve unfamiliar problems. No Communist system has as yet successfully passed through the post-mobilization phase; accordingly, as the foregoing analysis suggests, all such systems face a choice between isolationism (with economic stagnation) and

---

[40] This point was developed by Benjamin N. Ward in the seminars that preceded the writing of this volume.

[41] Robert C. Tucker, "Towards a Comparative Politics of Movement-Regimes," *American Political Science Review*, LV: 2 (June 1961), 281–89.

revolution unless a political leadership capable of managing reform comes to the fore.

To summarize this developmental pattern, many details of which are elaborated in the following papers, a Communist party in power adopts a transfer culture, which it expounds and defends as moving society toward a utopian goal culture but which in fact has as its first two priorities the preservation of the party's power monopoly and the maintenance of the social system. Third in priority, but still of decisive importance, are schemes thought to be necessary for achieving the goal culture—a classless society, the defeat of "imperialism," socialist construction, the "new socialist man," etc. It is the particular contents and precedents of the Marxist-Leninist goal culture that distinguish Communist from other revolutionary movements. All three goals of the transfer culture demand societal mobilization, a process that is inevitably alienating because at least the third-priority goals have never been legitimized among the mass of the population. The resulting state of mobilization resembles that of a resource-poor social system mobilized to fight an ideologically dictated, unpopular foreign war. The inevitable concomitant of Communist mobilization is thus totalitarianism.

Mobilization is never carried out to achieve all possibly attractive goals; it is intended instead to achieve a few high-priority goals determined by the leadership. Feeling themselves to be the agents of an ineluctable historical process, the Communist leaders readily accept the necessities of totalitarianism: ruthless mobilization in the designated sector and equally ruthless "demobilization" in the undesignated sectors. This strategy works: it does in fact bring about change in the designated mobilization sector. But it carries with it two sets of unintended developments for which there are neither ideological guidelines nor historical precedents offering acceptable solutions. One is the bureaucratization of the revolutionary elite, which has important consequences for second- and third-generation elites, for the unity of the elite corps, and for the regime's capacity to control events rather than be controlled by them. The other is a marked increase in societal complexity and functional differentiation, a result of success on the main mobilization front.

These unintended developments occur precisely because of the unpopular, unbalanced nature of totalitarian mobilization, and because of its success. Solving the old problems leads to new problems. In particular, mounting pressures to redress the system's basic imbalance lead to mounting resistance from the bureaucracies created by the mobilization effort, which often see pressure for change as a threat to their vested interests. The maze of problems thus created is further complicated by the fact that the party, as a result of its bureaucratic fragmentation, no longer speaks with one voice. It has become, in effect, an arena of politics.

In the outline presented here, we have assumed that the main mobilization effort will be made in the area of industrial development, as the Soviet case illustrates not only for the Western scholar but for all succeeding Communist leaders. It is possible that Communist China, since the failure of the Great Leap Forward and particularly since the Cultural Revolution, is experimenting with an emphasis on political development, with a consequent demobilization of the economic and social sectors; but it is too early to tell. It is equally possible that the Cultural Revolution constitutes only a huge shake-up in response to bureaucratization and that the basic priorities of mobilization have not been altered. However this may be, the eccentricities of China during the late 1960's are a good illustration of the problem of diversity in the Communist world, to which we turn next.

Diversity among Communist Mobilization Regimes

Differences of policy and political structure among the nations of the Communist world are harder to characterize than differences among constituents of other classes of social systems—e.g., democracies, new nations, planned economies. This is because diversity is itself a problem for Communist political leaders. Theoretically, diverse political and national interests should have disappeared in the Communist world with the elimination of classes. In practice, however, even when two Communist nations have very similar internal structures and records of achievement (e.g., Hungary and Rumania), fundamental differences among them remain—differences with profound consequences for the integrity of Communist ideology. As Adam Ulam observes:

Nothing would be more injurious to the attempt to revive ideology in the Soviet Union, and hence to the continued rationale of totalitarianism, than a convincing demonstration of the inability of Communism to provide a lasting link between states, short of domination by one of them. Communism may catalyze the people's energies for revolution, it may provide a short cut to industrialization and modernity, but it has not been able to provide the kind of society for which the revolution was fought or the sufferings of industrialization endured. The last illusion that provides the material for ideological enthusiasm in a society where other points of Marxism have lost their relevance is the claim of the ideology to provide the only basis for a peaceful world order.[42]

The obvious failure of proletarian internationalism to produce a true union of soviet socialist republics has led some observers to dismiss Communist ideology in discussing the differences among Communist states. They argue that Communism as such has only historical significance: i.e., it helps explain how a group calling itself Communist gained power in a given system. In their view the operative forces shaping the so-called Communist nations are no different from those shaping non-Communist nations, notably ethnic or religious identities, national aspirations, and international competition for power within the global balance of power. There is some truth to this analysis. All Communist states are in some sense the creation of authentic but non-Communist revolutionary movements that the Communists have merely harnessed to their own ends; all such states have seen the reemergence of "primordial loyalties" as the tide of attraction to Communist political novelties begins to ebb.

But does the exercise of absolute political leadership by a Communist party for a generation or more make no difference to the presumed course of change in a social system? Is the contribution of a Communist party only nominal, a datum for the archivist rather than for the social scientist? These are not merely rhetorical questions; only in recent years have the histories of the various Communist systems begun to suggest answers. Not long ago, many intelligent people thought that the Chinese Communists might be nothing more than "agrarian reformers,"[43] the Hungarian Communists nothing more than agents serving an occupying power, the Vietnamese Communists nothing more than anticolonial nationalists, and the Yugoslav Communists nothing more than defenders of the fatherland against fascist invasion. Today it is clear that whereas ruling Communist parties do to some extent play roles created by a national history, they play identifiably Communist roles as well.

There are Communist universals—ways of doing things that are common to all ruling Communist parties and not found in some non-Communist ruling parties. According to Ezra Vogel, all ruling Communist parties use the same general methods (1) of reorienting the party after coming to power, e.g., the gradual elimination of people

---

[42] *The Unfinished Revolution: An Essay on the Sources of Influence of Marxism and Communism* (New York, 1960), pp. 296–97.

[43] See Kenneth E. Shewmaker, "The 'Agrarian Reformer' Myth," *China Quarterly*, 34 (Apr.-June 1968), 66–81.

who supported the party in a united front; (2) of organization building, e.g., youth leagues and the candidate-member system; (3) of re-
solving the political problems of agricultural nationalization and
collectivization; (4) of structuring political life, e.g., the tensions between horizontal and vertical organizations; (5) of target-setting, e.g.,
five-year plans; and (6) of irregular replacement of personnel, e.g.,
purges.[44] It remains to inquire why these common modes of behavior
exist and why their outcomes differ so markedly from system to system.

In the two preceding sections we first discussed what appear to be
the characteristic orientations of new Communist regimes toward the
problems of government, and then noted some of the inherent consequences of these orientations and the responses these consequences
have evoked from advanced Communist regimes. In order to explain
the manifest diversity among Communist regimes, we shall now take
the set of characteristic Communist orientations as a parameter and
introduce a range of operative, or intervening, variables that tend to
produce different outcomes from the same original attempt to put the
parametrical orientations into practice.[45] Three operative variables
appear to be particularly significant: level of economic development,
type of political culture, and mode of coming to power.

To appreciate how the level of economic development affects the
mobilization process, it is necessary to distinguish between prerequisites and requisites for success in reaching the stage of unbalanced
development skewed in favor of the economy (i.e., the checkerboard
stage). Prerequisites must be satisfied before an economy can move
into a given stage; requisites must be satisfied before a given stage can
be completed.[46] In social systems that lack the prerequisites for carrying out Communist transfer-culture plans, such plans will have a different outcome from the one indicated by the model of unbalanced
development.

[44] This list grew out of the seminars that preceded the writing of this volume.

[45] In this analytical scheme, a Communist regime on which the typical Communist orientations seem to have little influence (e.g., Albania or Mongolia) should
be seen either as belonging to some non-Communist "order" or as constituting a
family within the Communist order different from the family of totalitarian mobilization regimes, depending on the level of abstraction at which an investigator
chooses to work. Needless to say, the choice of parameters is dictated by the particular set of problems addressed by comparative Communist studies. For other
problems this procedure might easily be reversed—e.g., in order to study the present state of the Chinese revolution, it might be more advantageous to conceive of
the social and intellectual history of modern China, within which all twentieth-
century Chinese political leaders work, as a parameter and to introduce the contributions of Chinese Communist leaders as an operative variable.

[46] Holt and Turner, *The Political Basis of Economic Development*, p. 44.

Consider, for example, the typical Communist agricultural program, which is designed to increase output sufficiently to sustain the rapid development of heavy industry. In such a program, the agricultural sector is expected not only to feed an expanding urban population, but also to provide raw materials for light industry and to produce an exportable surplus for purposes of earning foreign exchange —and to do all this by means of organizational rearrangements alone (e.g., obtaining economies of scale by collectivization). Such programs are realistic only if there is a considerable agricultural surplus or unused capacity, but ideological pressures may nonetheless lead to their being tried. When they are, Communist planners typically overestimate the advance in productivity obtainable by organizational engineering and underestimate the managerial skills and distributive capacity required for the successful operation of very large farms.

Communist China illustrates the difficulty precisely. During its first five-year plan, 1953–57, the Chinese regime launched a typical program of Communist revolutionary development. It placed primary emphasis on the rapid growth of heavy industry, and rested its hopes of increasing agricultural production on a political program calling for the collectivization and general rationalization of peasant agriculture. No direct investment in agriculture was undertaken—no programs for rural mechanization, electrification, water conservation, or agricultural chemistry. By 1957 industrial production had increased noticeably, but agricultural production was barely ahead of population growth. Not enjoying the Soviet Union's relatively favorable ratio of population to arable land, China had little chance of successfully applying the Soviet formula for economic development.

The Chinese response to this situation, a response entirely consistent with the Chinese party's ideological commitments, was an even more determined effort to make the Communist paradigm work— namely, giganticism in agricultural collectivization in the form of the unprecedentedly large "people's communes." When this experiment with an overdose of the basic strategy also failed, the Chinese regime began to rethink the entire problem. After 1961, it came up with a revised theory of development characterized by the analysis that "agriculture is the foundation and industry is the guide."[47] Its new priorities were based on a prerequisite-fulfilling strategy, one designed to lay the agricultural foundations within China's economic geography for a later thrust toward full industrialization. This strategy was suc-

[47] See Chalmers Johnson, "Building a Communist Nation in China," in R. A. Scalapino, ed., *The Communist Revolution in Asia* (Englewood Cliffs, N.J., 1965), pp. 47–81.

cessfully put into effect between 1962 and 1965, and although it has since been obscured by the Cultural Revolution, it has not been abandoned.

A nation's political culture, the second of our operative variables, refers to a combination of its ethnic and religious characteristics and its political style. The Communist transfer culture demands that the existing social system be kept functioning while the movement toward the goal culture is launched. If ideological programs are pursued without sufficient regard to the functioning of the system, the system may disintegrate into rebellion or anarchy or be transformed into a vast concentration camp. All Communists are ideologically opposed to ethnic particularism, religion, and political rights that encroach on the party's political monopoly. However, ideology must sometimes defer to preexisting social commitments, depending on their nature (e.g., the precise configuration of ethnic or religious cleavages in the society), their strength, and the short-term priorities of the mobilization regime.

Thus, for example, the Yugoslav Communists found themselves committed to an ethnically federal structure because there was no other way to keep a Yugoslav social system in existence. Thus also the Chinese Communists made use of the Panchen Lama so long as they thought he might help them control the Buddhist population of Tibet, and the long-standing anti-Semitism of Eastern Europe has sometimes proved a useful cover for eliminating party enemies of Jewish ancestry. Appeals to nationalism are made by all regimes when national aspirations or hatreds coincide with party policy, thereby reproducing in a Communist context the nationalistic sources of diversity among nations.

The political heritage of a nation presents both constraints and opportunities for the Communist party. It is constraining in the sense that it may exacerbate problems of control during the mobilization phase—for example, a heritage of democracy, as in Czechoslovakia, requires the expenditure of more resources to build a totalitarian political structure than does a heritage of authoritarianism, as was the case in China. On the other hand, a country's political heritage also offers opportunities to the Communist political leader, opportunities that are often treacherous because they can foreclose options and dilute the transfer culture. For example, in periods of stress brought on by policy failures or party splits, a leader may be tempted to enhance his authority by partly "translating" his official role into one already legitimized by the political heritage. Thus Mao Tse-tung, following the failure of the Great Leap Forward, saw fit to appear more like the Son of Heaven than the Chairman of the Central Committee of the Chinese Communist Party; thus also Stalin during World War II took on the "little father" role so familiar to the tsars of Imperial Russia. Such strategic changes of image have their cost. Mao's performance seriously damaged the foundations of Communist party rule in China, and the Communist Party of the Soviet Union has never completely recovered from the excesses of the so-called personality cult.

One of the most fascinating aspects of the political culture variable arises from the fact that Communist regimes are inevitably national but never merely national. Poorly trained basic-level cadres in China, for example, may copy the life style of an imperial county magistrate; and Mao Tse-tung, in purging them, may act more like a Confucian bureaucrat than a Communist revolutionary. Yet when similar types of behavior occurred in an exclusively Chinese cultural context, without the overlay of Communist orientations, they produced stagnation and failure rather than revolutionary change.[48]

Our third and final operative variable, mode of coming to power, is closely related to political culture. Both variables produce diversity because they leave open some options and foreclose others in the Communist revolutionary directorate's relations with the mass of the people. Communist parties that come to power as the leaders of popular movements—e.g., parties that win victories based on guerrilla revolutions—are in a sense trapped by their popularity. The Leninist doctrine of the united front, whether used to gain popular support for a coup d'etat or to win over a sustaining population for guerrilla warfare, draws the party into a relationship with the population that it cannot possibly sustain after coming to power unless it abandons its goal culture. Given the fact that no revolution has as yet been successfully based on the aspirations Marx attributed to the working class (hence the resort to "united fronts," i.e., to tactical alliances based on causes that really do motivate people to revolt), no such Communist party can successfully pursue its transfer-culture goals and still maintain unimpaired the degree of popularity it enjoyed when it came to power. (It may of course regain popularity to some extent after making an initial breakthrough.)

---

[48] For an analysis of the interaction between Communist orientations and Chinese political culture, see Tang Tsou, "Revolution, Reintegration, and Crisis in Communist China: A Framework for Analysis," in Ping-ti Ho and Tang Tsou, eds., *China in Crisis* (Chicago, 1968), Vol. I, Book 1, pp. 277–347.

This element of popularity is not a problem for the derivative Communist regime. The original planners of the Communist regime in Rumania, for example, regarded the population only as a resource; questions of the popularity of a given program never weakened their resolve. Theoretically, there is no reason why Communist regimes raised to power by mass movements should not behave the same way. Historically, however, all such regimes have done their best to maintain their popularity, and their efforts to this end have been a major source of diversity among them.

Populism has had a profound impact on the Chinese Communist regime. It has inhibited reliance on a thoroughly totalitarian police apparatus, led to monumental indoctrination efforts (e.g., "thought reform"), caused major embarrassments to the regime (e.g., the "Hundred Flowers" campaign), and at least once threatened its very existence (during the Cultural Revolution). In both Cuba and Vietnam, Communist regimes lost popularity by carrying out certain ideologically dictated policies; the results were faltering execution of the policies, attenuation of the regime's authority, and splits in the leadership over who was to be blamed for what had happened. The populist base of the Yugoslav regime became its most valuable (and virtually its only) political asset after the regime's 1948 break with the Soviet Union, and the preservation of this asset has tended ever since to keep the Yugoslavs from developing a typical Communist transfer culture. Instead, Yugoslavia has sought to develop a Communist transfer culture that is consistent with party popularity, and has thereby become the most deviant of Communist nations.

Numerous variables other than level of economic development, type of political culture, and mode of coming to power contribute to diversity. Diversity comes from the very fact that Communist political systems exist as national states in an age when global politics is still seen as a system of relations among such states. To give just one example, the mere fact that some nations are small and others large must influence, if not necessarily obliterate, many an attempt to put Communist ideology into practice.

Diversity is one aspect of the process that Richard Lowenthal has called "the disintegration of a secular faith."[49] In this paper we have tried to show the basis for the disintegration of this faith, in the form of the diverse and largely unintended consequences that result when the faith is used as a guide to mobilization for change.

[49] *World Communism: The Disintegration of a Secular Faith* (New York, 1964).

Development vs. Utopia in Communist Policy

RICHARD LOWENTHAL

Communist parties seek to seize and maintain power in the name of a program of thoroughgoing social changes—in the class structure, the economic system, and the values governing social action—that are intended ultimately to create a classless society without scarcity, exploitation, or the need for coercion. As a supposed precondition for bringing about these changes, victorious Communist parties, beginning with the Russian Bolsheviks after the end of the civil war, have everywhere established a new type of political system providing them with an unprecedented concentration of power—a system characterized by a single party's claim to permanent and monopolistic control of all organs of government, all organized social groups, and all media of information, as well as by the absence of legal limitations on the exercise of state power. In the Communist view, the long-term stability of this *political* system is indispensable for achieving the changes in the *social* system demanded by the ideological goal.

It is, however, inconceivable that any social system should undergo the kind of profound and repeated changes imposed by Communist regimes over a long period without causing major repercussions on the very political system that has set those changes in motion. Such repercussions are all the more inevitable because indigenous Communist revolutions have so far been victorious only in underdeveloped countries, and the resulting regimes have all felt compelled to use their power to spur development as well as to bring about the specific social changes demanded by Communist ideology. Hence all Communist regimes resulting from indigenous revolutions are faced with certain conflicts arising from this simultaneous effort at accelerated development and ideologically guided change—and the solutions they adopt for those conflicts are bound to influence the further evolution of the regimes themselves.

In this essay I shall discuss only certain typical conflicts and changes in Communist political systems that may be traced to this special type of politically forced development. Hence I shall deal only with Communist regimes that have come to power by indigenous revolutions in underdeveloped countries—as in Russia, Yugoslavia, Albania, China, Vietnam, and Cuba—and not with those that were imposed by the Soviet Union on countries forcibly incorporated into its power sphere, as in the rest of Eastern Europe, in Mongolia, and in North Korea. The comparative material will be confined to Russia, China, and Yugoslavia.[1]

I am aware that by so limiting both the problems and the countries to be considered, I am excluding from consideration at least two major causes of political change in Communist systems. One of these concerns the conflicts arising from relations between Communist states, especially where these reflect the struggle for national independence from a leading Communist power; such conflicts may have far-reaching effects on the internal development of both participants. The other concerns the personality of the leader and the unstable balance between personal and institutional power, which seems to constitute an inherent problem of Communist party regimes. In the actual history of any country under Communist rule, the effects of all these factors interact; and it is their interaction, together with all the other differences in the situations of the countries concerned, that accounts for the variety of solutions adopted to deal with essentially the same problems. It is not common solutions, but common problems with a range of different solutions, that a comparative study of change in indigenous Communist regimes can aim to identify.

Communism as a Special Type of Politically Forced Development

It is hardly accidental that indigenous Communist revolutions have hitherto taken place only in underdeveloped countries. Far from

---

[1] The fragmentary nature of my knowledge of Albania, Vietnam, and Cuba as well as the recent origin and highly special character of Communist rule in Cuba has forced me to limit my comparative material. The Cuban revolution was not led by the Communist party, but joined by it at a late stage. Though the old Communists became dominant in the united party following the merger with Castro's movement, revolutionary legitimacy attaches to Castro's person rather than to the party. The leading party organs meet on exceptional occasions only, and the *líder maximo* seems to regard the party at best as one among the instruments of his rule —not necessarily the most important one. In short, the Cuban regime may turn out

being responses to the "contradictions" of a highly developed capitalist system that has reached the utmost limit of its possibilities, these revolutions have typically occurred in countries whose traditional, precapitalist order had been effectively disrupted by the impact of foreign capitalism and of a limited modern capitalist sector, but in which certain essential preconditions for the all-round growth of a modern capitalist economy were lacking. Communist revolutionary movements in such countries have thus been analyzed—just like nationalist revolutionary movements in the same countries or in other countries faced with a similar situation—as the response of frustrated intellectual elites to the phenomenon of partial stagnation in the midst of disruptive social change, and to the continued rule of traditional elites whose legitimate function had perished and whose values were no longer generally credible, but for whom no effective "bourgeois" successors had arisen. Both types of movements are carried to power when important groups become convinced that poverty and backwardness, national humiliation and dependence, injustice and lack of hope, can be ended only if state power is used for a concerted effort to change the economic and social structure and the values governing conduct. Both rely on the demand for forceful measures against the traditional holders of power and privilege, and on a program advocating large-scale investment by the state and politically directed mass education. Both types of revolutionary movements, therefore, create political regimes that consciously seek to achieve by political means an advance in all-round development that their societies had failed to produce "spontaneously," i.e., by the uncoordinated actions of individuals following their own interests and beliefs. Political regimes that set themselves this kind of task, and that seek both to extend the power of the state and to activate the people in its service, while limiting the right of their subjects to engage in any public, organized advocacy of particular opinions and interests, are now often described as "mobilization regimes"[2] or, as I should prefer, "dictatorships of development." In the frequent cases where the dictatorship is exercised and the mobilization accomplished by a political party or mass movement enjoying a more or less monopolistic position, we may also speak of "movement regimes."[3]

---

to be as much of a pseudomorph of a Communist party dictatorship as many Latin-American regimes have been pseudomorphs of Western democracy.

[2] Following David E. Apter, *The Politics of Modernization* (Chicago, 1965); see also Chalmers Johnson's introductory essay to this volume.

[3] Robert C. Tucker, "On Revolutionary Mass Movement Regimes," *The Soviet Political Mind* (New York, 1963).

The Common Background for "Politics in Command"

The characteristic rise of both Communist and nationalist revolutionary movements under the leadership of the intelligentsia of underdeveloped countries, and the subsequent creation of movement regimes devoted wholly or partly to the task of politically forced development, can be understood only in terms of the structural and cultural differences between the decaying traditional societies of the countries concerned and the type of traditional society in which modern development first originated in the West. The crucial fact is that the difference between the advanced Western societies and those underdeveloped countries is *not* just that of different stages in a single evolutionary process, as if the underdeveloped countries were simply lagging behind the West on a basically similar road to modernization (as seems to be implied, for instance, in Walt W. Rostow's *Stages of Economic Growth*).[4] Rather it is a structural and cultural difference between their historical starting points: the underdeveloped countries have started from radically different traditional societies and therefore can achieve modernization, if at all, only by means of a radically different process.[5]

As Max Weber was the first to point out, the original growth of a modern society based on individual mobility and security, rational experimentation, and continuous efforts to increase and improve production was made possible in the West only by a unique combination of structural and cultural factors in its history.[6] These factors were the early development of rational speculation in Greece and the early struggle in Jewish and Christian prophetic religion against the influence of magic beliefs; the early growth of religiously sanctioned communities not based on ties of kinship, opening the way to cohesive social units transcending clan and tribe; the value placed on the uniqueness of the individual by Christianity, and on productive, physical labor by Western Christianity; the development of the Western medieval city as a nontribal community of self-governing, self-protecting, and self-improving individuals, leading eventually to the growth

[4] *The Stages of Economic Growth: A Non-Communist Manifesto* (Cambridge, Mass., 1960).

[5] I have developed this point more fully in my article "Government in the Developing Countries: Its Function and Its Form," in Henry W. Ehrmann, ed., *Democracy in a Changing Society* (New York, 1964), pp. 177–215.

[6] Relevant passages can be found in many parts of Weber's work, but above all in his essay on the Protestant Ethic in Vol. I of the *Gesammelte Aufsaetze zur Religionssoziologie*, in *Wirtschaft und Gesellschaft*, and in the posthumously published *Wirtschaftsgeschichte*.

of an independent urban middle class; the creation of the modern state, combining bureaucratic regularity and efficiency with respect for the codified rights of the subject and the validity of contract under the rule of law; and finally the subordination of the daily lives of Western men to the rational discipline of continuous productive effort and continuous saving and reinvestment of profits (the "spirit of capitalism") under the influence of the Reformation and the Counter-Reformation. Equivalents for each of these factors, or indeed for several of them, may have existed in one or more non-Western traditional societies, but the combination of all of them is unique to the West. Only this combination has made it possible for the uncoordinated efforts of countless people to "better themselves"—to improve their knowledge, their morals, their material well-being, and their social standing—to set in motion the modern dynamism of social change without the guidance of any politically imposed plan of development.

I do not, of course, mean to deny that political measures intended to promote economic development have played a role in Western economic growth; we need only recall the age of mercantilism and of the early colonial companies, the importance of educational and social policies for the rapid development of modern industry, and the role of protectionism and government enterprise in certain latecomer countries of Europe. In no Western country, however, have these measures been central to the overall process of modernization. Nowhere in the West did this process have to be conceived as a primarily political task to be achieved only by the deliberate enforcement of major changes in the economic and social structure by the state and by the deliberate reeducation of the people to the adoption of new values by a political movement. Yet both nationalist and Communist movements in underdeveloped countries justify their claim to a monopoly of political power by proclaiming the need to "put politics in command" in order to achieve development.

Nor can this need be denied in principle, for where the historic preconditions for spontaneous social change as displayed by Western societies are wholly or partly lacking, it seems obvious that effective modernization[7] can be brought about only with the help of a substantial measure of political coordination and initiative, whatever the

[7] Throughout this paper the term "modernization" is used to mean the economic, social, and cultural features of modern development, but no assumption is made about a necessary connection between successful modernization and a particular political system. In our context the question of what changes must take place in the political system as development advances is a subject of investigation, and will not be judged in advance. In particular, it is not assumed that successful moderni-

ideology of the modernizing political activists. If no modern state with a trained bureaucracy exists, one has to be created. If an enterprising middle class willing to invest in production is lacking, the government may find it necessary both to provide the enterprise and to extract the savings required for investment purposes. If the peasants are too poor to save and the landowners unwilling to invest, the peasants may have to be liberated and the landowners to be expropriated; at least, traditional life-styles must be changed by a combination of economic, fiscal, and educational measures. If primitive superstition, narrow tribal loyalties, caste barriers, or specific family forms sanctioned by traditional religion stand in the way of economic and social mobility and of nationwide communication and integration, the obstacles have to be overcome by a "cultural revolution" (in the sense of Bolshevik Russia or Kemalist Turkey in the 1920's, rather than of Maoist China in the 1960's), which in our century only political movements inspired by militant ideologies seem able to bring about. If traditional contempt for manual labor and low esteem for material values prevent the upper classes from taking a serious interest in production and the lower classes from accepting the need for continuity and discipline in industrial work, their attitudes have to be changed by some mixture of coercion and reeducation.

Though none of these tasks of politically forced development can be said to make one particular type of political system inevitable, it is evident that some types are better suited to the job than others. On the one hand, a traditional oligarchy is bound to be opposed to modernization, and a traditional autocracy can cope with it only if it manages to preserve autocratic authority while radically reinterpreting traditional values—a feat so far accomplished only by Japan, and unlikely to be repeated in our century. On the other hand, a pluralistic democracy of the Western type, with its built-in respect for minority rights and legal procedures, will find it very difficult to overcome the resistance to modernization presented by entrenched privileged classes, tradition-bound religious communities, and self-sufficient tribes. Most likely to succeed would appear to be political systems that combine strong governmental powers, severely limiting the representation of independent interests and the expression of independent opinions, with a modernizing ideology that legitimates these powers by invoking the urgency of material and national progress and the

---

zation necessarily implies an advance toward political pluralism. The concept of "politically forced modernization" is central to this study. The concept of "political modernization" is never used.

will of the people. This applies particularly if a government can base itself on a privileged political movement devoted to reeducating the people and to mobilizing them for participation in carrying out government and party policy—in other words, in changing society and themselves. There is thus a natural correspondence between the task of politically forced development and the rise of development dictatorships or mobilization regimes in general, and of movement regimes of either the nationalist or the Communist type in particular.

The Distinctive Consequences of Communist Ideology

The most effective dictatorship of development so far has been the Communist party dictatorship in the Soviet Union; in a number of respects, it has become a model for all others, Communist and non-Communist alike.[8] Yet in classical Communist ideology, the task of modernization played no central role. Lenin started from the Marxist assumption that the "dictatorship of the proletariat" would first be achieved in advanced industrial countries; when his party seized power in backward Russia, he attributed its success to one of the "zigzags of history"[9] and expected the Communists of Western and Central Europe soon to follow suit. It was only their persistent failure to do so that forced first the Bolsheviks and later the victorious Communist parties of other underdeveloped countries to attempt politically forced modernization.

Yet in Marxist ideology, the ultimate goal that gives meaning to all Communist effort is not the modernization of a particular country, but the attainment of the classless society on a world scale. That objective is defined as a social order in which, thanks to the expected rise in the levels of technical productivity and general education, there will no longer be any scarcity of material goods or any need for an occupational division of labor between those who carry out manual or subordinate tasks and those who perform intellectual or directing tasks. Because there will be neither problems of distribution nor a social hierarchy implicit in the structure of production, there will also be no need for any coercive apparatus and no distinction between

[8] See Richard Lowenthal, "The Model of the Totalitarian State," in Royal Institute of International Affairs, *The Impact of the Russian Revolution, 1917–1967* (London, 1967).

[9] See Lenin's report to the Seventh Congress of the Bolshevik party (March 1918) on the Brest peace treaty with imperial Germany: "The more backward the country which, owing to the zigzags of history, had to start the socialist revolution, the more difficult it is for it to pass from the old capitalist relations to socialist relations. To the tasks of destruction new tasks are added, incredibly difficult tasks, viz. organizational tasks...." (*Selected Works* [London, n.d.], VII, 285–86.)

rulers and ruled. The remaining tasks of social administration will be performed, just like the higher directing tasks of production, by all the members of society taking turns.

Of course, this vision of a classless and stateless society is based not on a scientific analysis of the trends of social development, as Marx and Lenin claimed, but on a number of ideological assumptions that are either unproven or demonstrably wrong. The expectation that the rise of productivity will eliminate the scarcity of material goods assumes a limited elasticity of human material wants and a limited growth of the world's population—hence it depends on future human decisions that may be influenced but cannot be foreseen with certainty. The view that the need for an occupational division between subordinate and directing tasks in production will disappear with advances in technology and education is contrary to experience in the century since Marx sketched out his prophecy. Technological progress has tended to make the "higher" tasks of production and administration more complicated, widening rather than narrowing the gap between them and the remaining tasks of manual or subordinate labor, and educational progress tends to equalize only people's chances— not their abilities—to acquire the knowledge needed for mastering the more complicated tasks. Finally, the belief that all need for social coercion will disappear once the problems of income distribution resulting from material scarcity are solved is based on an absurdly narrow view of the causes of social conflict.

In fact, far from being scientifically deducible from the Marxian analysis of capitalism's "laws of motion," the belief in the eventual disappearance of all social conflict was the axiom on which that analysis was constructed—an axiom derived from Marx's utopian heritage. The vision of a society without conflict has been the core of every utopia ever invented by philosophers and prophets in search of release from the unbearable personal and social conflicts of their time, and it is utopian also in the strict sense of being inherently impossible. But in its Marxist version, this utopian vision of the classless and stateless society is presented as a goal for political action whose attainment is guaranteed by the "laws of history": we are dealing with a secular religion, in which history is viewed as the movement of mankind toward its salvation on earth, and revolutionary practice as the way to fulfill this destiny.

Thus in contrast to nationalist movement regimes, which may have no higher goal than the achievement of complete independence and the effective modernization of their country (a pragmatic task limited in space as well as in time), Communist regimes are officially dedicated to the struggle for the utopian goal of a classless world society, a struggle that is not only worldwide but unending, since its goal can never be achieved. Yet there exists no equally fundamental difference in the circumstances under which these two types of movement regimes have come to power: both have led victorious revolutions in underdeveloped countries only, and both have been confronted after victory with the need to prove their effectiveness in the immediate tasks of politically forced development. Moreover, each type often finds it necessary to take actions commonly associated with the other. Nationalist regimes have frequently felt compelled both to take forcible measures against native privileged classes and to seek international support against privileged foreign capitalist firms and the imperialist powers protecting them. Communist regimes, for their part, have regularly discovered that in the interests of survival they have had to give priority to the immediate tasks of consolidating their power at home and developing their country's productive forces, even if they view these tasks as mere stages on the road to world revolution and Communist utopia. Indeed, the parallelism in the actual situations and immediate problems of both types of regimes, and the contrast between the utopian goals proclaimed by Communist doctrine and the limited range of policies available to Communist regimes in practice, are so striking that some analysts have properly raised questions about just how important are the effects of the ideological differences for the behavior of such regimes. Is the goal of the classless society really more than an energizing "myth" of limited operational relevance for the content of Communist policy?[10] Does it really make a difference that one type of regime claims to be carrying out revolutionary transformation at home and risking international conflicts strictly as a means of achieving national independence and development, while the other type claims to be promoting national development and power strictly as a means of fostering social revolution at home and abroad?

In fact, the different ideologies of Communist and revolutionary nationalist movements in underdeveloped countries do have observable consequences of crucial importance both before and after the seizure of power. First, though the commonly accepted view that both types of movement are led by the intelligentsia is broadly true, it must

[10] For the fullest statement of this view, see John Kautsky, *Communism and the Politics of Development* (New York, 1968). For an earlier critique by the present writer, see Richard Lowenthal, "Communism and Nationalism," *Problems of Communism*, XI: 6 (1962).

not be allowed to blur the substantial differences in leadership composition between the Communist and most of the nationalist parties. The intelligentsia of those countries typically consists of a mixture of sons of the traditional upper classes with educated people of lower social origin. But the share of the sons of landowners or even merchants, and of people with bureaucratic or military experience *before* the revolution, appears to be considerably higher in the central and provincial leadership of the nationalist parties than in that of the Communist parties.[11] Second, Communist ideology seems generally more effective than nationalist ideologies in preserving the newly privileged elites from corruption by the temptations that follow the conquest of power;[12] to this extent, Communism seems the better energizing "myth." But for our study, the crucial operational difference is the third: Communism and revolutionary nationalism in power tend to lead to different strategies of politically forced development, different kinds of imposed social change, and different unforeseen effects on the evolution of the movement regimes themselves.

In economic policy, all dictatorships of development, whether nationalist or Communist, are committed in principle to the struggle against vested interests that obstruct the nation's economic development, but the nationalist regimes are not ideologically committed to a precise model demanding all-out nationalization or collectivization. In practice, the victorious nationalists may well find that radical changes in land ownership and tenure are required to liberate the peasants, break the power of the landed oligarchy, and raise produc-

---

11 Comparative studies of Communist and national-revolutionary political elites are still extremely rare. John Kautsky quotes Robert C. North's pioneering analysis, *Kuomintang and Chinese Communist Elites* (Stanford, Calif., 1952), which refers to "the basic similarity in social origins of the largest portion of both Kuomintang and Communist leaders"; but North's own figures do not bear him out. Comparing the Kuomintang Central Executive Committees of 1924, 1926, and 1929 and the Communist Politburos up to 1945 in terms of the occupations of the members' fathers, he gets indeed a closely similar representation of the traditional upper class (wealthy landlord, scholar landlord, scholar official, scholar), with 34% for the KMT and 33.4% for the CP, and again 8.5% "other landlords" for the former and 8.3% for the latter. But for the bourgeois element (merchant scholars, wealthy merchants, other merchants) he finds 46.8% in the KMT and only 8.3% in the CP; whereas "wealthy peasants" and "other peasants" account for only 6.4% of the KMT and 41.7% of the CP leaders, with another 8.3% of workers' sons added in the Communist case (p. 47).

12 Though Communist regimes are hardly immune from corruption, I know of no Communist dictatorship in which corruption has been as blatant among the higher ranks as in Sukarno's Indonesia, Nkrumah's Ghana, or the later stages of Kuomintang rule in China. On the other hand, the army and bureaucracy of Kemal's nationalist regime in Turkey appear to have preserved a high reputation for integrity throughout.

tivity in the long run; and those who shy away from drastic measures in this field are likely to fail in their self-set task of modernization, as did the Kuomintang on the Chinese mainland. Nowadays most nationalist regimes impose state control over major foreign enterprises on their soil, for symbolic if not for practical reasons, by nationalization with nominal compensation or other equally effective measures. They make plans for the development of diversified national industries, and undertake substantial public investments where private funds and private initiative are not available, thus creating publicly owned and managed industries in key sectors. But they are unlikely to go beyond this program unless forced by circumstances that they perceive either as willful obstructions of their development plans or as technical necessities. For instance, they may be moved to nationalize native-owned industries and banks, as in Egypt, if the owners appear unwilling to cooperate with the national plan. Or they may hand over expropriated land to state-managed collectives if peasants with independent farming experience are lacking, as in Algeria, or more generally if division of the expropriated land would render existing types of cultivation uneconomical, and if conversion to other types would require a prohibitive amount of capital investment.

The Communists, on the other hand, are committed by their long-range aim not only to achieve economic development, but to prevent development "by the capitalist road" and more generally the consolidation of new classes. This means, first of all, that they will typically nationalize all private industry and may lose scarce managerial skills in the process; medium-size and small enterprises in particular are usually run by owner-managers, and their contribution to development is often difficult to replace. Nor does it help much if the Communist leaders are conscious of the problem and would like to wait. Once the owners perceive the implications of the Communists' long-term program and see them as enemies, they become a potential danger to Communist rule; at this point the Communists feel compelled to destroy their economic power base, even though they cannot yet replace their function. That is what happened in Russia during the early months after the October Revolution. Lenin had at first instituted a system of "workers' control" rather than immediately nationalizing most factories; but he soon found the resulting friction between workers and owners too risky in conditions of civil war. Hence the key industries were fully nationalized by the end of June 1918, and the nationalization of all industries was completed in December 1920.

The Chinese Communists, operating in far less developed conditions and gaining control of the main industrial centers only toward the end of the civil war, were at first able to win the cooperation of many private industrialists by a solemn assurance of long-term toleration.[13] Yet the strains of the Korean War led to a tightening of controls by the end of 1950, and in late 1951 to the "Five-Anti" campaign (in which workers and employees of private firms were called upon to denounce the owners for economic crimes, thus enabling the government to raise a heavy capital levy from them as "fines"). In late 1952, after announcing the end of the "rehabilitation period," the regime proclaimed as its policy goal the transformation of all private enterprises into "joint enterprises" under state direction, and this goal was in fact reached much faster than originally planned.[14] Nonetheless, the Chinese seem to have succeeded in retaining the cooperation of most of the former managers.[15]

The Yugoslav Communists started fastest of all. An estimated 54 per cent of Yugoslavia's industry was nationalized while World War II was in progress under a very broadly interpreted decree of November 1944, which provided for expropriating all persons who had collaborated with the Axis powers or fled abroad. A law ordering the complete nationalization of all industries of national importance (as well as of transport, banking, and wholesale trade) was passed in December 1946, and a second law covering the remaining industries in April 1948, on the eve of the break with the Soviets.[16]

In all these cases, the Communist regime's commitment to long-term ideological goals characteristically converged with its immediate interest in maintaining itself in power in such a way as to produce measures that would be premature or irrational in terms of "pure" economic development. Moreover, the situation is bound to recur. Thus, preventing development "by the capitalist road" also means preventing the unhampered growth of an individualistic peasant economy beyond a certain point, since such growth inevitably leads

[13] See the "Common Program" adopted by the Chinese People's Consultative Conference in September 1949; T. J. Hughes and D. E. T. Luard, *The Economic Development of Communist China, 1949–1960*, 2d ed. (London, 1961), p. 20; Ygael Gluckstein, *Mao's China* (Boston, 1957), pp. 192 *et seq*.

[14] The process was speeded up in 1955 and virtually completed by September 1956 (Hughes and Luard, pp. 93–95; Gluckstein, pp. 203–6).

[15] Franz Schurmann, *Ideology and Organization in Communist China* (Berkeley, Calif., 1966), p. 282; see also pp. 60–61 below. The flexibility shown by the Chinese Communists in retaining former owners as managers rather than liquidating them seems to have been due to their belief that people's consciousness may be transformed along with their social function—if the pressure is strong enough.

[16] George W. Hoffman and Fred Warner Neal, *Yugoslavia and the New Communism* (New York, 1962), pp. 90–96.

through competition to social differentiation and the emergence of a kulak class of incipient rural capitalists, a development perceived by the regime as a threat both to its future goals and to its present control.

Again, Lenin had hoped to avoid this danger by gradual, evolutionary methods, using the state's economic power to guide the peasantry along the alternative road of voluntary "cooperativization";[17] and as late as 1928–29, Bukharin was still convinced that the Soviet Union could both contain its kulak minority and use the peasants' surpluses to finance an industrialization program without resorting to the new revolutionary upheaval that forced collectivization was bound to mean.[18] Yet a growing sector of Bolshevik opinion came in the course of the 1920's to be alarmed by the increasing influence of the small minority of prosperous, "capitalist" farmers in the villages and by the limits that the growth of the peasants' informal organizations (the "land associations" based on the prerevolutionary communes) might impose on the extraction of funds by the state and hence on the pace of industrialization. Finally, Stalin came to share this alarm in the winter of 1927–28, when he found it nearly impossible to make the peasants sell at low, state-fixed prices the amounts of grain needed by the growing town population.[19]

Faced in this critical form with the economic difficulty of effecting the transition to industrialization, Stalin interpreted it as a political problem resulting from peasant obstruction under kulak leadership. Rather than tolerate any force that might push Russia toward development by a road other than that prescribed by Communist ideology, he decided to impose what he later described as another revolution, equal in importance to that of October 1917 but distinguished from

---

[17] Lenin, "On Cooperation," *Selected Works*, IX, 408–9. First published Jan. 4–6, 1923.

[18] See Nikolai Bukharin, "Lenin's Political Testament," *Pravda*, Jan. 21, 1929 (referring to Lenin's article "On Cooperation"); and see also Bukharin, "Notes of an Economist," *Pravda*, Sept. 30, 1928. A slightly condensed English translation of the latter is printed as an appendix to Bertram Wolfe, *Khrushchev and Stalin's Ghost* (New York, 1957), pp. 295 *et seq.*

[19] According to official figures, kulaks in 1927 amounted to only 3.9% of the village population, and accounted for 13% of the grain production. It was the increased grain consumption by poorer peasants rather than the kulaks' ill will that limited supplies to the towns. But there was evidence that the "land associations," typically led by well-off peasants, were more influential than the village soviets until they were officially dissolved by the Fifteenth Party Congress in December 1927 (Leonard Schapiro, *The Communist Party of the Soviet Union* [London, 1960], pp. 336–40). See also Alexander Erlich, *The Soviet Industrialization Debate, 1924–1928* (Cambridge, Mass., 1960); and Alec Nove, *Economic Rationality and Soviet Politics* (New York, 1964), pp. 17–39.

it by being accomplished "from above, on the initiative of the state"[20] —the "liquidation of the kulaks as a class" and the forced collectivization of the whole of Soviet agriculture within a few years. The next step toward utopia had to be taken, at once and regardless of cost, as soon as experience showed that the spontaneous development of society was tending to create increasingly powerful obstacles to the attainment of the goal.

The Chinese Communists in turn, aware of the terrible human and economic price the Soviets had paid for forced collectivization, originally hoped for a gradual and voluntary collectivization. As late as the end of 1952, their policy called for the socialist transformation of agriculture to be completed in the course of three five-year plans, starting at that date; by March 1954, less than 1.5 per cent of peasant households had been organized into Agricultural Producers' Cooperatives, with a target of 20 per cent for the end of 1957.[21] Yet during 1954, heavy flood damage reduced the grain harvest, and the state-controlled grain market was plunged into crisis as during the winter and spring of 1954–55 many peasants rushed to buy from the state stocks; the party and the government reacted by curtailing sales and sending out their cadres for "house-to-house appraisals" to judge the peasants' "real" needs and expose "hoarders."[22] It was in the light of this need for tighter control of the peasants that the government first started a speedup of collectivization: the number of Agricultural Producers' Cooperatives jumped during that same winter from 90,000 to 670,000. After a brief pause for consolidation, Mao gave the signal for all-out collectivization in July 1955; this coincided with the discovery that capital investments for industrialization were lagging behind the targets of the first five-year plan, and with the decision to increase investment dramatically during the following year. From then on, targets were constantly raised and overtaken, until by the end of 1956 some 96 per cent of all peasant households had been organized in producers' cooperatives—83 per cent of them in the fully collectivized type.[23] Mao had cast aside his gradualist long-term plans because in a critical economic situation tighter control of the peasants had suddenly become urgent; and once high-pressure collectivization had proved the most effective means of control, there was no turning back.

In Yugoslavia, there were hardly any kulaks to be fought following

[20] The formula comes from the official "Short Course" of the History of the CPSU, edited under Stalin's personal direction and first published in 1938.
[21] Hughes and Luard, p. 150.
[22] Gluckstein, pp. 136–41.
[23] Hughes and Luard, pp. 150–54.

the radical land reform of the early postwar years; nevertheless, the first five-year plan, adopted in 1947, called for collectivizing half the country's arable land by 1951. Progress toward this target was slow at first, and at the time of the break with the Soviets, in mid-1948, there were only 932 "rural working cooperatives," holding only 2.6 per cent of the arable.[24] But the regime's first reaction to the break was an effort to speed up both industrialization and collectivization. Though the country's precarious international situation precluded the use of terrorist violence against the peasant majority, the application of economic pressures succeeded in raising the number of collectives to nearly 7,000, holding almost one-fifth of the arable, by the end of 1950, before the introduction of economic reform policies first stopped and later reversed the movement.[25] The Yugoslav case, however, appears to be atypical because of the interaction of international and domestic factors both in starting and in limiting the movement of forced collectivization. Tito's original decision to embark on a more radical domestic policy in mid-1948 was probably motivated by the need to preserve the morale of his party cadres after the break with Stalin; yet the need to preserve popular support in the face of growing Soviet pressure subsequently limited the forms that policy could take and finally, together with the need for Western economic aid, contributed to its demise.

What seems to emerge from both Russian and Chinese experience is, however, a more general principle. This is that a party dictatorship committed to a utopian goal cannot be content with a single revolutionary upheaval, however radical and profound; rather it must attempt to impose on society repeated "revolutions from above" because the economic growth achieved by politically forced development is accompanied by spontaneous social changes that run counter to the utopian vision. The point is not that the Communist rulers are forcing the pace merely because they are impatient to reach the final goal: their Marxist readiness to work their way through a number of historic stages in order to create the economic and cultural preconditions for utopia is precisely what distinguishes them from less realistic utopians of the anarchist or millenarian type. The point is that members of a Communist-ruled society, in pursuing their interests within the framework set by the regime for the sake of economic development, tend to create new social stratifications, and that the more successful groups among them, in seeking to consolidate their advantage, usually

---

[24] Hoffman and Neal, p. 97.
[25] *Ibid.*, pp. 272–73.

form new centers of social power. It is for this reason that the Communist regime, in order to preserve both its freedom to approach its final goal and the monopoly of power needed for that purpose, feels compelled again and again to intervene forcibly to prevent the consolidation of ideologically undesirable new class structures. It cannot preserve its control of the direction of social development without repeatedly wrenching society from the path it would "naturally" take, since all natural paths lead away from the utopian goal.

In particular, the problem is bound to reappear as the growth of nationalized industry, with its attendant bureaucratic administration and planning machinery, leads to the emergence of a specialized stratum of engineers, managers, and economic administrators—people who must be given certain privileges to make them contribute to economic development, yet whose consolidation as a privileged class would threaten the attainment of the utopian goal. For a nationalist dictatorship of development, not committed to the utopia of a classless society, none of these problems need arise; hence there is no need for the kind of recurrent revolutions from above that occur in Communist political systems. This is why nationalist movement regimes may become "extinct,"[26] in the sense of ceasing to be revolutionary, much more easily than Communist ones.

The specific, long-term program of economic and social transformation and the repeated revolutions from above are not the only observable effects of the ideological commitment that distinguishes the Communist strategy of development from that of a nationalist movement regime. We must mention at least two other differences. The first concerns the cultural revolution. Communism, as a secular religion, is equipped with a militant atheist philosophy that enables it to attack the traditional beliefs obstructing modernization with a far more ruthless enthusiasm than most nationalist dictatorships of development can muster.[27] However, this also means that Communist regimes cannot be content with merely denouncing the obstructive aspects as such; the Communists are committed to a frontal attack on traditional religion, and such an attack can be difficult and dangerous. The second difference concerns relations with the advanced, capitalist West. For the nationalists, conflicts with Western imperialists are part of an uncompleted struggle for final emancipation from the rem-

---

[26] The evocative expression is from Tucker's article "Towards a Comparative Politics of Movement-Regimes."

[27] The exceptions are the Kemalist and Mexican revolutionary movements with their anti-religious fanaticism.

nants of colonial rule, particularly from Western economic privileges, to be continued as long as Western resistance to those limited objectives makes it necessary; for the Communists, these conflicts are part of a worldwide struggle that can end only with the total demise of the capitalist order.[28] Hence the Communist outlook, as distinct from that of the nationalists, implies a basic unremitting hostility to the Western powers which, though it need not lead to a major war, excludes the possibility of substantial Western capital aid and requires a long-term, high-priority effort in the field of armaments and the basic industries on which their production depends. The combined result of excluding substantial Western aid and giving long-term priority to arms production and basic industries is that a Communist regime will normally have to demand from its subjects heavier and more lasting sacrifices than a nationalist one in order to obtain the same degree of success in development.

It is now apparent why, though all regimes devoted to politically forced development are characterized by a concentration of great power in the hands of the government and limitations on pluralistic political freedoms, only regimes inspired by Communist ideology tend to acquire totalitarian powers in the full sense of an institutional monopoly over policy decision, organization, and information by the ruling party, and of the freeing of the state from all legal limitations in the exercise of its tasks. The attempt not merely to speed up development by political means but to enforce development of a special type along lines that society would not naturally take, requires beyond the original destruction of anti-developmental institutions and social forces the repeated "revolutionary" (i.e., violent) intervention by a dictatorial state to prevent or reverse the spontaneous growth of ideologically undesirable social phenomena. The effort to destroy not merely specific superstitions and anti-modern traditions, but traditional religion itself in the name of a "scientific" world view embodied in the official ideology, requires the monopolistic imposition of that ideology on all media of information and instruction. The decision to maintain for an indefinite time an attitude of basic, unremitting hostility to the non-Communist world implies the need for long-term economic sacrifices so great that no scope is left for a free expression of different interests and opinions. Communist regimes

[28] A few nationalist leaders, notably Sukarno in Indonesia and Nkrumah in Ghana, have gradually come to adopt a similar attitude, but only as a result of failures in development and the intensified ideological needs arising from those failures; such an attitude has emerged as a prelude to the collapse of their regimes.

thus constitute both the extreme, totalitarian form of a dictatorship of development and the specific form whose ideology does not recognize any built-in limits on its own function short of the attainment of utopia on a world scale. Yet contrary to the assumption of Communist ideology, experience has shown that such built-in limits do exist.

The Communist Dilemma: Utopia versus Modernity

In contrast to revolutionary nationalist movement regimes, then, Communist regimes in underdeveloped countries—the only Communist regimes that have so far arisen from indigenous revolutions—are characterized by a dualism of goals. Owing to the conditions in which they come to power, they aim at politically forced development; owing to Communist ideology, they aim at achieving the classless society. Both goals, moreover, are closely bound up with the power interests of such regimes. Their leaders see rapid, successful modernization as necessary for survival in a presumably hostile world; it is also likely to increase the number of nonparty citizens at home who loyally accept the regime for its contribution to their welfare, to general progress, or to the strength of the fatherland. The approach to utopia, on the other hand, serves to legitimate the Communist leadership in the eyes of party members, and thus to cement the internal cohesion of the regime; and the utopian goal can be invoked also to justify crushing any potential centers of independent social power that arise in the process of development.

In some respects, these commitments to utopia and to modernization reinforce each other. Not only is belief in the secular religion of Communism a source of inspiration to the party's cadres, immunizing them against the cynicism and corruption of power and assuring their continued ascetic dedication after victory, but also it may encourage the ordinary worker to keep up his effort while accepting prolonged material sacrifices in the hope of receiving some ultimate reward in the historical Beyond.[29] Conversely, practical successes in quickly increasing the nation's economic and military power may strengthen the cadres' confidence in the scientific truth of the ideology guiding the leaders and their conviction that further stages on the road to the classless society will be attained with similar promptness.

Yet in other respects, the two commitments are in stark, irreconcilable conflict: for development in the sense of catching up with the economic and military capacities of the advanced Western nations is

---

[29] The analogy with the influence of the early puritan religion on zeal for work was stressed in our discussions by Maurice Meisner.

achieved most speedily by subjecting people to the discipline and rationality of production by a combination of coercive threats and material incentives, whereas utopia can be approached only as more and more people are willing to work for the common good, not from fear of deprivation or hope for individual advantage, but out of an enthusiastic faith. This leads to opposite strategies for the planned reeducation of the masses: for the sake of the final goal, the Communist regime ought to aim at creating a "new man," a man free from the egoistic ambition and avarice characteristic of class society; yet for the sake of rapid development it must aim at educating and manipulating "economic man," the type that has created the modern industrial society precisely by pursuing his own self-interest. Communist doctrine may, of course, try to reconcile the conflict by arguing that the new, Communist man will emerge only as material abundance takes the place of scarcity, and that "economic man" and his self-interest are needed to enable society to traverse the intermediate stages quickly.[30] Yet on the one hand the need for self-sacrificing enthusiasm, at least among the active Communist minority, cannot be dispensed with in the earlier stage either; and on the other hand the materialist education of the masses may well make it increasingly difficult to reconvert them later to the ideals of Communist man.[31] The fact remains that the more successful the regime proves in inculcating materialist values, the faster national development is likely to advance—but the sharper the conflict between its long-term aims and the spontaneous interests of the masses, conceived now in an increasingly materialist frame of reference, is likely to be.

In the history of the Communist regimes in question, this basic contradiction between the goals of utopia and modernity appears in the form of a succession of concrete policy conflicts. As we have seen, development requires not only that expert managers and administrators be trained but also that they be given authority in production, security in the enjoyment of material privileges, and some influence on policy. Yet the security of a privileged stratum is incompatible with the goal of a classless society, and its influence on policy would tend to be conservative and inevitably come into conflict with the total power of a party committed to that goal. Hence Communist regimes in developing countries sooner or later experience conflicts between two kinds of elites: the elite of revolutionary veterans iden-

---

[30] Cf. the early Soviet criticism of the Chinese communes along these lines.

[31] This counterargument has been used not only by Mao, particularly since the Socialist Education campaign of 1964, but increasingly by Fidel Castro.

tified with the utopian orientation, and the new technocratic elite aspiring to influence in the name of rational economic development. Although the veterans' generation necessarily dominates the party apparatus at first, the party's interest in preserving its power may eventually cause some key leaders to take an independent position, leading typically to a "generation crisis" in the party and to a major change in its composition.

Again, the choice between the use of ideological and material incentives and of coercive measures in economic life is likely to cause different kinds of conflict at different stages of development. During the most dramatic phase of industrialization, one major issue is the need for inequality of rewards in order to stimulate both the growth of the new stratum of engineers and managers and the ambition of gifted workers to acquire skills, earn promotions, and initiate technical improvements; here conflict arises between the long-term egalitarian ideals of Communism and the need to raise productivity. At this stage, the consumption of the mass of unskilled workers new to industry has to be kept so low that their education to working discipline can be assured only by intense propaganda, increasingly supplemented by economic penalties and direct coercive threats. As the level of industrial productivity advances and the influx of untrained labor from the countryside slows down, mass coercion may become both less necessary because of the greater range of available goods and less useful because of the need to promote a sense of positive responsibility for the maintenance of machinery and the quality of the products, rather than mere submission to discipline. At this stage a major shift from the role of coercion to the use of material incentives, familiar from the history of capitalist industry, becomes rational. But if carried out in a Communist dictatorship, such a shift is likely to reduce the political power of the agencies of coercion; moreover, it will tend to reinforce the role of "economic man" and correspondingly to reduce the importance of Communist ideology in the life of the working masses. At this stage, therefore, conflict is likely to turn on the relative importance of economic tasks and ideological tasks in the activity of the ruling party.

Finally, once the structural obstacles to economic development have been removed, economic growth may be expected to proceed most rapidly if further violent upheavals are avoided and all productive classes can go about their daily business with a sense of both personal and social security, that is, without fear not only of new waves of terrorism but of further sudden, politically imposed changes in their social situation. Any revolution from above, undertaken by the regime in order to prevent the consolidation of new class differences and to preserve the party's freedom to work toward its long-range goal, is bound to disturb that sense of security, hence to interfere with the continuity of growth and to cause economic losses that may be severe. It follows that revolutions from above will be initiated only after serious policy conflicts between the advocates of renewed revolutionary change and the defenders of steady economic growth. In such conflicts, the supporters of a new turn of the revolutionary screw will typically argue that the economic losses caused by the break in continuity—say, by forced collectivization, or by a wholesale purge of managerial personnel, or by the introduction of the "communes" in China—will be merely temporary, since the new measures, besides assuring the party's hold on power and taking the next step toward the utopian goal, will also unleash new forces of popular initiative in production whose impact will more than compensate for the initial setback. But the closer the development of a Communist country approaches the level of a modern industrial society, the more difficult it will be to sustain such an argument.

The dynamics of Communist regimes in developing countries thus appear to be characterized by recurring conflicts not only between the two kinds of goals pursued by those regimes, but between two types of social change arising from their policies. As the Communists succeed in destroying the obstacles to modernization rooted in the structure and culture of the given traditional society, in inculcating a new discipline of production and new "materialist," achievement-oriented values, and in creating a framework for the operation of material incentives, the tendency to further economic development becomes increasingly spontaneous, or self-sustaining, in the sense of no longer depending on deliberate political action. However, this new type of spontaneous change, being based on the material self-interest of individuals, also tends to create new class differentiation, and thus comes into recurrent conflict with the other goal of the regime, the classless society. Hence the Communists seek again and again to undo those ideologically undesirable by-products of economic development and spontaneous social change by using their monopoly of state power to impose centrally manipulated social change guided by their ideology—in other words, by initiating repeated revolutions from above. For change in the direction of utopia never becomes spontaneous—that, indeed, is what is meant by calling a goal "utopian."

Yet in this persistent conflict between developmental and utopian goals, and between the tendencies of spontaneous social change and the policies of imposed social change, the balance of forces itself is changing in the course of time, and that in two different ways. On the one hand, we observe throughout the history of these indigenous Communist regimes a kind of natural alternation in which periods of revolutionary upheaval are followed by periods of consolidation and economic progress, and these in turn by new revolutionary upheavals, though the alternation does not seem regular enough to be meaningfully described as cyclical. On the other hand, it seems evident that the very success of economic development tends in the long run to strengthen the forces of spontaneous, self-sustaining change, which are typical of modern societies everywhere, while making the cost of further imposed revolutionary change not only higher and more obvious, but less likely to be recovered by a new upsurge of enthusiasm. Our argument, then, suggests the existence of a long-term trend toward the victory of modernization over utopianism: as Communist-governed developing societies approach the level of advanced industrial societies, the arbitrary reshaping of their social structure by ideologically guided political power—in Marxist terms, the reshaping of their "basis" by their "superstructure"—becomes increasingly difficult and ultimately impossible. But once a Communist party regime recognizes that permanent revolution has reached its limit, it becomes extinct as a movement regime and turns into an essentially conservative bureaucracy; and such a change of function and values is bound to affect its institutional structure as well.

The Dilemma in Practice

In the following pages, I shall examine the way in which the Soviet, Chinese, and Yugoslav Communist regimes have dealt with three types of policy conflicts arising from the clash between utopian and developmental attitudes—conflicts over the dualism of elites, over the use of different types of economic incentives, and over the continuation of the revolution from above—and shall try to show what effects the solutions chosen by each of them have had on their respective political systems.

Elite Dualism and Change in the Party

Russia. Soon after the October Revolution, conflict developed between the utopian demand for "workers' control" and the economic need for managerial authority in industry. The idea that factories could at once be taken over by their workers and run by elected committees had been no part of prerevolutionary Bolshevik doctrine; but the Bolsheviks had used the slogan of "workers' control" as a weapon in their final struggle for power. After victory, the new Communist trade union leaders came to identify "workers' control" with their own control, and pointed to union influence in the new management boards of nationalized industry as proof that the unions need no longer defend the workers' interests against "their own state." Their influence was reflected in the purely syndicalist clause in the new Bolshevik party program of 1919, claiming that the "unions must achieve the actual concentration in their hands of all management of the national economy."[32]

When Lenin embarked at the beginning of 1920 on a campaign to end committee rule in industry and restore one-man responsibility on all levels, the initial resistance of the Communist union leaders had much support from the rank and file, above all because the shortage of technically competent party men made it inevitable, despite the nominal authority of "red directors" selected by the party, that much of the restored power of decision would in practice be exercised by "bourgeois specialists." Yet the industrial situation was so desperate, and the dependence on non-Communist technicians so evidently temporary, that the party's top leadership at this time was united in putting economic necessity above ideological purity; at the Ninth Party Congress, in March 1920, Lenin's policy was adopted and union interference in management rejected as "syndicalist."[33] For one more year, a hard core of the defeated Communist trade unionists continued the struggle under the flag of the "workers' opposition." The consistently utopian platform of this group not only denounced the influence of the "bourgeois specialists," but anticipated later criticism of the bureaucratic and "bourgeois degeneration" of the party and even the demand that all party members, however highly placed, do manual labor for three months each year.[34] But the Tenth Party Congress of March 1921, which introduced the New Economic Policy and generally turned away from the utopianism of the early post-revolutionary period, adopted Lenin's motion formally condemning the views of this group as a "syndicalist and anarchist deviation" that was incompatible with the Marxist teaching on the leading role of the party, and therefore inconsistent with party membership.[35]

Henceforth, the issue was not *workers'* control, but *party* control

[32] Leonard Schapiro, *The Origins of the Communist Autocracy* (London, 1955), pp. 226–27.

[33] *Ibid.*, pp. 230–33.

[34] This platform owed much to the influence of an intellectual, Alexandra Kollontai (*ibid.*, pp. 293–94).

[35] *Ibid.*, pp. 317–19.

of management, and on this issue a very different alignment developed on the eve of the first five-year plan. Most nonparty experts in the state planning organs and in the higher administration and management of industry were known to be skeptical of the sudden spurt of industrialization envisaged by Stalin and to sympathize with the views of what was soon to become the Right Opposition.[36] When Stalin decided on his new installment of revolutionary violence, he was prepared to incur the costs of a partial purge and total intimidation of those insufficiently "red" experts along with the economic costs of forced collectivization, and to mobilize working-class resentment against the "bourgeois specialists" (many of whom were in fact ex-Menshevik intellectuals) no less than against the kulaks. The Shakhty trial of nonparty engineers in the Donets for "sabotage" was launched in the spring of 1928, at the same time as the first proposals for the new industrial targets were put forward. The trial was followed by a campaign encouraging people to develop a "healthy lack of faith in the specialists," which led to the arrest of several thousand of them in the course of the next few years; their professional association was dissolved in 1929.[37] Meanwhile, a campaign for the high-speed technical training of thousands of Communist officials and tens of thousands of working-class activists was launched in July 1928 in order to provide a new, reliable industrial elite;[38] it was these new technicians who were meant to benefit from the final establishment of managerial "one-man leadership" by a Central Committee decision of September 1929.

The first signs that the economic cost of this "class struggle" orientation in the selection of industrial personnel was getting too heavy for Stalin appeared before the end of the first five-year plan. In a speech of June 1931—the same speech that launched the campaign against "egalitarianism"—he called for the creation of a new technical intelligentsia from the ranks of the working class, but also for a "changed attitude toward the engineers and technicians of the old school," that is, for an end to the purge.[39] By September 1932, the curriculum of the new technical schools was broadened and lengthened, and admission to them was made dependent on an entrance

---

[36] Jeremy Azrael, *Managerial Power and Soviet Politics* (Cambridge, Mass., 1966), pp. 54–55.

[37] *Ibid.*, pp. 55–57; Schapiro, *The CPSU*, p. 363.

[38] Azrael, p. 127n; Gregory Bienstock, Solomon M. Schwarz, and Aaron Yugow, *Management in Russian Industry and Agriculture* (Ithaca, N.Y., 1944), p. 106.

[39] Stalin, "New Conditions: New Tasks in Economic Construction," speech given June 23, 1931, in *Pravda*, July 5, 1931; printed in Stalin, *Problems of Leninism* (Moscow, 1947), pp. 359–80.

examination because so many students were failing to complete the course; the requirement that two-thirds of the entrants must be workers was silently dropped, and their percentage declined in the following years.[40] By January 1934, when the second five-year plan was adopted by the Seventeenth Party Congress, reconciliation with the nonparty intelligentsia had become official policy, and in contrast to the parallel policy of reconciliation with the former inner-party oppositionists, it remained in effect after the assassination of Kirov at the end of that year. Indeed, the regime's success in creating a new Soviet intelligentsia of working-class and peasant origin and the need to accept this new stratum as "equal members" of the new society along with the workers and peasants became one of the main themes of the campaign for Stalin's new constitution in 1935–36.[41]

It was precisely at this point that the problem of a dualism of elites became acute: a political elite infused with revolutionary traditions and ideological commitment but lacking adequate educational and technical qualifications for running a modern society, and a new technical and managerial elite without those traditions and having only tenuous links with the ruling party. The gap between the two groups may be gauged from the fact that in 1928, on the eve of the first five-year plan, only 2.8 per cent of the "red directors" of state enterprises had a higher education, compared with 58 per cent of the nonparty directors;[42] altogether, only 138 engineers and 751 people with higher technical education were party members at that time.[43] In the course of the plan, parallel with the rushed technical training of Communists and the arrests of thousands of "bourgeois specialists," large numbers of "engineering-technical workers," among them old specialists as well as newly trained workers, were allowed or asked to join the party—according to one report, four thousand in 1930 alone.[44] However, the party role of those who were not of proletarian origin remained precarious, not only because of class discrimination in the rules of admission, but because of the party's ideological climate. As late as the Seventeenth Party Congress in 1934, 40 per cent of the delegates had been Bolsheviks since 1917 or before and 80 per cent since 1920 or before, whereas only 10 per cent had

[40] Bienstock, Schwarz, and Yugow, p. 108.

[41] See Stalin's speeches of May 1935, and see particularly "On the Draft Constitution," speech given Nov. 25, 1936, in *Problems of Leninism*, pp. 520, 540 *et seq.* (English text based on the 11th Russian edition).

[42] Merle Fainsod, *How Russia Is Ruled*, rev. ed. (Cambridge, Mass., 1963), p. 258.

[43] Azrael, p. 53.

[44] *Ibid.*

a higher education.[45] Meanwhile the organizers and engineers with a full technical training, comprising a minority of old "specialist" survivors and an increasing majority of Soviet-educated youth, were assuming an increasingly important role in the new industrial economy. Whereas in 1934 half the country's factory directors had had only a primary education, in 1936 only 40 per cent were in this category, and by 1939, at least in the defense industries and in ferrous metallurgy, the proportion of directors with a higher education had risen to nearly 87 per cent.[46] Even within the working class itself a similar dualism between cadres distinguished by technical competence and those representing the revolutionary tradition developed with the launching of the Stakhanovite movement in the second half of 1935. On both levels Stalin left no doubt about his view that eighteen years after the revolution the time had come to confer on the technically gifted members of the younger generation not only material rewards, but recognition of their leading role in the new society.[47] Indeed, the wish to justify this policy by announcing the disappearance of hostile classes seems to have been his principal motive for proclaiming the new socialist constitution.

Yet contrary to the expectation of his left-wing critics, Stalin was not willing to renounce the utopian goal and to dismantle the party dictatorship in favor of permanent rule by the new, privileged technocracy: he wanted to preserve the party's power to impose further social transformations in the future, yet to effect a radical change in the party's social composition so as to ensure improving economic performance in the present. The change did in fact come about—as a result of the Great Purge of 1936–38. This is not to say that the problem of elite dualism could not have been resolved, even by a Communist regime, in other, less sanguinary ways; or that this was the only, or even necessarily the principal, cause of the unprecedented wave of terror in which the bulk of the veterans of the Bolshevik revolution perished. In the light of the known facts, however, there can be little doubt that it was *one* of the major causes. For it can hardly be regarded as accidental that the Great Purge was preceded by Stalin's deliberate extolling of the new technical cadres over the tradition-bound veterans of the party; that it resulted in the mass liquidation of old Bolsheviks in general, and of the old generation of "red

[45] Bienstock, Schwarz, and Yugow, p. 29; Fainsod, pp. 267–68.
[46] Fainsod, pp. 505–6.
[47] Speech given at the First All-Union Conference of Stakhanovites, Nov. 17, 1935, in *Problems of Leninism*, pp. 526 *et seq.*

directors," as well as a considerable number of the younger party volunteers who had been hastily trained for management in 1928–31 in
particular;[48] and that it was followed by a change in the party statutes
adopted at the Eighteenth Party Congress in March 1939 that threw
the party's doors wide open to young, Soviet-trained managers and
engineers by ending all discrimination against nonproletarian elements.[49] In fact, even before the statute change the effort to enlist the
new technical intelligentsia was stressed by the party machine as soon
as recruitment was resumed with the first abatement of the purge in
1938.[50] Of the delegates to the Eighteenth Party Congress in 1939,
only 5 per cent had been party members since at least 1917 and less
than 20 per cent since 1920, whereas 43 per cent had joined in 1929
or later. The number of delegates still working at the bench was no
longer reported, but more than a quarter now had received a higher
education.[51]

The following years showed that the dualism of elites had been
effectively eliminated. The new managers became party members
almost to a man, and a number of them rose to positions of influence in the state administration. Their material privileges, like those
of other bureaucrats, were increased, and the introduction of fees for
secondary education even tended to make their status hereditary.[52]
Yet they were not allowed to forget that every man's position depended on his continuing loyal and efficient service to the regime. If
the elite of development had thus survived the elite of utopianism,
the basis of the revolutionary commitment to utopian goals was nevertheless still preserved in the institution of the party. It was on this
basis that Khrushchev was able, after Stalin's death and the subsequent restoration of the primacy of the party machine, to reduce the
privileges of the managerial establishment, to shake up its occupational security, and above all to reverse Stalin's educational policies.
Khrushchev's grandiose plans for making manual work compulsory
for all students were, in fact, an attempt to undermine the near-
hereditary privileges of the unified "new class" of bureaucrats and

[48] Azrael, pp. 98–102; Fainsod, p. 506.

[49] The new statute made the conditions of admission to the party independent of
class origin, on the explicit grounds that with the disappearance of the former exploiting class, class distinctions between workers, peasants, and intellectuals were
disappearing also. See A. A. Zhdanov's report to the Eighteenth Congress of the
CPSU, Moscow, 1939.

[50] Fainsod, p. 263.

[51] *Ibid.*, p. 264; Bienstock, Schwarz, and Yugow, p. 29.

[52] Fees were introduced in October 1940; grants for university students were reduced in number at the same time (Fainsod, pp. 290–91).

technicians by another major installment of applied utopianism, if a nonviolent one; and these plans certainly contributed to the steady accumulation of bureaucratic resistance to his leadership that ended in his fall.[53]

China. When the Chinese Communists set out to rebuild their country after the civil war, they started with a firm determination to harness not only managerial skills but also capitalist initiative to the urgent tasks of industrial rehabilitation and development. Their working-class following had been too insignificant for any serious problem of working-class utopianism to arise. Their political strategy had long appealed to the "national bourgeoisie" as one of the revolutionary classes, and that concept was now interpreted to include any businessmen who had not been personally linked with the old regime and who were willing to continue running their factories under the new one. In fact, the bulk of the business community cooperated at first because the Communists had pledged themselves to "protect private enterprise" and even to "clear the road for capitalist development" by eliminating the corrupt favoritism of the past regime.[54] Moreover, the Chinese Communists' initial ideas about management were copied readymade from contemporary Russia.[55] Hence undivided authority, free from interference by either the trade unions or the party, was granted in the interests of production not only to the managers of the big state-owned combines taken over from the Kuomintang and the Japanese, but also to the large numbers of owner-managers. The labor regulations for private industry issued in 1949 not only stressed the common interests of capital and labor and the need for labor discipline, but specifically upheld such traditional principles as compulsory arbitration, a ban on strikes, and the employers' right to hire and fire. Official propaganda even encouraged workers to accept "voluntary" wage cuts in the interest of combating inflation.[56]

This idyllic state of affairs was partly disturbed at the end of 1951 by the "Five-Anti" campaign against the "economic crimes" of private capitalists. The party's appeal to the personnel of all private firms to join in "investigating" the transgressions of their bosses must have considerably weakened the managerial authority of the latter.

[53] Khrushchev introduced this "educational reform" in 1958–59, stressing its egalitarian aspect (Fainsod, pp. 582–83).

[54] Hughes and Luard, *The Economic Development of Communist China*, pp. 89–90; Gluckstein, *Mao's China*, pp. 192–99.

[55] Schurmann, *Ideology and Organization*, pp. 239–50.

[56] Hughes and Luard, pp. 117–21; Gluckstein, pp. 195–96, 213–15.

But in mid-1952, after this campaign had thoroughly frightened the owner-managers and had netted the government substantial capital funds for their coming five-year plan in the form of "fines," it was stopped and the owners were given new assurances of the regime's goodwill. The later pressure to transform the private firms into government-directed "joint enterprises," with the former owner reduced at first to receiving a quarter-share of the profits, and later to a fixed interest on his capital, seems generally to have achieved its aims without a similar "mobilization" from below.

But it was above all in the state-owned modern industrial combines of Manchuria and a few east coast centers that the Soviet model of managerial authority and responsibility was systematically pressed, reaching its maximum effectiveness during the preparation and the early years of the first five-year plan. From 1952 to the first half of 1954, China's Communist planners, then headed by Kao Kang, urged the general adoption of the principle of one-man management instead of the more diffuse traditional forms of collective responsibility. To ensure the subordination of production in each industry and each factory to a single will, there was to be a direct flow of commands from the central ministry to the last factory and from the factory manager to the last workshop, and an equally direct flow of information upward, based on a precise technological division of labor within the factory.[57] This overriding Stalin-type concern for efficiency based on unity of command went, on the one hand, with plans for a substantial, but realistic, rate of industrial growth, and on the other with a steady, ruthless tightening of labor discipline. Norms were raised by means of "emulation" campaigns; punishments were introduced for absenteeism, lateness, and negligence, and administered by "comradely tribunals"; and under the "labor book" system, job changes were placed under the control of employers.[58] In the name of the primacy of economic development over "ideological" considerations, the manager was to be given sole power over piece-work norms and over hiring and firing, though in contrast to Russia, the manager, even in the state-owned factories, was normally still a technical specialist inherited from the pre-Communist period: the training of large numbers of new technical personnel in Soviet-type schools was seen as a task for the period of the first two five-year plans.[59]

[57] Schurmann, pp. 250–62.
[58] Gluckstein, pp. 215–22.
[59] Li Fu-ch'un's report on the first five-year plan to the National People's Congress, July 5–6, 1955, quoted in Hughes and Luard, p. 43.

In the early years the power of the managers had increased along with that of the central ministries and of the planning commission to whom they were responsible; but this trend was reversed when the party resumed effective control over the planning commission after the fall of Kao Kang. At the end of 1954, the party embarked on a new stage of accelerated transformation of society in both the industrial and agricultural spheres. Reasserting its collective supremacy over economic life, it now denounced the exclusive "vertical rule" of the economic ministries over their branches as a form of "dispersionism";[60] by mid-1955, the campaign for one-man management had stopped. The new political climate seems also to have affected the curriculum of the training schools for new managers; political loyalty and aptitude for improvising leadership of the type developed by the party cadres in their long guerrilla struggle now came to be valued over technical expertise.[61]

By the spring of 1956, however, the revolutionary spurt of nationalization and collectivization had been completed; in the party's official view all hostile classes had been liquidated and only hostile individuals were left.[62] The victorious party now sought to dispel the bitterness caused by its harsh measures. To this end it not only granted material concessions, ranging from private plots for the collectivized peasants to wage increases for the workers, but also sought to transform the consciousness of the intellectuals of bourgeois origin by permitting a frank discussion of their grievances in the "Hundred Flowers" campaign, and to recruit a large share of the intellectual elite, of which the managers, technicians, and economic bureaucrats formed an important part, for party membership.[63] The Eighth Party Congress, meeting in September 1956 in this atmosphere of domestic victory and reconciliation (but also in the shadow of Khrushchev's disclosures about Stalin's purges), adopted a new statute ending all discrimination by class origin in the rules of admission as having "lost its original meaning."[64] Thus the Congress opened the doors of the Chinese party to ex-bourgeois intellectuals just as the 1939 party congress of the CPSU had opened the doors to the postrevolutionary So-

[60] Schurmann, pp. 267–71.

[61] *Ibid.*, pp. 283–84.

[62] Cf. John W. Lewis, "Leader, Commissar, and Bureaucrat: The Communist Political System in the Last Days of the Revolution," in Ping-ti Ho and Tang Tsou, eds., *China in Crisis*, Vol. I, Book 2 (Chicago, 1968), pp. 463–65.

[63] See Chou En-lai's "Report on the Question of Intellectuals" (Jan. 1956), quoted in John W. Lewis, *Leadership in Communist China* (Ithaca, N.Y., 1963), p. 109.

[64] Quoted by Lewis, *Leadership in Communist China*, p. 106.

viet intelligentsia—and without a purge. Within a year, the number of intellectuals in the party rose by about half—indeed by over 600,-000 out of a total membership increase of two million—and overtook the number of workers in the party.[65]

The Eighth Party Congress had also replaced the Soviet model of one-man management by the ambiguous formula of "managerial responsibility under the leadership of the party committee"; but the question to what extent the former subordination of the managers to the central ministries would be replaced by subordination to regional party authorities or by genuine autonomy was left open. It was decided a year later under very different political conditions, for in the meantime the mounting flood of intellectual criticism of the regime had convinced Mao Tse-tung that the "Hundred Flowers" experiment had been premature and that a substantial part of the educated class remained unreconciled. The "Anti-Rightist" campaign against the critics followed; and the Central Committee ruled in the fall of 1957 that whereas managers should be autonomous in routine operations, they should be clearly subordinate to the party committee in all policy matters—notably matters concerning their factory's contribution to the five-year plan and the selection of personnel.[66]

It was this assertion of the Communist party's primacy first over the central planning bureaucracy and then over the industrial managers that set the stage for the adoption of the Great Leap Forward in the following year. Though the draft targets for the second five-year plan, worked out in 1956, had been somewhat more ambitious than those for the first, they foreshadowed none of the wild competitive increases now proclaimed in an orgy of party "subjectivism." The immediate pressure both for raising the targets and for trying to mobilize rural manpower on the spot in masses of small, improvised, low-capital "factories" may have arisen from the increasingly evident inability of urban industry to absorb, with the scarce capital available, more than a fraction of the rapidly growing population,[67] and from the Soviet Union's failure to supply massive new amounts of

[65] The figures are given by Lewis, *Leadership in Communist China*, p. 108. The number of "intellectuals" in the party rose from 1.26 million or 11.7% of the membership on June 30, 1956, to 1.88 million, or 14.8% on September 27, 1957. Even assuming a broad definition of "intellectuals," one that includes large groups of employees and minor bureaucrats, the sudden increase seems to have been motivated chiefly by the need for educated cadres.

[66] Schurmann, pp. 195–97, 284–92.

[67] Urban employment is estimated to have risen by "not much more than a million a year," compared to an annual population increase of 12–15 million (Hughes and Luard, pp. 124–25).

capital aid. But although the problem was real and urgent, the solutions adopted—competitive target-raising and rural communes—clearly reflected the proneness of the higher party cadres to relapse into the utopianism of their civil war days as soon as the decision to "put politics in command" freed them from the restraining influence of economic specialists. Though some of the more sober leaders still talked about the need for cadres who were at once "red" and "expert," the provincial party committees increasingly ignored the central planning experts and accounting authorities and bypassed the experienced industrial managers in their area, relying instead on inexpert party men appointed as deputy managers to carry out the committees' demands in a spirit of guerrilla autonomy and provincial autarky.[68]

As it became obvious that the Great Leap was leading to economic disaster, its component policies were abandoned piecemeal in the following years: the fantastic targets were cut, the rural furnaces closed down, the communes reorganized. By 1961, experienced managers were once more granted "independent operational authority" to get orderly production going again, and the planners were allowed to try restoring balance to the national economy.[69] Mao's authority was gravely shaken; but many of his critics in the party leadership must have felt that the party's authority as well was so closely bound up with the general line of the Great Leap that they could not possibly admit its overall failure. Hence P'eng Teh-huai's effort to have the program's utopianism condemned in principle in the name of economic rationality was rejected at the Lushan session of the Central Committee in 1959.[70] Yet the decision to go on defending the correctness of the utopian orgy in words while turning to opposite policies in deeds appears in retrospect to have accelerated the creeping demoralization of the party cadres that began with the Great Leap and that formed the background for the recent Cultural Revolution.

The Great Leap was, after all, an attempt to transfer the guerrilla traditions of China's revolutionary veterans to the field of economic construction. Its failure hit the veteran generation at a time when many of them were old or aging, discrediting the very traditions they

[68] Schurmann, pp. 293–96.
[69] Ibid., pp. 297–98.
[70] David Charles's account of this plenum, "The Dismissal of Marshal P'eng Teh-huai," China Quarterly, 8 (Oct.-Dec. 1961), 63–76, has since been confirmed by the official and semiofficial disclosures made in the course of the Cultural Revolution. See the Central Committee circular of May 16, 1966, in Peking Review, May 19, 1966, and the follow-up, ibid., May 26, 1966.

wished to pass on to the rising postwar generation. By 1961, 80 per cent of all party members were people recruited after the end of the civil war.[71] Many of the new rural cadres, let loose on the peasants with orders to create communes, had become notorious for brutal terrorism and even for common crimes;[72] and many of the middle-level administrators, caught between this ugly reality and the utopian dreams of their leaders, must have lost all faith in the applicability of the veterans' guerrilla spirit to the problems of China's economic development in the 1960's. It was this party crisis that raised the specter of a Chinese counterpart to Soviet revisionism and goaded Mao and some of his civil war comrades, from 1962 onward, into desperate efforts to achieve an ideological revival in order to train "millions of revolutionary successors" among China's youth.[73] But although the campaign to revive the guerrilla spirit seems to have largely succeeded in the army, thanks to the replacement of P'eng Teh-huai by Lin Piao and to the plausible presentation of China as a besieged fortress surrounded by enemies,[74] it apparently encountered growing apathy and even resistance not only among managers and administrators, but even in the party machine.[75] Thus the dualism of elites, familiar from the Russia of the middle 1930's, took rather a different form in China. Here, much of the party apparatus, particularly its postwar generation, backed the developmental realism of the managers and technocrats, whereas the leader was committed by his failure in the Great Leap to a position of utopian revivalism and supported in this by a following of political veterans and most of the army. The result of this constellation has been, first, a growing militarization of China's political and economic life (the "Learn from the Army" campaign); then the mobilization, carried out with army help, of millions of youngsters without production experience for an assault on the cadres of party and administration (the Cultural Revolution); and lately the attempt to rebuild the broken

[71] Lewis, *Leadership in Communist China*, p. 112.

[72] John W. Lewis, "China's Secret Military Papers," *China Quarterly*, 18 (Apr.-June 1964).

[73] See in particular the CCP's Ninth Commentary on the Soviet Party's "Open Letter," entitled *On Khrushchev's Phoney Communism*, New China News Agency, July 14, 1964.

[74] See John Gittings, "The 'Learn from the Army' Campaign," *China Quarterly*, 18 (Apr.-June 1964); and Lewis, "China's Secret Military Papers."

[75] See Tang Tsou, "Revolution, Reintegration, and Crisis in Communist China," and Franz Schurmann, "The Attack of the Cultural Revolution on Ideology and Organization," in Ho and Tsou, *China in Crisis*, Vol. I, Book 1, pp. 277 *et seq.*, Book 2, pp. 525 *et seq.*

and purged party from the top down, with army commanders and political commissars as regional leaders aided by a growing share of rehabilitated old party cadres and a declining share of newly mobilized
young enthusiasts. Whether this policy will succeed in temporarily restoring stability to the shattered political institutions of the regime
remains to be seen; that the dualism of elites cannot be overcome or
economic development successfully resumed while Mao's anti-expert
policy continues seems certain to the present writer.

Yugoslavia. The nationalization of industry, as we have seen, got
off to a much faster start in Yugoslavia than it did in China. The fact
that the first wave of expropriations was justified by broadly interpreted charges of collaboration with the enemy would seem to suggest
that few of the old managers were retained. In general, poorly educated party men with more experience in partisan warfare than in
industry took over as "red directors";[76] and, like their early Russian
models, they threw themselves with enthusiasm into their task of
achieving the "Montenegrin targets" set by the political leadership.
No ideas about "workers' control" from below hampered those early
efforts. In fact, the managers were strictly subordinated to bureaucratic control from above by an elaborate network of ministries and
branch associations that the Yugoslavs seem to have copied from the
machinery of Soviet planning without regard to differences in scale.[77]

The series of reforms that were to become characteristic of the
"Yugoslav road to socialism" from 1950 on arose not from any pressure by the working class, but from the effort of the Yugoslav Communist leaders to defend their independent revolution against the
encroachments of Stalinist imperialism and against the Soviet charges
used to justify their excommunication. After a period of vain attempts
to convince Stalin that he was "misinformed" about Yugoslavia, Tito
and his fellow leaders reluctantly concluded that it was not they but
the Soviets who had strayed from the true Marxist path, owing to the
"bureaucratic degeneration" of their social system. Responding to the
emergency with a revival of utopian fervor, they sought to prevent a
similar process in their own system: they took steps to cut down the

76 See Joseph T. Bombelles, *Economic Development of Communist Yugoslavia*
(Stanford, Calif., 1968), pp. 9, 68. Bombelles cites *Borba*, Nov. 27, 1966, for the
statement that even twenty years after the seizure of power there were still 17,000
directors without an elementary education and 2,500 technical directors without
"adequate" qualifications in their fields (*ibid.*, p. 205n).

77 Hoffman and Neal, *Yugoslavia and the New Communism*, p. 96, quote the
Yugoslav economist R. Bičanić for the statement that at this time, "217 federal and
republican ministers gave orders to directors (of industrial groups) and those in
turn to factory managers."

size of the bureaucracy and to eliminate the privileges of party members, but above all they proclaimed the right of the workers to run their factories through elected councils as the true socialist alternative to Russian "bureaucratic state capitalism."[78] The practical, as distinct from the ideological, importance of this first reform remained negligible so long as each enterprise was kept rigidly subordinate to central administrative planning; for under that system, the scope for managerial authority remained confined to the kind of day-to-day decisions in which no committee can possibly replace the man in charge. But two years later, at the end of the first five-year plan, the logic of the struggle against bureaucracy and the pressure for greater consumer satisfaction converged to beget the second reform—the replacement of central administrative planning by the bold experiment of a "socialist market economy," in which each enterprise was to be free, within the framework of basic proportions fixed by the government, to adjust its output and prices according to supply and demand. With this restoration of management autonomy, the task of the workers' councils and their management committees suddenly became real, indeed vital.

In fact, the reform contained both a developmental and a utopian element. The revival of competition between the nationalized enterprises, which carried with it both the risk of suffering losses, even bankruptcy, and the incentive of retaining some profits for improvements or bonuses, proved a powerful stimulus to development. Moreover, the linking of the enterprises' new autonomy with the slogan "The factories to the workers" enabled the Yugoslav Communists to present the cancellation of certain "gigantomanic" construction projects and unrealistic targets not as a retreat, but as an advance to a truer form of socialism.[79] Finally, the changes in managerial personnel made possible by the reform were on balance beneficial. Managers were now to be appointed by mixed commissions representing the workers' council, the local authority, and the government-controlled industrial chamber in the particular field concerned, and each of these constituent groups was also entitled to propose dismissals, and in certain conditions to force them. Since most of the personnel changes in the years following the reform were initiated by local authorities anxious for greater efficiency leading to better tax yields, a

---

[78] Josip Broz Tito, *Workers Manage Factories in Yugoslavia* (Belgrade, 1950). The thesis of Russian "bureaucratic state capitalism" was first developed in an authoritative series of articles by Milovan Djilas in the autumn of 1950 (see Ernst Halperin, *The Triumphant Heretic* [London, 1958], pp. 119–22).

[79] Halperin, pp. 125–29.

number of the less competent "red directors" were gradually replaced by younger and better trained men.[80] On the other hand, the principle of management's responsibility to the workers for job security, wage policy, and profits encouraged pressure from below to conceal losses by allowing insufficient depreciation and other accounting tricks, and the refusal of new credits to inefficient enterprises—the counterweapon of the central authorities—could easily be attacked as "bureaucratic interference with workers' management." In practice, this pressure from below to force the community to subsidize hidden losses, combined with the leadership's continued desire to maintain a higher rate of investment than Yugoslavia could afford, produced a recurrent inflation that may fairly be described as the price Yugoslavia has paid for the utopian element in her system of "market socialism."[81]

At the same time, the power, cohesion, and confidence of the party elite were gravely weakened by the decentralizing tendency of the reform, by its emphasis on economic competence rather than traditional loyalty, and by the shifting of utopian hopes away from the role of the party to that of the organs of workers' management. The Sixth Party Congress of November 1952 proclaimed the doctrine that de-bureaucratization and self-management required a basic change in the role of the Communists from a ruling party identified with state power to an ideological vanguard working by persuasion. As a result, the Congress not only changed the party's name to "Communist League," but dismantled much of the party's apparatus and loosened centralized discipline to the point of dissolving the units charged with implementing party policy in government organs and mass organizations.[82] The resulting disorientation of the party activists was further increased in February 1953, when the peasants were permitted to leave the collective farms. This decision, which was intended both to improve the economic performance of agriculture and to broaden the political basis of the regime, led in short order to the massive dissolution of the farms, which had been the party's main rural strongholds.[83]

---

[80] In 1956, 502 enterprises out of a total of 6,079 changed their managers, and this was a smaller proportion than in the preceding years. Of the dismissals, 168 were initiated by the workers' council, 314 by the authorities, and 20 by the party (Hoffman and Neal, pp. 241–42). But see Bombelles, p. 68, and the figures quoted in note 76 above for the limited range of this improvement.

[81] This point is much stressed by Nenad D. Popovic in *Yugoslavia: The New Class in Crisis* (Syracuse, N.Y., 1968). The evident bias and unconvincing main thesis of this book by a former highly placed Yugoslav official and diplomat do not detract from the value of its documentation.

[82] Hoffman and Neal, pp. 176–78.

[83] Halperin, pp. 182–83, 213 *et seq.*

Thus on the eve of Stalin's death Yugoslavia seemed set on a course that would have logically led to abandonment of the class struggle as an instrument for effecting further transformations of society, and thus to the "withering away" of the party regime.

In fact, however, the regime was not prepared for self-liquidation. In May it reduced the maximum permissible landholding for individual peasants from thirty hectares to ten,[84] thus reassuring the party cadres that even though it could not then resume the class struggle in the countryside because of Yugoslavia's precarious international situation, it was willing to restrict the kulaks in order to preserve the basis for future transformations. In June, the Central Committee warned against tendencies toward the party's "ideological and organizational dissolution."[85] When the inconsistency between these reflexes of self-preservation and the ideas of the Sixth Party Congress drove Milovan Djilas toward the end of 1953 to write that the only remaining hostile class was now the bureaucracy, and that there could be no place for a centralist and monopolistic party in a truly self-managing socialist society, he was himself condemned as a spokesman of the class enemy and stripped of all public positions.[86] By 1956, encouraged by the reconciliation with Khrushchev's Russia and by the progress of de-Stalinization there, Tito went even further in reversing the decisions of the Sixth Congress. In an effort to overcome the persistent apathy among the cadres, the apparatus of full-time party officials, directed by Aleksandar Ranković, was expanded, and party "aktivs" were once again placed in government offices and mass organizations so as to ensure their leadership. These measures of political recentralization remained in effect even when the Seventh Party Congress, meeting in April 1958 in a climate of renewed conflict with the Soviets, gave new impulses for economic reform and for the ideological renewal of the international movement.[87]

From about this time, however, the dualism of elites became increasingly visible in Yugoslavia. The basic measures of economic decentralization had remained in force even during the most active period of political recentralization, except for the restoration of central control over foreign trade and for occasional central credit restrictions during acute foreign exchange crises; and rejuvenation of the managerial stratum according to criteria of professional efficiency had continued slowly, with many of the young men joining the party

---

[84] *Ibid.*

[85] *Ibid.*; Hoffman and Neal, pp. 184–85.

[86] Halperin, pp. 222–28, 232; Hoffman and Neal, pp. 186–95.

[87] Hoffman and Neal, pp. 199–201, 204, 207–8.

only after completing their training. The party, on the other hand, had ceased to attract the young after the Djilas crisis; during the two years that followed, it lost more members by purges than it gained by recruitment.[88] And when young people, attracted by the party's new stress on Yugoslavia's independent ideological and international role,[89] began once again to join it in significant numbers, they found the path to responsible positions blocked by veterans of the Partisan War who had entrenched themselves at every level of the party machine, the army, and the secret police.

One consequence of this hardening of the party's arteries was the increasing alienation of the scholarly, literary, and artistic intelligentsia in the course of the late 1950's and early 1960's, which found expression not only in pro-Western or "cosmopolitan" tendencies, but also in a revival of the cultural nationalism of the various federated republics. Another was the growing tendency of public opinion to blame party centralism and its local exponents for the country's recurrent economic difficulties, particularly after the disappointment of the great hopes with which the new reforms accompanying the devaluation of the dinar in 1961 had at first been welcomed. The failure of these measures to overcome the inflationary tendencies seems largely to have been due to the regime's unwillingness to accept a temporary cut in investments and a corresponding increase in unemployment as the precondition for an adjustment of production costs to the international level;[90] and this political resistance to a painful but necessary rationalization was widely believed to have had its backbone among the apparatchiki, at both the local and central levels, who were untrained in economics.

In time, however, Tito and a majority of the top leadership came to see the power, age structure, and rigid centralism of the party apparatus as a danger to the regime's popularity, its economic performance, and harmonious relations among its nationalities. The first signs of this changed attitude appeared when the new constitution, introduced in 1963, both considerably expanded the rights of the national republics and introduced the principle of rotation for government jobs on all levels.[91] By 1964, it became obvious that rotation was

88 Some 72,000 party members or 10% of the membership had been expelled during the second half of 1953, and an additional 270,000 in 1954–55, leading to a decline of the total membership from a peak of 780,000 in mid-1952 to a low point of 635,000 in mid-1956 (Hoffman and Neal, pp. 196–97).

89 Of some 120,000 members who joined the party in 1957, 63% were classified as "young people" (Hoffman and Neal, p. 204).

90 Popovic, pp. 159–60.

91 *Ibid.*, pp. 121–22.

also being pushed in the local and regional party organs, thus weakening the cohesion and fostering the rejuvenation of the party machine; from that year on, one-third of the membership of municipal party committees and one-fourth of the party secretaries have been replaced annually.[92] Rotation was presented not only as essential for reviving democratic party life at the grassroots, but also as a weapon for breaking up the interlocking cliques of local bureaucrats in the party, the police, the administration, and economic life—the so-called Vrkhushkas, who were accused both of resisting reform and of obstructing communication between the top leadership and the rank and file.[93] Only after this political preparation did the top leaders decide to launch a new and major economic reform: in mid-1965 the regime announced for the first time a policy designed to effect a harsh deflationary adjustment of expenditures, including investment, to available resources and of production costs to the international level.[94]

Within less than a year it became obvious that the reform, though basically sound, was endangered by the widespread tendency of enterprises, backed by local authorities, to hoard their goods pending permission for new price increases rather than write off their losses.[95] Though this resistance to the government's deflationary policy was clearly motivated at least partly by the immediate interest of the workers' collectives in holding on to their jobs and improving their wages, Tito promptly denounced it, in early 1966, as a manifestation of the capitalist spirit;[96] specifically, most of the leaders now accused the lower party organs of interfering with economic self-management by "bureaucratic usurpation" and of sabotaging the economic reform even while paying lip service to it.[97] As the leaders' intention to turn popular discontent against the entrenched apparatchiki became obvious, Ranković seems to have sided with his veteran subordinates. The approach of the crisis was foreshadowed by Tito's appeal to the people to rally to him against "the enemies of socialism and self-management," while Ranković posed as the defender of "the leading role of the party" as "the guarantee of the continuity of the revolution."[98] Seen against this background, the purge of Ranković and his supporters in the summer of 1966 had a much wider significance than the dis-

---

[92] *Ibid.*, p. 74.
[93] *Ibid.*, pp. 81–90. (Popovic quotes press attacks on this phenomenon.)
[94] The dinar, devalued to 300 to a dollar (U.S.) in 1952, and to 750 in 1961, was now devalued to 1,250 (*ibid.*, pp. 169–71).
[95] *Ibid.*, pp. 172–77.
[96] *Borba*, Feb. 26, 1966, quoted in Popovic, p. 182.
[97] Edvard Kardelj in *Borba*, Mar. 13, 1966, quoted in Popovic, p. 188.
[98] Popovic, pp. 190–91 (quoting Ranković from *Borba*, Feb. 26, 1966).

covery of a secret police conspiracy within the party, by which it was justified, for Ranković had used the uncontrolled channels of the secret police not in a Stalinist manner to build a terrorist power above the party, but rather to maintain secretly the centralist discipline of the party apparatus while outwardly complying with the general line of decentralization. His defeat thus led not only to a drastic purge of the security police and its radical separation from the party machine,[99] but to a thorough, if bloodless, purge of the party's veteran elite and a dramatic rejuvenation of its leading organs.[100] On the lower levels, the party was "deprofessionalized"; full-time local secretaries were replaced by unpaid part-time volunteers, and the ban on the cumulation of party and state offices by one and the same person was strictly enforced.[101] At the same time, the privileges and sinecures of retired army and security officials, whom Ranković as president of the war veterans' organization had traditionally protected, were ruthlessly cut down, and the principle was proclaimed that no one, whatever his wartime merits, had a right to a senior position or a comfortable job independent of his ability and performance.[102] Only then was it disclosed how many technically untrained and poorly educated party veterans had succeeded in holding on to managerial jobs all along, often preventing the employment of better qualified technicians in their factories.[103]

More than twenty years after the Communist seizure of power, a generation and elite change in party leadership has thus been effected in Yugoslavia since 1966, being finally sanctioned by the Ninth Party Congress of March 1969. This changeover is no less comprehensive than that carried out by Stalin's Blood Purge in the Soviet Union or that attempted by Mao's Cultural Revolution in contemporary China. Yet in the different political climate of nonaligned and decentralized Yugoslavia, the purge of the veterans has been achieved, in contrast to Russia, without bloodshed, and the mobilization of the

[99] Figures ranging from 24% to 64% of security personnel dismissed or due for dismissal in the different republics are quoted from *Borba* and *Politika* for September 1966 by Popovic, p. 69.

[100] The republican party congresses of late 1968 and the Ninth Federal Party Congress of March 1969 have produced a turnover affecting the absolute majority of the memberships of the republican central committees and the federal presidium, and a remarkable lowering of their average age. Only in the federal party's executive committee of fifteen, the effective inner leadership, is there a high degree of continuity.

[101] Popovic, pp. 73–81.

[102] *Ibid.*, pp. 204–6.

[103] Bombelles, pp. 68–69 (figures and examples quoted from *Borba*, Nov. 4, 1966).

younger generation against the conservative apparatchiki has not assumed the form of a virtual destruction of the party organization itself, as in China. But as in Russia, the rejuvenation of the party cadres is likely to have been accompanied by a substantial improvement in their educational level and economic and technical expertise; and even though the specific economic problems that precipitated the crisis may still be far from solved, it seems probable that the changeover in leadership will lead to a further strengthening of developmental over utopian considerations in the party's policy.

Incentive Policies and the Role of Coercion

Russia. Even during the heyday of War Communism, the Bolsheviks, in their labor code of December 1918 and in their party program of March 1919, rejected the utopian notion of an immediate radical leveling of all incomes as impossible at Russia's stage of development.[104] Yet in practice, the demands of the trade unions for lower wage differentials (supposedly in the interest of the "average worker") were powerfully reinforced throughout the civil war by the need to ration food and consumer goods and the increasing replacement of monetary wages and markets by the distribution of supplies in kind. The proportion of such supplies in total real wages is estimated to have risen from 6.2 per cent at the end of 1917 to 93.7 per cent by the first quarter of 1920,[105] and distribution was carried out on a basis of equality. Thus whereas prewar wage differentials among Russian workers had a range of 2.32 : 1,[106] and the new wage scales were first fixed by the unions, in January 1919, with a spread of 1.75 : 1 (which by April 1920 was broadened to 2 : 1 in general and 2.8 : 1 for some key industries),[107] a later study by the Soviet economist S. G. Strumilin estimates that the range of actual differentials had been whittled down to 1.02 : 1 by the beginning of 1921.[108] As this amounted in effect to a drastic downward leveling enforced by extreme shortages, it is obvious that material incentives for work played only a marginal role during those years; and the growing difficulty of effectively replacing them by patriotic or ideological solidarity on one side and by requisitioning of labor under military discipline on the other, once the civil war and

[104] Abram Bergson, *The Structure of Soviet Wages* (Cambridge, Mass., 1944), pp. 190–91, 194–98.

[105] Alexander Baykov, *The Development of the Soviet Economic System* (Cambridge, Eng., 1947), p. 43.

[106] *Ibid.*

[107] Bergson, pp. 181–84.

[108] Baykov, p. 43.

the war with Poland had ended, was one of the major factors forcing the introduction of the New Economic Policy.

This policy meant, in Lenin's words, the achievement of higher productivity "not directly through enthusiasm, but with the help of enthusiasm through personal interest and personal motives."[109] With rationing disappearing fast, and with the unions freed from quasi-military control and enjoying considerable autonomy in wage negotiations, both the level of real wages and the range of differentials now rose substantially. From 1922 to the end of 1926, the range of wage differentials was fixed at 3.5 : 1 for industrial workers generally and 4.2 : 1 in key industries;[110] if managers and apprentices are included at the upper and lower ends of the scale, the spread was 8 : 1.[111]

By the time of the Seventh All-Union Trade Union Congress, in December 1926, pressure to allow the lowest-paid workers to participate in the generally improving standard of living combined with ideological worry over the fact that wage differentials were higher in Russia than in Western Europe. Natural though this difference was in view of the shortage of skills in a developing country, it was embarrassing for the image of Soviet "socialism." The differentials were thus considerably reduced during the next two years: on the eve of the first five-year plan, average real wages were above the prewar level, but differentials below it.[112] Nominal wage differentials even continued to decline somewhat during the first two years of the plan except for managerial salaries, and the actual decline was rendered even steeper by the return to comprehensive food rationing, a consequence of forced collectivization. Leveling thus continued in conditions when the increasing demand for skilled labor on the one hand and the sudden influx of illiterate ex-peasants into industry on the other should have logically led to greater differentiation in material incentives.[113]

Yet, in fact, Stalin, aware that the general level of wages was bound to decline under the impact of his new policy of "primitive socialist accumulation," i.e., of forced industrialization financed by restricting mass consumption, returned at this time to an emphasis on ideological, administrative, and outright coercive methods of raising labor productivity and strengthening labor discipline. The defense of the workers' immediate interests was once more proscribed as the expression of an opportunist and narrowly "trade-unionist" outlook; and

---

[109] From a speech made by Lenin in the spring of 1921, quoted in Baykov, p. 145.
[110] Bergson, pp. 187–89.
[111] Baykov, p. 145.
[112] Bergson, pp. 187–89.
[113] *Ibid.*, pp. 199–202; Baykov, pp. 149–50.

after the removal of M. P. Tomsky from the leadership of the trade unions in June 1929, the unions' autonomy in wage negotiations and their influence on management within the factory "triangle" were quickly broken.[114] The main task of the unions, it was now proclaimed, was to help management raise productivity by organizing campaigns of "socialist emulation." During the same period, the government introduced the continuous working week and assumed powers of directing labor.[115]

By mid-1931, Stalin felt that the positive effects on industrial productivity of "storming" and "campaigning" had reached their limit, and that a greater use of material incentives and material pressures along with penal sanctions was needed. His speech of June 5, 1931, opening the attack on "petty-bourgeois egalitarianism,"[116] was promptly echoed by the Ninth Trade Union Congress in April 1932, and a general revision of wage scales followed, leading to a clear though limited widening of differentials among manual workers and a considerable increase in the advantages of salaried personnel.[117] Rationing, too, was now differentiated, with preference given to key industries and cities, and the allocation of rations handed over to the enterprises themselves. The biggest and most important enterprises were favored in the supply of food to their canteens and of consumer goods to their shops, so that the workers' dependence on these advantages as well as on factory housing should provide an additional incentive for working hard and staying on the job. The permission granted to the collective farms in May 1932 to sell on local markets what surpluses remained to them after fulfilling their delivery quotas also benefited the few consumers who could afford the much higher market prices.[118] At the same time, harsh penalties for absenteeism and lateness, to be administered by "comradely tribunals," were decreed, and the "labor book" was introduced for all workers;[119] moreover, the rapid growth of the forced labor system in the camps to which millions of kulaks had been deported served to give reality to the threats and provided a sector of the economy in which coercion reigned supreme. Finally, the use of piece-rates was steadily expanded,

---

114 Bienstock, Schwarz, and Yugow, *Management in Russian Industry and Agriculture*, pp. 35, 40–41.

115 Baykov, pp. 213–17, 220–25.

116 Stalin, "New Conditions: New Tasks in Economic Construction," speech given June 23, 1931, in *Pravda*, July 5, 1931; printed in Stalin, *Problems of Leninism*, pp. 359–80.

117 Bergson, pp. 178–79, and tables, pp. 117–18.

118 Baykov, pp. 228, 236–38, 241, 246–48.

119 *Ibid.*, p. 229.

and in 1933 participation of workers' representatives in the fixing of these rates was abolished.[120] By the end of the first five-year plan, the system in force was characterized by a powerful combination of material and coercive motivations, with the role of ideological enthusiasm much reduced.

The return of peace to the collectivized countryside, followed by a gradual easing of food shortages, and the mild slowing down of the feverish pace of industrialization under the second five-year plan, formed the background of the slogan "Life has become happier," launched by the Seventeenth Party Congress in early 1934. There followed two major changes in the incentive structure: the abolition of food rationing in stages during 1935, and the launching of the Stakhanovite movement in August of that year. When rationing was ended, prices were set somewhat lower than the "free market prices" under the old system but considerably higher than they had been for rationed goods;[121] hence, real wages declined for the lowest-paid workers, who spent most of their earnings on basic foods. At the same time, the end of rationing made the nominal wage differentials fully effective. The Stakhanovite movement was sharply distinguished from earlier campaigns for "socialist emulation" by its emphasis both on combining technical proficiency and innovation with simple increases in the intensity of work, and on combining material rewards with the honors and public praise showered on the record-breakers. But above all it was linked with the introduction of a system of "progressive piece-rates" and with steady pressure for raising the "technical norms" on which both these and the remaining time-rates were based.[122] In the years after 1935, when collective wage contracts were no longer negotiated with the unions, even as a matter of form,[123] this raising of norms proceeded rapidly (by 15 to 30 per cent in 1936 alone) and not infrequently faster than the actual rises in productivity.[124] It thus amounted to another factor increasing differentials and tending to depress the income of the least-skilled workers.

The slogan "Life has become happier" must be interpreted in the context of this practice of the middle and late 1930's, in which Stalin's incentive policy assumed its final shape. It amounted to an announce-

120 Bienstock, Schwarz, and Yugow, p. 44.
121 Baykov, pp. 251–52.
122 *Ibid.*, pp. 335–39.
123 Starting in 1935, minimum wages were fixed by management and differentials were frozen; in 1938 the ministries began fixing differentials (Bienstock, Schwarz, and Yugow, pp. 40–44).
124 Baykov, pp. 251–52.

ment that the call for sacrifice was now being replaced by a frank appeal to material interest, but under circumstances in which the workers' standard of living could be maintained or improved only by extremely hard efforts. This material pressure was reinforced by the simultaneous tightening of family responsibilities—the increased difficulty of divorce and a ban on abortion—and by the subsequent introduction of fees for higher education. In short, material pressures and incentives became so highly developed that they not only largely replaced the appeal of ideology, but also relegated open coercion to a background role—where it nonetheless remained effective owing to the emasculation of the trade unions and the ever-present threat of the labor camps.

It was only after Stalin's death that Soviet leaders—Khrushchev in particular—came to feel that Russian industrial productivity had reached a stage at which extreme pressures were becoming harmful for further development, and at which raising the lowest-paid workers' standard of living was both possible and necessary. The disappearance of the labor camps as a major sector of economic life, the introduction of a number of basic social security measures, the raising of the minimum wage, and a gradual reduction in the range of wage differentials by an improvement in the earnings of low-paid workers and low-paid industries and by a decline in the importance of piece-rates—these appear to have been the major changes in the incentive structure of Soviet industry adopted in the post-Stalin era. But Stalin's basic option in favor of a highly differentiated system of material incentives, a system oriented to developmental needs rather than to utopian beliefs, is shared by his successors, and "egalitarianism" is still explicitly rejected. The changes are justified on such economic grounds as the overcoming of the former shortage of skills and the increasing difficulty of finding workers for low-paid, unskilled labor, thanks to the progress of development, and the inapplicability of the piecework system in fully automated factories.[125]

At the same time, the disappearance of coercion from the climate of daily economic life has also affected the working of the political system. By dissolving the labor-camp empire, the post-Stalin leadership has sharply reduced the independent power base of the security

[125] According to recent studies by Soviet economists, the relation between the average earnings of the top 10% and the bottom 10% of wage earners and salaried employees had by 1959 fallen to 5.8 : 1, compared to the 8 : 1 calculated by Bergson for 1934. For a discussion of post-Stalin wage policy, its justifications, and its results, see Murray Yanovich, "The Soviet Income Revolution," *Slavic Review*, XXII: 4 (Dec. 1963), 683–97.

police. This action also has lent substance to the proclaimed "return to socialist legality"—at least to the extent that political terror, in the sense of the extralegal imposition of penal sanctions by the state, is now applied only against individuals who are genuinely considered by the leadership as politically dangerous, but not as a general instrument of social transformation and on a mass scale.

China. In the field of incentive policy, as in that of management policy, the Chinese Communists started with a predominantly developmental orientation based on the Stalinist model. They stressed a combination of material incentives and coercion; "egalitarianism" was opposed and labor discipline emphasized right from the time of their seizure of power.[126] Because the main concern of wage policy during the early years was to stop inflation, a point system of index wages was introduced, with regional authorities empowered to adjust the money value of a "wage point" to the cost of living. The labor regulations for private enterprises, announced in 1949, permitted point scales to be varied by collective agreement according to industries and skills;[127] but the same regulations took care to keep the trade unions weak by providing for compulsory arbitration and a ban on strikes.[128] Instead of bargaining for better wages and conditions, the unions were to concentrate on educating the workers to state and labor discipline and to the need to increase production; besides, they were to administer social insurance and workers' saving programs, and to provide welfare benefits and cultural amenities.[129]

With the end of the rehabilitation period and the preparation of the first five-year plan, the importance of wage differentials as incentives increased. In 1952, the regime announced that it regarded the differentials customary under the Kuomintang as insufficient, and that the new scales should be constructed purely on the basis of skill and performance—without consideration for family needs, seniority, or political attitude.[130] New regional wage scales issued in the same year provided for seven or eight different grades for workers in each industry, not counting the separate grades for managers and technicians at the top and for general laborers and apprentices at the bottom; the average range within the workers' grades proper was still

[126] Gluckstein, *Mao's China*, pp. 225–26.
[127] Hughes and Luard, *The Economic Development of Communist China*, pp. 117–18.
[128] Gluckstein, pp. 213–15.
[129] These tasks were laid down in the Trade Union statute of May 1953 (Hughes and Luard, pp. 118–21).
[130] Gluckstein, pp. 225–26.

only 2.85 : 1, but the regime also pressed for the introduction of piece-rates and the assignment of precise technical "norms" for each job.[131] By 1953, when "emulation campaigns" had been extended to include 80 per cent of China's industrial workers, production norms came to be based on the performance of recognized "model workers." These constituted the upper 9 per cent of the labor force in late 1954, but their rating was subject to annual review, and the norms themselves were revised twice yearly.[132]

Parallel with this increase in material pressures, disciplinary sanctions were being tightened. The regulations for state enterprises of May 1954 provided a range of penalties for lateness, absenteeism, malingering, negligence, and "sabotage" in the handling of materials, to be administered by "comradely tribunals"; they also forbade workers to change their jobs without permission, and introduced the "labor book."[133] The analogy to the first Russian five-year plan is complete. It is hardly surprising in the circumstances that the average wage level of the Chinese workers does not seem to have risen substantially above the prewar level in that period;[134] in fact, real wages declined somewhat during 1954 and 1955 as the value of a "wage point" rose less than most prices, despite considerable advances in productivity.[135]

By that time, however, the excessive pressure on the workers had begun to be recognized not only as politically dangerous—there had been an outburst of slowdowns, which even the cowed trade unions attributed primarily to poor living and working conditions[136]—but as literally counterproductive. It was now argued that the material incentives were neither sufficiently differentiated nor sufficiently substantial to promote the rise of productivity. Not only were there

---

[131] Gluckstein, pp. 226–29; Charles Hoffmann, "Work Incentives in Communist China," *Industrial Relations*, 2 (1964), 84. The need to assign precise technical norms for each job was cited as one of the chief arguments for the internal reorganization of the factories discussed above, pp. 60–61 (Schurmann, *Ideology and Organization*, pp. 242–47).

[132] Gluckstein, pp. 229–30.

[133] *Ibid.*, pp. 215–22.

[134] Gluckstein, pp. 251–55, calculates the average monthly wage at 40–50 yuan ($17–20). Bernhard Grossmann, in *Die wirtschaftliche Entwicklung der Volksrepublik China* (Stuttgart, 1960), p. 323, quotes official figures giving an average wage for 1957 of 636 yuan yearly, or 53 monthly, *after* the 14.5% wage rise of 1956, which confirms Gluckstein's calculations for an earlier date. The official figures claim that the workers' real wages were 26% above the prewar level by 1955 (Grossmann, p. 312), whereas Gluckstein concludes from his calculations that they were about equal.

[135] Hoffmann, pp. 90–91.

[136] Gluckstein, pp. 222–23.

irrational and egalitarian elements in the wage structure, including a residuum of allowances in kind that amounted to an equalizing element of "disguised wages," but there were inadequate rewards for inventors and innovators, and above all an excessive disparity between increases in productivity and wage increases. If it was right, in the interest of the investment program, that wages should rise more slowly than productivity, it was no less right that they must not be allowed to stagnate or fall if the rise in productivity was to continue; but the nominal wage level had risen by only 2.3 per cent and 6 per cent, in 1954 and 1955 respectively, whereas productivity had risen 25 per cent during those two years! Nor was there any sense in raising production norms in a spirit of "shock work," for this could only lead to cheating or to one-shot records that could not be maintained.[137]

These were some of the considerations underlying the wage reform of June 1956, aimed at improving both the general wage level and the range of differential incentives. The general level was raised by 14.5 per cent at a single stroke; in November 1957 average earnings were given as 636 yuan ($261.00) per year. The wage-point system was abolished along with the remnants of rationing, and the average wage range was increased to 3 : 1 for the workers' grades proper and rather more for the salaried incomes. A piecework system, intended to be in effect throughout China by the end of 1957 and actually reaching 42 per cent of the country's workers by that time, provided for 80 per cent of the workers' wages to be fixed and the remaining 20 per cent to be tied to the norms, so that this part could rise or fall according to performance; the norms were to be revised only once a year. In addition, there were to be bonuses for innovations that reduced the cost of production, and provisions for overtime and hardship pay.[138] On the whole, it was the most rational system of incentive wages devised in the history of Communist China, a system based explicitly on "the socialist principle of pay according to work." It was also influenced by the political climate of the year of de-Stalinization in Russia and by the regime's desire to replace coercion by reconciliation with the defeated bourgeois and peasant classes now that the nationalization of industry and the collectivization of agriculture had been completed. The new system was accompanied by promises of a greater role for the unions in industrial management.

137 Hoffmann, pp. 90–91; Gluckstein, pp. 229–32.
138 Hughes and Luard, pp. 126–28; Gluckstein, p. 230; Hoffmann, pp. 84–85, 90–91; Grossmann, p. 323.

Before the end of 1957, however, it appeared that the improvement in the situation of the workers, limited though it was, exercised a dangerous attraction on the even poorer rural population. As peasants flocked to the towns in far greater numbers than urban industry could absorb, the regime responded by lowering the wages for new, untrained workers, lengthening apprenticeship to an average of three years, and fixing the retirement age for workers at sixty at considerable financial cost.[139] Finally, by the spring of 1958, the Great Leap Forward, with its attempt at creating industries in the countryside, was accompanied by a sharp turn away from the Soviet reliance on material incentives to the utopian belief that the right Communist consciousness could become a decisive factor in expanding China's productive forces. In the new view, what was needed was an effort to wean the workers and peasants from their concern with personal interest by massive indoctrination.

Such was the new line expounded by Liu Shao-ch'i at the second session of the Eighth Party Congress in May 1958—a line that was to remain in force to the end of 1960. As late as the National People's Congress of that year, the need to give preference to the political-ideological education of the masses over material incentives and to time-rates over piece-rates was argued by the head of the planning commission, Li Fu-ch'un, himself. In fact, the norms had been raised to such extravagant heights in the early months of the Great Leap that the piece-rate system had become unworkable; a movement was then organized for its restriction and quickly led to its virtual disappearance in the leading Shanghai industries. Henceforth, bonuses were paid almost exclusively to collective bodies, and a greatly increased emphasis was placed on moral incentives, notably such individual and collective honors as the awarding of banners to successful factories and the reception of model workers by Chairman Mao.[140] Of course, the abandonment of the principle of material incentives was far more radical in the new rural communes, whose members had most of their wages paid in kind under the "free-supply system." This system, which provided equal rations for all independent of skill and performance and which accounted at first for some 70 per cent of members' income, was hailed as a direct step toward full Communism. The shortages produced by this agricultural upheaval, combined with a series of natural disasters, soon produced the familiar leveling effect in the cities as well.

[139] Hughes and Luard, pp. 126–28; Gluckstein, p. 230; Hoffmann, pp. 84–85.
[140] Hoffmann, pp. 93–95.

Only in 1961, following the Ninth Plenum of the Central Committee, was the necessity to offer more pay for more work during the whole period pending the achievement of full Communism recognized once more, thus relegating utopia to the future. Private plots and rural markets were restored, free supplies to commune members were restricted to 30 per cent of their incomes, and piece-rates, though preferably for teams rather than for individuals, were again stressed in industry. By the end of the year, almost all Chinese industry was run either on a time-rate-plus-bonus basis or on a strict piece-rate basis.[141]

No studies are available yet on the effect of the Cultural Revolution on incentive policy. But we know that this renewed outburst of utopianism had been prepared by Mao Tse-tung's insistent warnings against the danger of China's following the Soviet Union back to "the capitalist road,"[142] and that the Chinese leader sees one of the principal proofs of this relapse of the Soviets in their thoroughgoing reliance on personal interest and material incentive as the means for achieving better performance in production. It is the burden of Mao's critique of the development of Soviet society that by relying on the motivations of "economic man" the Russian leaders have tended to perpetuate the capitalist mentality. By contrast, it is the core of his concept of "socialist education," which the Cultural Revolution is designed to promote, that the basic motivations for people's economic effort must be changed from selfish materialism to selfless service of the community before the classless society can be achieved.[143] It is therefore no accident that when Shanghai workers in early 1967 sought to use the climate of the officially encouraged "rebellion" in order to put forward demands for material improvement, these demands were bitterly denounced as "economism" by the leadership of the Cultural Revolution, or that the last stage of that movement took the form of the massive drafting of students and intellectuals to do "voluntary" work in the countryside. In the circumstances, we may conclude that the Cultural Revolution has amounted to one more major setback for the developmental use of material incentives in favor of a utopian reliance on a combination of ideological and coercive techniques.

Yugoslavia. The early period of Yugoslavia's postwar reconstruc-

---

141 *Ibid.*, pp. 96–97.

142 See note 73 above.

143 For this interpretation, see also Lowenthal, "Mao's Revolution," *Encounter*, Apr. 1967.

tion and of the country's first centrally administered five-year plan, both before and after the break with Stalin, recalls the early years of the first five-year plan in Russia. The general level of real wages was held down to finance the rapid expansion of industry; mobilization of "voluntary labor" for special projects played an important role; rationing and the distribution of free or subsidized services to ensure rough social justice at a time of grave shortages kept real income differentials low. The great economic reform of 1952 changed this situation dramatically: the new decentralized market economy made more and better consumer goods available, and labor mobilization, rationing, and free services were ended.[144] As a result, both the level of real wages and the range of wage differentials rose, leading to a substantial increase in the effectiveness of material incentives and a reduction in the role of ideology and coercion. In principle, the workers' participation in the profits of the enterprise under the new system could have offered a further increase; in practice their share was negligible in the early years, but later it rose to a fairly stable 8 per cent of their regular income.[145]

Yet even though the Yugoslav regime has never returned to an emphasis on ideological or coercive motivation, the effectiveness of the material incentives approach could not develop consistently owing to the consequences of recurrent inflation on the one hand and to the efforts to ensure a stable minimum of social security for the workers on the other. In an economic system committed to forcing industrialization by a high rate of investment, but neither able nor willing to reduce consumption by cutting wages, unplanned inflation became the effective method of forced saving, except during brief emergency periods of drastic credit restriction under the pressure of acute foreign-exchange crises. From the workers' point of view, this led to a kind of cycle in which their real wages increased for a time until the cost of living began to catch up with the rise in nominal wages, then stagnated or declined from the eve of the financial crisis to its immediate aftermath, after which the process was repeated— all this without any apparent relation to the workers' effort. Thus, according to official figures, real wages did not rise from the crisis year of 1957 to 1958, rose 20 per cent from then to 1960, remained unchanged during the next two years (which included the crisis and devaluation of 1961), rose by more than a quarter from 1962 to 1964 (because nominal wages rose by 50 per cent while the cost of living

[144] Halperin, *The Triumphant Heretic*, pp. 164–70.
[145] Hoffman and Neal, *Yugoslavia and the New Communism*, pp. 365–67.

rose only 17 per cent), and marked time again from 1964 to 1965, as a new inflationary climax led to a new crisis and devaluation.[146] After this devaluation the average monthly earnings of a Yugoslav worker were reckoned as equivalent to just over $40[147]—a figure that may give rise to some doubt about the reliability of the cost-of-living index on which the above statements on the growth of real wages are based.

At the same time, from a desire to guarantee the workers at least a secure minimum standard, the regime instituted a system of children's allowances that were equal for all and rather high in relation to the average wage—by the mid-1950's they amounted to one-third of the average worker's regular income.[148] As a result, though wage differentials according to figures for 1958 were 2.8 : 1 between skilled and unskilled workers and even 4 : 1 for the most highly skilled groups, the actual range of incomes was considerably less.[149] Moreover, upward adjustments in these allowances did not follow the inflationary process as quickly as did rises in wage rates, thus adding another element of uncertainty both to the statistical calculation and to the workers' actual experience of the rise in real incomes.

The low level of average real wages, its dependence on the inflationary cycle, and the importance of the share of income not related to work have thus combined to weaken the Yugoslav system of material incentives and to encourage an orientation toward sheltered security rather than toward heightened effort among the workers. For example, when the regime tried to introduce piece-rates during the monetary crisis of 1957, at a time of severe restrictions on total wage payments, it failed altogether. Piece-rates were successfully introduced only after the economic reform and devaluation of 1961, when a general relaxation of wage restrictions and an easing of profit taxation were coupled with the condition that wage increases should be granted only on a piece-rate basis.[150] At the same time, however, the authorities decided to reduce differentials by raising the minimum wage; and the combination of the two moves with a continuing policy of high investment clearly helped to cause a new round of inflation.[151]

Thus, whereas Soviet incentive policy from the time of the first five-year plan appears to have developed along a fairly straight line of increasing reliance on material rewards at the expense first of ideo-

---

[146] Statisticki Godišnjak SFRJ 1967, p. 268.
[147] 1965: 501 new dinars; 1966: 693 new dinars, at 12.5 to the dollar (U.S.). *Ibid.*
[148] Hoffman and Neal, pp. 366–67.
[149] *Ibid.*, pp. 366–68.
[150] *Ibid.*, pp. 255–58.
[151] Popovic, *Yugoslavia: The New Class in Crisis*, pp. 164–65.

logical motivations and later also of coercion, and whereas Chinese policy has zigzagged, so far without a clearly perceptible trend, between the extremes of a developmental emphasis on material rewards and of a utopian revivalism rejecting them, Yugoslav policy since the decentralizing reforms appears as a succession of halfhearted compromises: it has oscillated within a fairly narrow range between the recognized developmental need for material incentives and the effect of commitments that keep interfering with that need—commitments to investment goals overtaxing the national resources and to granting the workers a high degree of social security independent of performance. The persistence of these commitments, and the resulting indecisiveness of the Yugoslav Communists in this field, seems to be due to a combination of ideological and political pressures. Ideologically, it is related to their adoption of continuous high investment and stable social security as provisional substitutes for the utopian goals that had to be put aside in the interest of internal peace after the break with the Soviet bloc. Politically, it is linked to the early renunciation of massive coercion and to the relative political effectiveness of quasi-democratic pressures from below under the Yugoslav system of self-management.

Permanent Revolution and the Nature of Dictatorship

Russia. The adjustment of Soviet political institutions to the change in the social structure caused by Stalin's revolution from above —the forced collectivization of the peasantry—took the form of the so-called Stalin constitution of December 1936. The adjustment to the results of the Blood Purge—the virtual annihilation of the Bolshevik veteran elite—was embodied in the change in the party statutes adopted at the Eighteenth Congress of the CPSU in March 1939. Whereas the constitutional change, which granted peasants equal voting rights with workers in direct elections to the Supreme Soviet, was essentially symbolic, the change in the party statutes, which permitted members of the new Soviet intelligentsia to join the ruling party on the same terms as workers, had substantive significance for completing the evolution of the supposed vanguard of the working class into a bureaucratic state party. But ideologically both changes were interpreted as reflecting the same stage in the transformation of Russian society: the complete victory of socialism had been achieved in all spheres of the national economy. After the elimination of all exploiting classes there now remained only productive classes with nonantagonistic mutual relations—the working class, the collective peasantry, and the new intelligentsia of working-class and peasant origin. Since the economic and political contradictions between these three basic elements of Soviet society were declining and the dividing lines between them disappearing, the Soviet Union was supposed to have entered "the stage of the completion of the building of a socialist society and of its gradual transition to Communist society."[152]

Yet this triumphant interpretation of the achievements of the regime raised the problem of the need for its continued existence. If the surviving classes were nonantagonistic and the party was no longer specifically proletarian in composition, why should its rule still be described as the dictatorship of the proletariat? Indeed, if there were no hostile exploiting classes left, why should such a dictatorship, which Marx had envisaged only for a limited transitional period as a means to hold down the enemy, still continue to exist? If socialism had been achieved and the transition to Communism was on the agenda, had not the time come when, according to both Marx and Lenin, the state itself, this instrument of class oppression, should begin to wither away?

In his report to the Eighteenth Congress, Stalin answered these questions by frankly proposing a revision of Marx and Lenin in the light of Soviet experience. It was true, he argued, that the state's function of suppressing the former exploiting classes had become obsolete, as there was no one left to suppress; but the Soviet state had acquired other functions that Marx had not foreseen. Not only did it have to defend the socialist society against foreign attack and subversion by enemy agents at home in conditions of capitalist encirclement, but it had to organize the new, socialist economic system and to educate the people in the socialist spirit. These economic and cultural tasks of the state were becoming more rather than less important as society approached the higher stage of Communism; as for external and internal defense, that task would continue even under Communism until the capitalist encirclement had ended.[153] Although Stalin did not explain why the state charged with these tasks must remain a party dictatorship, his argument implied that such a dictatorship must hold power until all class differences had finally disap-

---

[152] See Stalin's speech "On the Draft Constitution of the USSR" (Nov. 25, 1936), in *Problems of Leninism*, pp. 540 *et seq.* See also the corresponding formulation in Stalin, ed., *History of the CPSU: Short Course* (first pub. 1938; N.Y. ed. 1939), pp. 343–46.

[153] Stalin's Report to the Eighteenth Congress of the CPSU (Mar. 10, 1939), in *Problems of Leninism*, pp. 596 *et seq.* See particularly pp. 636–38.

peared at home and Communism had triumphed throughout the world.

As it happened, the events of 1939–45 determined that the international aspect of the revolutionary task would dominate Soviet policy during the following decade. The annexation of eastern Poland and the Baltic states under the Hitler-Stalin Pact meant that Soviet institutions were imposed on these territories by revolutions from above, and even the attack on Finland, though chiefly motivated by the wish to acquire limited territories of strategic value, was at first accompanied by the attempt to proclaim a Communist government for that country. Again, from early 1943 onward, once the Soviet victory at Stalingrad had removed the risk of defeat, Stalin launched—parallel with the dissolution of the formal machinery of the Comintern—an active policy designed to prepare for the Communist seizure of power in all countries his armies were likely to reach.[154] Contrary to Western expectations, he was not content merely to ensure the formation of "friendly governments" on Russia's vulnerable western borders; he regarded only a government controlled by Communists as reliably friendly. Until the middle of 1947, his policy toward continental Western Europe, too, was geared to the hope that the upheavals of the war and the postwar period would offer opportunities for Communist takeovers after the expected early withdrawal of the American and British forces. Even when the announcement of the Marshall Plan threatened to thwart that hope, the Soviets tried for two more years to force such a withdrawal by pressure and threats, and thus to prevent a non-Communist consolidation in Western Europe, until the defeat of the Berlin blockade and the formation of the NATO alliance in 1949 convinced Stalin that the end of this particular wave of revolutionary expansion had come.[155]

Meanwhile the process of domestic transformation had been seriously set back by the war because the regime had temporarily relaxed its control over the peasants and made ideological concessions to patriotic and religious traditions for the sake of national unity. Accordingly, the early postwar period inside the Soviet Union was char-

---

154 Cf. Stalin's statement to visiting Yugoslav leaders in April 1945: "This war is not as in the past; whoever occupies a territory also imposes on it his own social system. Everyone imposes his own system as far as his army has power to do so. It cannot be otherwise." (Milovan Djilas, *Conversations with Stalin* [London, 1962], p. 105.)

155 I have developed this interpretation in my article "Soviet Foreign Policy since 1945," in Michael T. Florinsky, ed., *McGraw-Hill Encyclopedia of Russia and the Soviet Union* (New York, 1961).

acterized by tough measures to undo the wartime encroachments of the peasants' private plots and herds on the collective farms, to isolate and reeducate the returned prisoners in the labor camps so as to prevent them from spreading word of their experience of the outside world, and to restore ideological control in literature and the arts. But as soon as this internal consolidation had been accomplished and Soviet external expansion had been stopped, the first steps were taken toward another major transformation of Soviet society.

This change involved the structure of collectivized agriculture, and its conception seems to have been connected with the transfer of N. S. Khrushchev to the secretariat of the Central Committee in Moscow in December 1949. Khrushchev, up to then first secretary of the Ukrainian Communist Party, was soon to take over responsibility for agricultural policy within the Politburo from A. A. Andreyev. On February 19, 1950, a *Pravda* editorial censured Andreyev for having favored the organizing of collective farm workers into small teams to whom definite plots were assigned. This "Zveno" system, which had the advantage of assuring the personal responsibility of team members for results on their particular piece of land, was now condemned not only as inhibiting the mechanization of grain farming, which was said to require larger "brigades" as working units, but as "shaking the very foundations of large-scale, socialist agriculture"—in other words, as tending to break up the collective farm itself into smaller units. That the leadership was determined to move in the opposite direction became clear a fortnight later, when Khrushchev, in a signed *Pravda* article, launched the movement for merging the collective farms into still larger units on the grounds that this would facilitate mechanization, increase yields and deliveries to the state, and permit the selection of the best managers.[156] In fact, the number of collective farms was reduced by such mergers from 252,000 at the start of the campaign to 123,000 by the end of the year, and to 97,000 at the time of the Nineteenth Party Congress in October 1952.[157]

It seems hardly plausible, however, that this tripling of the average size of the collective farm within three years was due primarily to considerations of technical efficiency; in any case it did not prove justified in that respect.[158] More important, no doubt, was the insufficient number of basic party organizations in the countryside. In 1949,

---

[156] *Pravda*, Mar. 8, 1950.

[157] Fainsod, *How Russia Is Ruled*, pp. 539–40.

[158] Both grain output and cattle stocks were still hovering at about the same level three years later. For figures, see *ibid.*, p. 541.

on the eve of the merger campaign, only 15 per cent of the collective farms had a party unit;[159] by the time of the Nineteenth Congress, this figure had risen to nearly 80 per cent, though the absolute number of party units had barely doubled.[160] But Khrushchev disclosed his own chief reason for launching the new policy when in a speech in January 1951 he advocated resettling all the peasants of the new, enlarged units in central "agrotowns" with quasi-urban housing conditions and cultural amenities. This would be a major step toward the Communist goal of eliminating the essential differences between city and country; at the same time it would separate the peasants from their private garden plots in the old villages and force them to accept smaller plots to be tilled in common on the outskirts of the new settlements.[161] In other words, he was aiming at another major social change, not just at a technical one.

This new installment of applied utopianism, however, met determined resistance within the leadership. Khrushchev's January speech did not appear in *Pravda* until March 4, 1951, and on the following day the party organ printed an editorial correction apologizing for having failed to mention that Khrushchev's proposal was being published only as material for discussion. Soon afterward, an Armenian party leader attacked the proposal as "contrary to party and government policy,"[162] evidently because shifting and reducing the private plots might undermine the loyalty and productivity of the peasants. Finally, when the Central Committee issued a secret circular rejecting the resettlement plan as a whole[163] (for not even the building materials were available), Khrushchev's control of agricultural policy was ended for the time being. At the Nineteenth Congress Georgi Malenkov was still criticizing the proposal (without mentioning its author) for concentrating on cultural "amenities" to the neglect of the basic needs of production.[164]

[159] *Ibid.*, p. 537 and note 27, quoting an article by A. A. Andreyev, *Bolshevik*, Dec. 1949. However, Schapiro, *The CPSU*, p. 512, states that "by early 1948, already a third of all collective farms had their own primary party organizations." If Schapiro is right, the increase in the percentage due to the merger would not be so enormous, but still striking, from over 30% to 80% in four years.

[160] Out of 94,000 collective farms, 76,000 had party organizations by Oct. 1952 (Schapiro, *The CPSU*, p. 516).

[161] Khrushchev's speech as reported in *Pravda*, Mar. 4, 1951.

[162] G. A. Arutyunov in the Armenian *Kommunist*, Mar. 21, 1951, quoted by Fainsod, p. 540, and Schapiro, *The CPSU*, p. 516.

[163] Disclosed by L. F. Ilyichev at the Twenty-second Party Congress (*Pravda*, Oct. 26, 1961).

[164] Quoted by Fainsod, pp. 540–41, from *Pravda*, Oct. 6, 1952.

As Malenkov must have known, it was not just to provide amenities but to relaunch the social transformation of the Russian countryside that Khrushchev had made his proposal; and this, his real objective, was not repudiated. On the contrary, the Nineteenth Congress was faced with printed evidence that Stalin himself was actively concerned with resuming this process and had sketched out a different method for doing so. In his last pamphlet, *Economic Problems of Socialism in the USSR*,[165] published on the eve of the congress, the Vozhd stressed repeatedly that the transition to Communism was not a matter of mere quantitative advances in productivity, leisure hours, and the standard of living; it could not be brought about "if such economic factors as collective farm group property, commodity circulation, etc. remain in force." One of the conditions needed "for a real and not just declaratory transition to Communism" was "to raise collective farm property to the level of public property and also by means of gradual transitions to replace commodity circulation by a system of products exchange under which the central government or some other economic center might control the whole product of social production in the interests of society."[166] What was needed, Stalin explained, was to end what was left of the collective farms' right to dispose of their produce on the market; this was to be achieved by the gradual extension of barter between the collectives and the state based on "transformation contracts" such as existed already between cotton farmers and factories producing cotton goods.

Moreover, the pamphlet showed that in the course of discussions throughout 1952 Stalin had come to view this next turn of the screw of permanent revolution in an increasingly urgent light. In his first statement, on February 1, he had stressed that this task could only be undertaken in the future, once agricultural production was considerably more concentrated, and that for the present "commodity exchange," i.e., buying and selling, was still the only link with the cities acceptable to the peasants; nor was there any danger that this form of market production could under Soviet conditions lead to a restoration of capitalism. In his reply to the economist L. D. Yaroshenko, on May 22, he warned that it would be "unforgivable blindness" not to see that collective farm property and commodity exchange, though still useful in the short run, were already beginning to hamper the development of Soviet productive forces by obstructing the central, planned control of agriculture. Finally, in his rejoinder to

[165] Stalin, *Economic Problems of Socialism in the USSR* (Moscow, 1952).
[166] *Ibid.*, pp. 74 *et seq.*

the agricultural experts A. V. Sanina and V. G. Venzher, written on the very eve of the publication of the pamphlet and dated September 28, he quoted Engels to the effect that "commodity circulation must lead to the rebirth of capitalism," and demanded immediate, though gradual, measures for replacing the market relations between state industry and collective farms by organized barter. Thus what had seemed a distant dream in February had by the end of September become, in Stalin's eyes, an urgent measure needed to forestall the danger that out of the competition between the collective farms on the market, capitalist tendencies might be reborn.

But the idea of gradually replacing all market exchanges between city and country by centrally organized barter is clearly utopianism of a particularly antidevelopmental kind; if put into practice, it would have been bound to reduce the already low productivity of the collective farms, both by increasing the difficulty of calculating their production costs and by further reducing the peasants' incentive to work. One wonders whether objections of this sort from unpersuaded Soviet leaders were among Stalin's reasons for replacing the old Politburo, at the end of the Nineteenth Congress, by a large Presidium with many newcomers, and for his evident preparations to launch another purge of the top leadership at the end of his life.[167] In any case, Stalin's sudden death in March 1953 ensured that his 1952 plan for overcoming the class distinction between collective peasants and state-employed workers by yet another imposed social transformation would remain as abortive as Khrushchev's plan of 1951.

For the next few years, rivalry among the members of the Soviet Union's collective leadership led them to sponsor competitive measures for raising production and living standards. During this time little scope was left for utopian social engineering (if we except Khrushchev's vast scheme for the cultivation of virgin lands, which he seems to have initiated partly with a view to gaining a free field for experimenting with a new type of settlement). Once the struggle for the succession had ended, however, with the restoration of the uncontested primacy of the party over the other power machines and with the establishment of the personal primacy of Khrushchev over his colleagues, the first secretary after 1957 returned to his projects for transforming the social structure of the Soviet countryside, projects that now had assumed a more precise shape in his mind in op-

[167] See Khrushchev's Secret Speech at the Twentieth Party Congress, in the documentary collection *The Anti-Stalin Campaign and International Communism* (New York, 1956), pp. 84–85.

position to Stalin's alternative concept. Like Stalin, Khrushchev believed that full Communism could be achieved only by abolishing the distinction between collective and state ownership and eliminating all basic differences between rural and urban life. But unlike Stalin he understood that the necessary increase in agricultural productivity could not be brought about if market exchanges were replaced by barter; on the contrary, he believed in the need to eliminate existing features of a barter economy on the collective farms so that their costs and returns would be strictly measurable by "the yardstick of the ruble."[168] Nor did he accept the Stalinist dogma that state ownership of the existing type was necessarily superior to collective ownership and that the latter must be transformed into the former; instead, he envisaged a convergence of both forms into a new, higher type that would combine the rationality of existing state enterprise with some kind of participatory role for producers' organizations.[169]

In 1958 Khrushchev took the first two steps in this direction. He sold the machine tractor stations (mostly on credit) to the collective farms; and he replaced both the existing system of deliveries in kind to the machine tractor stations in return for their services, and the different types of sales to the state at different prices, by a single price for all sales to the government. These moves had the double economic merit of making the cost of the use of machinery and the value of farm produce calculable in money terms, and of giving the farms an interest in the most rational use of the former. At the Twenty-first Party Congress in February 1959,[170] Khrushchev further proposed that a fixed monthly cash advance be given to all kolkhoz members.

168 See Khrushchev's proposals and speeches on agricultural policy during 1958–59: in particular the theses of his report to the Supreme Soviet "On Further Development of the Kolkhoz System and Reorganizing of the MTS," *Pravda*, Mar. 1, 1958; the report itself under the same title, *Pravda*, Mar. 28, 1958; his report to the Central Committee "On Abolishing Compulsory Deliveries and Payments-in-Kind for MTS Work and on New System, Prices, and Terms for Procurement of Agricultural Products," *Pravda*, June 21, 1958; his report to the December session of the Central Committee in *Pravda*, Dec. 16, 1958; and his report on the seven-year plan to the Twenty-first Party Congress in *Pravda*, Jan. 28, 1959. For a full account of the inner-party discussion of these proposals, also see Sidney I. Ploss, *Conflict and Decision-Making in Soviet Russia* (Princeton, N.J., 1965), chs. 3 and 4, and Carl A. Linden, *Khrushchev and the Soviet Leadership* (Baltimore, 1966), ch. 4.

169 Evidence that the idea of a kolkhoz federation was pushed during 1958–59 by Khrushchev's closest political and journalistic supporters is presented by Ploss, ch. 4. For an indication that this may have been considered a first step toward a more comprehensive scheme of producer participation in the direction of the economy, see in particular the article by I. Vinnichenko, a writer often acting as Khrushchev's mouthpiece, in *Nash Sovremennik*, 4 (1959), quoted in Ploss, p. 158.

170 *Pravda*, Jan. 28, 1959.

This advance, corresponding to the monthly minimum wage received by workers on the state farms, was to make labor costs calculable as well, and to end the complicated and disincentive system under which collective farmers received rewards only once a year as a share in the farm's residual net income, and in proportion to the number of "labor days" credited to them. In practice, however, most collective farms lacked the means to pay such a minimum wage, and the Soviet government was not then prepared to raise their income to a level that would have allowed the plan to be carried out.[171]

Though the actual and projected reforms mentioned so far were clearly calculated to raise the level of collective farm productivity, Khrushchev also hoped they would help to persuade the peasants to consent to a reduction of their private plots and livestock. In the early post-Stalin period, the government had largely relieved this private sector of agriculture from tax and delivery obligations so as to encourage a quick increase in the cattle population as well as in the output of meat, milk, eggs, and vegetables. Now, at the Twenty-first Congress, described as the "Congress of the builders of Communism," Khrushchev argued that this private sector would have to disappear as the Soviet Union was transformed into a Communist society. He actually gave the signal for a campaign to persuade the peasants to sell their private livestock to the collectives, on the grounds that it would yield more meat and milk in big, modern collective stables: if only the peasants would spend more time in communal labor, they would be able to buy more food with their wages than they could ever produce on their little plots! Moreover, Khrushchev had persuaded the Central Committee in 1958 to annul the earlier condemnation of his agrotown project, and he now resumed his propaganda for this scheme, which called for rehousing peasants in new, urban-type settlements at the centers of their giant collectives. Pilot projects, he suggested, should be started at once in order to convince the peasantry quickly of the plan's advantages. As for the cost of the new housing and of the communal facilities, roads, and electrification necessary to make the agrotowns livable, the collective farms themselves would have to bear it; but much of the work could be done by joint enterprises to be founded by several farms.

---

[171] The funds for this were only approved under Khrushchev's successors by a decision of the Twenty-third Party Congress in March 1966, implemented by the government in July 1966. See Alec Nove, "Economic Policy and Economic Trends," in A. Dallin and T. B. Larson, eds., *Soviet Politics since Khrushchev* (Englewood Cliffs, N.J., 1968), p. 86.

Khrushchev also recommended the forming of "kolkhoz unions," at
the district and higher levels, which should both permit the subsidizing of poorer farms by more prosperous ones and take over some of
the functions of the agricultural administration.[172]

In fact, the material conditions for persuading the peasants to give
up their private activities and rely on communal labor did not exist;
nor did the financial conditions for building the model agrotowns.
Yet in the months following the Twenty-first Congress, these utopian
projects were featured in the party's propaganda, and successes in the
sale of private livestock to the collectives as well as in starting pilot
agrotowns were reported in the press. Clearly, Khrushchev had embarked on a new revolution from above, though in the changed conditions of the post-Stalin regime it was to be carried out without
violence and with minimal coercion. But the new push toward utopia
soon led to economic setbacks. It turned out that many "voluntary"
sales of private livestock to collectives had resulted in slaughter, and
that some of the temporary successes in increasing meat deliveries had
no other basis. Frauds of various sorts were common: one "model"
regional secretary whom Khrushchev had made a "hero of socialist
labor" in December 1959 committed suicide in 1960 before his false
reporting was discovered;[173] and Khrushchev's own secret subsidizing
of the agrotown experiment in his home collective at Kalinovka was
disclosed only after his fall. To other setbacks, Khrushchev reacted by
blaming local party officials for intimidating peasants instead of relying on persuasion; but as time went on, it became clear once again
that progress toward utopia could not be effected by persuasion—only
by using coercion and paying its economic price.

Khrushchev's report at the Twenty-first Congress had been intended to sketch the main points of a new party program for the period of
transition to Communism. But when the draft of that program was
published in 1961 in preparation for the Twenty-second Congress, it
showed that the choice between utopia and development had been
made—this time in favor of development. The goals of merging collective and state ownership and of eliminating all significant differences between town and country were still there; and so were the

172 See notes 169 and 170 above.

173 See Michel Tatu, *Power in the Kremlin from Khrushchev to Kosygin* (New
York, 1969), for the case of the Ryazan regional party secretary, A. Larionov, who
committed suicide in September 1960 after being highly praised by Khrushchev for
his alleged record achievements in December 1959. (Khrushchev in *Pravda*, Dec. 29,
1959; later Soviet accounts in *Voprosy Istoriya KPSS*, 3 [1963], and *Kommunist*,
13 [1963]).

means, namely a voluntary reduction of the private plots and herds and the creation of agrotowns. But these means were no longer presented as operative tasks for party action; instead they were seen as inevitable future by-products of a steady rise in productivity. The acceptance of this draft by the Twenty-second Congress[174] thus meant nothing less than the renunciation of further revolutions from above in the party program itself. Under Stalin, the use of state power to transform society had been a task for action, and the rise in the standard of living a vision of the future; by 1961, only the raising of productivity and the standard of living was the task for action, whereas the further transformation of society had become a mere vision of the future. After the failure of three successive attempts to keep the wheels of permanent revolution turning—Khrushchev's in 1951, Stalin's in 1952, and Khrushchev's in 1959—the oldest and most successful ruling Communist party had recognized that, at the stage of development reached by industrial Russia, it could no longer afford the active pursuit of utopian goals.

Along with his efforts to change the social structure of the Soviet countryside, Khrushchev had attempted to loosen the rigid, centralist structure of the Soviet bureaucracy by giving a greater role in economic life and social control to various "social organizations." The first major practical move in this direction—and the only one to be fully carried out—was the breaking up of the central bureaucracy of the economic ministries by his well-known regionalization of industrial planning in 1957. After the sale in 1958 of the machine tractor stations, which Stalin had conceived as organs of state control over the collective farms, Khrushchev had apparently intended to transfer the control functions of the agricultural ministries to a network of federations of collective farms to be formed shortly at a collective farm congress. The underlying theory, adumbrated in speeches and interviews since 1957 and developed in Khrushchev's speech to the Twenty-first Congress in 1959, was that whereas Stalin had been right to claim that the state was still needed to protect Soviet society against external enemies and their agents at home, he had been wrong to maintain that the socialist state could not be replaced in its economic and social tasks: in these fields, the state could begin to wither away as its functions were taken over by such organizations as volunteer militia units formed by the Komsomol members, "comradely courts" in factories and neighborhoods, trade unions, and evidently

---

[174] The draft appeared in *Pravda*, July 30, 1961; the final text in *ibid.*, Nov. 2, 1961.

also the projected kolkhoz unions. Some influence of the discussions with Tito during the Soviet-Yugoslav rapprochement of 1955–56 is visible in these ideas, though Khrushchev never went as far as Tito in advocating decentralized self-management.

But just as Khrushchev's plans for the transformation of agriculture ran up against the resistance of the peasants, so his plans for limiting the role of state power encountered the resistance of the bureaucrats; and just as he could not overcome the peasants' resistance by the methods of Stalin's forced collectivization (having renounced mass terrorism as inappropriate to the Russia of the late 1950's), so he could not overcome the bureaucrats' inertia by the methods of Stalin's Blood Purge. In dispersing the power of the industrial ministries, he had been able to rely on the support of the provincial party secretaries; but in seeking to transfer administrative control of the collective farms to self-governing kolkhoz unions, he was directly encroaching on the preserves of the provincial party apparatus. By December 1959 the Central Committee decided to shelve the plan for higher-level kolkhoz federations,[175] with the result that the "third congress of collective farms," proposed by Khrushchev at the Twenty-first Party Congress, was deferred for an indefinite period.[176] As for increasing the role of trade unions in the organization of industry, that idea never even got to the stage of a formulated proposal. Thus all that remained of Khrushchev's vision of a partial withering away of the state was the least progressive part of it—the transfer of some of the state's repressive functions to party-led organs outside all legal control, such as the Komsomol militia and the comradely courts; and even these courts have been downgraded by the post-Khrushchev regime in favor of the renewed use of direct party orders to the regular courts.[177]

Yet Khrushchev's very failure to maintain the momentum of the revolution from above has led to a major change of a very different sort: the final transformation of the party dictatorship into the rule of a postrevolutionary, conservative bureaucracy. Even in his own party

[175] See the full account in Ploss, pp. 172–79.

[176] The congress finally took place in November 1969. The new statute adopted by it has brought no substantial increase in kolkhoz autonomy. Instead of kolkhoz unions, which had again been much discussed in the late 1960's, an All-Union Kolkhoz Council under ministerial leadership and with purely advisory powers was set up, with similar councils to be created at lower levels (*Izvestiya*, Nov. 29, 1969).

[177] This can be seen from the systematic violations of Soviet law in the trials of Soviet writers since 1966. See Stephen Weiner, "Socialist Legality on Trial," *Problems of Communism*, XVII: 4 (1968), and the documentation on various trials in this and the following issue.

program of 1961 this change was reflected in the new, controversial proclamation to the effect that the Soviet Union had ceased to be a "dictatorship of the proletariat" and had become a "state of all the people." Logically, this formula could have been adopted as early as the time of the Stalin constitution of 1936, which was based on equal formal rights for the remaining productive classes; but at that time Stalin had to justify his Blood Purge by the absurd contention that the class struggle grows more acute as the "building of socialism" advances.[178] With Khrushchev's repudiation of this thesis in his Secret Speech to the Twentieth Congress of the CPSU in 1956, the "dictatorship of the proletariat" lost one more intellectual prop. As long as Khrushchev was actively involved in efforts to change the structure of Soviet society, however, no official attempt was made to redefine the nature of the state: it still might prove convenient to base the transformation of the collective farms on the leading role of the proletariat, even if that role was no longer enforced by terrorist violence. Only when the politics of the revolution from above had been abandoned as definitely as Stalinist methods of enforcing those politics— only when the ruling party had consciously accepted the fact that it could no longer continue the revolution but could merely administer its results—only then did the regime agree to have the Soviet Union described as a "state of all the people," rather than a "dictatorship of the proletariat." For now the change of name was to be understood as a pledge that Soviet workers, peasants, and intellectuals would henceforth be able to live normal lives without fear not only of sudden arrest and deportation, but of any sudden upheaval in their social situation imposed from above.

But by accepting the end of the revolutionary function of the party dictatorship, the 1961 program inevitably raised the question of the legitimacy of its continued existence. It was this question that Khrushchev attempted to answer by reorganizing the party in November 1962 so as to make guidance of the economic administration, in separate branches for industry and agriculture, the party's primary responsibility; but this plan did not correspond to the qualifications of many of the apparatchiki, nor did it offer a plausible reason for maintaining the party's "leading role." At the same time discontented top bureaucrats of party and state became increasingly aware

---

[178] The thesis was first put forward in Stalin's speech to the Central Committee session of March 3, 1937, published in English under the title *Mastering Bolshevism* (New York, 1937). It did not appear in his Collected Works (which stopped in 1934) or in the subsequent editions of *Problems of Leninism*.

that a postrevolutionary regime did not really require dynamic personal leadership of the type Khrushchev insisted on offering. When the disproportion between his leadership claims and his lack of political success became obvious to all, this top stratum finally found an opportunity to remove him and to undo both his latest party reorganization and the 1957 planning reform by which he had shaken up the administration of the economy. The overthrow of Khrushchev in October 1964, unprecedented in the history of Communist party regimes, and the establishment of a bureaucratic oligarchy in the name of institutional stability, thus marked the definite adjustment of the Soviet political system to the "extinction" of the "movement regime"—the running down of revolutionary dynamism corresponding to the stage of development reached by Soviet society.[179]

China. As we have seen, the Chinese Communists proclaimed in 1956 what Stalin had proclaimed twenty years earlier in Russia—that with the completion of agricultural collectivization (and in China of the nationalization of industry as well) a socialist economy had been created and no hostile classes were left. Similarly, just as Stalin went on within the next few months to justify his Blood Purge by announcing the illogical new dogma of the sharpening of the class struggle with the progress of socialist construction, so Mao Tse-tung, in the face of the use made by China's nonparty intellectuals of the freedom of criticism temporarily granted to them during the Hundred Flowers period, turned around in mid-1957 to announce a new "thought correction" campaign against "rightist tendencies." At this point, however, the parallel breaks down. For whereas Stalin's purge was primarily directed against the veteran elite of the party, Mao's antirightist campaign was primarily directed against nonparty elites and thus had a more nearly genuine class character. Moreover Mao's campaign was shortly followed, as Stalin's purge was not, by a further major effort to transform Chinese society by force—the creation of the rural communes as part of the Great Leap Forward of 1958.

The immediate pressure for creating the communes appears to have arisen from the need to tap the vast potential manpower surplus of the Chinese countryside. The idea of putting rural labor to work in low-capital industries on the spot, as well as drafting it for public works in the fields of transport and water control, was not irrational. But in the actual formation of the communes an attempt was made to mobilize rural manpower not only for use in light industries and

---

[179] I first put forward this interpretation in my article "The Revolution Withers Away," *Problems of Communism*, XIV: 1 (1965).

public works but for iron and steel production, military training, and ideological indoctrination at the same time; and this overreaching attempt required the effective militarization of labor under district-wide commands, the breaking up of the family household to mobilize womanpower, the liquidation of the peasants' private plots (because they led to a dispersal of labor), and the replacement of the main part of the family's cash incomes by rations in kind distributed equally to all. This type of military communism, based evidently on the Chinese Communists' experiences in supplying their forces in their rural fastnesses during the civil war and the war with Japan, but now forcibly imposed on the peasant population in peacetime, was justified by an explicit theory of "permanent revolution," expounded first by Liu Shao-ch'i during the second session of the Eighth Party Congress in May (before the public announcement of the commune policy) and later formally embodied in the Central Committee resolution of December 1958. This doctrine, later generally attributed to Mao Tse-tung himself, laid down that there must be no hiatus between the building of socialism and the transition to Communism just as there had been none between China's "new democratic" revolution and her "socialist" revolution—that the transformation of society in a Communist direction must be an uninterrupted process.[180] Accordingly, the new forms of communal life and work could be interpreted as a step in the transition to the higher stage of Communism; for a time even the tight rationing system was hailed as an expression of the Communist principle "To each according to his need"!

In the following years, the managerial organization, the economic program, and the wage system of the communes were all modified under the impact of economic disorganization, peasant discontent, and Soviet criticism; as early as the December 1958 resolution of the Central Committee, it was admitted that equal distribution might only be possible after fifteen or twenty years, and that full Communism was even further off. But the principle that the communes were a step on the road to that higher stage was never renounced, and by

---

[180] The germ of the Maoist theory of "permanent revolution" is contained in Mao's lectures of December 1939, "The Chinese Revolution and the Chinese Communist Party," *Selected Works*, Vol. III (London, 1954), pp. 72 *et seq.*, esp. pp. 96–97. The Wuchang resolution of the Central Committee, applying it to the transition to the "higher stage" of Communism, is in *People's Daily* (Peking), Dec. 19, 1958. See also Stuart R. Schram, *The Political Thought of Mao Tse-tung* (New York, 1963), pp. 52–54, 161–64, 252–54; Schram, *Documents sur la théorie de la révolution permanente en Chine* (Paris, 1963); and Enrica Collotti-Pischel, *La révolution ininterrompue* (Paris, 1964).

1960 urban communes were introduced as well, though chiefly for functions ancillary to industrial production itself.[181] The years 1961–62 were characterized by a growing divergence between an increasingly pragmatic policy geared to the needs of economic recovery and a basically unrevised utopian theory, apparently reflecting a deadlock in the party leadership between the unrepentant utopianism of Mao Tse-tung and the increasingly development-minded "revisionism" of his opponents.

In 1964, when Mao launched the "socialist education" campaign that was eventually to culminate in the Cultural Revolution, a new version of his theory made its appearance. Following the break with the Soviets, he had come to the conclusion that the achievement of full Communism in China might take "five to ten generations or one or several centuries"; but he also concluded from Soviet development that the danger of a restoration of capitalism would continue throughout this period preceding the attainment of the final goal, becoming more acute at particularly critical junctures.[182] The reason for this long-term danger of counterrevolution was the spontaneous reemergence of capitalist tendencies out of the unregenerated mentality of part of the people—in fact, the mentality of "economic man" —as well as the "embourgeoisement" of party and state bureaucrats in comfortable positions who allowed these tendencies to flourish instead of fighting them. That, in Mao's view, was what had happened in Khrushchev's Russia,[183] and the proclamation in the CPSU program that the dictatorship of the proletariat had ended was an ideological expression of that process. A similar development in China could be prevented only by unremitting political and ideological struggle against the capitalist outlook and all those who succumbed to it. This meant in particular a struggle for the education of the young, designed to train "millions of revolutionary successors," and also (as it came to be formulated during the Cultural Revolution) a struggle against "all persons in authority walking the capitalist road."

The Cultural Revolution inaugurated in 1966 was thus undoubtedly seen by Mao and his followers as yet another phase of their "permanent revolution"; but in contrast to previous phases, it was not aimed directly at transforming China's economic structure, however

181 Hughes and Luard, *The Economic Development of Communist China*, pp. 73–76. See also Schurmann, *Ideology and Organization*, pp. 380–99, esp. pp. 394–96.
182 See the CCP's Ninth Commentary on the Soviet "Open Letter," *On Khrushchev's Phoney Communism*, New China News Agency, July 14, 1964.
183 *Ibid.*

much it may have affected the functioning of the economy. Because of Mao's preoccupation with transforming the consciousness of the Chinese people in general and Chinese youth in particular, the campaign was directed first at the country's educational institutions; but the mobilized youth was soon incited to "bombard the headquarters," to attack the apparatus of party and government, sparing only the army and a few central ministries. Earlier we discussed the connection of these events with the alignment of "red" and "expert" elites at the time. But in the context of Mao's concept of the revisionist danger, they seem also to reflect his growing opposition to institutional stability as such—the conviction that not only "economic man" but also "bureaucratic man" represents a permanent danger to the achievement of utopia.

There can be little doubt that this conviction of Mao's developed after the failures of the Great Leap and the early communes had severely weakened his authority among the bureaucrats of party and state. Having retained control at times chiefly by army backing, he may well have remembered his experience in 1935 of rising to the top of the party over the objections of his entrenched opponents by the support of the military leaders.[184] At any rate, he seems to have drawn the conclusion that permanent revolution, as he understands it, is incompatible with institutional, bureaucratic stability, precisely as Khrushchev's colleagues and successors during the very same years came to the conclusion that institutional, bureaucratic stability was incompatible with further attempts at revolution from above. The result is that Mao's recent policy of mass mobilization against the party bureaucracy is as far removed from the "classical" Communist pattern of revolution from above under the leadership of the party as is the recent Soviet policy of postrevolutionary bureaucratic rule by the party. But whereas the new form of the Soviet political system is clearly recognizable, the new form of the Chinese Communist sys-

---

[184] According to the official version of the history of the CCP, Mao Tse-tung assumed the party leadership at an "enlarged meeting of the Central Political Bureau," held in the early stages of the Long March in Tsunyi in January 1935. (See, for example, the 1945 Central Committee "Resolution on Some Questions in the History of Our Party" in Mao's *Selected Works*, Vol. IV [London, 1956], p. 188.) Thus it seems that the decision to overthrow the previous leaders and replace them by Mao was made neither by the full Central Committee (part of whose members were not available on the spot) nor by the elected Politburo (in which Mao had no majority) but by an *ad hoc* meeting "enlarged" by the only people who could force a change—the military leaders present. For the latest scholarly account, see Jerome Ch'en, "Resolutions of the Tsunyi Conference," *China Quarterly*, 40 (Oct.-Dec. 1969), 1–38, particularly pp. 17–21.

tem is not; a new turn toward institutional stability and developmental priorities after Mao seems at least as conceivable as a continuation of utopian preoccupations and institutional crisis. The one thing that is clear is that the dilemma of utopia versus development has by now become as crucial for Communist China—despite its much lower stage of development, or perhaps because of its much greater difficulties of development—as it has proved for the Soviet Union at its advanced industrial level.

Yugoslavia. If in China conflict with the Soviet Union after 1958 helped to stimulate a renewal of permanent revolution, Stalin's break with Yugoslavia in 1948 had, after a short period of stimulation, the opposite effect of forcing a suspension of the revolutionary process there. As we have seen, in the first years following Yugoslavia's excommunication the Tito regime stepped up the pace of both industrialization and collectivization in an effort to prove its Communist orthodoxy, if not to Stalin, at least to its own rank and file. Indeed, the handing over of the Yugoslav factories to workers' management in 1950 was a way of proving that Yugoslavia was more truly a socialist workers' state than Stalin's Soviet Union, and it did introduce one more utopian element into the Yugoslav economy. But the economic reforms of the next few years, which led to the replacement of central administrative planning by a planned market economy, though justified as part of a new concept of socialist self-management, were clearly primarily efficiency measures determined by the immediate need for improvement in the living conditions of the people; and they were followed by the crucial turn in agricultural policy in early 1953, when the movement toward collectivization, which had gradually slowed down in the preceding years, was reversed and the peasants permitted to leave the collective farms.

The new agricultural policy amounted to recognition that the Yugoslav Communist regime, in its enforced isolation from the Soviet bloc, could not afford to conduct a class struggle for the transformation of the peasantry, but must make concessions to win its patriotic support. The subsequent decision to reduce the maximum private landholding to ten hectares was intended to assure the party cadres that no capitalist tendencies would be tolerated in Yugoslav agriculture; but though this deprived the freedom to leave the collectives of much of its immediate incentive effect on the peasants, it did not amount to another reversal of the trend. During the following years, the Yugoslav Communist leaders asserted repeatedly that they had not renounced the goal of fostering the growth of socialist agriculture, and they did indeed take a number of measures favoring the remaining collective farms as well as the state farms in the supply of machinery; but they also provided machinery for Western-style cooperatives formed by otherwise independent peasants.[185] On the whole, then, the Yugoslav Communists, even during later periods of rapprochement with the Soviets, which they never allowed to develop into a return to dependence on the bloc, have not carried their ideological devotion to the goal of voluntary collectivization to any greater lengths than the use of mildly discriminatory incentive techniques. In practice, this has meant that ever since the spring of 1953 Yugoslav agriculture has been predominantly based on individual farming, and has displayed neither the collectivist tendencies favored by the regime nor the trend toward a rebirth of capitalism expected in such conditions by orthodox Soviet and Chinese Communist theory. Since the Yugoslav government has made no serious attempt to change this state of affairs by the determined use of its power, we may conclude that it does not seriously regard further transformation of the social structure as its task.

This conclusion is borne out by the evolution of the official Yugoslav theory of socialism as expounded, for example, in the 1958 program of the Communist League. The theory stresses that socialism is not something that can be "built" as factories and railways are built, but that it consists of a type of relationship among the members of a given society. Political action may remove obstacles to the growth of such relationships by breaking the power of the exploiting classes, but it cannot by itself create the relationships.[186] On the contrary, attempts to use state power for the forcible creation of socialism will only consolidate the power of the bureaucracy, which, by developing into a new exploiting class, will become a new obstacle to the growth of socialist relations. Accordingly, to the extent that the Yugoslav Communists have sought to move toward utopia, their main effort has been directed not against the limited private sector of the economy, but against the power of the bureaucracy.

This effort has not, however, taken the form of an appeal to the masses to rise against the institutions, as recently in China. Rather, its aim has been to develop self-managed institutions, political as well as economic, in order either to replace or at least to control the bu-

---

[185] Hoffman and Neal, *Yugoslavia and the New Communism*, pp. 279–86, 297–98.
[186] See the official translation, *Yugoslavia's Way: The Program of the League of Communists of Yugoslavia* (New York, 1958). See also Edvard Kardelj's Oslo lecture of 1954, translated as *Socialist Democracy in Yugoslav Practice* (New Delhi, 1956).

reaucrats. In following this precept of democratic theory, the Yugoslavs have naturally come up against the contradiction between the needs of decentralized self-government and the monopolistic position of a party based on centralistic discipline. The characteristic political crises of the Yugoslav regime, ever since the Djilas affair of 1953–54, have always hinged on this contradiction. Over the long haul, however, with the waning of the veteran elite on the one hand and the growth of local and national self-confidence resulting from economic and cultural development on the other, the forces of decentralized self-government appear to have gained ground. President Tito's repeated warnings notwithstanding, the withering away of the bureaucratic state, inasmuch as that formula expresses an actual growth of self-government, appears to entail the withering away of old-style party discipline, even if not of the party itself.

On the whole, then, the course of economic, social, and cultural development, powerfully aided by the historical and geographical accident of Yugoslavia's early and lasting separation from the Soviet bloc, has stopped the forcible transformation of her economic and social structure by revolutions from above at an early stage, and has favored the loosening of her political structure by the growth of institutions of self-government. Though these bodies do not offer the clear-cut choice between political alternatives that one finds in a pluralist democracy, they are more than the simple transmission belts for decisions from above that one finds in a classical Communist party dictatorship. In Yugoslavia, then, the running down of the dynamism of the revolution from above has not resulted in the rule of a rigid, conservative bureaucracy as in Russia; instead it has given some scope to the dynamism of a groping political evolution from below that may hold democratic potentialities in the long run.

Comparisons and Conclusions

To compare the handling of a particular problem in different states and societies in isolation from the total flow of their history is always precarious. The more strictly we formalize the account for the sake of comparability, the more artificial and indeed superficial it may appear. But the closer we cling to the color and smell of the original context, the more difficult and seemingly arbitrary the comparison becomes.

In my account of the way the Soviet Union, China, and Yugoslavia have dealt with some of the problems arising from the dilemma of "utopia versus development," I am conscious of having fallen between these two stools. But as my personal bias is to favor the historical context rather than the abstract formalization of human actions as an approach to their understanding, some readers may well ask how any comparative generalizations at all could be based on such incommensurable and poorly predigested data.

Nevertheless, I propose to offer three sets of tentative conclusions based on precisely this material. The first concerns some of the common and distinctive features in the evolution of the three Communist regimes treated here, as well as some possible causal factors underlying them. The second set deals with the light this evolution may throw on the uses and limits of the totalitarian model for understanding Communist systems. The third set explores the directions in which a Communist system may change after the loss of its utopian inspiration—in other words, the possible political forms of a post-totalitarian Communism.

Common and Distinctive Features

Russia, China, and Yugoslavia are three countries vastly different in size, cultural background, and prerevolutionary level of development as well as in their historical role and geographical position within the Communist world. All they have prima facie in common is that they are ruled by Communist parties that came to power by independent revolutions in underdeveloped countries. Yet we have been able to show that recurrent conflicts between utopianism and development seem to be characteristic of all three countries, and to follow their manifestations in the fields of elite conflict, conflict over incentive policies, and conflict over the permanence or running down of the dynamism of the revolution from above. On the other hand, these conflicts have given rise over the years to a very different mix of solutions in each of the countries concerned, and even sometimes to the same solutions in different sequence; and those solutions in turn have tended to change the political systems of the countries in different directions. How are we to account for that? Can we hazard a guess about the operative factors?

Before trying to explain the differences, we should note that some of them are deceptive. In the first place, we have followed the three regimes from the conventional date of their seizure of power—their formal inauguration on a national scale. But the Yugoslav Communists held power over substantial parts of the national territory for two to three years before 1945, and the Chinese Communists for ten to twenty years before 1949; and during these periods of war and civil war both regimes exhibited the same sort of highly utopian egalitarianism that characterized Soviet War Communism between 1918 and 1921. To this extent, then, it is misleading to think that the Chinese and Yugoslavs started with a ready-made Stalinist attitude that the Bolsheviks acquired only after years of experience. In the second place, our cases are not as mutually independent as three experiments in a laboratory: the Yugoslav Communists after 1945 and the Chinese Communists after 1949 consciously imitated the model of Stalinist Russia, both because they were in awe of its ideological authority and because they were in need of Soviet aid and advice.

Next, we must keep in mind that the interdependence among the three countries had the effect of repulsion as well as attraction. For example, it was after and because of their conflict with Stalin over national independence, not before it, that the Yugoslavs developed their antibureaucratic model. Again, the Chinese might not have taken their radical turn toward utopianism in 1958 if Soviet capital aid had come up to their high expectations after the Moscow conference of November 1957; and certainly the desire to follow a road different from Moscow's was a major reason for Mao's consistent stress on utopian goals in later years. Finally, even Khrushchev's attempted revival of utopianism in 1959 was at least partly inspired by the atmosphere of ideological competition with the Chinese that followed Mao's announcement of the Great Leap Forward.

Besides the influence of relations with other Communist states, relations with the non-Communist world have at times been an important exogenous factor. This is most striking in the case of Yugoslavia because of its geographical position on the border between the Soviet and Western blocs, and because of its need for political "reinsurance" in the West during the period of Stalin's active hostility. The fact that the Yugoslav Communists, looking for a distinctive concept of nonbureaucratic socialism after the break with Stalin, endeavored to make their party dictatorship more democratically attractive by creating new organs of workers' management and self-government was certainly not unrelated to their need to win sympathy among the social-democratic parties and trade unions of the West. On the other hand, it is a commonplace of Western discussion that China's extremism should be explained by her diplomatic isolation, but it is not very convincing, for China was remarkably successful in overcoming that isolation by a non-extremist policy in 1954–55 at the time of the Geneva and Bandung conferences, and turned to extremism both at home and abroad in 1958 without any preceding change in the attitudes of the non-Communist world.

It thus appears, on the contrary, that China's grand utopian revival, the Great Leap Forward, which has remained basic for her later political evolution, is the major event that would require an explanation by mainly endogenous causes, leaving aside for the moment the possible contribution of the disappointment about Soviet aid. The first major factor that comes to mind here, in connection both with the lack of capital and with the growing importance of population pressure at the time, is simply the overwhelming difficulty of rational economic development in Chinese conditions. There did not and does not exist any way of developing China's industry fast enough to absorb her growing population.[187] There were not even enough technical cadres to train quickly the needed number of such cadres.[188] There was very little chance to increase the production of food and consumer goods fast enough for an incentive policy that offered the bulk of the workers and peasants more than the naked appeal to sacrifice. Utopianism, in short, may not just be a cause of failures in development—in certain conditions it may be their effect.

In the Chinese case, this vicious circle was powerfully reinforced by the strength of the "Yenan complex," the memories of War Communism that had remained alive among the veterans of war and civil war who still formed the leading stratum of the regime. But we may speculate also about the role of a cultural factor—a profound resistance to the acceptance of certain types of economic rationality and of institutional stability based on codified law that are seen as Western imports alien to Chinese tradition. However critical Mao has always been of the Chinese past, we cannot overlook the fact that ever since his assumption of the party leadership in 1935, Westernized or Russified intellectuals from the coastal cities have steadily lost influence in favor of a clan of leaders from the "backwoods" of Hunan, who consciously proceeded to "Asianize" Marxism. Under their guidance, the Cultural Revolution appeared for a time to have achieved the crucial transition from the familiar ambivalent attitude toward the West

---

[187] See note 67 above.

[188] Schurmann, *Ideology and Organization*, pp. 283–84: "China in 1949 was far behind Russia in 1917 as to levels of education and literacy. The Chinese Communists did not have sufficient educational facilities for the rapid training of a new technical intelligentsia.... Since they were unable to combine red and expert effectively in the form of a new worker-peasant intelligentsia, they turned over greater power to the red cadres."

that seeks to learn from it even while fighting it, to an almost total rejection of Western values that is hardly compatible with a serious effort at modernization.

Our consideration of the influence of a number of inter-Communist and exogenous factors as well as of the specific anti-developmental factors at work in the Chinese case seems to leave the Soviet pattern, in which a powerful, recurrent urge to utopian-motivated revolutions from above gradually loses momentum with the progress of economic development, as a plausible norm to be expected in the absence of such specific factors. Of course, we cannot claim to have proved this hypothesis; at best we may say that our examination of alternative outcomes and their possible causes still leaves it plausible. Indeed, the severely limited number of widely different cases examined excludes any thought of proving a general "law" for the evolution of Communist party regimes. All we can hope to do is confirm the usefulness of a model.

Uses and Limits of the Totalitarian Model

The foregoing analysis has in fact been based on a version of the much-criticized totalitarian model of Communist party dictatorship —a version that shares with other versions the selection of a "syndrome" of specific institutional features that may be used to define the concept. In our version, as introduced in the early part of this essay, there are only four such features: an institutional monopoly of policy decision, organization, and information for the ruling party, and the freeing of the state from all legal limitations in the exercise of its tasks.[189] (It will be seen that the last point, adapted from Lenin's definition of dictatorship, implies the possibility of terror.) But whereas some other versions, once influential and now widely criticized, portrayed totalitarianism as a political system essentially resistant to change,[190] we have followed those authors who emphasize

189 This version has been long used by me. See my articles: "Stalin's Testament," *Twentieth Century* (London), Mar. 1953; "Our Peculiar Hell," *Dissent*, Autumn 1957; "The Permanent Revolution Is On Again," *Problems of Communism*, VI: 5 (1957); "Totalitarian and Democratic Revolution," *Commentary*, June 1960; "Stalin and Ideology," *Survey*, July-Sept. 1960; "The Revolution Withers Away," *Problems of Communism*, XIV: 1 (1965); "The Model of the Totalitarian State," in Royal Institute of International Affairs, *The Impact of the Russian Revolution, 1917–1967* (London, 1967).
190 Hannah Arendt, *The Origins of Totalitarianism* (first pub. 1951); Carl J. Friedrich and Zbigniew K. Brzezinski, *Totalitarian Dictatorship and Autocracy* (first pub. 1956). In his revised edition (Cambridge, Mass., 1965), Friedrich has

the role of totalitarian dictatorship as a powerful agent of thorough-going, centrally manipulated, and recurrent social change imposed from above with a view to transforming society in the direction of a preconceived utopian goal—of "permanent" or at at any rate recurrent revolution from above.[191] We have further suggested that the specific dynamism of the revolution from above requires the extreme concentration of power in specific totalitarian institutions, which in turn require the utopian goal and the dynamism of imposed change for their legitimation.

Our underlying thesis is that although the conscious purpose of a totalitarian dictatorship is to change the social structure without changing the political system, the planned social change results inevitably in unintended and indeed unforeseen political change. In the foregoing, we have tried to describe and analyze how this political change comes about in cases where the ideologically guided transformation is accompanied by, and frequently conflicts with, the modernization of an underdeveloped society. For studying this question, the case of the Soviet Union is clearly of crucial importance as offering the longest period of the successful modernization and transformation of an underdeveloped country by a totalitarian Communist regime. We started with three hypotheses. First, that in the process of development, planned revolution from above leads to recurrent conflict with unplanned, spontaneous evolution from below, which tends to take a different direction. Second, that with the success of development, the forces of evolution from below tend to get stronger and the forces of revolution from above weaker until the process of recurrent revolutionary transformation loses its momentum and finally comes to a standstill because the cost of further imposed transformations to the regime itself, in terms of economic strength and international power, is seen by the regime as prohibitive. Third, that the loss of revolutionary dynamism, by depriving the totalitarian political institutions of their legitimation, is bound to become a major cause of change in these institutions.

The first of these hypotheses — the recurrent conflict between the two tendencies — has been confirmed for the three countries ex-

---

changed his account of the role of terror, but holds that the Soviet political system is still essentially totalitarian in the sense of his definition. Miss Arendt, on the other hand, states in her new introduction to the latest paperback edition (New York, 1966) that the Soviet Union ceased to be totalitarian after Stalin's death, but she indicates no other causes of the change.

[191] Above all Sigmund Neumann, *Permanent Revolution: Totalitarianism in the Age of International Civil War* (first pub. 1942; reprinted New York, 1965).

amined. The second hypothesis—the loss of revolutionary momentum as a result of successful development—clearly applies in the Soviet case, and less clearly, because of the precipitating role of exogenous factors, in the Yugoslav case. In the Chinese case, it has so far received an indirect and negative confirmation because the pursuit of permanent revolution appears to have stopped development at an early stage, but also because utopianism appears to have been reinforced by the extraordinary objective difficulties of development. The third hypothesis—crisis and change in the political institutions of the party dictatorship following an end of revolutionary dynamism—offers a key to the understanding of the post-Khrushchev replacement of one-man leadership by bureaucratic oligarchy in the Soviet Union, as well as to that of the continuing political experimentation in Yugoslavia; both systems, though preserving the political monopoly of the Communist party, have by now departed from the totalitarian model in different ways.

I should like to conclude these reflections by referring to a suggestion of Alex Inkeles. In discussing the need to integrate the study of Communist systems more effectively with the general body of the social sciences, he observed that whereas the totalitarian model has had its uses for an understanding of the former, at the present stage of our knowledge and of the development of Communist societies it must necessarily be supplemented by use of the "developmental model" and the "model of the industrial society."[192] In this essay, I have tried to show that where Communist dictatorships in underdeveloped countries are concerned, the totalitarian and developmental models do indeed describe two interconnected and conflicting aspects of one and the same process, but that where the model of the industrial society takes sway, the totalitarian model begins to lose its relevance.

Post-Totalitarian Communism

But if a Communist regime tends to lose the revolutionary momentum characteristic of totalitarian political systems as it approaches the level of an industrial society, how are we to describe the new political forms of its postrevolutionary, and therefore potentially post-totalitarian, phase? May we say that a new kind of political system has emerged?

We have described three kinds of typical conflicts between utopian and developmental tendencies in Communist regimes, and have examined in each case the political consequences of a victory of the de-

[192] Alex Inkeles, "Models and Issues in the Analysis of Soviet Society," *Survey*, 60 (July 1966).

velopmental approach. In the conflict between the revolutionary veteran elite and the postrevolutionary expert elite, a victory of the experts leads, in one form or another, to a major change in the party's composition, and hence in its outlook. In the conflict over the role of moral and material incentives, a victory for economic man leads to a growing acceptance of materialist values, and in due course to a major decline in the role of coercion, a corresponding decline in the political and economic power of the security police, and the disappearance of mass terrorism as an instrument of policy. In the conflict over the continuation of the revolution from above, the ultimate disappearance of revolutionary dynamism leads to a critical change in the party's image of its role in society and therefore to a crisis in its political legitimation.

Clearly, these three kinds of political change not only are rooted in the same process of development, but tend to reinforce each other. But they do not occur simultaneously or even necessarily in the same sequence in different countries. Thus the drastic change in the composition of the CPSU that followed Stalin's mass liquidation of the revolutionary veterans did not end the party's utopian commitment to permanent revolution (or indeed Stalin's own), though it helped to prepare the ground for resistance to later revolutionary projects based on a realistic recognition of their cost. The change in party membership also helped to reinforce the climate of materialism, but it took fifteen years of further industrial advances to bring about the disappearance of forced labor as a major sector of the Soviet economy. The end of mass terrorism, in turn, obviously made further revolutions from above more difficult, but by itself did not convince Khrushchev that he could not continue to launch such transformations by nonviolent means.

In Yugoslavia, the external threat from Stalin forced the regime by 1952–53 to discontinue both mass coercion and the attempt at permanent revolution; but whereas both changes must have weakened the position of the veteran elite, the veterans' defeat was not consummated until 1966! The example illustrates the truth that the effect of developmental pressures on Communist regimes makes itself felt slowly and not in a straight line; indeed, as the case of China shows, these pressures may not prove irresistible.

Let us now look at the combined effect of the three changes on a Communist political system.[193] When they have all taken place, we

---

[193] With respect to the Soviet Union, I have developed some of the points that follow in my papers "The Soviet Union in the Post-Revolutionary Era: An Overview," in Alexander Dallin and Thomas B. Larson, eds., *Soviet Politics since Khru-*

still find a Communist party holding a monopoly of political power. That party now largely consists of a postrevolutionary generation of fairly well-educated members, including a considerable number of economic and technical experts. The regime is neither using mass coercion nor trying to impose revolutionary transformations on society, but seeks simply to increase its national power and economic productivity. But although it has in practice renounced the specific goals of Communist ideology and the totalitarian dynamism that flowed from it, it has still preserved most of the totalitarian institutional framework. The monopolistic party is still in a position to control all mass organizations (though in Yugoslavia it does so less strictly than in the Soviet Union), and it may still act as a power above the law if it chooses (though in Yugoslavia it does so less frequently). The party's monopoly of information even in Russia has been weakened by the effect of foreign contacts, foreign technical and scholarly literature, foreign Communist newspapers, and foreign broadcasts; but part of those changes are still reversible, and though they suffice to make the official manipulation of opinion less than total, they do not permit the formation of independent opinions except by a very small elite.

Yet though the totalitarian institutional framework has in the main been preserved, the basic relation between the political system and the evolution of society has been reversed. Formerly the political system was in command, subjecting an underdeveloped society both to forced development and to a series of revolutions from above. Now the political system has to respond to the pressures generated by an increasingly advanced society. Formerly the Communist political superstructure was concerned with forcibly transforming the system's economic and social basis, contrary to the generalizations derived by Karl Marx from the evolution of the industrial society in the West. Now, the economic and social basis of the countries under Communist rule, having reached a state of development comparable to that of the modern West, is beginning to transform the political superstructure in the familiar manner described by the Marxist interpretation of history.

One of the first signs of this reversal of roles is a reduction in the range of government and party activities and an increase in the legal and social security of the average individual. As leaders lose the belief, and subjects the fear, that further major upheavals may be imposed on the social structure from above, and as the climate of mass coercion evaporates with the dismantling of the apparatus for imposing it, the regime loses the power to mobilize the people except in national emergencies. "Spontaneous" mass demonstrations and "voluntary" participation in political study groups disappear from everyday life, and the sphere of privacy and autonomous leisure, in which the party and its mass organizations do not normally intrude, is correspondingly extended.

Next to the autonomy of the private sphere, there develops a growing autonomy of intellectual life. The natural sciences, recognized as indispensable for the country's economic and military progress, are the first to win the struggle for independence from dogmatic ideological control. But as the society becomes more complex and the ideologists less secure, the need for sophisticated techniques of economic planning facilitates the autonomous development of economics as well; and as unplanned and unforeseen phenomena occur because of the society's spontaneous evolution, empirical social research has to be encouraged to enable the rulers to find out about them and respond to them. Finally, the decline in the authority of the official faith, and particularly the growth of moral problems unforeseen in its canonical writings, stimulates a desire for autonomous development and experimentation in literature and the arts, for which the growing autonomy of leisure provides a market. The regimes tend to respond by permitting a greater variety in form while only maintaining a censorship of content against ideas liable to foster political opposition or undermine social discipline.

In the most general terms, it is the growing differentiation of an advanced society that faces Communist rulers with new problems and demands: and though its spontaneous development in a framework of state ownership of the principal means of production no longer confirms, at this stage, their fear of a rebirth of capitalism, it does confront them with a variety of conflicts of opinions and interests that require policy decisions. In Soviet economic policy, the proponents of strict central planning with modern mathematical methods stand against the supporters of increased managerial autonomy oriented to flexible prices on the market; the advocates of priority for armaments and heavy industry against those who stress the claims of agriculture and chemicals or of industrial consumer goods. In military policy, the nuclear missile lobby is fighting the defenders of maximum conventional flexibility; in foreign affairs, the enthusiasts of all-out aid to national-revolutionary regimes in developing countries are opposed by the skeptics. In the handling of the scientific and literary intelligentsia, the bureaucratic supporters of rigid control are at odds with liberal spokesmen for those professions who assert that the most loyal of citizens cannot do creative work without some freedom to experiment.

Soviet political leaders, anxious to preserve their monopoly of decision-making, will not permit these conflicting interests and opinions to be represented by independent groups or organized factions; yet they know that well-informed decisions require the airing of conflicting arguments in their councils and at times even in public. As a result, they have established a variety of forums[194] for the discussion of such issues to supplement their discussion inside the top bureaucracy—a device amounting to the encouragement of interest articulation by informal and impermanent bureaucratic groups. The Yugoslav leaders, with their stress on "socialist self-management," have long gone much further in institutionalizing the articulation of interests in chambers of producers, but continue to prevent their aggregation by rival political tendencies or factions. In either case, the open voicing of disagreements on policy questions by party officials acting as informal spokesmen for conflicting interests has become a necessary element of the decision-making process, so much so that participants must feel assured that no serious harm will come to them if their cause is defeated. To this extent, policy conflict inside the ruling bureaucracy has become legitimate even in Russia, though the top leadership still reserves the right to decide which particular issues will be discussed and for how long.

What has emerged, then, is a political system in which both the spirit and the procedures of single-party rule—the regime's concept of its own role and its manner of governing—have been profoundly altered by the change in its functional relation to society. The Communist party can no longer claim that its task is to use state power to transform the social structure in accordance with its utopian goals;

[194] Under Khrushchev, the holding of enlarged Central Committee meetings with hundreds of outside experts—specialists in industrial planning and management, or in agriculture, or in cultural affairs, according to the subject—and the publication of the minutes of those discussions served this function, among others. Though this practice has been discontinued under his successors, the publication of opposing views in specialized journals and occasionally in the daily press has become even more frequent; but care is now taken that no member of the Politburo, the ultimate "arbitrating" body, should express personal opinions on controversial issues until a decision has been reached.

it knows it must react to the pressures and demands of society. But wishing to keep its monopoly of power, it is not resigned to conceive of government as a mere representative of the needs of society—for a truly representative regime would have to be a pluralistic regime, permitting independent, organized groups to struggle for their opinions and interests and to reach decisions by coalitions and compromises. Rather, the postrevolutionary party regime sees itself as an indispensable, authoritative arbiter of society's various interests, recognizing their existence but regulating their expression and limiting their representation while retaining for itself the ultimate right of decision. Unable to continue its revolutionary offensive against society and unwilling to be reduced to a mere expression of the constellation of social forces at a given moment, it is neither totalitarian nor democratic, but *authoritarian*: it is on the defensive against the forces of autonomous social development, a guardian clinging to his role after his ward has reached adulthood.

One symptom of this defensive situation of a Communist party ruling an industrial society is its search for a new ideological legitimation. No longer able to justify its rule as a dictatorship of the proletariat needed to achieve full Communism, it claims that its guardian role is necessary to assure a steady growth of production and welfare (which will eventually lead to Communism), to prevent the penetration of foreign influences hostile to the country's socialist achievements, and generally to maintain national unity, independence, and greatness. As the fate of Khrushchev's attempt to reorganize the party as an agency of economic super-management has shown, the argument that a party dictatorship is needed for steady economic progress has little plausibility in an advanced country—even for the party bureaucrats themselves. Accordingly, the tendency to give an increasingly nationalist interpretation to the old legitimizing slogans about the need for ideological unity and the defense of socialist achievements appears to become universal among post-totalitarian Communist regimes.

At the same time, the renunciation of further revolutions from above and the acceptance of the primary need for continuous economic growth lead to a strong emphasis on rationality, not only in the running of the economy but in the methods of bureaucratic government. The improvisations of dynamic, personal leadership come to be distrusted, while the predictable regularity of bureaucratic procedures—in the application of the party statutes, of the administrative rules, and of the law—comes to be stressed. A regime thus committed to bureaucratic rule necessarily shows a tendency to become both oligarchic and conservative, and to favor the consolidation of the privileges of the "new class."

Yet there exists an increasingly obvious conflict between the wish for bureaucratic rationality and stability on the one hand and the nationalist transmutation of Communist ideology on the other, a conflict that reflects the persistent contradiction between the requirements of legitimizing the party dictatorship and the growth conditions of an industrial society. The ruling bureaucracy will tend to be rational and legal in its methods so long as it does not feel threatened in its privileged position by pressures from below; but once such pressures make themselves felt, it will be quick to proclaim that the fatherland is in danger, and to tamper with legal guarantees in the name of a national emergency. This, at any rate, has been standard practice for post-totalitarian Communist systems up to now. It seems to reflect the basic dilemma of these new authoritarian dictatorships, which, in contrast to the totalitarian dictatorships they have succeeded, have found it necessary to tolerate certain limited elements of pluralism but are still seeking to keep them under tutelary control.

Types of Communist Economic Systems

JOHN MICHAEL MONTIAS

The political scientist's obsession with the "totalitarian model" as an image of Communist politics finds its counterpart in the economist's preoccupation with the integrally planned economy. Both constructs may once have been useful in bringing out the "essential differences" between Communist societies on the one hand and the politically pluralistic and economically atomistic societies of the West on the other. But it has become increasingly evident in recent years that such theoretical constructs have now become an obstacle to the deeper comprehension of these systems.

A new approach to the analysis of Communist political systems shifts the focus of attention to the dynamic properties of Communist regimes, in particular to their ability to mobilize the population for furthering party goals.[1] In the economic sphere, this mobilization takes the form of pressures on individuals and their families, usually channeled through local party cadres, to make them contribute as much as they can to the pursuit of the regime's economic goals. The contributions exacted from households may be in the form of work, consumption forgone, or participation in organized activities aimed at mobilizing others.

Postrevolutionary regimes go through a phase marked by a high

I am grateful to Gregory Grossman for a number of perceptive comments on an earlier draft of this paper and to Richard Lowenthal for his useful suggestions on terminology.

[1] Chalmers Johnson in his essay in this volume refers to high- and low-mobilization phases in the evolution of Communist regimes and to the dynamics of societal change that bring about the transformation of one phase into the other.

degree of popular mobilization as they attempt to launch their first grandiose schemes, inspired by a Marxist conception of utopia.[2] As revolutionary regimes mature, their pent-up energy gets dissipated, and they become more bureaucratized or routinized in their operations. Yet Communist systems are capable of reverting to a high-energy phase, as the Chinese Communists have demonstrated on at least two occasions, at the time of the Great Leap Forward of 1958-59 and in the initial stages of the Cultural Revolution of 1966–69. We may speak therefore of high- or low-mobilization regimes without prejudging the existence of any necessary sequence of phases. As a matter of historical record, it happens that the endogenous forces working for the transformation of one regime into the other are sometimes checked and sometimes accelerated by exogenous factors, including external threats to the survival of the system.

In this essay I attempt to distinguish the salient traits of four main types of socialist economic systems: (1) mobilization, (2) centralized-administered and (3) decentralized-administered, both of which are characterized by having hierarchically structured bureaucracies for effecting the party's economic policies, and (4) market-socialist. I conclude by speculating on some of the factors that may cause the transformation of an economic system from one basic type into another or into a hybrid.

My initial principle of classification hinges on three coordinates: the degree of mobilization for the promotion of regime goals of participants in the system, particularly of peasants, workers, and employees by lower-level party cadres; the degree of reliance by central authorities on hierarchically transmitted commands for furthering regime goals; and the relative importance of markets for producer goods.

In the accompanying diagram the first, or mobilization, coordinate is shown vertically; the second, or reliance-on-commands, coordinate, horizontally; and the third, or reliance-on-markets, coordinate, obliquely, to suggest a dimension in depth. Each coordinate is divided into two segments representing a low or a high score.

In this simplified schema, the centralized- and decentralized-ad-

---

[2] On utopian elements in the economic policies of the Soviet, Chinese, and Yugoslav Communist parties at various historical phases, see Richard Lowenthal's paper in this volume. To minimize duplication and because of my specialization in Eastern European affairs, I have drawn my examples of policies pursued in mobilization systems and my accounts of the gradual changes in these systems mainly from Eastern Europe.

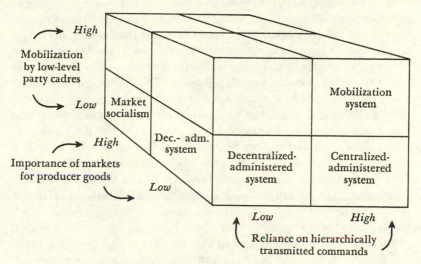

Classifying Socialist Economic Systems

ministered systems differ only in the extent of their reliance on hierarchically transmitted commands (both score low on mobilization and the reliance on markets). The mobilization system is obviously high on the mobilization coordinate and low on the market coordinate; it is also given a high score on the command coordinate, although as we shall see this is not a necessary characteristic of the system.

In the diagram the decentralized-administered system, labeled on two of its facets, scores low on all three dimensions. This system is decentralized in the sense that detailed input and output decisions (in natural units) are made by the enterprise or association (or trust) rather than by higher authorities. Hierarchic channels are used by central coordinators to impose *aggregated* targets (such as gross output, value added, and tax remittances) or to set upper limits to the value of certain resources allotted to enterprises or associations (such as investment funds, foreign exchange allowances, or the wage bill). Although prices of both consumer and producer goods are centrally set, this does not necessarily create severe shortages or disrupt production, especially in the absence of competition among producers,[3] as

[3] In a somewhat different institutional context this point has been persuasively argued by J. K. Galbraith on the basis of his experience with price controls in the United States during World War II (*A Theory of Price Control* [Cambridge, Mass., 1952], ch. 2).

long as fiscal and monetary policies are employed to keep the aggregate demands for inputs in check. To the extent that excess demand for individual commodities persists because of inefficient prices, producers may be allowed to ration off available supplies informally, according to the previous volume of business transacted with each customer or on a first-come, first-served basis. The disadvantage of tolerating uncoordinated rationing decisions may be offset by the advantage of allowing close contact between producers and consumers, who may reach mutually advantageous agreements despite the rigidity of prices. If import and export decisions remain centralized in such a system, as they are likely to, they may be used to correct some of the remaining disequilibria. In 1967 and 1968, the Czechoslovak economic system, which provided for price flexibility only in relatively unimportant areas, bore some resemblance to the decentralized-administered model I have just described. I shall return to the question of the stability of such a system in the last part of this essay.

The unlabeled boxes in the diagram are not necessarily empty but cannot be filled with convincing examples of formerly or presently functioning Communist systems. Two interesting possibilities should, however, be mentioned. First, a mobilization system need not rely heavily on hierarchically transmitted commands. During the Great Leap Forward campaign in China, for example, the decisions of local cadres may not have been guided very closely by specific orders from the top leadership. Second, market socialism may be compatible with a fairly high degree of mobilization of the population by local cadres. Yugoslavia in the mid-1950's, at a time when party cadres still exerted considerable influence on lower-level economic decisions, may be a case in point. For both these variants, however, the evidence available is too slim to warrant an extension of the basic classification.

If we analyze Communist systems through history, we find that few can be neatly pigeonholed. We may choose then to treat our four basic systems as *Idealtypen*, which may happen to have fairly good actual representatives, and to view other Communist systems as combinations of these types.[4] The mobilization system, for example, is

---

[4] To be accurate, we should speak of combinations of the individual elements in the column vector of system coordinates (as in the table below, in which scores have been entered into the individual cells), since a combination of the vectors themselves would imply that each element in the vector should be given the same weight. In other words, there are existing systems that have traits resembling the mobilization type and others resembling the centralized hierarchic type. Such hybrids could not be represented by any combination of columns if each column were assigned a unique weight.

fairly well represented by China during the Great Leap Forward, by Cuba in the 1960's, or by War Communism in Soviet Russia in 1918–21.[5] The Soviet Union during the first years of its first five-year plan and the people's democracies in the period 1948–51 may be said to have gone through mobilization phases, although in both cases the central authorities were trying with increasing success to develop hierarchic commands and controls that would make producers more responsive to detailed directives from above. Despite these efforts, full-fledged "administered systems" were not established until the late 1930's in the Soviet Union and the mid-1950's in Eastern Europe. We have already cited Czechoslovakia in 1967–68 as an example of a decentralized-administered system. The German Democratic Republic created a hybrid system in the mid-1960's that was decentralized in some respects but that retained a larger measure of central control of input and output decisions than was the case in Czechoslovakia or Hungary.

The Soviet Union during the period of the New Economic Policy and Yugoslavia since 1952–53 are the only representatives of market socialism that can be cited: the scope of free prices seems to have been greater in these instances than in any decentralized-administered system, and producing units organized as enterprises in Yugoslavia or as trusts during the NEP were to a significant extent free from centralized commands conveyed through an administrative hierarchy.

In the table below the list of system traits has been extended beyond the three basic coordinates used in the diagram; some of these traits require an explanation. Instead of scoring economies according to the relative importance of markets for producer goods, I show separately the prevailing mode of allocation for these goods—type of rationing or market process—and the basis for setting prices in the four *Idealtypen.*

Planning "from below" or counterplanning refers to the procedure in effect in the Soviet Union until the late 1930's, in Czechoslovakia until 1953, and in Poland and East Germany until 1954:[6] the preliminary output targets and limits on materials and the inputs issued for the coming year by the planning commission were parceled out to

---

[5] In the period of Soviet War Communism, however, there was no development strategy, whether of a teleological or genetic character. (See the accompanying table.)

[6] The evidence for counterplanning in Eastern Europe from 1949 until 1952–53 is plentiful. For a detailed description, see *Plánované hospodářství*, 4 (Prague), Apr. 1952, 243–47.

System Traits for Four Basic Types of Socialized Economies

	Mobilization	Administered Systems		Market Socialism
		Centralized	Decentralized	
Organization	Hierarchical, functional, and/or regional	Hierarchical, functional or regional	Hierarchical, functional	Polycentric or regional
Mobilization of peasants and workers by low-level party cadres	High	Low	Low	Low
Reliance on hierarchically transmitted commands	High	High	Low	Low
Incentives	"Moral"	Material	Material	Material
Distribution of producer goods	By rationing on basis of priority	By rationing according to plan	Insufficient evidence	Through markets or by informal rationing
Prices of producer goods	Centrally set, arbitrary	Centrally set, at average cost	Partly decentralized, set at "full cost"	Market, subject to central and local controls
Consumer goods	Rationed	Sold at approximately market-clearing prices set by center	Sold at market-clearing prices, some of which set by enterprise	Sold at market-clearing prices
Type of planning (participation of enterprise in planning process)	"From below," counter-planning	"From above"	"From below"	Insufficient evidence

Coordination of short-term allocation decisions	Through priority system	Through central yearly and quarterly plans	Through central plans and informal contacts among producers and their organizations	Through market and informal contacts among producers and their organizations
Development strategy	Teleological	Genetic	Genetic	Genetic
Managerial latitude	Medium	Low	Medium	High
Tranquility of enterprise	Low	Medium	Insufficient evidence	High
Financial relationship of enterprise to state	Budget relation	*Khozraschet* with state as residual claimant	Pays taxes to state	Pays taxes to state
Tolerance for remnants of private enterprise in agriculture, retail trade, etc.	Low	Medium	Medium to high	Medium to high
Macroeconomic policy	Passive (inflationary in effect)	Budget-active, credits-passive; macroeconomic stability	Active, especially via banking system	Active, especially via banking system
Effect of system on innovations	Diffusion of foreign technology, occasional adoption of "crank ideas"	Diffusion of foreign technology plus innovation in favored sectors	Insufficient evidence	Insufficient evidence
Organization of factory workers	Shock workers' battalions and emulation drives	Stakhanovism	Insufficient evidence	Insufficient evidence
Reliance on "volunteer" (unpaid) workers in harvesting, reconstruction, etc.	Frequent	Rare	Absent	Absent

industrial ministries, by ministries to chief administrations or central boards, and by these intermediate organs to the enterprises themselves, which were then expected to offer counterbids committing them to producing a higher output with the same inputs as they had been tentatively allotted. "Bolshevik ingenuity" on the part of party members in uncovering reserves at the plant and at the enterprise level was supposed to be the key to these "mobilizing" counterplans. The abandonment of this typical mobilization feature of a socialist economic system and its replacement by planning "from above," which cut the enterprise out from preliminary planning and thrust the chief burden of framing consistent estimates on the planning commission and the ministries, marked an important turning point in the bureaucratization of planning.[7]

In the idealized mobilization system, allocation decisions are made at various levels in the hierarchy by functionaries who are in effect custodians of current production and who determine on the basis of the dominant priorities established by the highest party organs which claimants will receive allotments of materials or other inputs and in what amounts. The provisions of the yearly plans for the allocation of the materials and capacities that were supposed to be produced during the year are only tangentially relevant to these ad hoc decisions. The plan serves as a loose framework rather than as a set of operational directives. In the centralized-administered system, the plans are sufficiently consistent to guide allocations; ad hoc decisions are confined to the distribution of unexpected additional output or to coping with unforeseen circumstances. In practice, errors in planning make a good deal of improvisation necessary, even in the most stable centralized-administered systems, but the influence of quarterly and yearly operation plans in these systems is great enough for us to discriminate between the two types on the basis of this trait.

In decentralized-administered systems, as we have seen, taxes, credits, and other macroeconomic instruments are used to induce enterprises and their associations to fulfill at least the main provisions

---

[7] One of the chief reasons given in Czechoslovakia's shift from planning from below to planning from above was that when the counterplans submitted by enterprises were aggregated by production sector, it usually turned out that they were mutually inconsistent to such a degree that they had to be completely recast, starting from the original directives. If the Czech planners really felt that the consistency of plans mattered, as they apparently did as early as 1951–52, then they could well have dispensed with the ritual of participatory planning. For an early and candid discussion of this problem, see *Problémy nové soustavý plánování a financování Československého průmyslu* (Prague, 1957), p. 38.

of the yearly and long-term plans. In the absence of markets brought into equilibrium by flexible prices, coordination is also effected through informal contacts, barter, and exchanges among producers. Such systems have also been marked by the absence of competition, each sector being organized as a hierarchically structured monopoly. Under market socialism, prices tend to be flexible, or at least more flexible than in a decentralized-administered system, and competition among producers is fairly frequent, if not the general rule. Another distinction is that in the decentralized-administered systems the central authorities try to get enterprises to behave so that the main conceptions of the plan will be realized, whereas in the market system enterprise decisions deviating from the plan are more likely to be allowed, since the market may be expected to lead to a better pattern of allocation than would have been attained if the plan had been followed strictly.

The strategy of development, insofar as rather vague concepts and notions can be dignified by the name of strategy, is said to be teleological in mobilization systems and genetic in all others, a distinction that arose in the mid-1920's, when the optimal strategy for industrializing the Soviet Union was under discussion. The teleologists, who favored *industrialisation à outrance,* argued for the central authorities' setting ambitious output targets that would draw every effort from party cadres, managers, and workers toward their fulfillment; the material means for carrying out the plans might not be clear at the outset but would emerge as the creative potentialities of the masses were released;[8] finely balanced plans, the teleologists thought, were not as likely to mobilize the population and promote rapid industrialization as were more imaginative, albeit less meticulously elaborated schemes. The partisans of genetic planning favored a careful husbanding of resources and the setting of targets consistent with the best available estimates of capacity, foreign exchange, and other limitations. When the teleologists wished to caricature the genetic approach to planning, they claimed that the genetic method was essentially a conservative projection of past trends.

We may score an actual system on this trait with two indicators: the average level of fulfillment of plans and the variance around this average. If a teleological plan had been fulfilled "on the average" by deflecting scarce inputs from low- to high-priority sectors, a high vari-

---

8 "To plan," wrote Hilary Minc in 1949, "means first of all to mobilize the masses whose creative energy and enthusiasm are the most important factor in the realization of the plans." (*Nowe Drogi*, 8 [Warsaw], Aug. 1948, 36.)

ance in the percentage deviations from the initial targets around this average would presumably result.

In the evolution of the centrally coordinated economies from a mobilization to a centralized-administered system, the abandonment of teleological in favor of genetic planning is gradual and uneven, with striking lags in certain sectors. Plans for the agricultural sector, in particular, continue to be idealistic and optimistic long after the planners have settled on fairly firm estimates for the industrial sectors, or at least for those not depending on the farms for their inputs. And this for two reasons: first, the party's role in "mobilizing the masses" is usually greater in agriculture than in industry, if only for organizational-hierarchic reasons; second, shortfalls in agriculture have repercussions limited mainly to the food and textile industries, consumer-goods sectors that may be at least temporarily sacrificed, whereas errors in planning for any branch of heavy industry are likely to trigger off a whole sequence of shortfalls in priority sectors.

Managerial latitude refers to the freedom an enterprise manager has in making decisions about the variables under his control in typical circumstances; tranquility of enterprise, a related but distinct trait, is a measure of the stability of centrally imposed constraints. In measuring managerial latitude, we view the external environment of the enterprise as average or modal for the years; when we study tranquility, the focus shifts to the variability in this environment, as it is affected by decisions by superiors in the hierarchy.

It is not obvious how managerial latitude and tranquility should be measured. Let us suppose that the success of a manager of an enterprise in pursuing the objectives he has set himself on the basis of the targets and other constraints imposed by higher authorities can be gauged in terms of one or more value indices (e.g., the gross value of the enterprise's output, profits, or the volume of managerial bonuses for fulfilling the plans). We may now ask how much better the manager would do on this scale if the targets and other orders concerning his inputs or the structure of his output that presently hem him in were suddenly removed (while the constraints set by the enterprise's capital stock and other resources remained as before). The ratio of the value of these indices (suitably aggregated), computed for the actual situation of the enterprise and for the hypothetical case where the "organizational restraints" were removed, might serve as an indicator of the manager's latitude during a given period of time. If this indicator could be computed frequently, on the basis of the current orders received by the enterprise during a longer period such as a year, its variance over the period would yield an inverse measure of the enterprise's tranquility. A simpler and cruder approach would consist in building up a tranquility indicator from the number and relative importance to the enterprise of the countermanding orders it had received during the year.

The mobilization system has a medium score on managerial latitude because managers in these systems tend to acquire a good deal of de facto power despite, or perhaps even because of, the numerous and sometimes contradictory orders and prohibitions the enterprise receives from higher levels in the hierarchy. In practice the manager can often withhold information about detailed circumstances at the plant level from superiors; thus he can choose to comply with the commands that happen to suit him, disregarding some that do not. Nevertheless, tranquility in such a system is low because of frequent plan changes and countermanding orders, some of which have to be complied with.

The financial relationship of the enterprise to the state clearly affects the latitude open to managers, but it is sufficiently distinct to be analyzed separately. In a mobilization system, enterprises or "trusts" cover their expenses from and pay all their receipts into the state budget. They operate like a government department with virtually no financial autonomy.[9] In centralized-administered systems, enterprises are on a cost-accounting system (*khozrashchet*): they cover their expenses from their receipts, dealing with the treasury only on a net or residual basis. The state, however, usually levies all but the part of the profits earmarked for rewarding the enterprise for fulfilling or over-fulfilling its industrial-financial plan. In a decentralized-administered system, as well as under market socialism, if we may infer from the 1967–68 reforms in Hungary and Czechoslovakia and from the experience of Yugoslavia, the enterprise keeps any profits that are left over after it has paid to the central and regional government all taxes on "gross income" (value added), wages, capital assets, profits, and other financial activities.

A sensitive indicator of the level of mobilization in a system is the

---

[9] Gregory Grossman in his analysis of what he calls "siege systems," which more or less coincide with what I call mobilization systems, singles out the relationship of the enterprise to the budget, together with the type of incentive scheme in operation, as distinguishing characteristics. He observes that in contemporary Cuba, which is a good example of a siege or mobilization system, enterprises and trusts are run "on budget." See "Continuity and Change in Centrally Planned Economies," in A. A. Brown and E. Neuberger, eds., *Perspectives in Economics* (McGraw-Hill, forthcoming).

attitude of the regime toward private enterprise. A coercive policy aimed at liquidating petty retail trade, collectivizing agriculture, and within collectivized agriculture curtailing the size of peasants' private plots and the scope of free peasant markets is highly symptomatic of a mobilization phase. Both centralized- and decentralized-administered systems are more tolerant of private initiative, especially if it can play an inconspicuously positive role in mitigating the adverse effects of an excessively centralized public sector. A good example would be East Germany in the 1960's. In Yugoslavia, decollectivization in agriculture accompanied decentralization in industry, although at least until recently private initiative in the industrial and distribution sectors was about as narrowly circumscribed as in a centralized-administered system.

In his essay in this volume, Chalmers Johnson gives a number of reasons why mobilization systems should gradually subside into centralized-administered systems. Supporting his points with references to Anthony Downs's work on bureaucracies, he also finds convincing explanations for the frequent reforms in administered systems, which oscillate by a sort of dialectical process between their centralized and decentralized forms.[10] Proceeding from Johnson's argument, we may distinguish several groups of factors making for system change. First, there are factors inherent in the system whose dysfunctional effects become evident with the passage of time and eventually compel the "system directors" to launch fundamental reforms. Second, developmental variables only indirectly influenced by the prevailing system may make the system appear to be increasingly ineffectual as industrialization and economic development proceed. Third, exogenous factors such as war, internal disorders threatening Communist rule, or other "siege conditions" may cause the leaders to accelerate industrialization and rearmament and thus force them to resort to quasi-military methods of running the economy. Conversely, the removal of these external pressures or threats may allow the leaders to abandon these methods. Finally, there are subjective political factors, such as the predilection of a top leader for utopian solutions to economic problems or his reluctance to tolerate the growing powers of the administrative bureaucracy (especially at the expense of local party activists) after a period of relative economic stability.

[10] See Johnson's discussion of mobilization and bureaucratization, pp. 15–26 above.

In general, the creation or the revival of a mobilization system seems to hinge mainly on subjective and exogenous factors, although we should remember that totalitarian leaders are given to exaggerating and distorting danger signals from without. The nature of the system itself leads to the transformation of a mobilization system into a centralized- or decentralized-administered system. Developmental variables play a major role in bringing about the change from either a mobilization or a centralized-administered system to a more decentralized form of economic management.

Consider, in connection with the first group of variables, the effects of a protracted period of teleological planning and of the application of the priority system of allocation. Imbalances in the plans have created bottlenecks and shortages. As the current allotments received by the low-priority sectors and their resources drop toward zero or a tolerable minimum, the contribution of these sectors as buffers or as sources of "primitive accumulation" declines.[11] In Eastern Europe, for instance, the Communist planners initially economized on capital "by minimizing expenditures on the modernization of railroads, the construction of a modern road network, the expansion of warehouse space and the satisfaction of consumer demand for housing. This strategy could be sustained for some years because to a point the use of capacity in these services is quite elastic."[12] Eventually, capacities gave out; no more people could be squeezed into existing housing, and bottlenecks in transportation, storage, and communications raised the marginal costs of operating with congested capacities to prohibitive levels. The planners were forced to redress some of these imbalances and fill the most conspicuous gaps in the infrastructure of their economies.

Furthermore, a Communist regime cannot go on forever promising "jam tomorrow" without supplying "jam today." Promises predicated on the fulfillment of teleological schemes set up claims that must eventually be honored to some degree if the masses are not to become apathetic, rebellious, and "demobilized." Moral incentives and calls

[11] In Cuba, for instance, the number of private automobiles is said to have dropped by two-thirds since 1959. Some of the cars that are left are likely to be owned by people who, in the regime's eyes, deserve to keep them. The economies in foreign exchange that would have been used to import spare parts, gasoline, and oil before the revolution must have dwindled to a relatively small sum today.

[12] Maurice Ernst, "Postwar Economic Growth in Eastern Europe," in U.S. Congress, Joint Economic Committee, *New Directions in the Soviet Economy* (Washington, D.C., 1966), pp. 875–916.

for voluntary work may be effective and beneficial to the economy for a period of time, but they are likely to lose their strength as the masses experience protracted discomfort.

If only for these reasons, periods of intense mobilization must eventually be followed by periods of consolidation or retreat. Whatever may have been Stalin's natural penchant for mobilization methods, he understood the need for breathing spells. He did not hesitate to introduce basic elements of an administered system from 1933–34 to allow the Soviet economy to recover from the excesses of the previous period. In Eastern Europe the mobilization phase, the onset of which had been precipitated by the Cominform break with Yugoslavia and by the Korean War, showed signs of coming to a close as early as the end of 1951 or the beginning of 1952, a year before Stalin's death. No doubt the start of negotiations to settle the Korean War had some effect on this transition, but economic necessity would have wrung reforms in the system from even the most sanguine planners sooner or later.

In Poland the rationing of consumer goods was abolished, and more rational prices for producer goods were introduced in early January 1953. In Czechoslovakia the planning commission's directives replacing counterplanning by planning from above were issued (and, counter to precedent, published) in the spring of 1952.[13] The new directives seemed to imply that national economic plans would henceforward be framed on the basis of a more sober assessment of the capabilities of enterprises and of the limitations in existing resources. Without explicit reference to teleological planning, the language of the introduction to the document and the commentaries published in economic journals at the time signaled that the Czech planners at that time entertained a more genetic conception of their tasks.[14]

Whether or not these changes were prompted by Soviet advisors—and some of them undoubtedly were—the timing of their introduction and the evident relief shown by harassed officials still suggest they should be treated as rational responses to the pressure of circumstances rather than as the result of blind adherence to Soviet advice or precepts.

However we may interpret these first harbingers, the "new course"

[13] Státní úřad plánovací, *Metodické pokiny a formuláře k sestavení státního plánu rozvoje národního hospodářství ČSR na Rok 1953* (Prague, 1952).
[14] See in particular the articles by Z. Puček and J. Balaban in *Plánované hospodářství*, 4 (Prague), Apr. 1952.

introduced in Eastern Europe in the months following Stalin's death must certainly have hastened the extinction of the mobilization system. The overambitious long-term plans were for all practical purposes discarded. Relatively sober yearly plans were drawn up, geared to the short-term objective of redressing the imbalances created in the preceding period, particularly in the production of consumer goods and in agriculture. Institutional reforms went hand in hand with changes in strategy and planning style, so that by 1954 the process of mutation was virtually completed.

But the momentum of change did not cease once an administered system had been set up, for in the more advanced countries of the Soviet bloc the developmental variables that had reinforced the factors within the system making for demobilization continued to pull in the direction of basic reform. These more developed countries increasingly depended on technical progress and the successful absorption of innovations in large-scale manufacturing to maintain their competitive position in foreign markets and to offset or mitigate the shortages of primary materials and labor that accompanied their higher-stage industrialization. To achieve this progress, enterprises needed tranquility and a measure of autonomy to nurse new products through the long period of design, experimentation, and final sale. Managers had to be offered the right incentives to bend their efforts to these ends.

Centrifugal pressures for greater sectoral and managerial autonomy quickly began to be felt in several of the people's democracies, including Hungary, Poland, and Czechoslovakia. The first moves toward the delegation of certain detailed responsibilities to lower organs were made so early in this demobilization process that one may legitimately ask whether a full-fledged centralized-administered system was anything but the ephemeral and unstable product of the transformation. It may be argued that the equilibrium of an administered system, characterized by the existence of a hierarchy of functionaries for transmitting the orders and commands of top authorities to producers and for channeling information from producing units to these authorities, is upset by the extremes of centralization and decentralization. The extremely centralized variant is unstable because the planners' information collecting and processing capacities are not sufficient to embrace all the activities they would wish to control from the center: their reach exceeds their grasp. To achieve successful guidance of the economy by the highest party authorities, the enlightened system directors advocated "centralization in the solution of the main problems and decentralization in the solution of individual questions."[15] During the "new course" period after Stalin's death this formula, attributed to Georgi Malenkov, served as a pretext for unburdening the central organs of a host of petty responsibilities and for transferring them to lower organizations, including enterprises. Yet when the center delegated responsibility to lower organs for targeting and distributing an unduly large portion of industrial output, it also lost some of its ability to guide the economy, especially in a crisis, so that wherever the devolution of tasks went too far it had to be held in check or reversed by centripetal measures.[16] The reforms and counterreforms that took place in the Soviet Union and in Eastern Europe from 1953 to the present, with the probable exception of the most recent Czechoslovak and Hungarian experiments, had little effect on day-to-day procedures at the enterprise level.[17] Given the absence of clear efficiency criteria and the ideologically determined limits within which institutional change could take place, it is not surprising that reforms oscillated "dialectically" between centralizing and decentralizing measures.

Two important transformations that are probably least open to economic rationalization remain to be discussed. We can imagine a system at one end of the "totalitarian" scale in which mobilization is revived after a stretch of centralized administration; at the other end of the scale, we can conceive the possibility of the dismantling of a decentralized system to create a variant of market socialism.

"Remobilization" may occur in the face of a real or imagined external threat; it may be bound up with a new injection of utopian elements in the party ideology, in a frantic effort to arrest organizational ossification and the formation of self-seeking cliques in the hierarchy. It would be hard to disentangle these factors in Khrushchev's reforms of the period 1957–60, some of which at least signaled

---

[15] *Wirtschaftliche Wissenschaft*, 4 (East Berlin), Apr. 1954, 488.

[16] According to Czech economists writing in 1957–58, the material balances that the planning commission actually worked on at that time and that served as a basis for setting its physical targets, embraced a little less than half the value of total industrial output. The remaining part of gross output was usually planned on the assumption that each ministry's output would go up in roughly the same proportion as the aggregate of its centrally fixed targets. When the proportion of the latter to a ministry's total output was small, this planning method was liable to lead to grave errors—to avoid or correct which officials in central organs pressed for recentralization. Cf. J. Kolář, *Plánované hospodářství*, 8 (Prague), Aug. 1957, 621.

[17] See Downs as cited in Johnson's essay in this volume, p. 17.

a shift toward a mobilization system (e.g., partial return to teleological planning, more vigorous mobilization of workers and farmers by provincial party organs, curtailment of collective farmers' private plots). Similar motives have also been adduced for the Great Leap Forward campaign of 1958–59. In China's case, however, overpopulation, natural calamities, and the ever-present menace of famine may have acted like external threats to the security of the regime, threats that could be dealt with only by the most drastic means. Where the rulers' plans to remobilize are thwarted by a party apparatus that will not sedulously obey the orders of the leaders and carry out their grandiose schemes, as in China in 1966–69, alternative channels for communicating these impulses to the population must somehow be opened (e.g., Red Brigades, the army, or any other available nation-wide grouping).

The gap between a decentralized-administered system and market socialism is wider than the idealistic intellectuals who provide the rationale for reforms in Communist countries often seem to assume. The thoroughness of the conversion cannot be gauged merely by the scope of the market for producer goods. Market socialism also assumes the radical curtailment of the government and party hierarchy through which commands are transmitted from the center to all member organizations. But this dismantling goes counter to deeply vested interests and is extremely hard to achieve without a "revolution from above" buttressed by suitable changes in ideology. In Yugoslavia, where a breakthrough took place between 1950 and 1952, Boris Kidrić, Vukmanović-Tempo, and other members of Tito's leading group supplied ideological support for the reforms by inveighing against state capitalism, monopoly, and bureaucratization, which were said to be the hallmarks of Soviet degeneration (at a time when the whole country was mobilized against its former ally).[18] In this period, the hierarchic lines that once tethered Yugoslavia's enterprises to the planning commission and the Council of Ministers were severed.[19]

In Czechoslovakia and Hungary, by contrast, the reforms were grafted to the old system. An influential Czech economist and re-

18 See, for example, Boris Kidrić's forceful speech to the 1952 congress of Yugoslav economists, where domestic reforms are linked with an attack against Soviet bureaucratization. *Ekonomska politika* (Belgrade), Apr. 18, 1952, pp. 42–43.

19 The severance of these hierarchic lines did not, however, liberate producers from all interventions. Central policy directives could still be channeled through party lines or through the socialized banking system, which acquired greater powers after the basic reforms of 1950–52. But these controls were much less constraining than the old ones and could be evaded more easily.

former, writing in the journal of the Communist party's Central Committee four months before the Soviet invasion, explained why the reforms had not produced the results that had been expected of them in his country:

The fundamental reason for the survival of the old practices ... was that the direct methods of administration—the structure of institutions and of the relations among them—were not disturbed. The hierarchic structures through which the leading personnel of lower organs were appointed and dismissed by their superiors continued to exist, as did the responsibility of the leading personnel of enterprises to superior organs.... The 1965 reorganization was not adapted to the needs of an effectively functioning market mechanism and was only the continuation and the extension of the tendencies peculiar to the old system of (centralized) administration."[20]

Without a change in the old political leadership, it is evident that the transformation to market socialism could not occur. There was considerable doubt a year after the Soviet invasion whether the Czechoslovak regime had the power and energy to break the institutional mold in which the economy had been encased for over twenty years.

This is a suitable point to conclude my taxonomic exercise. I have tried to sort out a fair number of system traits observed in Soviet-type economies and to group them into as few homogeneous classes or "types" as possible. My remarks on the coordinates along which change has taken place in postwar Eastern Europe may have convinced the reader that my four types were too heterogeneous to contain the various historical examples of systems I have made reference to. This lack of neatness in the four-way classification, however, may be a price worth paying for the sake of allowing instructive generalizations, at least in a first investigation. A finer classification, possibly based on some other salient system traits, may eventually prove useful in analyzing the complex process of change in the Eastern European economies, and particularly in assessing the operational impact on their systems of the reforms they are now going through.

[20] T. Kožušník, "Rozhodující krok dalšího rozvoje ekonomické reformy," *Nová mysl*, 5 (Prague), May 1968, 590.

Varieties of De-Stalinization

JEREMY R. AZRAEL

The past decade or so has been a period of extensive political change for almost all of the fourteen countries under Communist rule. What is truly notable, however, is not the occurrence of such change but the fact that it caught so many analysts by surprise. Nevertheless, surprise gradually gave way to criticism (in some cases, even self-criticism) and to a growing demand for a reevaluation of the "conventional wisdom" in the field. In particular, an increasing barrage of criticism has been directed at the "totalitarian model" originally elaborated by Friedrich and Brzezinski and subsequently adopted by most of their colleagues.[1] Serious doubts have been expressed not only about the current relevance of this model but also about its utility for historical analysis and comparative taxonomy.[2]

Certain analysts had always been disturbed by the static character of the totalitarian model, but the onset of a period of conspicuous large-scale change in Communist systems has made this deficiency seem particularly grave. Furthermore, the fact that change has pro-

[1] Carl J. Friedrich and Zbigniew K. Brzezinski, *Totalitarian Dictatorship and Autocracy* (Cambridge, Mass., 1956). Friedrich and Brzezinski's "model" was in fact a syndromic trait list and was presented as such. However, subsequent authors have regularly used the term "model," and we shall follow this inflated and somewhat misleading usage here.

[2] See, for example, R. J. Groth, "The Isms in Totalitarianism," *American Political Science Review*, LVIII: 4 (Dec. 1964), 888–901; Allan Kassof, "The Administered Society," *World Politics*, XVI: 4 (July 1964); T. H. Rigby, "Traditional, Market, and Organizational Societies," *World Politics*, XVI: 4 (July 1964). It is worth recalling that one of the first published criticisms of the static character of the totalitarian model was by Brzezinski himself. See "Totalitarianism and Rationality," originally published in 1956 and since reprinted in the author's *Ideology and Power in Soviet Politics* (New York, 1962).

ceeded in different directions in different Communist countries has suggested that the uniformity of the preceding period existed largely in the eye of the observer—an observer whose vision was clouded by a model that stressed formal institutions at the expense of dynamic nationally and culturally differentiated processes. Finally, the growing (and/or increasingly visible) differences within the Communist world have lent currency to the view that reliance on the totalitarian model deterred students of Communism from exploring many rewarding comparisons between Communist and non-Communist systems. Although the model may originally have been designed precisely to facilitate such comparisons, the principal result, according to a growing number of critics, was to establish a misleading identity between Communism and Nazism and to encourage a tendency to cast other comparisons in the form of a value-laden "we-they" dichotomy.

One of the main purposes of this volume is to air views on whether or not the "mobilization system" is a more appropriate paradigmatic concept for the comparative study of Communism. Compared with "totalitarianism," "mobilization system" seems a relatively nonpolemical concept. In addition, it seems to incorporate a much wider range of political activities and processes and to call attention to social and economic variables that clearly influence and may determine the rate and direction of political change. Finally, it suggests numerous similarities between Communist and non-Communist countries, including countries that have approached analogous developmental problems by different means and countries that have adopted Communist techniques without subscribing to Marxist ideology.

Although the strength of these appeals is obvious, it may still be appropriate to warn against the dangers of overcommitment and premature closure. If nothing else, a cautious response is warranted because of the frequent failure of those students of Communism who have embraced the mobilization system to designate its empirical referents. This failure would be less serious if the substantial general literature on mobilization had established a more or less standard definition, but this literature in fact yields a variety of definitions, some of which are mutually incompatible.[3] Thus, there are authors

---

[3] See, for example, David E. Apter, "Political Religion in the New Nations," in Clifford Geertz, ed., *Old Societies and New States* (New York, 1963), pp. 57–104; J. P. Nettl, *Political Mobilization* (London, 1967); Karl Deutsch, "Social Mobilization and Political Development," *American Political Science Review*, LV: 3 (Sept. 1961), 493–514; Amitai Etzioni, *The Active Society* (New York, 1968). Actually, only Apter uses the term "mobilization system"; the other authors refer to dominant processes or characteristics within systems.

for whom one of the defining characteristics of a "mobilization system" is its inability to achieve an industrial breakthrough, and other authors for whom mobilization is virtually inseparable from economic modernization. Some include within their definition only systems that are dominated by a self-perpetuating revolutionary elite; others include stable democracies or associate mobilization with progressive democratization. These usages may be equally valid, but they vary significantly and cannot be indiscriminately lumped together; nor, if serious confusion is to be avoided, can any of them be tacitly excluded or ignored. Rather, those who propose to make the "mobilization system" a paradigmatic concept in Communist studies must explicitly recognize the concept's ambiguous connotations and specify the precise configuration they have in mind.

Although many students of Communism have begun to question the established boundaries of their field, those who advocate the substitution of the "mobilization system" for the totalitarian model usually proceed on the assumption that most Communist-ruled countries belong—or belonged—to the same (generic or specific) type. Given this premise, however, there appears to be a strong prima facie case against any taxonomy that is not primarily based on political criteria. To put the case summarily, if one agrees that countries under Communist rule share—or shared—important features in common and that the task is to design a model that identifies and relates these common traits, then efforts to encompass a large number of socioeconomic variables are likely to be counter-productive and ultimately abortive. There is no doubt, of course, that students of Communism should take account of urbanization, industrialization, per capita income, education, and all of the other nonpolitical indicators that figure so prominently in the general literature on mobilization. The point is not that these indicators are irrelevant but that they throw the differences between Albania and Czechoslovakia or China and the Soviet Union into such sharp relief that the entire idea of a distinctive universe of Communist systems is called into question. One may nonetheless conclude that this idea has substantial merits, but it is difficult to see how these merits can be concisely and persuasively conveyed in a model that puts a premium on disaggregating indicators. With sufficient ingenuity it might be possible to overcome this difficulty, but those who propose to do so clearly bear the preponderant burden of proof.

If nonpolitical properties are not considered integral to the mobilization model, then its supposed advantage over the totalitarian model is substantially reduced. It too then emerges as a "mere" regime model, and its claim to preferment comes to rest largely, if not entirely, on the proposition that it comes closer than its more static, institutionally oriented rival to capturing the reality of "totalitarian" politics. This contention also requires more amplification than it has thus far received, but the crux of the argument seems to be that the totalitarian model overemphasizes bureaucratic centralism and administrative regimentation at the expense of such properties as charismatic leadership, ideological militancy, mass activism, organizational dynamism, and the domination of party cadres ("reds") over state officials ("experts") in the formulation and implementation of public policy. When one studies actual Communist regimes, however, it is not clear that these latter properties, which are at least recognized in the totalitarian model, deserve such heavy stress.

If one takes the Soviet Union between 1938 and 1953 as a test case and surveys the standard secondary sources for pertinent data, one cannot fail to be impressed by the recurrent references to conservatism, inflexibility, inertia, and stagnation. To some extent these descriptions may be tainted by reliance on the totalitarian model, but they undoubtedly capture significant operational realities. More precisely, one can refer to such traits as a highly ritualized adherence to a series of carefully selected ideological formulae designed to justify the status quo and curb chiliastic or "utopian" expectations; a highly conservative educational system in which progressively less time and energy was devoted to ideological indoctrination; the theoretical and actual downgrading of the party relative to the state; extreme bureaucratic rigidity and a low degree of organizational innovation; and highly formalized popular participation in public affairs, with little real involvement, especially in the case of the peasantry, whose participation was largely confined to compulsory voting. Furthermore, a similar though not completely identical trait list could be compiled for the vast majority of postwar Communist regimes during the first decade of their existence.

The informed reader will recognize that the foregoing picture is highly selective. Nevertheless, the perspective is neither arbitrary nor irrelevant, since the implicit standard of comparison is either a prior phase of Soviet history or the more or less "normal" situation under revolutionary regimes at an equivalent stage of development. Accordingly, it seems reasonable to conclude that at least one common (albeit imperfectly articulated) version of the mobilization regime model does considerably less than full justice to the complex political situation that obtained during the apotheosis of "Communist totalitarianism." Since no general model can replicate reality, the indicated omissions might be justified for certain analytical purposes. When the purpose is to facilitate a more sophisticated and discriminating analysis of "Communist totalitarianism" or to identify a baseline for "post-totalitarian" change, however, a model that underestimates the degree of political *immobility* is in danger of doing great violence to important facts.

The ambiguities and deficiencies of the mobilization model are highlighted when one attempts to view the changes that have been occurring in the Communist world as steps toward demobilization. If demobilization implies a deceleration of socioeconomic modernization, then it clearly misrepresents the situation in the majority of Communist states, although it may be relevant in the case of China. If, on the other hand, demobilization is defined politically, China provides a clear-cut negative example and numerous counter-indicators can be found elsewhere. China has been caught up in a veritable paroxysm of political mobilization, and many other Communist regimes have become *more* mobilized in some respects. Certainly it is difficult to capture the reality of Khrushchev's Russia without reference to ideological revivalism, increased party militancy, and the reactivation of the masses, and the same is true of much of contemporary Eastern Europe. In a long-term perspective an argument can still be made for characterizing the overall trend in the Communist world as political demobilization. But any such argument must be highly qualified if it is not to obscure some of the most challenging problems posed by the question "How and why do Communist systems change?" Rather than continue to pursue this question by discussing problems of taxonomy, however, it seems advisable to adopt a more direct approach. In doing so, there will be occasion to make a number of almost simplistic observations. Nevertheless, there is something to be said for even a low-level ordering of the data when the observed reality is sufficiently complex and the construction of a fully satisfying explanatory paradigm is not yet completed.

During the late 1940's and early 1950's, all of the regimes of the Communist bloc employed Stalinist techniques. In the years following, most of these regimes began a process of selective de-Stalinization during which many of these techniques were downgraded or abandoned. Among the techniques affected were: extreme administrative centralization, strict "one-man management," control through "parallel competing bureaucracies," priority investment in heavy industry at the expense of light industry and agriculture, rigid intellectual regimentation, and arbitrary mass terror. Although these techniques were not equally well developed throughout the bloc, they were everywhere firmly enough entrenched to make their modification an extremely arduous process. Nevertheless, the impetus to change was great, and efforts at reform were duly launched in almost every country under Communist rule. While it is impossible to specify exact dates, one can speak of the onset of active reformism in Yugoslavia in 1951 (after an initial post-expulsion effort to "perfect" Stalinism), in the Soviet Union and China in the period 1953–55, and in the Eastern European "satellites" around 1956.

According to many Western analysts, de-Stalinization was reluctantly inaugurated in response to compelling social pressures and economic imperatives. Implicitly or explicitly, there is an assumption that one is dealing with fiercely embattled, highly conservative regimes. Chalmers Johnson supports this view in his introductory essay, in which he characterizes incumbent Communist leaders as typically lacking in creativity and vision and speaks of their having been *forced* to relax controls.[4] If nothing else, the very prevalence of this view makes it essential to emphasize those instances in which the initiative for de-Stalinization came from elite cadres and established leaders who were not unduly subject to external duress. To adopt this perspective is not to deny that numerous leaders throughout the Communist world viewed change as anathema and did their utmost to preserve the status quo. Nor is it to deny that many reforms were precipitated by unanticipated crises to which the regimes were compelled to respond on an ad hoc emergency basis. The East Berlin revolt of 1953 and the Hungarian revolution of 1956 are obvious cases in point, and these are but extreme examples of a widespread and persistent condition. Even these examples, however, must be interpreted with care. If such explosive manifestations of popular discontent and disaffection necessitated a reevaluation of past policies and practices, the brutal suppression of the insurrectionary forces made it possible to limit participation in this reevaluation to elite cadres and to disregard reform proposals that the most powerful of these cadres considered inimical to their vital interests. And what was true in East Germany and Hungary was even more true in the other Communist countries, including, most particularly, Yugoslavia, China, and the Soviet Union.

The point, once again, is not that the reforms that were introduced

4 See above, pp. 24–25.

in these countries were evolved in a socioeconomic vacuum or were adopted without reference to public opinion or expert advice. If the regimes in question did not have to contend with imminent or actual insurrections, they did confront severe social tensions and economic strains. Nevertheless, their circumstances were not desperate, and they retained extensive room for maneuver. Although pressures for reform were difficult to resist, they were not self-evidently irresistible, and many were in fact resisted. Of those that were not resisted, in turn, a significant number were generated within official circles, and still others were cordially received and/or effectively accommodated by programs that conformed to the priorities and preferences of those in power. In short, a great many measures of de-Stalinization were the result of deliberate decisions made by incumbent leaders and elites under conditions that permitted real choice, not only the choice of sponsoring more limited reforms or different reforms from those that were actually introduced but even the choice of maintaining Stalinism more or less intact. Over the longer run, the exercise of these options might have spelled disaster, but they were still options, and on a number of occasions—especially in the Soviet Union—the protagonists of a more conservative approach came within a hairsbreadth of victory in the intra-elite conflicts that accompanied or were engendered by de-Stalinization. That it was generally the less conservative leaders who emerged victorious doubtless indicates that socioeconomic conditions were propitious for relatively far-reaching reform. But the narrow margin of their victory and the highly selective character of their response to socioeconomic pressures indicate that change was far from inevitable.

To the degree that the origins of de-Stalinization can be traced to the activities of comparatively independent innovational oligarchies, questions concerning the motives and goals of the reformist leaders obviously acquire increased importance. In spite of the limited information we have, it is certainly possible to improve upon the common practice of treating "power" as an adequate reply. This answer is at best too general, and in some cases it seems positively misleading. Its deficiencies are most evident in the case of Yugoslavia, but it is also too simple an explanation for the conduct of the Chinese and Soviet reformers. Indeed, if power means "the possession of [direct] control or command over others,"[5] then one of the attributes that differentiated the reformers from their more conservative colleagues seems to have been their willingness to delegate power and to accept a more

[5] *The American College Dictionary* (New York, 1955), p. 950.

circumscribed span of command and control. At the same time, it should be stressed that there are exceptions to this generalization and that few of the reformers sought to liquidate their own power or sacrifice their status as members of the ruling elite. Yugoslavia is the only country in which the leadership included advocates of something approaching collective abdication, and even there they were isolated figures who were quickly silenced and vigorously condemned. But unwillingness to surrender power is one thing, and an exclusive concern with power quite another.

If political self-preservation and self-aggrandizement belong in any comprehensive catalogue of the goals and motives behind elite-sponsored de-Stalinization, then so do ideological bad conscience, revulsion against mass terror, longing for personal security, concern for popular welfare, commitment to economic efficiency, national pride, and a desire for international influence and prestige. Even this enlarged list probably contains significant omissions, but the real challenge is not to fill the remaining lacunae but to estimate the relative influence of various desires and objectives on the conduct of different national and subnational elites with respect to particular aspects of reform. Provided such estimates are empirically well grounded and are not mere extrapolations of the presumed logic of "interests" that have been more or less arbitrarily imputed to hypothetical groups, they should make a substantial contribution to our understanding of why Communist systems change. In particular, it should be possible to make far more sophisticated judgments about the instrumental rationality of various reform policies and hence about the factors responsible for the continuation or modification of such policies over time. "All" that is needed is a great deal more detailed, empirical research conducted with a minimum of fixed preconceptions and *a priori* assumptions.

Although the existence of different "mixes" of elite goals and motives, as well as of different objective conditions, led different Communist regimes to establish different timetables and priority scales for de-Stalinization, there were marked similarities of approach. In part, these similarities can be explained by the desire of the Soviet and some satellite leaders to preserve the "monolithic solidarity" of the Communist bloc. As a result, there was considerable mutual emulation, accompanied by a willingness to bring strong pressure to bear on those regimes that proved too eager to follow "separate roads" to reform. In addition, some parallelism was implicit in the presence of structures that had been built from almost identical blueprints and were hence likely to be "dismantled" in roughly the same fashion whatever the international situation. Finally, certain similarities derived almost necessarily from the fact that the various regimes were led by men who came from comparable backgrounds, shared many ideological premises and commitments, and based their legitimacy as leaders on their adherence to the same body of doctrine. These latter points are especially pertinent in explaining the common features of de-Stalinization in Yugoslavia, China, and the Soviet Union, none of which were satellites or even, strictly speaking, members of a single bloc.

In these three countries, the early stages of de-Stalinization appear to have been characterized by the following measures: stress on the more messianic aspects of Marxist-Leninist ideology; the adoption of more collegial leadership practices; the curtailment of the autonomy of the secret police; increased operational independence for middle-level managers and administrators; expansion of the functions of the regional or provincial party apparat; the transfer of significant resources from heavy industry to light industry and agriculture; the active solicitation of "constructive" but genuine criticism from experts and intellectuals; efforts to invigorate the life of officially sponsored "public organizations" and secondary associations and to stimulate mass participation in the implementation of official policy; and pursuit of a more egalitarian social policy. Many of these measures had precedents in Communist history, and some involved almost no formal change. However, most of the precedents had been devalued or ignored for many years, and in all cases the actual changes were quite extensive.[6]

Up to a point, these measures can be viewed as operational counterparts or corollaries. Thus, proclamations about the more or less imminent realization of full-fledged Communism would have carried little conviction, either domestically or within the international Communist movement, if they had not been accompanied by some concrete steps to increase popular participation, to reduce wage and status differentials, and to debureaucratize the "state machine." For better or worse, Lenin had written *State and Revolution*, and it was impossible to ignore his prescriptions about the "second stage" of socialism while simultaneously professing to be true Leninists whose policies were about to culminate in the practical realization of the

---

[6] For present purposes the "early stages" of de-Stalinization are considered to have lasted until the late 1950's or early 1960's in the three countries under direct scrutiny.

mentor's theoretical principles and scientific plans. Similarly, so long
as there was a general elite consensus in favor of relatively orderly
change, administrative decentralization was bound to involve some
increase in the authority of regional party cadres, who were now in a
position not only to control the implementation of policy but to
directly influence policy decisions. In the same vein, it would have
been extremely difficult, if not impossible, to allocate more resources
to the fields of light industry and agriculture, with their vast number
of relatively small and geographically far-flung units of production,
without a reduction in the scope of central economic planning and
control. Finally—to cite but one more of many similar examples—it
would have been virtually impossible to elicit genuine criticism without curbing the arbitrary power of the secret police.

Although these relationships are well worth noting, it is essential
to stress again that we are dealing with political decisions and not
with the disembodied logic of events. More particularly, we are dealing with decisions that often represented expedient compromises or
trade-offs among factions and groupings that, although jointly dedicated to overhauling the Stalinist system and hence prepared to maintain a united front against powerful champions of the status quo, did
not necessarily agree on all, or even most, principles of reconstruction.
Almost inevitably, therefore, de-Stalinization was accompanied by an
escalation of conflict among its leading sponsors. As the resistance of
the arch-conservatives was overcome and the process of change acquired a certain momentum, inhibitions on mutual recrimination
began to relax, and there was growing recognition of and concern
over the contradictory implications of various approaches to reform.
The overall trend can be illustrated by a few slightly idealized examples, not all of which are equally applicable to all of the countries
concerned but each of which can be generalized.

An alliance that proved particularly fragile was that between "technocrats" who had reconciled themselves to the revival of chiliastic
expectations by focusing on the practical implications of such utopian
visions as the replacement of political domination by scientific management and militant ideologues who tended to take other utopian
visions equally seriously and to sponsor policies designed to eradicate
the difference between mental and physical labor, to substitute moral
for material incentives, and to subject the state machine to "workers'
control." For their part, the ideologues discovered that many industrial executives were "vulgar pragmatists" who looked on administrative decentralization, which the ideologues could justify as a step

toward the "withering away of the state," as a prelude to the introduction of a quasi-market economy. Similarly, party secretaries who had made common cause with plant and factory directors in attacking administrative centralism learned that their erstwhile allies were very reluctant to exchange the "petty tutelage" of ministers and planners for that of local apparatchiki. Conversely, the directors learned that their secretarial counterparts were apt to be more interested in asserting the primacy of the party than in following the dictates of economic rationality. Finally, party and state officials who had joined forces with leading members of the cultural and scientific intelligentsia to loosen the hold of obscurantist dogma found that even "constructive" criticism was often hard to take, while would-be "responsible" intellectuals began to realize that most of their political patrons continued to think of them as indentured "mental workers" whose only proper task was to fulfill officially prescribed tasks in a disciplined and unequivocal manner.

As these various conflicts and others like them became more acute, all of the regimes concerned showed signs of succumbing to political atrophy. These signs were initially less visible in China than in Yugoslavia and the Soviet Union, but in all three countries mutual antagonism began to replace mutual compromise, with factions and groupings that had previously submerged their differences now vetoing each other's policies and blocking each other's initiatives, thereby preventing authoritative action on any front. In consequence, it became progressively more difficult both to prevent the political activation of potential counter-elites (including chastened but basically unreconstructed Stalinists) and to subject "spontaneous" social and economic processes to "conscious" political management and control. In each case, however, vigorous countermeasures were taken before the decisional logjam became hopelessly impacted and incipient political paralysis gave way to political degeneration and/or socioeconomic "drift." More precisely, in each case, the regime's principal leader personally intervened to push through major policy decisions. These interventions could scarcely have had more distinctive foci, centrally oriented as they were to political liberalization (in Yugoslavia), economic renovation (in the Soviet Union), and cultural transformation (in China). But they all involved the selective extension and acceleration of trends that were closely associated with the onset of de-Stalinization and can hence be viewed as variations on a common theme.

In light of our earlier comments on mobilization, it is noteworthy that all three leader-initiated "breakthroughs" were accompanied by significant increases in mass political participation. These increases obviously took very different forms and had very different meanings in each of the countries concerned. In Yugoslavia, there was a genuine turn toward communal self-determination and local self-government. In the Soviet Union, democratization was far more nominal than real, but there was a vast proliferation of para-political "public organizations" and "volunteer" auxiliary formations attached to official bodies. In China, there was a para-military, mass-based ideological crusade, a marching, chanting plebiscite in arms. In all three cases, however, there were certain common denominators. In particular, there was an effort to use pressure from below to secure the compliance of recalcitrant local officials and to mobilize a highly vocal popular constituency whose support could be cited to legitimize the newly adopted decisions. These functions were of more than ordinary importance because Tito, Khrushchev, and Mao all had to contend with strong opposition reaching to the highest levels of power— so strong, indeed, that they were sometimes unable to win the unqualified endorsement of regular decision-making organs.

The major source of opposition in all three cases was the party apparatchiki. One reason for this opposition was the propensity of the apparatchiki to view any decisive personal initiative as a derogation of the principle of "collective leadership." This principle was valued by most members of the ruling elite, irrespective of their particular institutional affiliations, but it had a special meaning to elite cadres for whom politics was a full-time profession and whose high status was justified largely, if not exclusively, by their ability to make political decisions. In addition, the apparatchiki were aroused by the fact that the initiatives in question all included measures specifically designed to limit the institutional hegemony that the apparat had acquired during the early stages of de-Stalinization. In part these measures were inspired by high-level power-political considerations (e.g., by a desire to undermine the power base of leading oppositionists), but all three top leaders also appear to have been convinced that the apparatchiki were basically unqualified to preside over any program involving fundamental change. There is little question, moreover, that this judgment was well founded.

Although most leading apparatchiki had been in favor of de-Stalinization at the outset, their primary objective had been to reclaim the prerogatives they had lost to the state bureaucracy and the secret police during the consolidation of full-fledged Stalinism. Once this objective was attained, the majority of them adopted a distinctly conservative stance. In effect, they challenged any reforms that could conceivably jeopardize their gains, either by direct encroachment or by placing a premium on technical skills that they could not provide. Since it was easy to believe that any but the most marginal, incremental changes posed such a threat, it was virtually a foregone conclusion that the prevailing decisional logjams could not be decisively broken unless the apparatchiki were dislodged not only from their positions of political leadership but also from their positions of entrenched administrative power. It was for this reason that all three "breakthrough" programs sought to restrict the institutional jurisdiction of the apparat. And it was largely for this reason that most apparatchiki took such a strong oppositionist stand. In all cases, however, their resistance was at least temporarily overcome. Their span of command and control was drastically curtailed, and their high-level representatives and spokesmen were either purged, like Ranković and Liu Shao-ch'i and their associates, or so effectively outmaneuvered, like Khrushchev's presidial opponents in 1961 and 1962, that they were incapable of fighting anything more than a sporadic rear-guard action until their overbearing antagonist suffered a series of major (largely self-imposed) debacles.

By successfully implementing their "breakthrough" programs in the face of such powerful opposition, Tito, Mao, and Khrushchev demonstrated that de-Stalinization had not eliminated the strong tendency for Communist regimes to vest ultimate power in the hands of a single individual. Indeed, one is tempted to go further and suggest that even "reformed" Communist regimes ultimately require decisive one-man leadership in order to survive. However, it might have been possible either to "muddle through" the decisional logjams that emerged in the middle stages of de-Stalinization or to overcome them by less highly individualistic interventions. Moreover, there is no reason to believe that equally severe logjams are inevitable in the future. In this connection, the experience of the Soviet Union in the years since Khrushchev's ouster (October 1964) seems quite germane, although the time involved is admittedly brief. It has become commonplace to refer to the present Soviet leadership as irresolute and unpredictable, but in fact the Brezhnev-Kosygin regime has adopted and successfully implemented a great many far-reaching decisions and has often done so on the basis of clear-cut policy guidelines stated well in advance. This is true both domestically and internationally, and failure to come to grips with this fact is one of the major weaknesses of current "Kremlinology," academic or applied.

What the regime has *not* done is to confirm the predictions of those who argue that the sole alternative to political degeneration—the inevitable result of a completely impacted decisional logjam—is self-transformation from an oligarchic regime exercising far-reaching social control into a pluralistic regime articulating and aggregating the demands of a relatively open society.[7] On the contrary, the narrow group of presidial conspirators who deposed Khrushchev have kept power tightly concentrated in their own hands and have, if anything, subjected Soviet society to greater political regimentation. Although the designation "neo-Stalinist" overstates the case, many of the policies of the Brezhnev-Kosygin regime have been quite repressive, including, most particularly, its policies toward the politically critical intelligentsia. To date, however, the overall result has been not increased social protest but rather increased resignation and a general withdrawal from politics into professional and vocational self-realization within the framework of existing opportunities, opportunities that are sanctioned by the regime and contribute to its power and authority.[8] Eventually, of course, full-fledged political degeneration may emerge as so clear and present a danger that intelligent occupants of the Kremlin will try to avoid it by imitating the nineteenth-century English aristocracy and admitting the classes and masses to a significant share of power. But the prospect for the short and middle runs seems to be for a continued oligarchic rule by reasonably effective leaders who will apply their intelligence in the first instance to the preservation of their own collective power. In sum, we would suggest that the Soviet regime at least has probably passed through what de Tocqueville correctly described as the period of maximum peril for any "bad regime"—the period when it attempts to reform itself without losing its basic political identity.

That the Chinese Communist regime has also passed the point of utmost danger seems considerably more doubtful. Mao and his lieutenants have certainly subjected their regime to thoroughgoing reform, but the combination of Mao's old age and the extreme dislocations caused by the Cultural Revolution make the future most uncertain. Given that Mao's death will probably create both a major

[7] See Zbigniew Brzezinski, "The Soviet Political System: Transformation or Degeneration," *Problems of Communism*, XV: 1 (Jan.-Feb., 1966), 1–15.

[8] See Jeremy R. Azrael, *Managerial Power and Soviet Politics* (Cambridge, Mass., 1968), ch. 2, for a discussion of the decision by the late-nineteenth- and early-twentieth-century Russian intelligentsia, especially the technical and scientific intelligentsia, to abjure political activities in favor of the professional exploitation of "existing opportunities." See *ibid.*, ch. 5, for a fuller discussion of a parallel trend among the contemporary intelligentsia.

power vacuum and a major legitimacy crisis (because of the difficulty of transferring charismatic authority and/or maintaining a posthumous cult of personality) and that he is likely to die before the new political structures that have emerged during the Cultural Revolution can be fully institutionalized, a period of social chaos and political violence may ensue and be followed by the establishment of a very different regime, a regime that will have different leaders, different symbols of legitimacy, and different modes of organization. Among other things, one can envision a regime that would rely on Stalinist techniques of rule, thereby providing an interesting example of the reversibility of historical processes (in this case de-Stalinization) and posing interesting problems for those who argue that the abandonment of these techniques by the Chinese Communists was dictated by the functional requirements of the Chinese social system and economy. All this once said, however, it is worth recalling Mao's remarkable success as an organization-builder, and his demonstrated ability to prevail against the most adverse odds. Judging from recent evidence, he does appear to be taking some steps to arrange an orderly succession and to ameliorate the most socially and economically disruptive consequences of his own extremism. If he lives long enough and persists in this course, and if his successors prove reasonably skilled and astute (as skilled and astute, say, as Stalin's successors in the Soviet Union), the regime Mao has created may well survive.[9]

If neither the Soviet Union nor China provides much comfort to those who believe (or hope) that political pluralism and social democracy are the wave of the future, Yugoslavia provides a substantial amount. During the past several years, Tito appears to have devoted almost all his energies to transforming Yugoslavia from a latitudinarian "people's democracy" into a "tutelary democracy" with genuinely democratic content and real prospects for further liberalization. To be sure, Tito is over seventy-five years old, and the "new democracy" is still too new to be safe from the political turmoil that could follow his death. Unlike the structures created during the Cultural Revolution in China, however, those associated with the "new

[9] As the parenthetical comment in this sentence suggests, Mao bears many resemblances to Stalin despite his abandonment of a variety of Stalinist techniques of rule. Indeed, as many Soviet polemicists and numerous Western analysts have pointed out, virtually the only historical parallels for the Great Leap Forward and the Cultural Revolution are the collectivization campaigns of 1929–32 and the Great Purge of 1936–39. In many respects, these parallels seem more worthy of exploration than the parallels that we have emphasized in the course of viewing Mao as a "de-Stalinizer," but that is not our present task.

democracy" appear to enjoy wide popular support and to be reasonably well adapted to their socioeconomic environment. The gravest threat to their survival is probably not Tito's disappearance from the scene but the gradual reemergence of intense conflict among the nationalities. Precisely because they are genuinely democratic, they would inevitably become deeply implicated in such conflict and would be prime candidates for suppression by the military leaders who would probably intervene to preserve the unity of the country and restore civic discipline. Without ruling out this possibility, however, a good case can be made for Tito's having created a sufficiently strong sense of Yugoslav patriotism that nationality demands can be effectively accommodated within the framework of the existing federal constitution. As popular political participation becomes freer, this constitution will be severely tested, but in view of what Tito has already accomplished, it is likely that the ability to air national demands in public and to process them through generally accessible but mutually cross-checking channels will have an integrative effect and will strengthen political consensus. Certainly this was Tito's hope in introducing and broadening the "new democracy," and there is a good probability that his hope will be vindicated and that the "new democracy" will develop into genuine and responsible popular self-government. If this happens, we will have an almost "ideal-type" example of the transformation of a Communist regime. It will be a transformation, though, that will testify to the importance of political entrepreneurism and risk-taking and the ability of certain leaders to reshape society according to their own distinctive visions, not a transformation in which the political superstructure bows to the dictates of an imperious socioeconomic base.

To our remarks on how and why contemporary Communist systems change we have now added some remarks on current situations and possible outcomes. By so doing, we have, in effect, returned to our original point of departure—namely that what once seemed to be broadly similar, if not "essentially" identical, regimes have become highly differentiated and show signs of becoming even more so. We have suggested that this has happened despite the fact that the techniques of change have often been similar and that many of the decisive stimuli have come from a common source, i.e., from incumbent leaders and elites. We have also argued that the political differences that have emerged cannot be satisfactorily explained by the existence of different socioeconomic conditions to which the regimes were required to adapt. All of these points clearly underscore the inadequacy of established theoretical paradigms and analytical models, not only in the field of comparative Communism but in the broader field of political development and change. At the same time, they underscore the extreme difficulty of finding any plausible alternatives that are not confined to a far lower level of generality.

The Rationalization of Party Control

PAUL COCKS

The party machine has long functioned as the hub of Communist political systems. How and in what direction these systems evolve depends in large measure, then, on the nature and success of party reform.[1] Surprisingly, however, although virtually everyone agrees on the central importance of the role of the party apparat, little attention has been given to the efforts at institutional change and reform in and by the party apparat since Stalin's death. On the contrary, though Soviet specialists are willing to concede a change in the political climate in the Soviet Union since 1953, they emphasize the absence of basic institutional development in the political sector. It is precisely this sector, and above all the party machine, that seems to accord with Alex Inkeles' conclusion that the Soviet system "is fixed, relatively unchanging. It is everything implied in the concept of structure, frozen in its units, forms and relations."[2] The apparatchiki and apparat are generally viewed as being not only opposed to but indeed impervious to the process of change. Seeing the party bureaucracy as unchanged and unchanging, moving only by ineptitude and inertia rather than by any adaptive capacity, has caused us to lose

I wish to acknowledge the generous support of the Harvard Russian Research Center, which made possible the research on which this essay is based.

[1] While recently assessing the prospects for the future of Soviet society, Jeremy Azrael aptly concluded, "The really decisive question, therefore, would appear to be how, not who—not the political potency of the apparat, but the apparat's potential for *internal* transformation. Here, above all, is where the critical unknowns lie; here, above all, one must penetrate in order to estimate the forces of continuity and change that will shape the development of the Soviet system for the foreseeable future." "The Party and Society," in Allen Kassof, ed., *Prospects for Soviet Society* (New York, 1968), p. 71.

[2] *Social Change in Soviet Russia* (Cambridge, Mass., 1968), p. 55.

sight of experimentation and change where in fact they have occurred —at the heart of the Soviet polity, in the apparat of the CPSU.

In this essay I shall discuss the process and problems of institutional innovation and change in the machinery of party administration and control in the post-Stalin period. I shall try to show not only that the party apparat has been subjected to change but that party administrative reform has had a specific nature and direction. For Stalin's heirs the fundamental problem has been how to eliminate or mollify the worst grievances, abuses, and techniques of Stalin's system of terroristic and personal rule while preserving the substance of totalitarian power.[3] It is within this perspective that the policy of directed change has been pursued. In the eyes of the Soviet leadership the problem of change has been conceived basically as a question of techniques, not of politics, of modifying administrative means, not political ends. The whole process of adjustment and adaptation of the Soviet political system in the post-Stalin era, therefore, can be best described as the "rationalization" of Stalinist totalitarianism. The term "rationalization" is particularly relevant not only from the point of view of Western theories of bureaucracy and organization but, even more important, because it is precisely the term used in the Russian dictionary of administration and Soviet historical experience to refer to the process of retooling faulty and archaic administrative machinery and methods.

In general, however, little attention has been given to the semantic relevance and historical roots of rationalization in Soviet experience, even by those who have talked about the possibility of a "rationalized" totalitarianism. This historical legacy, moreover, so impinges on both the theory and the practice of post-Stalin rationalization that our discussion necessarily begins with an exploration of the past.

Bureaucracy, Rationalization, and Control

Use of the term "rationalization" in Western organization theory dates back to Max Weber, who associated the term with the general process of adaptation and adjustment within bureaucratic structures. Although at times he used the word very ambiguously and broadly, Weber essentially distinguished two meanings of the term. In one sense, "rationalization" refers to the appropriateness and adaptation of means to ends. In the other, more abstract sense, it is identified with the demystification of the world in man's thinking and with

---

[3] Merle Fainsod, *How Russia Is Ruled*, rev. ed. (Cambridge, Mass., 1963), p. 580.

what Weber called the "routinization" of charisma. Given the nature of Stalinist totalitarianism with its highly personal element—indeed, with its cult of personality—its rationalization in the context of post-Stalin politics necessarily acquires overtones of Weber's second meaning of the term. It is important to stress, however, that in Russian *ratsionalizatsiia* has a much more limited usage and meaning. Defined as the process of improving the organization of activity, ratsionalizatsiia is applied generally to administration and economic production. Concerned narrowly with techniques and making a cult of efficiency, it is geared to perfecting, not to liquidating, existing machinery. Basic systemic change remains outside its purview.

Whereas Weber tended to see in the process of rationalization a general unfolding of not only a law of progress but indeed the rule of law, ratsionalizatsiia is devoid of any normative content. For this reason it is a more acceptable and accurate term than, for example, "liberalization" or "democratization" to describe the development of the Soviet system since Stalin's demise. Though the rationalization of Stalinist totalitarianism has included measures that appear to be steps toward political liberalization, in fact the thrust of rationalization policy and the intent of Stalin's successors have been to build not a more democratic order, but a more efficient totalitarian leviathan without the Stalinist excesses and aberrations.

Equally important for our analysis is clarification of another term, the always thorny and highly abused word "control." It has generally been pointed out that in Russian this word, *kontrol'*, has a much more limited and far less ambiguous meaning than in English. Whereas English usage of the term connotes both a check and a restraint, kontrol' strongly emphasizes the more narrow checking aspect. By reducing kontrol' essentially to verification of performance and the execution of orders, however, we have failed to recognize that kontrol' also implies restraint, especially restraint on the abuse of bureaucratic and personal power. We have neglected the ambiguity that did, in fact, exist in the 1920's in the meaning of the word and in the perception of its institutionalized expression, the party control commission.

More significantly, semantics has seriously obscured our interpretation and perspective of the complex nature and changing character of the function and the instrumentalities of party control in the history of the Soviet regime. Although the party control establishment originally emerged as a device to arrest and check bureaucratic power, its transformation by Stalin's hand into an instrument of bureaucratic control has received our dominant attention. Indeed, the control commission has been remembered almost solely as the ruthless purging arm of the party apparat and the club by which Stalin personally browbeat Trotsky, Bukharin, and others into submission and forged his totalitarian order. The original mission and heritage of the control commission as an organ designed to struggle against the evils of bureaucracy have been virtually forgotten in our histories of this important party institution. Needless to say, the idea has not been seriously broached that this organ, which has been epitomized as the quintessence of Stalinist terror, could at the same time have functioned as an organ with an anti-Stalinist complexion promoting rationality in the Soviet system. Yet this is precisely the institutional profile that emerges from a closer examination of the history of the Central Control Commission (CCC) and the Workers' and Peasants' Inspection (the Rabkrin or RKI), which served as the organizational center of the party control establishment from 1923 to 1934.[4]

Of particular interest for our study is the fact that administrative rationalization was conceived and practiced as an important means of checking the incubus of bureaucracy during the first decade of Soviet power. On one hand, bureaucratism was seen as a personal malady and an ethical question. That Lenin also continued to view the problem partly from this perspective is evident from his final "testament," in which he made Stalin's rudeness adequate cause for his removal from the post of party general secretary. On the other hand, bureaucratism was believed to be primarily a "technical" problem—the bad habits of an incompetent rather than a corrupt officeholder—whose solution lay in reorganizing the office and improving the system of administration along rational and scientific lines. The prescribed medicine for curing creeping and crippling bureaucratic decay, then, was not so much a lesson in party ethics as in administrative skills and organization theory. Indeed, it was this technical conception of and solution to the Communist bureaucratic phenomenon that dominated Lenin's thinking during his last days and his struggle against Stalin and the party bureaucracy. More and more he saw the ultimate remedy for Russia's bureaucratic ills as rationalization, as an administrative revolution from above by experts. Moreover, he sought to make the party controllers his primary agents of

4 See Paul Cocks, "Politics of Party Control: The Historical and Institutional Role of Party Control Organs in the CPSU" (unpub. Ph.D. diss., Harvard Univ., 1968).

change. According to his final plan, the CCC and RKI were to be fused and transformed into a super-control agency against all forms of bureaucratism and staffed predominantly with rationalizers, efficiency experts, and administrative specialists. In contrast to the purely negative and punitive aspects of control that stress the "purge" and disciplinary measures to cope with bureaucratic wrongdoing, ratsionalizatsiia emphasizes the positive and preventive character of control activity and the importance of control as a major vehicle of institutional change.

Ratsionalizatsiia came to occupy such a prominent place in the work of the control center that the RKI earned the sobriquet "Commissariat of Organization." The CCC-RKI not only issued a monthly journal entitled *Za Ratsionalizatsiiu (For Rationalization)* to provide overall guidelines for this work but also sponsored a host of other specialized periodicals devoted to questions of organization theory and the science of administration. Valerian Kuibyshev, who served as chairman of the CCC and RKI from 1923 to 1926, dubbed rationalization "the basis, the soul of our work."[5] A reorganization of the control machinery in early 1926 resulted in nearly two-thirds of the members of the CCC being sent to work in the field of rationalization. Kuibyshev, in fact, was soon complaining that everyone in his organization wished to be a "rationalizer" and deprecated the punitive and police-related activities of the control organs as "dirty business" that seemed dishonorable to members of the CCC.[6]

Although he did not oppose rationalization in principle, Kuibyshev did have serious reservations about its short-run value and regarded it as "too weak a medicine" to cure the immediate ills of the Soviet state. He likened the Soviet bureaucratic machine to a rough and gnarled stump and said that the rationalizers were trying to shave it with a plane, whereas in fact it was necessary first to lay in with an axe to get rid of the rough protrusions. At the same time, he emphasized that the controllers should not forget about the plane and the need to use its blade gradually.[7] In reality, however, the tendency he decried—to forget the axe in favor of the rationalizer's plane—in-

[5] *Zadachi TsKK i RKI po Ratsionalizatsii Gosapparata v Plane Rabot RKI na 1925–1926g (Doklad no Kursakh Rabotnikov RKI 16 Iiunia 1925g)* (Moscow, 1925), p. 7, and *VI Plenum TsKK Sozyva XIII S"ezda VKP(b) 11–13 Dekabria 1925g* (Moscow, 1926), pp. 58–59.

[6] *Vtoroi Plenum TsKK Sozyva XIV S"ezda VKP(b) 2–4 Aprelia 1926g* (Moscow, 1926), pp 4, 8, 43, 71–73.

[7] "Pervyi God Raboty," *Voprosy Sovetskogo Khoziaistva i Upravleniia*, 4–5 (Moscow, April-May 1924), 8.

creasingly appeared among the workers in the control center. Resent-
ing the efforts of the rationalizers to turn the RKI into a "scientific
research center" and steer it down the path of academic deviation,
Kuibyshev harshly criticized those who wanted to apply only scientific principles and not punitive measures to control work. He
stressed that the controllers must not be "impartial cold onlookers,
preoccupied with contemplating the white clothes of the perfect state
apparat," which was still far in the future. Above all, he reminded
his subordinates that "passion and blood" must be in their work.[8]
In the following months his frustration with the rationalization
group mounted, and in May 1926 he jotted down in his diary that
the rationalizers were either "crazy maniacs or blind people to whom
it is impossible to entrust serious practical state work."[9] The whole
control establishment was becoming in his view something like a
"crazy house."[10]

Kuibyshev was not alone in his criticism of the academic, apoliti-
cal, and excessively mechanistic outlook and models of the rationalizers. In the fall of 1923 Trotsky rebuked those who regarded bureaucratism as only "the aggregate of the bad habits of officeholders."
"Bureaucratism," he pointed out, "is a social phenomenon in that it
is a definite system of administration of *men* and *things*."[11] Two years
later Felix Dzerzhinsky also insisted that it was time to recognize that
the work of leadership and administration could not be mechanized.
He reminded the rationalizers, "It isn't offices that work. It is people
that work in offices."[12] Such warnings, however, fell on deaf ears and
closed minds. In devising their various schemes, the rationalizers continued to wear their Marxist blinders and to take literally Engels'
distinction that "under Communism the governance of men will be
replaced by the administration of things." Concerned entirely with
things and not with men, the rationalizers remained preoccupied
with administrative techniques, and they sorely neglected politics.
Theory for them remained the guide to action, and that proved to

[8] *Ibid.* See also Kuibyshev's *Zadachi TsKK i RKI (Lektsii Chitannye v Univer-
sitete imeni Ia. M. Sverdlova v Aprele 1924g)* (Moscow, 1925), p. 73.

[9] Quoted in R. V. Gataullin, "Voploshchenie Leninskikh Printsipov Kontrolia
v Deiatel'nosti OKK-RKI Tatarii v Vosstanovitel'nyi Period (1921–1926gg)" (unpub.
diss., Kazan State Univ., 1966), p. 74n.

[10] Quoted in *Valerian Vladimirovich Kuibyshev: Biografiia* (Moscow, 1966), p.
231.

[11] *The New Course and the Struggle for the New Course* (Ann Arbor, Mich.,
1965), p. 45.

[12] Quoted in R. W. Davies, "Some Soviet Economic Controllers, II," *Soviet
Studies*, XI: 4 (April 1960), 389.

be their fatal error. As Stalin pinpointed the issue himself at the Sixteenth Party Congress, "Our difficulties are not difficulties of petty and accidental mismanagement but difficulties of class struggle.... Behind our difficulties are concealed class enemies."[13] The rationalizers, however, did not take into account the class struggle in their administrative schemes.

By the end of 1930 the whole rationalization movement as a policy and strategy for Soviet political and economic development came under heavy attack. Those engaged in this work were criticized for having been engrossed only in "fruitless scholastic exercises," "games in abstraction," "superficial know-it-all-ism," and "futile bustle." Much "bourgeois ideological rubbish" was exposed in rationalization theory, which had come under the strong influence of Western schools of public administration led by such men as Henri Fayol and Frederick Taylor.[14] Indeed, the broader movement for the "scientific organization of labor" (*nauchnaia organizatsiia truda*, or NOT), which developed with the outburst of technocratic zeal in Soviet Russia during the 1920's and with which the rationalization movement was closely associated, was marked by a strong foreign accent. The superiority of capitalist technology was officially recognized, and the rationalizers were encouraged to borrow and make use of its advances. Throughout the 1920's the CCC and RKI sent a number of emissaries to Western Europe, Japan, and the United States to gather the latest scientific information on administration and economic management. Indeed, it must have seemed strange for many to see these Old Bolsheviks and revolutionaries canvassing the West for ideas on how to put in order the administrative chaos they had created and how to build a more efficient Soviet state system. Even Stalin himself frankly admitted to the Sixteenth Party Congress, "We have never concealed the fact that in the sphere of techniques we are pupils of the Germans, the English, the French, the Italians, and first and foremost, the Americans."[15]

Just as the rationalizers had deficient vision at home in recognizing politics in their applications of rationalization techniques, they also had poor powers of political discrimination when selecting these techniques from abroad. Borrowing from the West had to be on a highly selective basis. As Sergo Ordzhonikidze, the head of the CCC-

[13] *XVI S"ezd VKP(b): Stenograficheskii Otchet* (Moscow, 1930), p. 86.
[14] "Vsesoiuznoe Soveshchanie po Uluchsheniiu Gosapparata," *Organizatsiia Upravleniia* (Moscow), 1 (1931), 57; M. Shul'gin, "Chto Delat' Zhurnalu?" *ibid.*, p. 1.
[15] *XVI S"ezd VKP(b)*, p. 106.

RKI from 1926 to 1930, clearly explained, "We need to adopt American and European techniques in our plants, factories, and railroads, to build our foundries, forges, blast furnaces, and mills in the American way. *But we cannot in any way adopt the administrative system of the capitalist states. Techniques of administration we can and must borrow from them, but their administrative system we cannot and must not adopt.*"[16] Although politics and techniques were again sharply separated, he failed to point out how, in fact, it was possible to separate the techniques from the system. Obviously having in mind the rationalizers in the old CCC-RKI, Lazar Kaganovich, whom Stalin had installed as head of the reorganized party control machinery in 1934, told the Seventeenth Party Congress, "Many of our officials, even good honest ones, and leaders do not understand the *basic differences between organizing administration here and organizing it in bourgeois countries.*"[17]

A full history of the rationalization movement is outside the scope of my essay. Suffice it to say that by its foreign spirit, its caste of experts, and its genetic evolutionary design the movement and its institutionalized standard bearer, the CCC-RKI, were politically and psychologically out of tune with the needs, the mood, and the mentality of Stalin and those who advocated "building socialism in one country—Soviet Russia." Stalinist totalitarianism had outgrown, or more properly speaking, outdistanced, the rationalization movement. Stalin was impatient to get on with modernization. And as Lenin warned, "In matters of culture, haste and sweeping measures are the worst possible things." Ironically, one of the first sweeping measures was the abolition of Lenin's appointed agency of rational modernization, the CCC-RKI. Efficiency and rationality, which continued to be the ends of the organizational model of the rationalizers, were no longer the primary goals or operative means of the evolving Stalinist system. The arbitrary political and economic policies and methods that he forcefully advocated indeed defied rationality and efficiency. The axe was a much more appropriate tool than the plane for implementing his totalitarian formula for Soviet development.

Consequently, the attacks against the rationalizers were vigorously renewed at the beginning of 1932. Not only was the charge repeated that rationalization theory included "a bouquet of anti-Marxist theories," but it was now declared to be a "right deviation" in politics and linked to Bukharin's *Economics of the Transition Period.* The

16 *Ibid.*, p. 312; italics mine.
17 *XVII S"ezd VKP(b): Stenograficheskii Otchet* (Moscow, 1934), p. 532.

Institute of Administrative Techniques, the "think tank" on rationalization for the CCC-RKI, was closed down along with its local affiliates. In July 1932 responsibility for publishing the severely criticized *Organizatsiia Upravleniia*, the main journal on rationalization theory and practice, passed from the RKI to the Commissariat of Heavy Industry. Indeed the change was significant, for thereafter rationalization was no longer applied to administration (politics) but was limited primarily to the organization of production (economics). Administration disappeared as a science and entered the realm of the Stalinist art of politics.

Bureaucracy, Popular Participation, and Control

Although rationalization figured as a prominent form of control activity during the 1920's, it was not seen as the only means of checking bureaucratic evils. Deeply rooted in Marxist thought and Lenin's ideas on the state, administration, and bureaucracy was the notion that direct democracy and popular participation in administrative affairs provided the best antidote to bureaucratism. Bureaucracy Lenin originally envisaged as a specific product of bourgeois society that would disappear when the old order was overthrown and would be replaced by self-administration of the masses. "Under socialism," he pointed out, "*all* will administer in turn and will quickly become accustomed to nobody administering."[18] Such ideas derived from his view that administration was a relatively uncomplicated function. Indeed, capitalism, he held, had reduced it to the "uncommonly simple operations of checking and accounting" and to "a knowledge of the four rules of arithmetic," of which every literate person was capable. Within a very short time, however, this utopian image of administration as a simple affair readily within the reach of the masses was admitted even by Lenin to be "a fairy tale."[19] The Workers' and Peasants' Inspection, which had arisen in 1920 as a channel for drawing the broad public into control work and as a school of state administration, remained little more than a wish and rapidly became a forgotten and disappearing commissariat in the Soviet government.

Wrestling with the baffling and stubbornly recurring problems of administration and bureaucracy after the seizure of power, Lenin increasingly came to appreciate the difficulties and complexities of administration, although he still viewed it as essentially a function of

---

[18] *Polnoe Sobranie Sochineniia* (Moscow, 1958–65), XXXIII, 116.
[19] *Ibid.*, XLII, 253.

technology. In this way Lenin could theoretically explain the Russians' lack of any administrative ability or "culture" in terms of Russia's technical backwardness. The task, then, as he came to see it, was to learn organization theory and principles of scientific management from the most advanced capitalist countries with their technological superiority. Whereas before Lenin had taken an oversimplified view of administration and underestimated the expertise required for its conduct, his growing recognition of its complexity led him to overemphasize the importance of modern techniques in simplifying and changing the administrative process. These were the ideas, moreover, that dominated his thinking when he was devising his final scheme in the winter of 1923 for reorganizing the control edifice. In his last article he explicitly dismissed the possibility of improving the administrative machine through the workers. "These elements are not sufficiently educated. They would like to build a better apparat for us, but they do not know how. They cannot build one. They have not yet developed the culture required for this; and it is culture that is required."[20] Not revolutionary enthusiasm and voluntarism but the capacity to organize and administer became the overriding political priority. The RKI was transformed from an organ of mass control into an institution of specialists in organization with a redefined mission of improving the state machine through an administrative revolution from above. For some years, the RKI remained a Workers' and Peasants' Inspection in name only.

Until 1928 few efforts were made to establish close ties between the control organs and the masses. The predominant method of recruiting workers into control work, if they were drawn in at all, was to select a person living near a particular factory or office to be investigated and to use him three or four times a month in his nonworking hours. The sole expense incurred was paying for his streetcar tickets.[21] Shortly before leaving the CCC-RKI, Kuibyshev, in fact, expressed aloud his worry that so little had been done to enlist the masses into RKI work. He even confessed that perhaps the workers and peasants knew less now about the RKI than before, lamenting, "Now it's as if they are beginning to forget."[22] A check of the control network in early 1927 disclosed that very few control commissions and RKI organs had any contact at all with the public. Only in Mos-

20 *Ibid.*, XLV, 390–91.

21 *Vtoroi Plenum TsKK Sozyva XIV S"ezda VKP(b) 2–4 Aprelia 1926g* (Moscow, 1926), p. 38.

22 *VI Plenum TsKK Sozyva XIII S"ezda RKP(b) 11–13 Dekabria 1925g* (Moscow, 1926), pp. 54–55.

cow province were peasants and workers from party cells and Komsomol organizations occasionally drawn into RKI investigations. The enlisting of women into control work was not practiced at all.[23]

As concern mounted over the academicism of the rationalizers in the CCC-RKI, greater stress was gradually given to widening the public base of control activity. Checking-verification work (*proverka ispolneniia*) was recognized as a more suitable channel for enlisting the masses than rationalization, which necessarily required experts to interpret and apply it. Indeed a common complaint was that the masses simply did not understand what rationalization was all about with its abstract schemes and complex vocabulary. A shift away from rationalization and toward public checking was already evident in May 1926, when a top control official asserted bluntly that the work of improving the state apparat did not "presuppose the presence of 'geniuses.' "[24]

For the most part, however, over the next two years various measures designed to strengthen the ties between the control organs and the local population never left the paper on which they were written. The whole question of public participation remained a burning political issue. Efforts by the CCC-RKI to establish a lower *aktiv* of volunteer controllers by recreating the cells of assistance to RKI that had existed during the early years of the inspection at individual factories and plants met stiff resistance from both the trade unions and the economic managers. The fiasco of workers' control was only too fresh in everyone's mind. In 1927 Michael Tomsky, the head of the trade unions, who soon became a leader of the Right Opposition, tried to dismiss any fears of a return to the old workers' control by claiming that the working class had "grown up." At the same time, he staunchly opposed the setting up of even "temporary" control commissions at individual enterprises. In reply to those who wanted the control establishment more directly involved in checking production and management, Tomsky sarcastically quipped, "For God's sake, don't get tied up with the RKI! Nothing will come of this. In doing one thing you will undo another."[25]

Having achieved his victory over Trotsky and the United Opposition and growing more impatient than ever to begin his plans of building socialism in one country, Stalin at the Fifteenth Party Con-

---

[23] "O Sostoianii Sviazi KK-RKI s Delegatskimi Sobraniiami Rabotnits i Krest'-ianok," *Biulleten' TsKK VKP(b)* (Moscow), 1 (Jan. 30, 1927), 44–45.

[24] "Neskol'ko Zamechanii," *ibid.*, 4–5 (May 15, 1926), 7.

[25] *Piatnadtsataia Konferentsiia VKP(b) 26 Oktiabria–3 Noiabria 1926g: Stenograficheskii Otchet* (Moscow, 1962), pp. 301, 343.

gress in December 1927 gave notice that he was contemplating a drastic shift to the left and a new upsurge of revolutionary action, both
from above and from below, for socialist construction. Various forms
of mass participation in control work soon developed as part of his
general offensive to reorganize thoroughly the administrative machinery and to purge the bureaucracy. A broad campaign of mass
criticism was initiated against bureaucratism in order to make it possible, Stalin said, for the masses "to go for" their leaders by criticizing mistakes and exposing defects.[26] He felt it was necessary to
arouse the fury of the masses against all corrupt elements and to give
them the opportunity "to send such elements packing."[27] Thus, Stalin momentarily switched the political priority back to revolutionary
enthusiasm and zeal. The masses could help improve or, more properly speaking, destroy the old state apparat after all.

By the end of 1930, however, Stalin was already calling a halt to
the campaign for mass participation in administration with its disruptive, indeed destructive, results. Industrialization created its own
imperatives, and Stalin was soon again courting the specialists though
not the rationalizers. But on paper the volunteer and vigilant aktiv
around the control organs not only continued to exist but even increased in number after 1930. In reality, this "flowering" of mass control represented only statistical fantasy. Everywhere, including at the
center, the control machinery was increasingly staffed with "dead
souls."[28] Lenin's hopes for a genuine workers' and peasants' inspection remained a dream.

In 1934 the RKI was formally abolished, and its former aktiv was
dissolved. The control organs under Stalin became highly bureaucratized with virtually no ties with the masses. Andrei Vyshinsky, one
of Stalin's old cronies, succinctly expressed the view that became
dominant for more than two decades when he sneeringly said, "The
old talk about mobilizing the public aktiv and assistance groups
should all go you know where!"[29] In 1948 Lev Mekhlis, the Minister
of State Control, reportedly issued an order categorically forbidding
the enlistment of persons from outside the ministry to participate in
its checking activities.[30] Neither public participation nor scientific
rationalization had a place in Stalin's system of rule and instrumentalities of control.

---

[26] *Works* (Moscow, 1954), XI, 35.
[27] *Ibid.*, p. 76.
[28] See Cocks, "Politics of Party Control," pp. 457–58.
[29] Quoted in *Pravda*, May 8, 1964.
[30] *Ibid.*, Dec. 26, 1962.

For Stalin's heirs the problem of rationalizing Stalinist totalitarianism, which may be understood as de-Stalinization in the broad sense, has been viewed and pursued as part of the much larger question of the strategy for building Communism and the future of Soviet society. We have seen two divergent approaches to this problem, which have clearly mirrored the diverse political perspectives, leadership styles, and personalities of Khrushchev on the one hand and of his successors on the other hand. For Khrushchev—the impulsive adventurer, fervent ideologue, "democratic popularizer," and restless pragmatist—the means of sociopolitical organization and advance emphasized public-spiritedness and participation in societal and administrative affairs. By contrast, for the more cautious, faceless, and systematic Brezhnev and Kosygin, who have been fittingly called the "grey directoire of post-revolutionary administrators,"[31] the solution lies in bureaucratic instrumentalities perfected according to the principles of scientific Communism and laws of economic development. Thus, the conflicting strategies of popular and participatory control versus control through bureaucratic rationalization and scientific organization, which were combined though never resolved in the activity of the CCC and RKI in the 1920's, have again appeared in the 1960's. The Central Control Commission and the Workers' and Peasants' Inspection have themselves been not only historically "rehabilitated" but also institutionally resurrected—by Khrushchev in the form of the Party-State Control Committee and by his successors as the reorganized People's Control Committee. Moreover, both the Khrushchev and the Brezhnev-Kosygin regimes have sought to use the experience of the CCC by emphasizing one of these areas, rationalization and public participation, while de-emphasizing the other. The purpose of the following discussion is to explore the nature of these two strategies of relying on voluntary public participation and scientific organization as ways to rationalize Soviet totalitarianism, to check bureaucracy, and to resolve the problem of party control.

Khrushchev's Populist Formula for Rationalization: Obshchestvennye Nachala

The importance and spirit of the policy of *obshchestvennye nachala*[32] in Communist construction were most fully expressed in the

---

[31] See Richard Lowenthal, "The Soviet Union in the Post-Revolutionary Era: An Overview," in Alexander Dallin and Thomas P. Larson, eds., *Soviet Politics since Khrushchev* (Englewood Cliffs, N.J., 1968), pp. 23–40.

[32] The phrase obshchestvennye nachala unfortunately has no exact English equivalent. Literally translated as "public principles," it approximates in the

1961 party program, Khrushchev's blueprint for Soviet development, which declared:

All-round extension and perfection of socialist democracy, active participation of all citizens in the administration of the state, in the management of economic and cultural development, improvement of the government apparat, and increased control over its activity by the people constitute the main direction in which socialist statehood develops in the period of the building of Communism. As socialist democracy develops, the organs of state power will gradually be transformed into organs of public self-government.[33]

Constant party, state, and public control figured as a prominent and pervasive feature of the developmental process. In his particular model of totalitarianism, with its strong populist overtones, Khrushchev sought to mobilize the energies and active participation of the masses for purposes of building Communism as well as for ensuring social control through institutionalized "public scrutiny" as a substitute for Stalinist terror.[34]

Even more central to the rationalization of the Soviet system, however, was the application of the policy of obshchestvennye nachala to the party and, above all, to the party apparat. As the program explicitly affirmed,

There must be a new, higher stage in the development of the party itself and of its political, ideological, and organizational work that is in conformity with the full-scale building of Communism. . . . The party . . . must serve as an example and model in developing the most advanced forms of Communist public self-government.[35]

Among the measures outlined for promoting internal party self-government were the steady reduction and "withering away" of the sal-

---

broad sense the notion of "public participation" in Western political literature. However, both the direct English translation and approximation are misleading and inadequate in that both of them are too vague and at the same time fail to suggest the specificity of the Soviet term. In its Khrushchevian ideological context obshchestvennye nachala broadly related to such concepts as "socialist democracy," "Communist principles," "Communist public self-government," and "self-administration by the masses." More narrowly, it signified a policy of involving nonprofessionals, nonofficials, in the affairs of the apparat with a view to their performing voluntarily and without pay administrative work that was usually conducted by salaried functionaries. As used in this context, the word *obshchestvennik*, i.e., the individual engaged in such volunteer work, was almost interchangeable with the term *vneshtatnyi rabotnik* (nonstaff worker).

33 *Programme of the Communist Party of the Soviet Union Adopted by the 22nd Congress of the CPSU, October 31, 1961* (Moscow, 1961), p. 92.

34 For a discussion of Khrushchev's totalitarian model, see Fainsod, *How Russia Is Ruled*, pp. 580–86, and Azrael, "The Party and Society," pp. 59–75.

35 *Programme of the Communist Party, 1961*, pp. 123–24.

aried party functionaries and the drawing in of Communists as non-salaried workers doing voluntary staff work. Such a practice if genuinely applied constituted a direct encroachment on the privileged and dominant position of the party apparat. The development of any extensive intra-party democracy necessarily represented a real threat to the power of the party bureaucracy. Indeed, Khrushchev's emphatic and impulsive use of "public principles" in and against the state and party apparat was an instrumental factor in his downfall.

The drive for greater participation by party members in the conduct of party affairs was partly motivated by reasons of administrative convenience and necessity. As one high-ranking party official attested, "Today it is impossible to cope with the tasks that face party organizations through the forces of the staff officials alone."[36] By making the party his primary instrument of rule, Khrushchev extended its control and direction over all sectors of Soviet life. He used the broadly enlisted party public as the proliferated nonstaff adjunct of the regular party apparat, which remained the backbone of his machinery of control. It would be a mistake, however, to view Khrushchev's policy of "public participation" only and even primarily as the disguised effort of the new totalitarian leader to enhance his own power and the hegemony of the party in the political system. The rise and development of the policy were inseparably linked to the emphasis on the restoration of "Leninist norms" and to the revitalization of the party after Stalin's death. Greater participation by the rank-and-file members has been seen as the key to increasing the activeness and vitality of the party. Under Stalin the role of the party member was reduced simply to occupying a stool at the party meeting from which he left without being internally changed. This passivity, moreover, often engendered a lack of discipline. For this reason in the post-Stalin period active participation by party members has been conceived as a mechanism for control.[37]

It is difficult to overestimate the gulf that had developed by the early 1950's between the party apparat and general party membership. Whereas in the 1920's any member could enter the building of the party committee, including the Central Committee, simply by showing his party card, by the 1930's an elaborate pass procedure had

[36] P. Pigalev, "Obshchestvennye Nachala v Rabote Partiinykh Organov," *Kommunist* (Moscow), 7 (1962), 60–69.

[37] See N. Lomakin, "O Leninskikh Normakh Partiinoi Zhizni," *Partiinaia Zhizn'*, (Moscow), 7 (1963), 15–24, and N. Dovbysa, "Vnutripartiinaia Demokratiia—Vazhneishee Uslovie Razvitiia Aktivnosti Kommunistov," *Kommunist Moldavii* (Kishinev), 3 (1960), 28–31.

been established, and armed guards stood at the doors. Only in 1958–59 were the guards removed. In many places party meetings became a rarity, the party aktiv dwindled and was not utilized, all business was handled by the apparatchiki, and there was little regular communication between higher and lower party organs. Even within the apparat complaints were heard that party work was "divided into shelves," with some workers responsible for economic affairs and others for purely party matters. The notion spread that party information, the central ingredient of control and of any system of feedback, was a matter for only the Party Organs Department. In many party committees even the ties between the staff and the party secretary weakened. In Archangel, for example, as late as 1956 the secretaries did not meet with the workers of the apparat even after the plenary sessions of the provincial party committee and had not once in the previous eighteen months met with all the department heads and talked with them about the activities of the apparat. It was not surprising, then, that the secretary of the party committee felt himself to be "lord of the region"—a little Stalin—and decided all questions by himself.[38] Needless to say, after Stalin's death the party machinery was in need of rationalization.

Ossification of party institutions was merely one aspect of devitalization of the party under Stalin. Equally important was the depersonalization, even dehumanization, of party life and affairs, which related particularly to the area of party disciplinary policy and to the consideration of personal cases of individual members. Under Stalin this business was turned into a technical matter of third-rate significance. A disciplinary case, complaint, or appeal would move from office to office, from pocket to pocket, and would receive only superficial attention. There was a strong tendency simply to brush aside the living person. Any meaningful code of party ethics had long disappeared from Communist human relations. The arbitary use of party penalties and lack of comradely concern became such salient features of Stalinist totalitarianism that a common complaint was that "the party secretary has no soul." Revitalizing the party and rationalizing the apparat through "public participation," Khrushchev sought also to infuse back into the party a dose of humaneness long lacking in the organization.

Only on September 30, 1958, did the Central Committee authorize party committees to resurrect the institution of nonstaff instructors,

38 See "Povyshat' Organizatorskuiu Rol' Partiinogo Apparata," *Partiinaia Zhizn'*, 5 (1955), 7–13; "Za Bolee Glubokuiu Partiinuiu Informatsiiu," *ibid.*, 17 (1955), 32–33; B. Borisov, "Partiinaia Demokratiia i Vospitanie Kadrov," *ibid.*, 8 (1956), 20.

which had disappeared from the organizational practice of the party years before.[39] This was the first application of obshchestvennye nachala, but it was soon followed by other forms of enlisting party members to perform staff work without pay. By early 1962 the practice had assumed the character of a campaign, the scope of which according to one high party official "exceeded all expectations."[40] Before long there existed a motley of nonstaff departments and organs virtually paralleling the regular structure of the party committees.[41] As the campaign developed, the Central Committee was forced to warn against certain extremes. For example, *Partiinaia Zhizn'*, the party's organizational journal, pointed out that there was no need for a nonstaff party council to be formed alongside the district party committee to exercise a check on the district party authorities.[42] Similarly, the "mechanical exaggeration" of the nonstaff apparat, it was said, could only harm party committees by creating confusion and parallelism. The Karaganda city party committee, for instance, set up such elaborate nonstaff machinery that "it created its own kind of small 'party *sovnarkhoz*.' "[43] A few organizations even took the novel step of creating the post of nonstaff party secretary to handle much of the work of the regular secretary on hearing complaints and receiving visitors.

Of greater significance for the rationalization of political techniques and party politics were other forms of "public participation." In 1963 councils of secretaries of primary party organizations began to be organized under party committees in large cities.[44] Existing as strictly consultative organs with no statutory or administrative rights, these councils have, nevertheless, introduced a new dimension into party communications and patterns of decision-making. One of the most successful new nonstaff organs has been the so-called Methodological Office or council under the district party committee, which functions as a consultation and information center for party members and lower party secretaries. The office contains a card file and reference library on questions of party structure, extracts of important decisions, model cases on admission and personal cases, proto-

[39] See *Spravochnik Partiinogo Rabotnika* (Moscow, 1959), p. 555.

[40] Pigalev, p. 61.

[41] By the summer of 1962 there were already over 4,000 nonstaff departments in district, city, provincial, and regional party committees, 80,000 nonstaff instructors, and 140,000 nonstaff lecturers and reporters. *Ibid.*, pp. 62–65.

[42] *Partiinaia Zhizn'*, 5 (1962), 74.

[43] *Ibid.*, 15 (1963), 27.

[44] See A. Vader, "Sovershenstvovat' Obshchestvennye Formy Raboty," *Kommunist Estonii* (Tallin), 10 (1964), 11.

cols of party meetings, procedures for collecting membership dues, and information on a host of other internal party organizational subjects. The importance of these new forms is difficult to overemphasize, since they were completely lacking in Stalin's system of party rule. In 1958 secretaries of primary organizations were complaining in droves that they needed seminars, advice, and training in the art of leadership "as badly as we need air."[45]

An important innovation by Khrushchev in the sphere of intraparty control was the creation of so-called nonstaff party commissions under district and city party committees.[46] Consisting of party volunteers who are not on the paid rosters of the party apparat, they act as assistants to the committees by preliminarily reviewing questions of party admission, disciplinary cases, and appeals that arise in primary party organizations. The nonstaff party commission, in effect, then, is the nonofficial functional counterpart of the party commission, the regular disciplinary body in the party, which exists at the provincial, regional, and republic levels. Since 1934 special party control organs have been absent on the lower administrative levels, and all disciplinary business and matters of party admission have fallen within the jurisdiction of the bureaus of the district and city party committees. In fact, these questions have been the privileged domain of the party secretaries. A study of the nonstaff party commission, therefore, provides an excellent example of the difficult process and problems of institutional innovation in the party and its apparat. Above all, it reveals how tenaciously unwilling the party bureaucracy is to share, let alone to surrender, its zealously guarded functional prerogatives. At the same time, it shows that even the party apparat has not been completely impervious to change and that the nonstaff party commission has introduced a new dimension into party affairs.[47]

Of primary interest to our discussion is the rationalizing role of the nonstaff party commission in party disciplinary policy. Again reasons of administrative efficiency figured as the paramount factor in the creation of this new body. The agendas of district committee bureau meetings had become so overloaded with party admission and disciplinary cases that often at one session forty to fifty people

---

[45] *Partiinaia Zhizn' Kazakhstana* (Alma Ata), 1 (1958), 49.

[46] These were first set up on a trial basis in the cities of Moscow and Leningrad and in Moscow Province according to a decision by the Central Committee on December 13, 1960. In January 1962 the Central Committee authorized that they be established on a nationwide basis.

[47] Cocks, "Politics of Party Control," pp. 597–611.

may have been judged in the most perfunctory manner. Adoption procedures became extremely simplified; usually a short biographical sketch was read and one or two questions were asked the prospective candidate. Frequently, the bureau was forced to hold special meetings, sometimes two and three times a week, to consider questions of admission and personal cases.[48] Responsibility for preparing the cases had formerly rested on the instructors in the organization department of the district party committee. However, this work had always been the last item of business on their busy daily schedules and occupied up to 30 per cent of their time, "laying them up within the walls of the district committee."[49] The investigation, preparation, and analysis of cases had long been treated as unimportant and bothersome matters. The formation of the nonstaff party commissions has allowed the district party leadership to give more attention to its economic and political responsibilities and has freed the instructors so that they can spend more time directly in the primary party organizations. It thus facilitates and reflects functional specialization in the party apparat.

At the same time, turning over the bulk of the business of party admission and disciplinary infractions to the commissions has facilitated a more thorough screening of party applicants and more careful examination of disciplinary offenders and appellants. As a result, the commission has served to rationalize and improve the purging process. Although on the one hand it has helped to rationalize the purge by decreasing the possibility of glaring abuses and arbitrary actions simply out of neglect and lack of information about the personal affairs of Communists, on the other hand the nonstaff party commission has tended to increase party supervision over individual members. In conducting their work, the commission members visit the living quarters of Communists, meet with their friends and neighbors, and talk with their families and work associates. If each instructor was previously responsible for not fewer than thirty primary party organizations, now each member of the nonstaff commission is usually attached to only five to ten organizations and has more time to become familiar with the party and personal lives of their members. In some areas once a penalty has been inflicted on a certain party member, a representative from the commission is assigned to observe him personally for several months. This form of surveillance, hounding, and follow-through on disciplined members has even been la-

[48] *Partiinaia Zhizn'*, 15–16 (1961), 106–7.
[49] *Ibid.*, 19 (1965), 53–54.

beled the "service" of the nonstaff party commissions, which, it is claimed, "relentlessly look after their wards" until punishment has achieved its aim.[50] The institution of the nonstaff party commission, therefore, provides an excellent example of why rationalization should not be equated and identified with liberalization.

Of course, the most important example of Khrushchev's use of obshchestvennye nachala as a rationalizing and checking force in and against the party and state apparat was the Party-State Control Committee, established in the fall of 1962. The resurrection of a potentially powerful super-control agency designed to struggle against all forms of bureaucratism was undoubtedly one of the most sensitive issues and important political choices of the post-Stalin period. For the first time in three decades a hierarchy of control organs was formed that extended not only below the provincial level but directly into the primary party organizations of virtually every government, economic, and public institution. The PSCC had its lowest links of control—the groups and posts of assistance—not only at all construction sites, in production enterprises, and in kolkhozes and sovkhozes, but also in academic and government institutions, in state committees and ministries and departments subordinate to them, in legal courts and offices of the procuracy, in the militia, in the correctional labor camps, and in military and naval units. Even the party organizations in educational and governmental institutions did not have the formal right to check on administrative activity in these organs, and no special party checking commissions had been set up in them after 1959 as in production enterprises. The organs of party-state control, moreover, were assisted by staffs and detachments of the "Komsomol Searchlight," which were a fusion and expansion of previously existing Komsomol checking posts, raiding brigades, and "light cavalry" units. By the fall of 1964 there were already more than 260,000 groups and 500,000 posts of assistance encompassing an army of 4,300,000 public activists as well as three million Komsomol members engaged in checking for the PSCC.[51] Clearly such a web of controls and controllers was designed, according to Khrushchev, so that "even a mosquito will not fly by unnoticed."[52]

Significantly, however, Khrushchev's extensive use of the policy of "public participation" as the means to build his populist model of rationalized totalitarianism increasingly encountered resentment and resistance from bureaucratic elements both inside and outside the

---

[50] Ibid., 20 (1964), 37; and 15 (1965), 44.
[51] Kommunist, 13 (1964), 123.
[52] Pravda, Nov. 23, 1962.

party and contributed to the eclipse of his power. From the beginning his innovations in party organizational affairs, which have long been the guarded monopoly of the party apparat, provoked fears in many party functionaries. The obshchestvenniki were almost always regarded with distrust by the apparatchiki. There was a strong tendency to view and use them as merely special appendages of the staff workers. Although theoretically equal in status with the apparatchiki, they have been received generally as second-rate officials who perform foreign work. Others have treated them as just auxiliaries in the apparat to patch up official gaps. Sometimes they have been neglected altogether, or as one disgruntled nonstaff worker put it, "confirmed and forgotten at the same time."[53] That the application of "public principles" to party work was already causing alarm in some party quarters by the time of the Twenty-second Party Congress in October 1961 was disclosed by the second secretary of the Moscow Party Committee. He remarked, "Sometimes one hears objections to this practice. Are party organs not being depersonalized? Is their leading role not declining? Aren't too many different commissions and councils springing up and aren't they being set up artificially?"[54]

Similarly, the idea of the nonstaff party commission met opposition from some local party leaders who did not want to share their jurisdictional mandate with even a nonstaff, fully subordinate organ, and there were many who looked upon the commission as "an uneasy and unnecessary venture."[55] Some were more favorable to assigning the commissions the preliminary handling of personal affairs of Communists but believed that party admission was by "established tradition" the special charge of the party secretary.[56] Others felt that the new appendage would only complicate the movement of cases.[57] Regarding it with suspicion, the local party authorities did not everywhere readily accept this new institution. Members of the commission in Dneprodzerzhinsk recalled in 1964, "In the beginning, not everything went smoothly with us. People tried to turn members of the commission into assistants of the apparat for technical work on documents. Thus, instructional conferences for us assumed the character of seminars for clerks."[58] Such an attitude reflected more than the disparaging opinion of the district party authorities toward the

[53] *Partiinaia Zhizn'*, 6 (1960), 55.
[54] *XXII S"ezd KPSS: Stenograficheskii Otchet* (Moscow, 1961), III, 57.
[55] *Partiinaia Zhizn' Kazakhstana*, 11 (1961), 73.
[56] *Partiinaia Zhizn'*, 20 (1961), 45–46.
[57] *Partiinaia Zhizn' Kazakhstana*, 1 (1963), 45.
[58] *Partiinaia Zhizn'*, 20 (1964), 34.

members of the nonstaff commission. It also reflected the fact that
this work, which above all touched the lives and fate of party members, had generally and simply been reduced to an impersonal, technical function. In some places there was no room made for the nonstaff commission in the party committee, and its members had to wait
until one of the staff workers went on a business trip and freed his
office so that they could have a place to meet. Several district committees adopted the practice of turning over only the noncontrover-
sial and unimportant cases to the commissions while assigning the
more "special cases," especially those involving members and friends
of the party apparat, to trusted staff instructors for preparation. In
some instances neither the secretary nor his deputy bothers to attend
the meetings of the nonstaff commission despite a formal ruling by
the Central Committee that they should.[59] In other districts even
though one of the secretaries may attend the meetings, the commission does not have daily ties with the departments of the party committee and with its staff workers. Commission members are often not
invited to meetings for apparat personnel and are not informed of
apparat affairs. Although in most places the nonstaff party commissions have been consolidated and integrated into the local party structure, it is still not uncommon to hear complaints from their members
about lack of support and trust from the district party committees.
For example, the deputy chairman of a nonstaff commission in Novo-
sibirsk wrote to *Partiinaia Zhizn'* in the winter of 1968 that during
the previous six years the bureau of the city party committee had not
once found time to discuss the work of the commission with its members. The secretary allegedly said that he had "more important matters" to attend to.[60]

It was the use and abuse of "public principles" in the Party-State
Control Committee, however, that caused the greatest bureaucratic
opposition and reaction. As Khrushchev's super-control agency steadily expanded its sphere of operations and ominously developed into
an independent pillar of power,[61] fears and resistance mounted in
the party apparat and among Soviet administrators against encroachments into their jealously guarded preserves of power and privilege.
The initial fears of some party apparatchiki were probably confirmed

[59] V. Liakhov and O. Maltsev, *Vneshtatnye Partiinye Komissii* (Moscow, 1964),
p. 32; *Partiinaia Zhizn'*, 9 (1965), 42.

[60] *Partiinaia Zhizn'*, 5 (1968), 70.

[61] See Christian Duevel, "The Dismantling of Party and State Control as an
Independent Pillar of Soviet Power," *Bulletin*, 3 (Munich, 1966), 3, 18; and Cocks,
"Politics of Party Control," pp. 626–36.

when several party-state control organs almost immediately began overstepping their authority by intruding into internal party affairs. For example, there were instances of checking by the lower-level groups of assistance to the PSCC on whether or not Communists were paying their dues on time, on how decisions of party meetings were being implemented, and on the quality of the political information being passed among party members.[62] Similarly, some members who had been expelled from the party began to complain and protest to the PSCC.[63] Such involvement in intra-party questions during the early stages of activity of the PSCC could be explained in terms of its functional roles not yet being clearly delineated and understood. However, in light of Brezhnev's blunt warning at the time of the reorganization of the PSCC into the People's Control Committee in December 1965 that the latter body was not to "control the work of party organs,"[64] it appears that Shelepin's agency continued to overstep its proper jurisdiction and to intervene in purely internal party organizational matters. Such actions could only sow seeds of fear and alarm in the party apparat.

Equally disquieting to the party bureaucracy must have been the increasingly high status and role of the groups of assistance to the PSCC. By the summer of 1964 the opinion was voiced that these groups should be granted administrative and disciplinary powers, an action that would have substantially altered the locus of power in lower party units and facilitated the autonomy of the lowest link in the control hierarchy from the party apparat.[65] Some groups of assistance even began issuing their own wall newspapers and exposure sheets instead of using the existing press organs of their party, Komsomol, and trade-union organizations.[66] Growing efforts by the PSCC to influence and control the elections of the chairmen of the groups of assistance brought the PSCC into the highly sensitive area of internal party elections and inevitably into conflict with the primary party organizations and local party committees.[67] That the party-state controllers were increasingly demanding, exercising, and abusing the right of coordination and the role of coordinating center for all forms of checking further exacerbated fears over the PSCC's intrusive pow-

[62] B. A. Zheleznov, *Osnovnye Prava i Zadachi Komitetov Partiino-Gosudarstvennogo Kontrolia* (Kazan', 1964), pp. 66–67.
[63] *Partiinaia Zhizn'*, 8 (1963), 56.
[64] *Pravda*, Dec. 7, 1965.
[65] Zheleznov, p. 78.
[66] *Spravochnik Narodnogo Kontrolera* (Moscow, 1965), p. 77.
[67] See Duevel.

ers; it was seen as usurping a role that had been traditionally claimed by the party itself.[68] Significantly, with the growth of Shelepin's organization, nearly half the primary party organizations dissolved their own checking commissions and transferred their members to the groups of assistance to the PSCC, which became the principal checking agency in almost all organizations and enterprises.[69] Needless to say, these developments must have made many party apparatchiki literally tremble with fear.

The expansive and intrusive posture of the Party-State Control Committee also began to weigh heavily on other bureaucratic structures and groups. The obtrusive meddling and tendency of the controllers to supplant organs of administration and economic leadership provoked open resentment from economic managers after the fall of 1964. Hostility against the party-state controllers grew in the trade unions. Similarly, the PSCC began to usurp and interfere in functions properly belonging to the procuracy, a situation that caused grumbling among its workers about the need to delimit the competence of the PSCC. Indeed, in general there was mounting bureaucratic opposition against the democratic intrusions and public pressures associated not only with the PSCC but also with Khrushchev's whole system of populist totalitarianism. The spirited momentum of amateurish and at times unruly public checking that was spurred by the spontaneity and voluntarism of obshchestvennye nachala constantly led to a blurring of the fine line between the vigilant activist and the unrestrained vigilante. Efforts by the public checkers frequently replaced organizational work with numbers and noise. Most of the time they were occupied in superfluous bustle and would merely get on people's nerves. Increasingly, it was stressed that public checkers must learn the technology of inspections and acquire the ability to decipher figures. There was a growing number of members of the groups of assistance to the PSCC that would break away for a few days in order to participate in checks and raids that resulted al-

---

68 Cocks, pp. 629–32.

69 For example, in Tadzhikistan 40 per cent of the party checking commissions were abolished. (R. G. Umetbaev, *Obshchestvennye Nachala v Partiinoi Rabote* [Dushambe, 1966], p. 36.) In Moscow the number of checking commissions in production party organizations had declined from 2,000 to 1,112 by the spring of 1964. In Belgorod Oblast, out of 697 primary party organizations that had the right to check on administrative activity, only 83 commissions were preserved, and in the sovkhoz party organizations only half were preserved. ("Partiinyi Kontrol' na Proizvodstve," *Partiinaia Zhizn'*, 6 [1964], 40–43.) In places where the party checking commissions were preserved, their work was considerably curtailed; they were restricted to examining long-range questions, and the task of daily operational checking was assigned to the groups and posts of assistance to the PSCC.

legedly in the loss of tens of thousands of working days. With the rising number of "mass pilgrimages" and "invasions" of controllers, checking, it was charged, was turned more and more into control for control's sake. This in turn caused unnecessary duplication and waste, and disrupted production and the normal functioning of organizations.[70] Needless to say, there quickly developed a desire to curb the PSCC and to control the controllers. The economic managers and professional party bureaucrats spoke with one voice of the need to tone down substantially the practice of "public principles" after Khrushchev's fall. For them this was merely another expression of his harebrained scheming and super-voluntarism.

Having described Khrushchev's policy of relying on obshchestvennye nachala to change, improve, and perfect the administrative machinery of Soviet totalitarianism, we may legitimately ask how effective this strategy of rationalization was in the long run. It is clear that the public control edifice was making inroads into the domains of established institutional structures and increasingly exerting pressures everywhere on bureaucratic elements. Yet, despite the popularizing effects of public participation in political and supervisory affairs, the policy as a rationalizing force appears to have been a failure. This was clearly brought out in a lengthy review article that appeared in April 1967 in the official philosophical journal of the party. The article, "Research in the Field of Political Organization of Socialist Society," strongly criticized the relevant literature of the Khrushchev period. The reviewers concluded that in general there had been a tendency "to run ahead in this matter, which disorients the reader and hampers a correct understanding of the immediate theoretical and practical tasks, since Communist self-government is still in a very early stage." They went on to say that some authors frequently strove only to ascertain the characteristics of the "state of the entire people" that distinguish it from the state of the dictatorship of the proletariat, "forgetting the common nature of these forms and the continuity in the political organization of a society building socialism and one building Communism." Others had taken the expression "mass participation in administration" to mean any kind of voluntary public work, such as planting trees and shrubbery in the countryside. One researcher had even concluded that already 55 per cent of the working masses were engaged in administering the affairs of Soviet society.[71]

[70] Cocks, pp. 632–33.

[71] V. V. Varchuk and V. I. Razin, "Issledovaniia v Oblasti Politicheskoi Organizatsii Sotsialisticheskogo Obshchestva," *Voprosy Filosofii*, 4 (1967), 136–37.

In overemphasizing "public principles" and forms of public participation, the theorists under Khrushchev tended to neglect the question of how to improve and rationalize the apparat in practice. In many respects the policy of "public participation" did not confront the problem of changing the existing structure but simply created a new, nonstaff apparat alongside the old one. Apparently it was rather seriously but naively assumed that the public apparat would simply replace rather than change the old structure as the latter gradually "withered away." Thus, in a cogent summary of the character and consequences of the policy as practiced under Khrushchev, the authors of the article cited above noted:

There was talk about drawing the public in and in rare instances about the public's activity, but never about improving the work of the state apparat, nor about improving its structure, reducing its size.... We thus have *two apparatuses*, as it were. One is the regular apparat, sufficiently large and basically stable. It exercises the function of power, is not free from bureaucratism, and, as a rule, is not the object of research. The other apparat is the public one. It is poorly organized, unstable, operates on the basis of enthusiasm alone.... We must conclude that the enlistment of the public is being conducted for the sake of the enlistment itself, for the sake of a good showing. We find that it yields no effect and at times merely distracts the energies of party and state officials.[72]

Since Khrushchev's fall the new leadership has reexamined and curtailed the excessive practice of drawing rank-and-file party members and the general public into the work of party and state organs. As *Partiinaia Zhizn'* concluded, many party committees had simply been "carried away by the quantitative aspect of the matter" and had created many unnecessary nonstaff bodies.[73] Instead of the policy of "public participation," those who assumed leadership after Khrushchev have adopted a different strategy and different tools for rationalizing the Soviet system. It is to their rationalization efforts that we now turn.

The Post-Khrushchev Bureaucratic Formula for Rationalization: Nauchnaia Organizatsiia Truda

In contrast to Khrushchev's alleged "harebrained scheming," the dominant tone of the Brezhnev and Kosygin regime has been to emphasize the need for a scientific and businesslike approach to the eco-

72 *Ibid.*, p. 143.
73 *Partiinaia Zhizn'*, 16 (1967), 59. Among the forms of nonstaff work that have been recognized to be of positive value are the nonstaff party commissions, the councils on party organizational work, and the councils of lower party secretaries.

nomics and politics of building Communism. They have deemphasized the voluntarism and populism of *obshchestvennye nachala* and have stressed instead bureaucratic reform along rational and scientific lines through *nauchnaia organizatsiia truda* (scientific organization of labor). Thus, they have again taken up the plane of scientific rationalization to make smooth what in their eyes is a workable and developed system.

Since Khrushchev's fall and largely in conjunction with economic reforms there has been a renascence of NOT—nauchnaia organizatsiia truda—which lay dormant in the Soviet Union for three decades. An official in Sverdlovsk province, which has been a pioneering center in both sociology and rationalization theory, affirmed in March 1966 that "not so long ago many workers in industry did not know what was hidden behind the short word NOT."[74] Nine months later the first secretary of the Sverdlovsk provincial party committee observed, "In our day NOT is acquiring first-rate importance as an instrumental factor in building Communist society.... NOT is becoming an important party matter."[75] The rising significance of scientific organization of labor and rationalization was dramatized in June 1967 by the convening of a national conference on problems of economic rationalization, the first conference on NOT since 1924. Though the main focus of NOT has so far been on the rationalization of production and on the creation of the material technical base for Communism, its importance for economic management has also been recognized. The need to apply NOT to administration as well as to production was voiced at the June 1967 rationalization conference. One delegate stressed that NOT could not be divided by a "Chinese wall" into the organization of production and the perfection of administrative techniques.[76] Similarly, I. V. Paramanov, an old economic manager, in his memoirs published in early 1967 regretted that there was simply no "methodology of management" worked out for young Soviet administrators. *Pravda* also acknowledged that the courses on "organization of production" offered in Soviet universities did not provide young specialists with knowledge of how they should manage people or how they should act in a complex situation.[77] In fact, in 1962 out of eight hundred higher educational and technical institutions only six included course offerings on NOT.[78] Conse-

---

[74] *Sotsialisticheskii Trud*, 3 (1966), 64.
[75] *Ibid.*, 1 (1967), 9.
[76] *Ibid.*, 9 (1967), 55.
[77] *Pravda*, May 31, 1967.
[78] I. Petrochenko, *NOT* (Moscow, 1967), p. 59.

quently, the systematic study of business management and administrative science has received increasing attention from Soviet rationalizers.

Of particular interest to us is the broader relevance of NOT for rationalizing Soviet politics and reforming the administrative machinery and techniques of the Communist party. Since in a Communist system politics and economics are inseparably linked, rationalization in the economy has been seen by some progressive party elements in Eastern Europe as the first step toward (or back door to) political rationalization and even liberalization. As a Czech writer has put it:

A connection between economics and politics is absolutely clear in this respect, and our present efforts cannot be limited to questions of economic management but must aim at the creation of general conditions for a more democratic administration and of a rational political system with strictly defined powers.[79]

Although such views have not been as forcefully and explicitly expressed in the Soviet Union, still a political relevance has been increasingly ascribed to NOT. For example, shortly after Khrushchev's fall *Pravda* carried an article by Fyodor Burlatsky entitled "Politics and Science," in which he proposed that the field of "political science" should be developed in the Soviet Union. Defining it basically as the technique of leadership and administration, he stressed its value as a means for "perfecting the forms and methods of guiding society." Taking the Brezhnev-Kosygin line that "scientific guidance is a necessary quality of socialism," Burlatsky strongly argued for the development of scientific "political technique" in contrast to the voluntarist and subjective political style of Khrushchev. Interestingly, Burlatsky had come to his ideas in part by rediscovering the rationalization efforts of the CCC and RKI in the 1920's. Referring to the old journals of the control establishment, he acknowledged, "One cannot but be amazed to see how profoundly problems relating to improving economic management and the machinery of state administration in general were studied back in those years."[80]

Indeed, since that fateful plenum of the Central Committee in October 1964, "harebrained scheming" seems to have given way gradually to a more sophisticated attitude toward politics and system-building. Like Lenin at the end of his life, Khrushchev's successors have come to recognize and appreciate the complexities and difficulties of administration and the need to avoid, if possible, simple solutions.

[79] J. Fojtik, "Does a Socialist Man Exist," *Rude Pravo* (Prague), Jan. 5, 1967, quoted in Michael Gamarnikow, *Economic Reforms in Eastern Europe* (Detroit, Mich., 1968), p. 15.

[80] *Pravda*, Jan. 10, 1965.

Now in vogue is the idea attributed to Lenin that politics is "more like algebra than arithmetic and even more like higher mathematics." Recognition of the complexity of politics in turn produces the corollary that greater political skills and knowledge are needed to cope with emerging and changing political problems. Consequently, it has been authoritatively stated that the party official must "know more than the four rules of arithmetic."[81] Similarly, Lenin's famous remark that a well-run organization is like a precision orchestra is held up as the ideal administrative model. In such a model, it is emphasized, experience and skill above all are required "in order to distribute correctly the parts, in order to know to whom to assign the sentimental violin, to whom the gruff doublebass, and to whom the conductor's baton." Significantly, in December 1968 Burlatsky chose for the subject of an article in honor of the forthcoming centennial of Lenin's birth the theme "Lenin and the Art of Management." That he should also have selected the lines I have just quoted from Lenin was not accidental, for they well convey the spirit of post-Khrushchevian rationalization policy.[82]

Most significant of all, there is growing recognition that the party apparat must also be subjected to the blade of scientific rationalization in order to make its rule more effective and responsive, if not more palatable. Just as Khrushchev stressed that the party must show an example of Communist self-government through applications of obshchestvennye nachala, Brezhnev has maintained that the party must base its organizational life and leadership techniques on scientific principles to accord with the demands of Communist construction. Not only has the construction of Communist society been emphasized as "a scientifically administered process," but also the most important feature of the Leninist party is said to be precisely its "scientific approach."[83] Consequently, the party leadership has been engaged especially since early 1968 in a major effort to introduce NOT into the party apparat in order to improve and perfect the style and methods of party work. For example, long-term planning (up to two years) has been instituted in party committees on all levels in order to put party work on a more scientific basis. Under Khrushchev only quarterly work plans were drawn up, and these could not always take

---

[81] *Kommunist*, 9 (1967), 54.

[82] Fyodor Burlatsky, "Lenin and the Art of Management," *New Times* (Moscow), 51 (Dec. 25, 1968), 6–9.

[83] V. Afanas'ev, "Stroitel'stvo Kommunizma—Nauchno Upravliaemyi Protsess," *Kommunist*, 14 (1967), 63–74; G. Popov, "Sovershenstvovanie Stilia i Metodov Partiinoi Raboty," *ibid.*, 13 (1968), 64–76.

into account long-range developments and problems.[84] The party's organizational journal, *Partiinaia Zhizn'*, has opened its pages to discussion of the problems and defects of the apparat, especially on the city and district levels, and has entertained suggestions about how indeed to apply NOT to party organizational practice. Prominent among the rationalization proposals is the demand for greater functional specialization in all areas of the apparat and among all levels and categories of party apparatchiki, not just in the secretarial hierarchy. The old notion that the party worker, especially the instructor who has served as the organizational nerve of the party committees, can be a "jack of all trades" has been roundly criticized.[85] Indeed, since the Twenty-third Party Congress a massive campaign has been launched to retrain virtually the entire administrative corps of party and government officials—from party secretaries to newspaper editors—from the central to the district level. In January 1968, on the republic, regional, and provincial levels, permanently operating one-month refresher courses were established, through which, it is planned, 50,000 officials will pass annually. Thus, as a rule all party and government workers will undergo retraining in the art of leadership and science of administration once every three years.[86]

Rationalization has been directed especially at updating and modernizing the obsolete organizational machinery and techniques of the apparat, and above all, its primitive information gathering and processing facilities. In order to solve the increasingly complex problems of building Communism, both policy-makers and controllers have raised a chorus of voices in demanding more and better information. On the need for complete and accurate information they are quick to point to Lenin's painfully relevant statement: "Without it, we have neither eyes, ears, nor hands." Some have adamantly insisted that the time has come when the party must install computers, teletype machines, adding machines, and dictaphones in all offices of the apparat. Surprisingly, until very recently only the Central Committee of the CPSU has used these more advanced technical means of data processing. Even the republic central committee was without its computer and had to rely chiefly on the abacus.[87] Equally significant is

[84] Popov, p. 68; N. Fedorov, "Perspektivnyi Plan Gorodskoi Partorganizatsii," *Partiinaia Zhizn'*, 12 (1968), 28–37.

[85] I. Gladchenko, "O Chem Govorit Nash Opyt," *Partiinaia Zhizn'*, 15 (1968), 41–42; "Novye Usloviia—Novye Trebovaniia," *ibid.*, 17 (1968), 35–40.

[86] See "Kursam po Perepodgotovke Partiinykh i Sovetskikh Rabotnikov—Neoslabnoe Vnimanie," *Partiinaia Zhizn'*, 12 (1968), 16–19; and "Kursy po Perepodgotovke Partiinykh i Sovetskikh Kadrov," *ibid.*, 17 (1968), 22–26.

[87] A. Liashko, "Partiinaia Informatsiia—Vazhnoe Sredstvo Sovershenstvovaniia Raboty Partorganizatsii," *Partiinaia Zhizn'*, 15 (1968), 16–25.

the change in values that is being brought about by the new spirit of rationalization in regard to administration and office work. Along with growing recognition that administration is a science, a more favorable attitude is being adopted toward office work in general. In the past this work was always derogated and depreciated, and associated with bureaucratic red tape, needless bustle, and even sedition. Indeed, it came to denote a certain political style of declarative leadership by the bureaucrat sitting in his office; hence, it was always contrasted with a more activist-oriented, "living" style of work. Now, however, it is increasingly recognized that the party worker will spend a certain part of his time at his desk and that this work is a necessary side of the activity of the party apparat.[88] Given the highly personalized nature of Stalin's system of rule, such a change in the value structure of Soviet "political culture" is a prerequisite for any trend toward the institutionalization of power and function in the Soviet Union. At the same time, present rationalization policy has the effect of not only depersonalizing the affairs of the apparat but indeed dehumanizing the basic machinery of the Soviet system. Clearly Khrushchev's populist variant of rationalized totalitarianism has given way to a new and different model, which in its leviathan-like design is awesome.

The Rationalization of Totalitarianism: Overview and Prognosis

Perhaps it is not too much of an exaggeration to say that much of Soviet history has been a frenzied workshop attempting to rationalize the Soviet system and to overcome the inheritance and consequences of the October Revolution. Defined basically as the process of improving and perfecting the organizational machinery of the Soviet system, rationalization in the 1920's was concerned with the cumbersome and archaic administrative structure and bureaucracy inherited from the Tsar. During the 1950's and 1960's the Soviet leaders have similarly tried to rationalize the equally obsolete organizational edifice built by Stalin. We have seen that in general two contradictory strategies of "rationalization" have been pursued both before and after Stalin. On the one hand, scientific rationalization based on the scientific organization of labor has aimed at administrative reform from above by experts. Extensive public participation in administrative affairs and pressure from below, on the other hand, have constituted a more primitive and amateurish form of populist rationalization. Each strategy, moreover, has its own set of tools. In general,

[88] Gladchenko, p. 41.

the administrative mechanics of Stalinism with its instruments of terror and purge allowed little room for either scientific rationalization or public participation. With Khrushchev's policy of obshchestvennye nachala, the tools assumed more the shape of a mallet, more blunt in its blow than an axe but equally rough in its swing. Abandoning the mallet, Brezhnev and Kosygin have taken up the rationalizer's plane. Nevertheless, the scope of rationalization remains narrowly focused on perfecting techniques and does not formally extend to politics and basic systemic change.

The road of rationalization has indeed been an arduous one with many turns and even full circles. Looking at the process and problems of institutional innovation and at the organizational responses of Stalin's successors, one is immediately struck by the paramount importance of the "historical" dimension of change and how it has dominated the political perspectives of Soviet leaders when facing challenges and choices in the area of rationalization and control. Every passionate search for something new is in many respects a search for something lost. One senses that the Soviet leadership in moving forward is constantly looking back. In its solutions to present ills, it has sought assistance from past experience and examples. Thus, in light of this merging of the past with the present, it may be useful to suggest a prospectus for the rationalization of Soviet totalitarianism by way of an overview of past and present efforts.

The more sophisticated character of rationalization theory today augurs more fruitful results than did NOT in the 1920's. Much of the trouble with early rationalization work was that it was a primitive approach to scientific reorganization. Administration was highly oversimplified and was viewed as essentially a technical process capable of automation. Rationalization focused on the administration of things and not of men. The rationalization movement and models lacked the human element and were not grounded in political, economic, and social reality. Even though much of the tone of NOT today strongly emphasizes computer technology, cybernetics, systems operations, and other scientific techniques, the human and behavioral dimensions have been explicitly recognized as part of the organization syndrome.[89] The slow but steady growth of social sciences in the Soviet Union in the 1960's and talk about the need to develop political science, political sociology, and engineering psychology promise

[89] Perhaps taking a lesson from the past, the 1967 conference on rationalization defined NOT as the organization of labor that facilitates "the best way of combining technology *and people* in a single production process." See *Sotsialisticheskii Trud*, 9 (1967), 106; italics mine.

to give a deeper meaning to rationalization. Most important, there is a greater awareness of the perplexing problems to which rationalization must ultimately address itself.

Equally significant for the favorable development of NOT in the 1970's are the changed economic conditions in the Soviet Union. In contrast to the 1920's the level of technology and the economy can sustain and indeed demand the application of more advanced techniques. Earlier rationalization failed in part because of the overriding desire and impatience to industrialize even at the expense and in defiance of rationality. Now that the economic revolution of the early five-year plans has taken place, the functional imperatives of future industrial progress dictate systematic economic reform. As a refined instrument, rationalization is more appropriate for reform than for revolution. In this regard it is significant that the recent economic reforms and the rebirth of NOT are closely related. If earlier administrative rationalization was to precede and be the prerequisite for industrialization, economic production today propels the rationalization of economic management and political administration.

Similarly, political conditions appear to be more conducive to a rationalization of totalitarianism in the 1970's. Not only Stalin but Khrushchev, the ebullient experimenter and impulsive adventurer, is behind the present rationalizers. The arbitrary excesses and abuses of the cult of personality have been denounced and renounced. De-Stalinization has produced its own fruits and forces that make any major reversals increasingly more difficult. Moreover, the failure of Khrushchev's policy of "public participation" to effect the necessary changes and improvements in the apparat and to solve the problem of control, discipline, and responsibility dramatizes the need for a more rational approach to political development.

In spite of these positive signs, however, there is no guarantee that the present leadership and strategy will be any more successful than Khrushchev's policy in rationalizing the Soviet system. The viability of the collective leadership of Brezhnev and Kosygin still remains to be seen. The alliance of the economic managers and party bureaucrats, which was forged out of a common interest and desire to maintain their own institutional structures against democratic intrusions and mass pressures, gives no guarantee of being long-lasting. Indeed, the throwing over of excessive public participation was done out of a mutual desire for stability and security for the party and economic bureaucracies, not out of a desire to institute change in these bureaucratic structures.

History has provided few examples of reforming bureaucracies capable of changing from within. Yet change from within is what the present emphasis on NOT attempts to achieve. In the 1920's the controllers, who were responsible for checking and eliminating abuses of power and bureaucratism, were theoretically separate from the administrators. The recognized corrupting influence of power and the necessarily contagious character of the administrative process dictated that rationalization of the apparat come from outside the bureaucracy, which was deemed incapable of reforming itself. But the history of the Soviet regime and of its control organs has revolved precisely on the pervasive and permanent fear in the party bureaucracy of any outside checking-rationalizing force, since such a force necessarily threatens the power, privilege, and survival of the party machine. These fears were well expressed in the rise and fall of the Party-State Control Committee. Dismantling the PSCC as an increasingly independent pillar of power, the Brezhnev-Kosygin regime has reaffirmed that rationalization of the apparat is to take place from within and under the direction of the party bureaucracy. Moreover, although greater efficiency and economy remain the goals of rationalization, they may be cast aside as in the past for higher political goals and interests.

Above all, the forms and spirit of rationalization through scientific organization, just as through "public participation," should not be confused with its essence and direction. The aim of rationalization is to preserve the substance of totalitarian power while perfecting its methods. Like Khrushchev's vision, that of Brezhnev and Kosygin remains total. The control structure of the political system is to be all-inclusive and all-pervasive. Rationalization seeks to erect, in effect, what Allen Kassof has called "the administered society: totalitarianism without terror."[90] Khrushchev described in detail the extent and degree of control that he sought to ensure with the assistance of a vast army of public checkers in which every citizen was turned into a policeman:

Like the good mechanic whose ear is attuned to the working of an enormous engine and who is able from a scarcely audible sound to tell where the trouble lies, who seems to see every little speck of dust that might cause the engine to stop running, we too are obliged to listen day by day and hour by hour to the heartbeat of the huge Soviet land, to eradicate evidence of bureaucracy and red tape and be prompt to notice and clear out of our way every obstacle to our successful progress.[91]

---

90 See his "The Administered Society: Totalitarianism without Terror," *World Politics*, XVI: 4 (July 1964), 558–75.
91 *XXII S"ezd KPSS: Stenograficheskii Otchet* (Moscow, 1961), I, 117.

Similarly, speaking about NOT, *Partiinaia Zhizn'* in January 1968 stressed that this would help to organize the people with the "precision of a watch mechanism."[92] Though the analogy is somewhat more sophisticated, the meaning is the same. Indeed, a recent innovation of NOT in party disciplinary policy and an example of new instrumentation for control purposes has been the creation and use by some party committees of an elaborate computerized accounting and surveillance system of punch cards to direct and detect the activity of party members, especially potential "troublemakers." This system is designed so that "not one Communist remains outside the field of vision of the party organization and beyond comradely control."[93] Again rationalization is not to be confused with liberalization.

By the same token, there has been virtually no change in the attitude of the political leadership about the necessity for continuous control. A basic distrust of human nature, which reached paranoid proportions under Stalin, continues to characterize the political mind of Stalin's heirs. In 1934 Lazar Kaganovich, whom Stalin had just installed as head of the revamped control apparat, aptly expressed the attitude of the General Secretary:

Even the good worker, if from time to time we do not "wipe the dust off which has settled on him," can go bad and "grow moldy." Any person, even a Solomon and the most outstanding fellow, if he is placed in conditions of complete lack of control and we blindly trust him will inevitably go downhill. There are no ideal persons, no people without shortcomings.[94]

Nearly three decades later Khrushchev echoed in the same vein: "Control is needed even for the work of honest people, because control is above all order. It disciplines workers, prevents errors, and increases their responsibility for assigned work."[95] Nor have Khrushchev's successors disparaged the need for a strong prophylactic control function in the Soviet system: as the editors of *Partiinaia Zhizn'* asserted in early 1969, "Systematic and fundamental control prevents mistakes and slips, holds people in a constant state of creative stress, and does not leave room for such manifestations as placidity, complacency, and conceit."[96] Needless to say, scientific rationalization fits well with the compulsive dream of beehive order and total control.

At the same time, it is important not to overdraw the strict division between obshchestvennye nachala and nauchnaia organizatsiia truda

[92] *Partiinaia Zhizn'*, 1 (1968), 22.
[93] *Kommunist Estonii*, 1 (1968), 52.
[94] *Partiinoe Stroitel'stvo*, 22 (Nov. 1934), 3–4.
[95] *Partiinaia Zhizn'*, 9 (1962), 5–6.
[96] *Ibid.*, 2 (1969), 3.

as we have applied them to characterize the dominant complexion of the control and rationalization strategies pursued by Khrushchev and his successors. Khrushchev was not opposed to economic rationalization. On the contrary, he sought a more rational solution to the problem of managing an increasingly complex economy by promoting technically trained people to administrative posts, decentralizing operational decision-making, rationalizing agricultural controls, etc. Similarly, Brezhnev and Kosygin instead of rejecting all forms of public participation have sought to rationalize and discipline the applications of "public principles" by curbing the excesses of unrestrained enthusiasm, unnecessary parallelism, and superfluous bustle. They have retained and even augmented the vast army of public checkers in the people's control organs and continue to use them in the extensive web of controls. Interestingly, the People's Control Committee itself has recently been set onto the path of scientific rationalization and is to be made "an example of businesslike efficiency, carefulness, exactingness, and effective operation," i.e., a model of rationalization and NOT.[97]

Finally, it may be argued that no matter how successful it is in promoting greater efficiency, rationalization can only be insufficient as a policy answering the developmental needs of the Soviet system. Some would contend that not just the perfection of techniques, fine adjustments, and reform are needed, but indeed fundamental systemic change—even revolutionary change—is required. The demands of change go beyond efficiency. Moreover, there seems to be a certain inherent contradiction between a policy of static and short-run efficiency and rationality and the requirements of rapid movement, change, and transformation.[98] Thus the axe may again be needed in place of the plane to effect necessary changes. To some extent, like applied social science in other organizational systems, rationalization in the Soviet Union is being used as a planned functional substitute for the spontaneous adaptive mechanisms by means of which the rational organization responds to external threats, reduces internal disruptions, and controls various forms of social deviance.[99] Although it fits

[97] See I. Shikin, "Leninskie Printsipy Narodnogo Kontrolia v Deistvii," *ibid.*, p. 13.

[98] See the comments by Alexander Eckstein in Gregory Grossman, ed., *Value and Plan: Economic Calculation and Organization in Eastern Europe* (Berkeley, Calif., 1960), p. 262.

[99] See Alvin W. Gouldner, "Organizational Analysis," in Robert K. Merton, Leonard Broom, and Leonard S. Cottrell, Jr., eds., *Sociology Today: Problems and Prospects* (New York, 1959), II, 408.

well the traditional predilection of the party leaders for planned rather than spontaneous adaptation, rationalization comes at a stage in the evolution of the Soviet system when comprehensive planned change is becoming increasingly difficult, if indeed it has not become impossible.

In our opinion, however, those who insist that the rationalization of totalitarianism is necessarily doomed to fail because it contemplates only technical adjustments and not systemic change underestimate the potential of rationalization to spawn unconsciously such systemic transformation. At the same time, the Soviet leadership overestimates the power of rationalization to forestall and consciously prevent any systemic transformation. Neither view recognizes the possibility that extensive quantitative changes in techniques can eventually produce qualitative change. Again lessons from the past are painfully relevant for the present and future. In the 1920's it was naive for the Soviet leadership to assume that the rationalizers could entirely separate Western administrative techniques from their derivative administrative systems. Equally today it is deceiving to believe that the Soviet system can be completely impervious to the broader rationalizing effects of substantial changes in its techniques and mechanics. Yet, surprisingly we see a strange convergence in the thinking, though not the vision, of present-day Western and Russian observers of the Soviet Union. Whereas one group regards rationalization as the panacea for perfecting and preserving Soviet totalitarianism, the other sees it only as an ineffectual remedy for the Soviet system, which inevitably requires another revolution before basic change is possible. Probably neither extreme view is warranted, for the potential of rationalization to effect change will ultimately depend on how much and how far the political leadership is willing and required to use it. As ever, rationalization remains caught in a crossfire between politics and techniques, a tool to be molded by political will and political hands.

One senses that the most viable model for the Soviet system must somehow strike a balance between the populist and the bureaucratic formulas for rationalization. Public participation and institutionalization must figure as integral and inevitable features of the model. Having said this, however, we have already extended the scope and import of our analysis well beyond the rationalization of Soviet totalitarianism. Indeed, the persistent and baffling problem of properly mixing mobilization and organization is not peculiar to the rationalization of Communist and other totalitarian regimes but is the basic dilemma constantly facing all developing political systems, Communist and non-Communist. Thus, in the final analysis, the choices and challenges involved in the rationalization of totalitarianism must be viewed within the broader perspective of comparative politics and modernization theory.

Political Terror in the Post-Mobilization Stage

ALEXANDER DALLIN AND
GEORGE W. BRESLAUER

Political terror has been called the linchpin of totalitarianism.[1] Indeed, its use as an instrument of public policy in the Stalin era was unprecedented; and, with some significant variations, other Communist regimes have also resorted to using extensive and intensive terror, both after coming to power and later, during the phase of coercive mobilization. But what is its place in Communist systems once they pass beyond the mobilization stage? Although the evidence is still slim, we can observe that the incidence of political terror tends to decline sharply at that stage; moreover, the tendency toward its disuse is congruent with other things in the system that together characterize the dynamics of the post-mobilization stage.[2] Whether or not the use of terror is in fact abandoned in any particular case depends, of course, on a variety of intervening factors, such as the political culture, the rationality of policy-makers, and exogenous pressures, but the preconditions for such a shift are typically created at the post-mobilization stage.

This paper is based on a chapter from the authors' more comprehensive book, *Political Terror in Communist Systems* (Stanford, Calif., 1970).

[1] For interpretations stressing the centrality of terror in totalitarian systems, see, for example, Hannah Arendt, *The Origins of Totalitarianism*, rev. ed. (New York, 1968); Carl J. Friedrich and Zbigniew Brzezinski, *Totalitarian Dictatorship and Autocracy*, rev. ed. (Cambridge, Mass., 1965); and Merle Fainsod's valuable analysis *How Russia Is Ruled*, rev. ed. (Cambridge, Mass., 1963), ch. 13. Stimulating discussions are to be found in Barrington Moore's *Terror and Progress—USSR* (Cambridge, Mass., 1954) and Zbigniew Brzezinski's *The Permanent Purge* (Cambridge, Mass., 1956). See also Thomas P. Thornton, "Terror as a Weapon of Political Agitation," in Harry Eckstein, ed., *Internal War* (New York, 1964), pp. 71–83.

[2] The stages we refer to—takeover, mobilization, and post-mobilization—amount to a taxonomy of periods in Communist development, identified by the processes dominant in each stage. See also Chalmers Johnson's introductory chapter.

Coercion and Control

We take political terror to mean the arbitrary use, by organs of political authority, of severe coercion against individuals or groups, the credible threat of such use, or the arbitrary extermination of individuals or groups.[3] Terror as an instrument of power is best seen as a form of coercion, which in turn is one major instrumentality of political control.[4] Not all coercion, of course, is terror. Coercive means other than terror lack the elements of arbitrariness and unpredictability that are the distinguishing marks of terror.[5]

By political control we mean the shaping and channeling of political behavior either to secure compliance with particular directives or to mold attitudes so as to assure political stability through the effective acceptance of a given authority structure, its norms of social conduct, and its directives.[6] Thus conceived, all political control requires a system of sanctions that consists of "normative" power (positive, or

[3] Our definition is broadly consistent with the prevailing use of the term. Some of the insights in recent writings on political violence have proved useful for this study. See, for example, Henry Bienen, *Violence and Social Change* (Chicago, 1968) and the literature reviewed therein. An important contribution is Eugene V. Walter's *Terror and Resistance* (New York, 1969), which appeared after this paper was completed. Although some of Walter's conclusions seem questionable to us, his approach corresponds in many respects to that employed in this paper. But whereas Walter considers all terror to be violence designed to control (p. 14), and Alfred G. Meyer speaks of terror as "violence, applied or threatened" (*The Soviet Political System* [New York, 1965], p. 318), terror in our usage does not necessarily include violence: just as some violence involves no terror, some terror (e.g., intimidation) requires no violence.

[4] For a discussion of the concepts as here used, see Franz Neumann, "Approaches to the Study of Political Power," in *The Democratic and the Authoritarian State* (New York, 1957); Moore; and especially Amitai Etzioni's *A Comparative Analysis of Complex Organizations* (New York, 1961), pp. 3–27, and his *The Active Society* (New York, 1968). A somewhat similar approach is used in Ezra Vogel, "Voluntarism and Social Control," in Donald W. Treadgold, ed., *Soviet and Chinese Communism* (Seattle, Wash., 1967), pp. 168–84.

[5] Thornton (pp. 81–82) correctly suggests that terror is most effective when it is indiscriminate in appearance but highly discriminate in fact. We distinguish between victims of coercion and target groups meant to be affected by the process. The two groups are identical when the liquidation is kept secret (in what might be called "hermetic terror"); on the other hand, "demonstration terror" (or "reverberating terror") may induce diffuse terror reactions even well beyond the intended target groups. We should note, too, the semantic confusion stemming from the use of the term "terror" to refer to a policy, a process, a system of relationships, or a condition of felt anxiety.

[6] This use of the term does not, of course, include outright physical extermination.

symbolic, power), commonly called persuasion and including, for example, education, socialization, and the offer of prestige, recognition, or love; "material" power (also referred to as technical or utilitarian power), commonly called incentives and including wages, rewards, bonuses, bribes, and promotions; and "coercive" power (also referred to as negative or physical power), including such forms as penalties, terror, and regulatory and police power.

Any society with a division of labor and of social roles requires power to assure the acceptance of dominant values and the implementation of policy decisions. Thus any government may normally be expected to use all three types of power. As Franz Neumann has pointed out, it is precisely their mix in the system of sanctions that constitutes a central problem for the political scientist as well as for the practitioner.

Whereas coercion is most effective in securing short-term compliance, it is least effective in securing subjective commitment over long periods. Normative power, in contrast, is the most economical and thorough but also the most difficult to manipulate with discrimination. Coercion is most effective in deterring and punishing behavior; it is least effective in promoting voluntary cooperation and commitment. Yet, as Amitai Etzioni has shown, complex modern society tends to require resources, such as goodwill, creativity, and critical intelligence, that cannot be harnessed by coercive means alone.

Rational policy-makers in any system may be expected to prefer to avoid the costs and penalties of widespread coercion, but to do so they must presumably be able to draw on other forms of power—in particular, on effective socialization. Yet, because coercion maximizes alienation even when it secures compliant behavior, it tends to make more difficult the regime's task of achieving popular legitimacy and thus executing a shift in emphasis from coercive to normative relations with its citizenry. Terror thus represents for the regime both an effective tool and a costly challenge.

Terror and the Developmental Hypothesis

Developing polities, in which class most Communist systems can be included, experience certain characteristic dynamics, in the course of which political terror proves to have a number of purposes and functions.

In the period immediately following the seizure of power, especially in relatively poor and underdeveloped countries, a revolutionary regime tends to rely heavily on coercion to consolidate its power by effectively eliminating actual and potential enemies within the territory under its control and by deterring hostile acts. Even if it comes to power with a measure of popular support, a revolutionary regime may have no meaningful alternative to the use of coercion, for it does not possess the base for adequate material incentives (which moreover, may be ideologically unacceptable to Communist elites, particularly in the regime's early phases); and it cannot quickly create sufficient normative dedication to the regime or to common values, because indoctrination and socialization at best require time. But the use of political terror for the assurance of survival and the consolidation of power in the first stage of a revolutionary regime is inherently limited: if the system survives, the success of the operation renders superfluous further resort to it for this function.

It is at the next stage that purposive terror becomes a dominant feature of the system: fear becomes an organizing principle of "permanent revolution" (to use Sigmund Neumann's phrase), of what social scientists have more recently labeled a mobilization regime. Mobilization, as a process, entails the acquisition of power by the state over the resources within the society; by the "mobilization stage," however, we mean that stage in which the regime mounts a major effort toward reaching one or more critical middle-range goals, such as industrialization, by directing all the needed resources toward this purpose at the expense of other goals and needs. The process of mobilization then becomes a central means toward this end. As a result, political control at this stage is extended to all members and associations of the society. Here terror comes to serve the two major objectives of the regime: on the one hand, political control; on the other, change, with the leadership typically attempting to carry out drastic transformations of society, the economy, and the citizen.

But the elite, committed as it is to such radical changes—whether for ideological or for power-political reasons—is bound to encounter and generate resistance and alienation, since the changes it is determined to carry out will necessarily clash with the values and perceived interests of significant sectors of society. Anticipating such hostility, the authorities, in line with their preconceptions and images of class or group loyalties and grievances, may identify certain strata as requiring suppression, intimidation, or removal. Typically such measures require the use of terror.

Massive transformation programs under Communist regimes, such as rapid industrialization and the collectivization of agriculture, have been characterized by intense commitment and short timetables. To secure the crucial "breakthrough"[7] requires a mobilization and reallocation of human and natural resources that will impose considerable strains and stresses on society and the economy. And, as Barrington Moore argues persuasively, everything else being equal, the more rapid and more extensive the change, the greater and more bitter the alienation of the population. Organized terror now serves to ensure compliant behavior during such a period of change, and to this extent has a rational base.

Communist practice, however, has typically moved beyond these paroxysms of directed change, with totalitarian features increasingly shaping the system. Most instances of massive political terror under Communism appear to have served the functions of destroying or inhibiting all rival authorities and of insulating the population from all incongruent value systems. The net effect is to eliminate all organized political opposition and to facilitate socialization by exposing the population to a single, unchallenged system of values.[8]

But this process tends to have a dynamic of its own. Reaching beyond actually or potentially culpable individuals who become the victims of terror, the process begins to engulf entire social groups on the basis of "negative loyalty indicators" and automatic arrest categories. As Alfred G. Meyer has aptly remarked, this process amounts to the bureaucratization of class warfare. In turn, from specific categories of "open enemies," whether real or imagined, it is extended to other sectors of society by a regime firmly committed to the pursuit of monolithic authority, the total control of all subgroups, and the suppression of all divided allegiance. But whereas the Maoist strategy defines the "out-group"—those who, in Bolshevik jargon, are destined for the garbage heap of history—so narrowly as to leave open the possibility of reeducating most "class-alien" elements, the Stalinist per-

[7] A "breakthrough" refers to the process by which an elite overcomes restraints on its ability to implement a program of revolutionary change. See Otto Kirchheimer, "Confining Conditions and Revolutionary Breakthroughs," *American Political Science Review*, LIX: 4 (Dec. 1965), 964–74. A more specific definition describes it as "a process designed to alter or destroy values, structures, and behaviors which are perceived by a revolutionary elite as comprising or contributing to the actual or potential existence of alternative centers of political power." Kenneth T. Jowitt, "A Comparative Analysis of Leninist and Nationalist Elite Ideologies and Nation-Building Strategies" (mimeo., Berkeley, Calif., 1968), p. 1.

[8] For a discussion of political terror at the mobilization stage, see Dallin and Breslauer, *Political Terror in Communist Systems*, chs. 3–5. A related aspect is what has been labeled a "passion for unanimity." For a thorough discussion of its various roots and functions see Edgar Schein, *Coercive Persuasion* (New York, 1961), esp. pp. 62–110.

ception of the malleability of human nature imposes a far narrower definition of the "in-group"—those who can be trusted as, and those who can be "transformed" into, good Stalinist Communists. The momentum of political terror is thus further increased by additional variables, such as the personality of dictators like Stalin.

Over time, however, the relative priority of the two objectives— control and change—tends to shift, and so does the place of political terror relative to other means that can serve the same functions. As other essays in this volume argue, the more the system succeeds in attaining its middle-range objectives, the more it generates forces that require its own modification. Particularly as a result of these unintended consequences of modernization the counterproductivity of political terror becomes clearer as the system moves beyond its mobilization stage.

The Characteristics of the Post-Mobilization Stage

Political terror may well persist in a variety of ways—as the residual product of surviving institutions and processes of coercion sometimes fitfully resorted to, as a diffuse anxiety based on the lively memory of the prior application of terror, or as the *ultima ratio* that remains available to the state. Nevertheless, the dramatic change that typically occurs at this stage is one of kind, not only of degree. Such a change may come about in three ways. Calculable forms of coercion may be substituted for arbitrary forms; this is seen, for example, in the role of the judicial system and legal norms, the routine tasks of the uniformed police, and various (at times, less predictable) forms of social pressure and public intimidation. There may occur a shift in the balance among the three alternative sanction systems and, more specifically, a relatively greater reliance on normative and material instead of coercive power. Finally the total scope of political control or the assets expended for it by the ruling elite may decrease. One or more of these processes may be involved in the rearrangement of the political control system at this stage.

The changes relevant to the fate of political terror are outcomes, either desired or unintended, of the prior forced-modernization process and of earlier policy choices. Thus at the mobilization stage the elite aims at a fundamental transformation of socioeconomic relations and of individual human nature, whereas at the post-mobilization stage it tends to realize that economic development has become increasingly self-sustaining and no longer dependent on inefficient coercive mobilization. One may posit, moreover, that all industrial societies tend to require or ultimately generate a stable matrix of role expectations. Finally, whatever its rhetoric,[9] the elite tends in practice to end up neglecting or ignoring other transformation objectives previously accepted as ideologically "given."[10]

Whereas at the mobilization stage Communist policy-makers may resort to social prophylaxis and the system-wide "institutionalization of universal suspicion," at the subsequent stage entire social strata are no longer subject to elimination or isolation. On the one hand, regime and society now tend toward a "substantial consensus,"[11] and coercion now serves largely to control dissent, not to consolidate or extend power. On the other hand, no more transformation breakthroughs are usually contemplated or attempted.[12] Whereas mobilization for fundamental change requires substantial coercion, the maintenance of a system of effective political control does not normally demand an equal amount of coercive power. This distinction appears to be congruent with the dichotomy between a prescriptive and a restrictive system: directed transformation requires the prescription of courses of action, and more terror, but a system that has eschewed coercive mobilization requires only restriction within certain boundaries of the tolerable, without specifying mandatory behavior.

Moreover, the greater resource base that has meanwhile developed makes possible a partial shift from coercive power to material power, or incentives, while the socialization process vigorously promoted by the regime presumably assures enough acquiescence to make possible a similar shift toward normative power: ideology gradually turns into a stable value system (to use Chalmers Johnson's formulation), which, despite prior alienation, becomes a source of normative support.

To be sure, the decision-makers are confronted with the necessity of making new and difficult choices. Pressures for the abatement of terror abound, a fact reinforcing the impossibility of a total prescription of behavior. But to curtail terror is to permit more overt dissent. There is independent support for the proposition that mild coercion

---

[9] See Robert C. Tucker, "The Deradicalization of Marxist Movements," *American Political Science Review*, LXI: 2 (June 1967), 343–58.

[10] In Chalmers Johnson's terms, the "goal culture" is silently abandoned as the "ideology" is transformed into a stable system of values. See also Moore, *Terror and Progress*, pp. 190 *et seq.*

[11] Carl J. Friedrich, "Totalitarianism: Recent Trends," *Problems of Communism*, XVII: 3 (May-June 1968), 34.

[12] The Eastern European experience does not entirely conform to this "ideal type," since collectivization in most countries took place in the post-1956 period. These years can properly be considered a twilight phase before the "derivative" systems fully passed beyond the mobilization stage.

tends to be more effective than extreme terror in producing desired performance.[13] Furthermore, when severe terror abates, the strain within the individual citizen to bring his attitudes into consonance with his compliant behavior is likely to increase. Such an adjustment may take one of two forms: a change in attitudes producing greater support for the regime, or a change in behavior producing greater manifest dissent or deviance. The experience of the post-mobilization stage in the Soviet Union and in Eastern Europe tends to bear out this view, for the reduction of political terror has both strengthened the legitimacy of Communist regimes and significantly increased the amount of overt dissent. But especially in instances where the shift in policy follows a change in leadership or evidence of the leaders' "good faith," even previously alienated elements of the population may now be prepared to give the new leaders a chance to promote precisely the kinds of changes likely to increase the regime's legitimacy.

Still, terror as an instrument of purposive policy does not erode or wither "on its own," even as a consequence of systemic changes. The decline in its use requires active or passive, explicit or tacit, decision-making. Whether, when, or in what form such decisions are made in a given polity cannot be predicted. In essence, the decision-makers' assessment of the possibility or necessity of dispensing with the use of political terror depends on a combination of events at the time, elite perception, and elite priorities. Changes in these factors may be expected to bring about a changed assessment of the relative costs and benefits of political terror.

We find, for example, that the elite, and to an even greater extent the increasingly articulate corpus of experts, now tend to put a higher premium on criteria of regularity and predictability, such as legal norms and procedures. As Max Weber wrote,

Bureaucratization offers above all the optimum possibility for carrying through the principle of specializing administrative functions according to purely objective considerations. . . . The "objective" discharge of business primarily means a discharge of business according to *calculable rules*, and "without regard to persons." . . . The peculiarity of modern culture, and specifically of its technical and economic basis, demands this very "calculability" of results.[14]

Likewise, the elite typically gives greater weight than it earlier did to considerations of economic efficiency, to the rationalization of production, distribution, and administration, and to technological and sci-

---

[13] We show this in Dallin and Breslauer, ch. 7.

[14] Max Weber, *Wirtschaft und Gesellschaft*, trans. in H. H. Gerth and C. Wright Mills, eds., *From Max Weber: Essays in Sociology* (New York, 1958), p. 215.

entific innovation. It is also likely to be more aware of the inverse relationship between information and coercion, which David Apter, among others, has pointed out. The need for a freer flow of objective information "upward" is now likely to be perceived more keenly, and there is likely to be greater recognition that political terror, because it paralyzes the information flow, tends to make an objective assessment of the system's operation doubly difficult.[15]

In any polity, as the structure of society changes in the course of modernization there tends to be greater role specialization and interest aggregation. At this stage many of the arguments of informal subgroups tend to be mutually reinforcing in their negative attitude toward mass terror. A part of the creative intelligentsia may advocate a greater concern for socialist "humanism"; military men may be more conscious of or more outspoken about the consequences of political terror for military competence and capabilities; managerial personnel, planners, and scientists may be more keenly aware of the costs of terror in economic growth, the waste of skilled manpower and scarce resources, and the inhibition of innovation and invention.

Thus the political elite, increasingly obliged or willing to recognize such attitudes, is likely to reevaluate the use of terror in terms of changing elite priorities; and, weighing the costs of terror as it knows them against the possible costs of doing without terror as it foresees them, if it feels secure enough it is likely to opt for a drastic reduction in the use of terror.[16]

If the leadership finds that political socialization has progressed to the point where the regime's legitimacy may be taken for granted and "more and more citizens have obviously accepted the values of the regime as their own, the Party can rely more . . . on peer-group pressure" and can substitute "majority tyranny" for overt terror.[17] Under

[15] See David E. Apter, *The Politics of Modernization* (Chicago, 1965), pp. 40 *et seq.*; see also Friedrich and Brzezinski, *Totalitarian Dictatorship and Autocracy*, p. 129, and Moore, *Terror and Progress*, p. 170.

[16] Of course the choice need not be so explicit: it may well be existential or incremental; but the ingredients are likely to be those suggested here. Moreover, if the transition to the post-mobilization stage is accompanied by, or is the consequence of, a change in leadership, the successors may be eager to dispel any "guilt by association" as heirs to a regime widely identified with the use of terror.

[17] Meyer, *The Soviet Political System*, pp. 331–32. One may of course conceive of situations in which the counterproductive, alienating consequences of terror in the mobilization stage are so disastrous as to preclude the production of such legitimacy. By the same token, such a regime may or may not have successfully achieved, or abandoned, its "transfer goal," which we posit as a condition for the transition beyond the mobilization stage. A more balanced allocation of resources to multiple goals is the process that distinguishes the post-mobilization stage.

such conditions decision-makers typically conclude that political terror—such as the extermination or persecution of individuals and
groups without due process or cause, and with pervasive popular
anxiety as its outcome—has become, or threatens to become, counter-
productive.[18] Although such a conclusion and its "organizational consequences" are likely to be resisted by some elements within the elite,
either because of ideological and bureaucratic rigidity or because of
their own vested interests, the trend toward unintended but irreversible pluralism in the elite and in the society militates for a decline in
the use of terror.

After Stalin

The experiences of the Soviet Union and Eastern Europe show that
whereas in the post-Stalin years there was indeed a striking change in
the use of political terror, the transition to a new stage may itself be a
drawn-out process full of zigzags, ambiguities, and contradictions.

The fact of Stalin's disappearance as an authority figure had a powerful liberating effect on his successors, making it virtually impossible for any of them to use or risk using physical violence against intra-
elite rivals.[19] Those who favored a drastic cut in the role of the secret
police and the use of coercive measures were fortunate that a broad
coalition so promptly agreed on the forcible removal of Lavrenti
Beria, for this action led to the extensive dismantling of the terror
apparatus and the subordination of the security services to the party;
it was also important for the satellite countries, for it triggered a
similar weakening of Soviet security control in Eastern Europe. Although the Beria affair was but a specific expression of the elite's
insecurity, it had significant systemic consequences; in fact, it is hard
to think of other circumstances that could have been equally effective
in creating the preconditions for the changes in the role of terror that

---

[18] Terror may or may not have been dysfunctional at an earlier point without
this circumstance having been perceived, much less acted upon, by a committed
leader.

[19] Robert A. Dahl has argued that "the prospects of successful coercion decline
when opposition groups improve their own opportunities to resort to defensive
violence if they are threatened with coercion." One of the key factors in the transition to nonviolent political relations between government and opposition is the
perception of the "limited preponderance of coercive forces" available to the government. The implication is that tolerance of political opposition increases as
available instruments of force, such as police and army, become relatively weaker,
and similarly the perceived threat to the government lessens. Robert A. Dahl, ed.,
Political Oppositions in Western Democracies (New Haven, Conn., 1966), pp. xiii–
xiv.

ensued in the following decade. But the underlying trends followed essentially the pattern outlined on the preceding pages.

Some of the major trends of the Khrushchev era were the rejection of Stalinism, an attempt to foster an ideological revival, and what the Maoists were to assail as "economism," i.e., the priority of economic over political goals. Functionally, all three were inversely related to the use of terror. Reacting to the experience of the Stalin era, at least some leaders thought terror had exacted what now seemed an excessive price: a paralyzing atomization of society reflecting its members' fear of communicating with each other, diffuse anxiety within the elite as well as throughout the population, and a stifling of creativity and candor. They tried now to kindle a new utopian commitment with greater stress on participation, on voluntary (even extra-legal) administrative and control mechanisms, mirroring the alleged beginnings of "withering" state institutions as the system ostensibly moved toward the higher stage of Communism. The new leadership responded likewise to pressures for decentralization in administration and to a lesser extent in economic planning, pressures for autonomy in management, for encouragement of controlled initiative and innovation, and for a style of experimentation that presupposed some tolerance of error and failure. All of these goals were incompatible with reliance on terror. Furthermore, the new concern with such values as efficiency, rationality, and predictability, even if logically incompatible with some of the above ends, also worked against the persistence of terror.[20]

In brief, the Soviet Union has since 1956 witnessed four significant, albeit inconsistently implemented, changes with regard to coercion: the abatement of coercive mobilization; the disappearance of diffuse violence as transformation breakthroughs are no longer attempted; the de facto disappearance of atomization thanks to both the objective constraints that "society" has begun to impose on the organs of government and the lessening of anxiety in interpersonal relations; and the halting, zigzagging, but dominant tendency to move from a highly prescriptive system to an essentially restrictive one. Even if the regime has continued to feel a need to reaffirm its traditional com-

[20] Among accounts of the Khrushchev era, see, for example, Merle Fainsod, *How Russia Is Ruled*, pp. 447 *et seq.*; Fainsod's "Transformation in the Communist Party of the Soviet Union," in Treadgold, *Soviet and Chinese Communism*, pp. 65–72; Wolfgang Leonhard, *The Kremlin after Stalin* (New York, 1962); and Michel Tatu, *Power in the Kremlin* (New York, 1969). On the changing role of ideology, see Kurt Marko, *Evolution wider Willen* (Graz, 1968).

mitment to unanimity, even if Khrushchev felt impelled time and again to threaten and cajole dissident intellectuals and inveigh against the "conspiracy of silence" on their part, even if the bureaucracy still often responded in a Stalinist manner to nonconformity, the compliant mass of the Soviet population has been generally immune from terror.

It may be well here to remind ourselves of our initial definition of terror as a policy of severe and arbitrary coercion or its credible threat. We do find in recent Soviet practice the substitution of selective intimidation for mass terror, accompanied by widespread uncertainty about the intended scope of the intimidation and the credibility of threats. Especially in the post-Khrushchev years, severe coercion has again been applied but largely against certain fairly well-defined zones of society, such as dissidents among the cultural intelligentsia. However distasteful this coercion may be, it is generally not "arbitrary" but predictable. Its victims have usually been aware of the risks they have taken by, say, sending manuscripts to be published abroad or protesting against the Soviet occupation of Czechoslovakia. Whereas terror as a felt condition is no doubt experienced by some citizens, political terror as a matter of general public policy, severe and arbitrary, is no longer employed.

In the years following Stalin's death most of the forced-labor camps were emptied and abandoned; many secret-police officials were replaced or purged; various former functions of the MGB and MVD were transferred to other agencies; and many prominent victims of the Stalin era were posthumously rehabilitated. However, especially since Khrushchev's ouster in 1964 many victims have not been cleared of spurious charges; the rhetoric of Stalinism persists to a disquieting extent; and various dissenting individuals and groups continue to be repressed. No doubt there are significant variations in the way different people perceive the new situation. Some citizens are clearly intimidated by threats and by examples of deterrent action. "Here, too, memory plays a key role, leading many people to exaggerate the intensity of threats and to assume that they are intended to apply broadly rather than narrowly even when this is not the case."[21] Yet others evidently ignore the pressures for conformity and are able to adapt themselves rather successfully to the new conditions. It is true that there remains a "credibility gap" between threat and action, an uncertainty that engenders insecurity because in large measure the

21 Jeremy Azrael, "Is Coercion Withering Away?" *Problems of Communism*, XI: 6 (Nov.-Dec. 1962), 16.

regime is unable or unwilling to define the boundaries of tolerance and deviance. The system continues in a state of tension between the powerful pressures to adjust, tolerate, and let live, and the recurrent impulse to clamp down, enforce, and control. Perversely the diminishing of fear, especially on the part of the oldest and youngest generations, who feel they have the least to lose, stimulates the expression of nonconformity and dissent—in works of art, in private and group petitions, in manuscripts circulated but not published, and occasionally but rarely in public demonstrations—that in turn tempts officials committed to conformity to respond with a "backlash" of greater repression.

In this regard Soviet domestic policy toward members of the intelligentsia as well as toward spokesmen of certain sectarian and ethnic groups has paralleled Soviet vacillation between tolerance of diversity and violent enforcement of conformity in Eastern Europe. Many of the "liberal" currents of the Khrushchev era proved remarkably easy to reverse after his ouster. And although political mass terror has by no means returned, the techniques employed to deal with dissent—such as "political justice," confinement in mental institutions, exile from specified places of residence, threats of dismissal from employment, and public intimidation—are at times terroristic in impact even if (and this is of course all-important in terms of our definition of terror) their application remains generally quite restricted and predictable.

In Eastern Europe, the analogous process began as a "derivative" echo of the Soviet changes; but indigenous and autonomous elements soon asserted themselves, especially as Soviet control weakened.[22] Most dramatically, the process was marked by attempted riots, revolts, and revolutions, consequences of a situation in which terror was scarcely used but the regimes had not gained much legitimacy. Terror may generate alienation, and the abandonment of terror may paradoxically permit the expression of such alienation in the form of organ-

[22] In Yugoslavia the leadership—before Stalin's death—chose to desist from political terror, not because "objective conditions" (such as substantial industrialization) forced it, but because of the general relaxation made possible by the legitimacy it enjoyed, made necessary (in its view) by exogenous circumstances and made desirable by its effort to present Yugoslavia as the paragon of undeformed socialism. On this point, see also the chapter by Lowenthal, above. Another suggestive perspective on the developments in Eastern Europe is H. Gordon Skilling's "Background to the Study of Opposition in Communist Eastern Europe," *Government and Opposition*, III: 3 (Apr.-July 1968).

ized resistance or revolt, or more mildly in various forms of civil dissent. In Eastern Europe, most regimes have been faced with this dilemma.

Terror, Authority, and Stability

What are some of the unintended consequences for the stability of Communist systems of policy choices leading to the decompression of political control and the disuse of terror? Here the distinction between intra-elite behavior and mass patterns of behavior becomes important.

The decline in the use of terror was a precondition for such intra-elite challenges to the incumbent leadership as that of the so-called "anti-party group" against Khrushchev in June 1957, the successful challenge to Khrushchev in October 1964, and the replacement of Antonín Novotný by Alexander Dubček in January 1968. If after the execution of Beria and his associates the new pattern of quiet retirement of defeated leaders was welcome to those involved, it also reduced the risks of vying for power. Whether or not the assurance of survival results in a stronger tendency toward collective leadership or more frequent changes in leadership is an open question. But it is probably true that

the elimination of violence as the decisive instrumentality of political competition—a move that was perhaps prompted by the greater institutional maturity of Soviet society, and which was in any case made inevitable by the downgrading of the secret police and the public disavowals of Stalinism—meant that Khrushchev, unlike Stalin, could not achieve *both* social dynamism and the stability of his power. Stalin magnified his power as he strove to change society; to change society Khrushchev had to risk his power.[23]

The post-mobilization leader tends to be caught in a web of conflicting interests, and—lacking the coercive apparatus of his predecessors —he is likely to find himself obliged, much in the manner of a leader in a pluralistic polity, to form coalitions and "pay off" others to secure acceptance and implementation of new policy departures whenever they conflict with the vested interests of competing groups and bureaucratic factions.

But whether the stability of a regime's leadership is impaired or enhanced by the abandonment of terror as a means of conflict resolution, there remains the question of the stability of the system as a whole. We have earlier argued that the coercive methods of Communist mobilization regimes tend to produce substantial alienation with-

[23] Zbigniew Brzezinski, "The Soviet Political System: Transformation or Degeneration?" *Problems of Communism*, XV: 1 (Jan.-Feb. 1966), 6.

in the population; we would suggest that the higher the level of terror relative to the normative and material power used, the greater the alienation (other variables being held constant). It appears that widespread alienation is only one necessary precondition for revolutionary initiative "from below"; evidently signs of elite weakness or divided leadership are also necessary to spark the masses to protest action. Such a division within the elite may have various causes; conflict over the wisdom of using terror may well be one such cause.

The use of terror against those outside the elite can generally be rationalized by the "establishment," but its use within the elite group typically causes considerable strain among the members: it may engender insecurity; it may lead to a questioning of the normative power on which the elite is based; it may invite further violations of the group's code of behavior; it may give rise to counter-elites denouncing the use of coercion by those who had also provided the normative power upon which the organization was based.[24]

To prevent or overcome such a crisis of organizational integration, the elite must strive not to dilute the power of its symbols and norms and, to this end, must safeguard a high degree of "consistency of command." By this we mean that "all commands in a system are consistent among themselves, whether they originate from a single source or from several sources."[25] Clearly an inconsistency of command may threaten the integration of the normative subsystem and in turn create conditions for a mass revolt. Whereas in authentic post-mobilization regimes the relaxation of terror presupposes the availability of normative and material assets that may be used as functional equivalents of terror, the reduction in the use of terror in derivative Communist systems need not presuppose the availability of such equivalents and—in their absence—may create the preconditions for a revolutionary situation.

In the Czech and East German riots of 1953 an alienated mass

---

[24] We are assuming that we are dealing here with a largely normatively-integrated organization, for which, as Chalmers Johnson observes, "the use of force in the exercise of authority must be rare and carefully circumscribed." By definition, the use of terror against members of such an organization cannot normally be deemed legitimate by the other members. See Chalmers Johnson, *Revolutionary Change* (Boston, 1966), p. 31. We do not mean to suggest that strains or guilt stemming from terror against elite members are the only basis for normative disintegration. The norms and values that define the organization's identity and mission may, over time, show themselves to be irrelevant or incorrect reflections of reality.

[25] Karl W. Deutsch, "Cracks in the Monolith," in Carl J. Friedrich, ed., *Totalitarianism* (Cambridge, Mass., 1954), p. 310. This refers not to bureaucratic orders but to the "authoritative allocation of values."

faced a more or less united elite and a loyal armed force. The "consistency of command" was successfully maintained, and the popular challenges were easily quashed, sometimes with resort to violence. The situation was significantly different where crises of self-legitimation developed simultaneously within the elite: in Hungary under Imre Nagy in 1954–55; in Poland after Józef Swiatlo's defection and Gomulka's reappearance in 1954–55; in the Soviet Union after the Twentieth Congress of the CPSU in 1956. In all three instances, profound doubt and in some cases a sense of guilt was felt by members of the elite when the leadership was no longer able to maintain ideological unity among "captive minds" and felt obliged to denounce previously sacred symbols.[26] In 1956 the Hungarian and Polish mass revolts readily found allies and leaders within the elite. In 1968 the Czechoslovak elite opposition, in turn, found a ready and sympathetic response in the population. In these three instances, the alliance was an essential condition for successful revolution, whatever its ultimate fate.[27] In contrast, when terror was reduced in the Soviet Union, Rumania, and Yugoslavia, compensatory normative appeals either existed or were generated in time to avoid a crisis.

In the Soviet Union, the longevity of the regime itself contributed to its survival; there had been time for the routinization of behavior and the reinforcing ritualization of belief, essentially an acceptance of official norms of conduct; the bulk of the population had been successfully socialized to the goals of the leadership; economic hardships and political repression had been mitigated somewhat; and there existed such pacifiers as "pride in jobs well done . . . the psychic rewards of self-respect gained from altruistic behavior, the feeling of serving the common good and being approved by the party [leadership]";[28] finally, the regime had led the country through an arduous war to national victory. In Yugoslavia, because of its role in World War II, the regime had a broad popular base that it managed to extend and strengthen as a consequence of its "hard" line vis-à-vis the Soviet Union and its "responsive" line at home after the Stalin-Tito break in

[26] The elite's trauma of legitimacy, aroused by doubts about terror, was further compounded by the effects of inconsistency of command on the elite's confidence in the leadership's ability to move toward the attainment of economic abundance and to maintain the integration of the party organization.

[27] This argument leans on the masterly analysis in Paul Kecskemeti, *The Unexpected Revolution* (Stanford, Calif., 1961), esp. chs. 9, 10. Inconsistency of command need not necessarily produce a revolutionary situation. The experience of Yugoslavia supports the view that an elite pattern and a mass pattern are needed for successful revolution.

[28] Kecskemeti, p. 96.

1948. Finally, in Rumania, by asserting autonomy and courageously standing up to the Soviet Union in 1958–64, a leadership imposed on a hostile population managed to gain the support and legitimacy it needed to become the symbol and champion of the national cause.

Two variables thus emerge as crucial for the stability of Communist polities after the abandonment of mass terror as an instrument of national policy. Everything else (including political culture, personalities, economic constraints, external pressures and threats) being equal, there must be organization (consistency of command) and compensatory incentives (functional equivalents of terror).[29] These conditions are also crucial for economic efficiency and political institutionalization even when such extreme challenges as riots and revolts do not occur.

So far, we have not dealt with the experiences of all Communist systems; in particular we have neglected China, which, like Cuba and North Vietnam, has neither completed its stage of coercive mobilization nor abandoned its commitment to far-reaching transformations at home. Furthermore, even if the objective conditions for an abatement of terror were present in China, they would not be likely to be translated into a significant change of policy as long as the Chinese leadership remains effectively committed to and capable of attempting attitudinal transformations, as exemplified by "thought reform." This orientation differs significantly from the Stalinist orientation, which was essentially directed toward securing compliant behavior, whatever the resulting dissonance between an individual's values and behavior.[30] If for Stalin a prescriptive strategy was in effect a timeless perspective, for Mao the task has been a far more utopian one—of remolding man, i.e., of changing underlying attitudes so that coercion could ultimately be abandoned without risk of deviance. There are reasons to think that sooner or later China's

[29] We advisedly leave out of consideration other dimensions of propitious revolutionary situations, since the introduction of variables not relevant to our argument would complicate and obscure the presentation. We have likewise chosen not to account for the varying patterns of economic conditions and demands. As for the level of economic development, the four countries in which riots and revolts occurred were more highly developed than Rumania, Bulgaria, and Albania. But the experience of Yugoslavia and the Soviet Union, where such outbreaks did not occur, shows that this is not in itself the decisive variable. Similarly, the role of intellectuals was considerable in Hungary, Poland, and Czechoslovakia; it was not in Rumania; on the other hand, it was also substantial in the Soviet Union and Yugoslavia, where no comparable mass pattern of revolt developed.

[30] For a discussion of terror in China, see Dallin and Breslauer, *Political Terror in Communist Systems*, ch. 5.

leaders will recognize the failure of their efforts to create a society in which the "new man" is ruled by means of normative power. But it remains to be seen when and how this utopian commitment will wither, and whether, more generally, China will then move to pursue a development strategy essentially similar to that of other Communist polities.

Functional Equivalents of Terror

It is a major theorem of functional analysis that "just as the same item may have multiple functions, so may the same function be diversely fulfilled by alternative items."[31] To prove the dispensability of political terror, we must show either that the functions it performs are no longer required or that there are alternatives, functional equivalents, ready to perform them.

To this end, we shall briefly review the major functions of terror, as we see them, in Communist systems. The survival and consolidation functions in operation at the takeover stage are, by definition, no longer required in the subsequent development of Communist polities. The transformation function, too, has no operational application once the mobilization stage is passed. Presumably any future effort to carry out fundamental transformations in the society, unlikely as it seems, would require a new mobilization under unforeseeable circumstances.

We have earlier referred to certain ancillary functions of terror. Indirectly, terror may contribute to mobilization and to the circulation of sub-elites by creating opportunities for the upward mobility of talent; it may also have normative effects, such as deflecting the blame for failures ("scapegoatism"). At the post-mobilization stage most of these functions—to the extent that they are needed—should be able to be served adequately by other techniques. In any event, coercive mobilization at this stage is abandoned, by definition; and terror was probably crucial to the fulfillment of only one of these functions, namely, the replacement of revolutionary cadres by younger specialists—by its very nature a nonrepetitive process.

The economic functions, forced labor for instance, are almost incidental in the total context of coercion; served by political terror in a highly inefficient and politically costly fashion, they can be better fulfilled by other means. As for the function of atomization, the very nature of the social processes characteristic of post-mobilization

---

[31] Robert K. Merton, *On Theoretical Sociology* (New York, 1967), pp. 87–88.

development makes atomization no longer practicable in fact, no longer desirable in the elite's judgment, and no longer functional in theory. The natural tendency of the system is to overcome the previous elements of atomization—a tendency reinforced by demands from within the system for better information and communication.

What remains to be examined are the political control and compliance functions of terror. These can best be seen in the framework of the three processes of substitution outlined in our discussion of the characteristics of the post-mobilization stage, on p. 196, above. The Khrushchev era provides a fine example of a many-faceted drive (resisted by bureaucratic and orthodox elements) for new "norms of legality" and due process. Whereas the courts continue to operate as agencies of political coercion, the trend has been in the direction of predictable and binding rules and procedures, beginning with the abolition of the Special Boards of the MVD and the abolition of the provisions in the Criminal Code permitting sentences "by analogy."[32] Though somewhat in conflict with the tendency toward due process but typical of the Khrushchev era, experimentation with volunteer bodies to bring social pressure to bear to secure conforming behavior provided another partial functional substitute for terror. The "people's militia" and the "comrades' courts" were examples of this effort, in part ideologically manipulated, in part intended to mobilize new resources in the struggle against deviance, and in part intended to absolve the government of direct involvement in the handling of minor misdemeanors.[33] Symptomatically, the further rationalization that came in the wake of Khrushchev's retirement led to the virtual replacement of these improvisations by regular judicial processes.[34] At the same time, the attempts to "turn back the clock" with regard

[32] See, for example, Harold J. Berman, *Justice in the USSR*, rev. ed. (New York, 1963); George Feifer, *Justice in Moscow* (New York, 1964); Darrell Hammer, "Law Enforcement, Social Control and the Withering of the State," *Soviet Studies*, XIV: 4 (Apr. 1963); Eugene Kamenka, "The Soviet View of Law," *Problems of Communism*, XIV: 2 (Mar.-Apr. 1965); and Ivo Lapenna, *Soviet Penal Policy* (London, 1968). For a thorough discussion of these trends, see John N. Hazard, *Communists and Their Law* (Chicago, 1969), esp. chs. 4 and 16.

[33] See, for example, Leon Lipson, "The New Face of 'Socialist Legality,' " *Problems of Communism*, VII: 4 (July-Aug. 1958), and "Socialist Legality: The Mountain Has Labored," *ibid.*, VIII: 2 (Mar.-Apr. 1959); Harold J. Berman and James W. Spindler, "Soviet Comrades' Courts," *Washington Law Review*, XXXVIII: 4 (Winter 1963); Dennis O'Conner, "Soviet People's Guards: An Experiment with Civic Police," *New York University Law Review*, XXXIX: 4 (June 1964).

[34] For the latest "Principles of Corrective-Labor Legislation" and the statute on "Preventive Detention in Custody," see *Pravda*, July 12, 1969, trans. in *Current Digest of the Soviet Press*, XXI: 29 (Aug. 13, 1969), 3-13.

to political nonconformity have led a leading British student of Soviet affairs to comment that in a modern industrial society,

if it is to operate to the full extent of its capacity, contracts must be observed, political considerations must be kept within strict limits, individuals must be able to do their work in circumstances which guarantee their security as long as they fulfill their obligations to the enterprise. As compared with Stalin's era, there has been enormous improvement already in these respects. Characteristically, while in the past few years legality has sadly declined in other areas, it has remained unaffected, or has even improved, in the technical and economic spheres. But since legality is indivisible (whatever the present rulers of Soviet Russia may think) it will be necessary to extend its operation to all aspects of life without exception before there can be any certainty that it will operate reliably in the area where it is so essential to the technocrats and the planners.[35]

A second and perhaps obvious process, again best illustrated in Soviet practice, is the shift from coercive to normative power. The pervasive machinery of political persuasion, the many instrumentalities of political socialization, and the sustained efforts to inculcate official values and attitudes in the citizenry are not new. What was novel in the Khrushchev era was the effort to stage an ideological revival and to sponsor a new utopianism. After a generation of cynicism and neglect of utopian perspectives, the new era reflected both naiveté and a quest for simpler answers, purer goals, and more glamorous targets. Accordingly the 1961 CPSU Program terminated the "dictatorship of the proletariat" and foresaw a selective "withering" of state institutions, although the party and its powers were to remain unchecked. As a high Soviet official explained the orientation of the moment,

The party as an ideological-political organization depends completely and exclusively on persuasion of the masses, whereas the state depends on force as well as on persuasion. . . . The methods of persuasion . . . are gaining more and more ground in the life of Soviet society, and under Communism they will become the sole regulator of relations among people.[36]

---

[35] Leonard Schapiro, "Collective Lack of Leadership," *Survey*, 70–71 (Winter-Spring 1969), 200.

[36] G. Shitarev, "Partiia i stroitel'stvo kommunizma," *Politicheskoe samoobrazovanie*, 8 (1960), 22–23. A programmatic forecast of the continual shift from coercion to persuasion, as the Soviet Union ostensibly moves closer to full Communism, concluded that, although agencies of coercion were still essential, "the sphere of coercion . . . is now being narrowed. . . . Direct administrative coercion is increasingly being replaced by other forces of economic, political, and moral suasion. State coercion is getting ever closer to social coercion, to various forms of persuasion." P. S. Romashkin, "O roli ubezhdeniia i prinuzhdeniia v Sovetskom gosudarstve," *Sovetskoe gosudarstvo i pravo*, 2 (1960), 26–29. For an analysis of the problems of coercion and persuasion in the Khrushchev era, see Herbert Ritvo, "Totalitarianism without Coercion?" *Problems of Communism*, IX: 6 (Nov.-Dec. 1960).

In various forms and to varying degrees, education and persuasion have continued to be stressed as means of political control, albeit in recent years with less millennial and extravagant expectations.

But, above and beyond the simple fact of a person's membership in a community, and disregarding for the moment mere habit as well as the elements of specifically Communist education and propaganda, what would lead citizens to do voluntarily what they had been or would otherwise have been coerced to do? Of necessity, the answer must be impressionistic and highly generalized. Such voluntary commitment usually has roots in experiences or attitudes that give rise to emotions either of pride and satisfaction—such as achievement or a shared sense of purpose and direction—or of insecurity, whether from threats or fear of external or internal forces. Both are apt to produce greater identification with and reliance on the system and its leadership.

National identification is one such sentiment. One might differentiate between manipulated and spontaneous national emotions, between reactive nationalism aroused in response to external threats, as in the Soviet Union in World War II and in Rumania and North Vietnam more recently, and authentic nationalism, which is part and parcel of the values and myths with which the regime comes to power, China being the outstanding example. Yet it is impossible to specify just how much diffuse support a regime needs, or thinks it needs, to dispense with terror. At the crucial stage of sanction substitution, numerous intervening variables may alter the outcome from case to case.

Another source of positive identification is belief in the system's effectiveness, especially when reflected in economic growth evidenced by the system's capacity to satisfy consumer demands and to raise living standards. Finally, positive identification may be produced for some groups by social and political participation. This may be true of those relatively few (except in Yugoslavia) who participate in making rules and decisions; but it may also be true of the many more citizens who are involved in ritual ratification, in various forms of implementation, and in mass organizations, or what has been labeled "participatory bureaucracy."[37] We should add that these possible forms and degrees of identification may be expected to vary considerably. Things are likely to be a good deal more complex than, say, a simple correlation of regime effectiveness with regime legitimacy. In practice, positive responses may well range from tacit and rou-

[37] Alfred G. Meyer, "USSR, Incorporated," *Slavic Review*, XX: 3 (Oct. 1961), 369–76.

tinized acquiescence in norms of social conduct on the part of those who support the system as a matter of self-interest, for example, to diffuse support based on the internalizing of the regime's values.[38]

In the 1960's Soviet officialdom apparently concluded that the heavy reliance on "moral suasion" had been misplaced. Ideology seemed to meet with widespread skepticism. After Khrushchev's ouster most of his doctrinal innovations were ignored. The rate of economic growth slowed for a time, and vertical mobility became more restricted. Despite the continuing esoteric argument over moral vs. material incentives—both in the Soviet Union and in Communist Eastern Europe—a growing effort was made to provide more "material incentives," tangible, nonpolitical rewards in the form of additional compensation, bonuses, goods, and services for increased productivity or efficiency and for loyal, rational, and innovative performance.[39]

Although conflicting emphases in public pronouncements appeared to reflect different views among Communist officials on the preferred balance of normative, material, and coercive power, such speeches and articles would typically stress all three. Curiously, they would often include a fourth element—organization. As early as 1961 the head of the Central Committee's Department of Administrative Organs declared that in the Soviet state the "main method of governing is through persuasion, education, and organization" (adding that this "does not of course exclude the use of compulsion . . . [which] remains an important means of eradicating crime" but must be resorted to "only when all other methods have failed or when violation is particularly dangerous").[40] Similar references to organization were made even more frequently in the post-Khrushchev days. Whether or not bureaucratic organization per se creates support is a matter for further study. For our purposes, bureaucratic organization is best thought of as situated at the threshold of normative and coercive power, possessing characteristics of both. As an instrument

---

[38] Personal success in, or anticipation of, job satisfaction or advancement, educational opportunities, improvement of status, leisure, and creature comfort may have similar consequences, but these do not necessarily assure a more willing or eager acceptance of the regime's values. On the contrary, they may well generate "rising expectations," privatism, and a stronger quest for release from political control.

[39] It should be noted that the increase in material incentives is meant to serve purposes other than those served by terror. It may nonetheless be functional in building diffuse support.

[40] N. Mironov, "O sochetanii ubezhdeniia i prinuzhdeniia," *Kommunist*, 3 (1961), 64–69.

of political control, organization has since Lenin's time ranked high among Communist values.[41]

The third process by which we suggest political terror may be curtailed is by reducing the assets for or the total scope of political control. Only in Yugoslavia, where terror was abandoned largely for other reasons, has this process been explicitly acknowledged, though in Czechoslovakia the short-lived changes of 1968 showed how fast and how far the process can go. Yet conceptually such a retreat from totalism follows from the differentiation of state and society, from the development of greater subgroup articulation and autonomy— in short, from the gradual transition from a prescriptive to a restrictive system. But precisely because it clashes with so major and traditional an orientation, Communist elites have difficulty in acknowledging the necessity or desirability of meaningful autonomy, pluralism, or zones of depoliticization.

Official prescription in certain fields, such as science, has considerably lessened in post-Stalin Russia and Eastern Europe, and close observers have identified the demand for greater "party-free spheres" as a continuing object of political dispute.[42] Kádár's formula, "He who is not against us, is with us," implies a similar zone of indifference. It is true that the Soviet regime, although it has become "less repressive," has not demonstrated any explicit willingness to become "less comprehensive."[43] But in practice the reduction in scope has occurred more often by dint of inefficiency than by political design, especially in Eastern Europe; and, more important, the leadership finds it increasingly difficult to focus its attention on all arenas that it would like to control. It is, in fact, functional for the leadership to avoid "overloads" by waiting for incidents to draw its attention to a given arena. Thus,

maintenance of "ideological purity" in the arts—whatever that means—is rarely at the center of Party attention for long. Occasionally, owing to a juncture of political circumstances, it can briefly become so. As soon as the leaders

[41] See, for example, Leonard Schapiro, *The Communist Party of the Soviet Union* (New York, 1959); and Philip Selznick, *The Organizational Weapon* (New York, 1951).

[42] Wolfgang Leonhard, "Politics and Ideology in the Post-Khrushchev Era," in Alexander Dallin and Thomas B. Larson, eds., *Soviet Politics since Khrushchev* (Englewood Cliffs, N.J., 1968), pp. 67–78. An authoritative editorial in the Warsaw *Trybuna Ludu*, Nov. 3, 1968, declared in condemning the Dubček regime: "It is impossible to grant the slogan of 'free play of forces' in a socialist society.... [Yet the Dubček regime] inclined to the concept of 'free play of forces' as a constitutional form of the socialist state."

[43] Leon Lipson, "Law: The Function of Extra-Judicial Mechanisms," in Treadgold, *Soviet and Chinese Communism*, p. 165.

turn away to a more pressing crisis or a more practical dilemma, officials of the second and third rank are left to cultivate political pastures of their own in the atmosphere the leaders have established. . . . That the regime may be distracted from its more intangible goals in the future as well is all the more probable in view of the continued ascendancy of economic over ideological tasks.[44]

Without terror, the costs of total enforcement or prescription are prohibitive.

How well Communist elites have learned this lesson is an open question. Just as Communist systems as a whole have found neither a stable equilibrium nor any clear formula of governance for the future, so the mix of sanction systems that they may employ remains in flux. Moreover, even in the absence of a single dictator able to project his own idiosyncrasies onto the entire society at will, there may be strong obstacles to the rational and irreversible abandonment of terror. As we have seen, bureaucratic rigidity, traditionalism, vestiges of ideological commitment, insecurity, suspiciousness, and the need for scapegoats, as well as overriding exogenous forces, may all delay, distort, and complicate the system's adaptation to the post-mobilization stage; and in the process Communist systems may experience fits of terror, like those exemplified recently by the treatment of "revisionists" in post-Dubček Czechoslovakia, of Jews in Poland, and of intellectual nonconformists in the Soviet Union.

But the Communist experience suffices to confirm the strength of the secular trend away from political terror—above all, owing to the growing pluralism and the awareness of the costs of terror. It shows, moreover, that functional equivalents can be substituted for terror without impairing the system's stability.

[44] Priscilla Johnson, *Khrushchev and the Arts: The Politics of Soviet Culture* (Cambridge, Mass., 1965), pp. 59–60.

Group Conflict and Political Change

H. GORDON SKILLING

Group conflict is present in every society and manifests itself politically to varying extents in all systems, Communist or non-Communist. This is an inescapable consequence of two ubiquitous realities of social and political life: first, the social heterogeneity of every community, whatever its political nature, and second, the diversity of opinion among men everywhere. Social differences, based for example on sex or age, on nationality or religion, or on occupational differences, are likely to produce some degree of political activity by what are often called "interest groups," each of which expresses demands common to a social category. Similarly, diversity in values or in attitudes toward public policy frequently produces politically active groups of like-minded persons, which we shall term "opinion groups." No political leader can ignore such interest and opinion groups, which constitute one of the ever-present realities of politics.[1]

Of course, the social and intellectual pluralism present in every social system does not necessarily generate political pluralism in the sense of a free and unfettered articulation of interests and opinions. The ideal type of pluralism would presumably consist of a universe of equal and autonomous political groups determining public policy as a result of their interplay, a kind of perfect political market in which policies reflect an automatic adjustment of conflicting interests and values. In fact, of course, no political system is pluralist accord-

[1] For a fuller discussion of groups in Communist systems, see H. Gordon Skilling, "Interest Groups and Communist Politics," *World Politics*, XVIII: 3 (Apr. 1966), 435–51; and the forthcoming book by Skilling and Franklyn J. C. Griffiths, eds., *Interest Groups in Soviet Politics* (Princeton, N.J.). Both sources provide extensive bibliographical references.

ing to such criteria. If political groups are active and significant they always differ in character, in strength, and in their degree of autonomy of action, and hence in their capacity to affect the making of policy. Moreover, groups are not the sole actors in the political process and must share the stage with other elements, such as leadership, in making and implementing decisions. Nor is the relationship of leadership and groups a one-way street, since leaders may influence and manipulate groups as well as be affected by them.

Nonetheless, whatever reservations may be made, it remains true that there will probably be some amount of group activity, and therefore some degree of pluralism, in any political system, no matter how authoritarian it may be. Communist systems will, however, differ profoundly with regard to the types of political groups present and active, their nature and strength, their relationship with each other, and their correlation with leadership. They will, that is, vary in the degree and kind of political pluralism present in each of them. A Communist system, it may be assumed, will never be fully totalitarian, nor will it be fully pluralist. It may, however, be anywhere between the two extremes: an ideal totalitarianism, where no groups exist or have relevance in politics, and a full pluralism, where many groups operate and exercise a decisive influence. The spectrum is a shifting one, too, as the relative importance of groups to each other and to those in power, and their salience in the system as a whole, change over time. In discussing Communist systems in terms of political groups we make no prior assumptions about the influence of groups in general or of particular groups, or about their significance in the working of the system as a whole. Above all, we do not assume that there is a necessary unilinear evolution toward greater and greater pluralism. Here I shall suggest some criteria for assessing the greater or lesser role of groups in a given Communist system and for differentiating Communist systems from each other.

The Nature of Political Groups

Political groups in Communist societies may be divided roughly into five categories according to their relative ability to articulate their interests. At the top of the pyramid of power are the "leadership groups" or "factions," which play a central and decisive role in policy-making. Below them are the "official or bureaucratic groups," such as the military, the security forces, the party apparatchiki, the state bureaucrats, and the managers, whose proximity to the first group and the power that they possess as part of the governing apparatus usually afford them ample opportunity to articulate their own interests and values, and those of other groups. At a lower, intermediate, level are the "intellectual groups," such as writers, journalists, scientists, economists, and scholars generally, who have no official authority but may sometimes exert considerable influence as a result of their knowledge and the opportunity to express their interests and values, and those of others, in the written and spoken word. At the base of the pyramid are "broad social groups," such as the workers and farmers, the nationalities and religious groups, and others based on age, sex, or region. These groups have much less chance of articulating their interests and values, since they have no direct access to those in positions of authority or to the media of communications, and do not possess the expertise of the elite groups. Finally, within each of these four categories are "opinion groups," differing from each other in values and viewpoints on public issues and often loosely allied with like-minded persons in other occupational or social categories. All these groups, whether they are based on common interests or common opinions, may in a sense be considered "political groups," since they constitute a factor in decision-making, if only as an object of consideration by others. More strictly, however, they should be regarded as political groups only if they have some opportunity to express their interests and opinions. This capacity for articulation is treated here as the defining characteristic of a political group, making it something more than a mere social category.[2]

My purpose here is to examine and compare the nature of political groups in the Soviet Union, China, and the Communist countries of Eastern Europe, to classify these ten countries at various periods in terms of the nature of group activity, and to estimate the relevance of these groups to political change.[3] Attention will be concentrated

[2] For a more detailed exposition, see Skilling and Griffiths.

[3] Citations are limited to sources in which a group approach has explicitly been attempted. For the Soviet Union, see Zbigniew Brzezinski, "The Soviet Political System: Transformation or Degeneration?" *Problems of Communism*, XV: 1 (Jan.-Feb. 1966), 1–15. Note Brzezinski's classification of groups into "policy groups," "specific interest groups," and "amorphous social groups," and his spectrum of opinions ranging from systemic left to systemic right. For Eastern Europe, see Jovan Djordjević, "Interest Groups and the Political System of Yugoslavia," in Henry W. Ehrmann, ed., *Interest Groups on Four Continents* (Pittsburgh, Pa., 1958), 197–228, 292–94; and H. Gordon Skilling, *The Governments of Communist East Europe* (New York, 1966), ch. 11. For China, see the papers by Michel Oksenberg, "Occupational Groups in Chinese Society and the Cultural Revolution," and Ezra F. Vogel, "The Structure of Conflict," both of which were pub-

on the groups below the highest level, leaving out of consideration the leadership groups or factions.[4] This does not imply that the latter are of little or no importance. On the contrary, the supreme power of decision-making in all Communist countries rests with the topmost leaders; thus conflicts between rival factions are extremely relevant to the political process. Moreover, as we shall note, the leaders have a significant role in articulating the interests of other groups as well as aggregating them in ultimate policy-making. Occasionally individual leaders may derive their power from certain political groups, such as the police, the apparatchiki, the intellectuals, or a particular nationality, and may give special consideration to that group's interests. On the whole, however, political leaders are independent makers of policy and are not members of other political groups, so that analysis of their role belongs more properly to the study of leadership.

Focusing on the other political groups listed above, then, we shall describe some of the salient features that distinguish them in the several Communist countries.

First, there is the question of legitimacy, or rather the presumed lack of legitimacy sometimes stressed as a reason for not acknowledging the existence of political groups in the Communist systems. Certainly Marxist-Leninist theory has traditionally denied the right of political groups to exist and to express their own interests and values, particularly when these interests or values contradict the prevailing party line. Even the apparatchiki as an occupational group are regarded as articulating not a special group interest but the general interest as determined by the party, i.e., the leadership. Similarly, societal organizations like the trade unions have a recognized status but are expected to defend a similar party-defined interest. Other groups whose existence as a social fact cannot be denied, such as the military, the writers, and the various nationalities, are not authorized to formulate distinctive interests of their own. Nonetheless, in the post-Stalinist era, especially in certain Eastern European countries, theoreticians have shown a greater readiness to recognize the exis-

---

lished in *Communist China in 1967: Review of the Year* (Center for Chinese Studies, Univ. of Mich., Ann Arbor, 1968). Oksenberg centers attention on seven occupational groups. He notes that groups based on other criteria may also be significant and that groups may be internally divided on various grounds, such as differences of opinion.

4 For a discussion of Soviet interest groups that focuses on leadership, see Sidney I. Ploss, "Interest Groups," in Allen Kassof, ed., *Prospects for Soviet Society* (New York, 1968), pp. 76–103.

tence of partial interests and of divergent opinions that ought to be considered in the elaboration of policy. The general national or social interest, needless to say, is still regarded as paramount and is to be embodied in the policy ultimately laid down. At the same time, however, the leadership is said to be at fault if it attempts to make decisions without a full airing of diverse viewpoints and conflicting interests.[5] The Chinese Communists have similarly recognized the existence of contradictions and the legitimacy of "nonantagonistic" contradictions, the overcoming of which is regarded as the art and the science of leadership.

In certain Communist systems, then, some political groups are entitled to articulate special opinions or interests within the limitations set by the framework of the leading role of the party. There is in fact a fairly wide spectrum among Communist systems in the degree of legitimacy accorded political groups, ranging from complete denial, as in the mature Stalinist period in the Soviet Union, through various degrees of acceptance, as in post-1953 Hungary, to almost complete endorsement, as in Czechoslovakia after January 1968. Even when legitimacy is denied political groups, they may function de facto as significant political phenomena.

Second, there is the question of group autonomy, i.e., a group's actual capacity for independent action in defense of its interests and opinions. Traditionally, official doctrine and practice have sought to circumscribe severely the freedom of group activity, thus reinforcing the idea among Western scholars that political groups do not exist in a Communist system. In fact, however, groups have often evaded the apparently all-embracing control of the party and have proved capable of articulating their own interests and opinions. In the post-Stalin period of the Soviet Union, for instance, some groups, such as the economists, have been authorized or encouraged by the leadership to debate questions of economic reform; other groups, such as the writers, have taken the initiative in presenting distinctive viewpoints on public issues. In the chaotic conditions of the Cultural Revolution in China radical students and the military have been able to reduce, if not destroy, the power of the party and state apparatchiki.

[5] For a Communist exposition of this point of view, see Z. Mlynarzh (Mlynář), "Problems of Political Leadership and the New Economic System," *Problemy mira i sotsializma*, 12 (Dec. 1965), 90–99, also available in *World Marxist Review*, VIII: 12 (Dec. 1965), 58–64. See also P. Kopnin, "On the Question of Contradictions in Social Development," *Pravda*, Feb. 10, 1966; and G. Smirnov, "The Struggle for the New—The Law of Movement Towards Communism," *Kommunist*, 1 (Jan. 1963), 36–48.

In Eastern Europe, students and writers have actively espoused oppositional attitudes, in Poland leading to severe repression in March 1968 and in Czechoslovakia contributing to the overthrow of the leadership in January 1968. The Catholic Church in Poland and the nationalities in Yugoslavia and Czechoslovakia have frequently challenged specific policies of the central party and state authorities. This is not to say that in any of these cases there has been "a free play of opposing political forces," such as the Russians complained of in Czechoslovakia.[6] It does indicate, however, that whatever may be claimed by doctrine or attempted in practice, some groups have vindicated these claims to autonomous action to a degree that varies according to time, country, and group.

This brings us to the third consideration, the extent to which political groups have become organized or institutionalized in Communist states. On the whole, political groups in Communist countries have lacked formal organization and have pursued their objectives through informal procedures. Certain groups, such as the police, the military, and the apparatchiki, have, of course, been institutionalized in the form of government or party agencies, but as we have noted, they have not been authorized, in their official capacities, to express dissenting interests or opinions. Other groups, such as writers and journalists, the workers, and the youth, have had their own associations and media of communication, but these have usually functioned as "transmission belts" for party policy rather than as spokesmen for the groups they purportedly represent. Opinion groups, such as "liberal" writers or "decentralizing" economists, have usually not had their own organizations but have used conferences and journals of the associations to which they belong as vehicles for the expression of their views. In the fluid conditions of China during the Cultural Revolution groups expressed themselves in many unstructured forms, including demonstrations, wall newspapers, strikes, and the use of violence. In Hungary and Poland in 1955–56 dissident groups were able to gain control of organizations that had previously been subservient instruments of official policy or formed new institutions to present their views. In Hungary in the mid-1960's more or less moribund organizations such as the trade unions were given greater power by the authorities and were urged to become genuine pressure groups defending the interests of their constituents. In several Eastern European countries new organizations—for example, of the collective farmers—have been established by the authorities for similar pur-

---

[6] Y. Zhukov, "What They Wanted," *Pravda*, Dec. 28, 1968.

poses. In Czechoslovakia after January 1968 a rare situation occurred when a host of institutionalized pressure groups sprang up, often with legal sanction.

The fourth consideration brings us to the problem of change in Communist societies: it is that political groups have varied greatly in their general purposes and specific objectives. Whereas some have sought to buttress and protect the status quo, others have criticized particular official policies or have more fundamentally opposed the regime in power. Still others have pursued more radical, even revolutionary, goals.[7] In Poland in 1968, for example, basic oppositional tendencies among the intellectuals were crushed by the combined forces of the apparatchiki and the police. Similar examples can be cited from other Communist countries. In Russia under Khrushchev various groups of economists defended their particular proposals for economic reform, and groups of writers debated the issues of literary and artistic freedom. In Czechoslovakia in 1967 a number of groups, such as the writers, journalists, students, and Slovaks, were locked in bitter strife with the Novotný regime, ultimately combining with sections of the party apparatchiki to overthrow it. In China during the Cultural Revolution groups such as the Red Guards attempted to bring about a thorough renovation of public life, and in particular to destroy the dominant position of the party and state bureaucrats. These few random examples of group action suggest that a systematic analysis would disclose a wide array of objectives among different groups in different countries at different times.

I will not discuss at great length the variety of political groups that have existed in Communist systems. One might, for instance, classify groups in terms of the techniques of action employed, whether verbal or nonverbal, violent or nonviolent, and whether applied through direct contact with the authorities or indirect influence on public opinion. One might differentiate between groups whose main purpose was a positive influence on the outcome of policy, and those whose purpose was the negative one of preventing official policy from being carried out.[8] One might weigh the relative significance of

[7] I have attempted a detailed analysis of opposition, including a classification in terms of the "specific," "fundamental," "integral," and "factional" nature of opposition, in "Background to the Study of Opposition in Communist East Europe," *Government and Opposition*, III: 3 (Summer 1968), 294–324.

[8] See Jaroslaw Piekalkiewicz, "Communist Administration in Poland within the Framework of Input-Output Analysis," paper presented at the Mid-West Association for the Advancement of Slavic Studies, Mar. 30, 1968. Piekalkiewicz analyzes the actions taken by the provincial people's councils to block the implementation of decisions made at a higher level.

groups based on occupational or other social distinctions and those based on common opinions. One might also, of course, evaluate the relative importance and effectiveness of political groups in attaining their ends under various conditions. These and other studies would not only contribute to a more precise knowledge of the nature of group conflict in Communist systems but also provide a tool for more precisely differentiating these systems from each other as well as from those in the non-Communist world.

The Diversity of Communist Systems

Although the rudimentary stage of research on these matters prevents an exhaustive or reliable classification of the Communist states in terms of the concepts mentioned above, a rough initial sketch may be valuable as a stimulus and guide to further research. Here I shall propose a classification of Communist states into five types. A sixth type, represented by Poland, Hungary, and Czechoslovakia in their first stage of evolution from 1945 to 1947–48, and perhaps China prior to 1949, is omitted inasmuch as these systems, in spite of substantial Communist participation, antedated the establishment of full Communist power. The existence of this "pre-totalitarian" type reminds us that the Stalinist, or so-called "totalitarian" phase, has not always been the initial stage of Communist rule; it has sometimes been preceded by a freer system in which group activity was pronounced and influential. It is important to note, too, that the political systems within a given category may vary widely in certain respects, and that a given system may shift from one category to another in the course of its evolution. It will also be self-evident that the classification does not represent a chronological sequence.

The first category, frequently termed "totalitarianism," may better be called "quasi-totalitarianism," inasmuch as the exercise of power is always affected to some extent by the existence of political groups. Here belong Stalin's Russia from 1929 to 1953; Mao's China prior to the Cultural Revolution; and the Eastern European states after World War II (in the case of Yugoslavia prior to 1948, and in that of Hungary, Poland, and Czechoslovakia after 1947–48). Czechoslovakia may be regarded as belonging to this category until the early 1960's, and Albania to the present. In the quasi-totalitarian state political groups are treated in theory as illegitimate, and in practice are severely limited in their capacity for independent action. In some cases the leadership consciously sets out to destroy political groups, in others to infiltrate and emasculate them. If organized groups such as trade unions exist, they are manipulated and controlled by the leadership and do not articulate the interests of their constituency. In general the official groups, especially the party, are superior in power and influence to the intellectuals, who are bereft of any real power. Even the official groups are relatively weak and are used as instruments by the leadership. The police may, however, play an important role. In the Soviet Union, and in most Eastern European states of this category, the police were able to subjugate the party and state bureaucrats. Broader social groups, such as the youth, constitute "problems" for the leadership and are the subject of the latter's political concern and decisions. However, their interests are articulated, if at all, by the leadership, and not by the groups themselves.

A second category, which normally follows the first chronologically but, as Albania demonstrates, may not occur at all, may be called "consultative authoritarianism," to use the term suggested by Peter Ludz in reference to the German Democratic Republic after the Berlin Wall was built.[9] In addition to the GDR, this category would include Rumania, Bulgaria, and in certain respects Hungary in the 1960's; Poland after March 1968; and the Soviet Union after Khrushchev. On the whole this type of state is not characterized by vigorous group conflict. When group activity occurs spontaneously and expresses fundamental opposition, it is firmly repressed, and the dominant role of the top leadership is kept intact. Although the police remain an important force, the prominent position they held in the quasi-totalitarian state is occupied here by such bureaucratic groups as the party and state administrators. These groups are valued for their expertise and thus acquire an opportunity to articulate their own and other groups' interests. There is also an increasing willingness to bring some of the professional groups, such as the economists and the scientists, into the decision-making process, although the party apparat continues to play the superior role both in theory and in practice. Creative intellectuals in the arts and humanities are subject to strict control, but occasionally slip the leash and assert their own viewpoint. Broader social groups continue to be impotent, and their interests are expressed, if at all, by the more powerful official groups and the leaders who claim to represent their interests. Mass associations such as unions or youth leagues are kept under rigid control by the party.

---

9 *Parteielite im Wandel* (Cologne, 1968), esp. pp. 324 *et seq.*

Although this type of system is primarily post-totalitarian, it may include certain states, such as Hungary, Poland, and the Soviet Union, that have regressed from an earlier, more advanced stage of pluralization. In these cases there are pronounced differences in development. Hungary, for example, shifted in the 1960's back toward a somewhat more pluralistic authoritarianism, whereas the Soviet Union after 1964 and Poland in 1968 moved in the reverse direction. In Hungary at present there is a greater official readiness to recognize that special interests and different opinions exist, and to permit some freedom of expression and group activity, although always within the limits of the party line. In contrast, the Soviet regime since the fall of Khrushchev has imposed stricter controls on the articulation of group interests; even so, it still is confronted with oppositional tendencies among the intellectuals. These regimes are somewhat different from the consultative authoritarian type proper, and bear some resemblance to the category to be considered next.

A third category, "quasi-pluralistic authoritarianism," includes Hungary and Poland during the thaw of 1953–56, the Soviet Union under Khrushchev, and Czechoslovakia and Poland in the mid-1960's.[10] This type is distinguished by a greater degree of group conflict, resulting usually from the initiative of the groups themselves. Although the party leadership remains the dominant factor in politics, there is greater interaction between the leaders and political groups, and greater likelihood of some influence by the latter on the political process. Group conflict is often accompanied, and may be encouraged, by sharp factional conflicts among the leaders and serious divisions of opinion within the party as a whole. Although bureaucratic groups, especially the party hierarchy, remain powerful, they cannot entirely exclude the intellectual groups and opinion groups in general from participation. Both types of group show a greater determination to express interests and values in opposition to the party line, advancing alternative policies, criticizing official decisions and actions, and in some cases challenging frontally a whole series of official policies. Ironically, these active groups continue to be for the most part noninstitutionalized, whereas organized groups such as the trade unions remain impotent.

[10] Russia under Lenin might also be included in this category. See Morton Schwartz, "Czechoslovakia: Toward One-Party Pluralism?" *Problems of Communism*, XVI: 1 (Jan.-Feb., 1967), 21–27; Stanley Riveles' letter of comment, *ibid.*, XVI: 4 (July-Aug. 1967), 83–84; and Michael Gamarnikow, "Poland: Political Pluralism in a One-Party State," *ibid.*, 1–14.

The regimes of this type have varied in their willingness to recognize conflicts of interest and diversity of opinions. Khrushchev's regime in the Soviet Union, for example, accepted political groups as inescapable realities and permitted them to articulate their interests and values to a limited extent. By contrast, Novotný's regime in Czechoslovakia was more reluctant to authorize or permit group activity, but was unable to stop it completely. The element of spontaneity in Khrushchev's and Novotný's regimes, and in others like them, produced an opposing tendency toward coercion, and hence a politically unstable situation. Thus in Czechoslovakia group action paved the way for the fall of the regime and the development of much greater pluralization from January 1968. After the August invasion group action continued but was steadily limited and reduced by an increasingly authoritarian regime, especially after the replacement of Dubček by Husák in April 1969. Similarly, in Russia after Khrushchev, and in Poland after the spring of 1968, there was a reversion toward a more controlled system.

Poland, indeed, presents a unique case, difficult to classify with exactness and shifting from one category to another. Prior to 1956 it was characterized by vigorous group conflict that persisted for several years after 1956 in spite of increasing curbs. Throughout the 1960's students and writers continued their resistance in the face of increasing official condemnation, so that Poland could still be considered quasi-pluralistic. Repression reached a high point in the spring of 1968, indicating the regime's retrogression to a less pluralistic form of authoritarianism. Even now, however, the peculiar position of the Roman Catholic Church, which through its own institutions has the opportunity to articulate religious and political interests and to function as a powerful oppositional group, introduces a quasi-pluralistic element unique among Communist systems.

A fourth category, so far rare in the history of Communist states, and difficult to designate, includes Czechoslovakia between January and August 1968, and Yugoslavia after its break with the Soviet Union, and most particularly after 1966. This category may be termed "democratizing and pluralistic authoritarianism." Although these regimes were neither fully democratic nor fully pluralistic, but remained essentially authoritarian, a serious effort was made in both cases to democratize the political process to a far greater extent than in other Communist systems. With the endorsement of the leadership, political groups were to a substantial degree institutionalized, and they played a significant role in policy-making. However, the two regimes differ strikingly from each other, thus corroborating again the infinite variety of group conflict in Communist systems and emphasizing the need to analyze the two cases separately.

In Czechoslovakia intense group conflict undermined the Novotný regime and led to its replacement by the regime of Alexander Dubček.[11] What followed under his leadership was an unusual combination of centrally directed change, designed and elaborated by the party leaders, and of powerful spontaneous forces from below, pressing the regime toward even more radical reform. As a result of almost complete freedom of expression, change-oriented intellectual groups, among them writers, journalists, and radio and television personnel, freely articulated a wide array of group interests and opinions. Broader social groups, notably the Slovaks and the youth, actively pressed their own views and needs on the leaders. Many groups infused existing associations with life, and created new institutions to defend special interests. Even the long-dormant trade unions were moved to become more active, and an organization of farmers was formed. Opinion groups with distinctive political objectives, such as the Club of the Nonparty Committed (KAN), were formed. All of these groups, in one degree or other, functioned in a manner similar to pressure groups in democratic countries, urging alternative policies on the leadership. Some official groups, such as the police, were pushed into the background; others, such as the party apparatchiki, were subjected to intense pressure, and were themselves split into conflicting opinion groups.

In some respects this outburst of group action resembled the process that had taken place in Hungary and Poland in 1955–56. In Hungary and Poland, however, group action, which was more informal and less institutionalized, was often strongly opposed by the leaders. Eventually new leaders, Kádár and Gomulka, brought the situation under control and restored more rigid authoritarian systems in their respective countries. The Czechoslovak leaders, who were predisposed toward significant change, were ready to accept the legitimacy of group action and even to grant it a legal basis. Nonetheless, they were under heavy pressure from more conservative forces, and were themselves seeking to direct and set some limits to the process of

11 See H. Gordon Skilling, "Czechoslovakia's Interrupted Revolution," *Canadian Slavonic Papers*, X: 4 (Winter 1968), 409–29, and Skilling, "Leadership and Group Conflict in Czechoslovakia," in R. Barry Farrell, ed., *Political Leadership in Eastern Europe and the Soviet Union* (Chicago, 1970). See also Morton Schwartz, "Czechoslovakia's New Political Model: A Design for Renewal," *Journal of Politics*, XXX (1968), 966–84.

change. In spite of the relatively radical changes envisaged by political groups and to some extent articulated by the leadership, the entire process of democratization was an evolutionary one, occurring within an orderly framework and averting such results as the revolutionary outbreak in Hungary or the severe crisis in Poland. Although Czechoslovakia was still in an early transitional stage, until the Soviet invasion in August 1968 there was some likelihood that the system would eventually develop into a more democratic and institutionalized form of Communist pluralism.

During the 1950's and 1960's Yugoslavia moved much more gradually and less fully toward a pluralistic system.[12] This development was largely a result of an initiative taken by the leadership, however, without the kind of large-scale spontaneous group pressures that occurred in Czechoslovakia or even in some quasi-pluralistic systems. Over more than a decade the powers of the police and the party apparatchiki were greatly reduced, but not to the extent that this was achieved in Czechoslovakia in only eight months. The intellectual groups, such as the writers, although enjoying greater freedom of expression, did not emerge as influential pressure groups or oppositional forces. Nonetheless, the Yugoslav leaders went further than leaders in most other Communist states in recognizing diverse interests and viewpoints and in permitting them to be expressed through formal institutions. In particular, the decentralization of public administration and the introduction of workers' councils in the factories institutionalized the means of expressing local and regional interests, and those of managers and workers, at the expense of the central authorities in Belgrade. Under the constitution of 1963, representation of economic interests was embodied in the elected assemblies, which were based on a kind of group corporatism. Similarly, the federal system made it possible for the republics to articulate both regional and national interests in a manner unique in the Communist world. Even the party was organized to facilitate the defense of these interests through the several republican party organizations.

The process was slow, however, and was hindered by the opposition of powerful conservative leadership groups, which were eliminated only in 1966 with the purge of Ranković and the reduction of police power. Moreover, though pluralization advanced significantly in the economic realm, and in nationality relations, it was not pronounced

---

12 See Benjamin Ward, "Political Power and Economic Change in Yugoslavia," *American Economic Review*, LVIII: 2 (May 1968), 568–79. See also Djordjević, "Interest Groups and the Political System of Yugoslavia."

in the cultural or intellectual spheres. The absence of vigorous oppo-sitional action by intellectuals and journalists, and until 1968 by the youth and students, and the regime's unwillingness to tolerate oppo-sition from these quarters, made the system less pluralistic in these respects than Czechoslovakia, or even Hungary and Poland in the months before October 1956. Yugoslavia represented, therefore, an unusual combination of institutionalized action by the nationalities, the workers and managers, and the localities and regions, and limited activity by intellectual groups and opinion groups generally.

Finally, a fifth and even rarer category, represented primarily by China during the Cultural Revolution, may be described as "anarchic authoritarianism."[13] Although during the two or three hectic years of the Cultural Revolution Mao's personal authority as the supreme ruler of Communist China was maintained, the system was severely shaken by the intense clash of competing groups. This situation was in part a product of Mao's own initiative in launching the Cultural Revolution and in part a result of the chaotic conditions thus created. During the course of this ferment the party's ruling position was al-most completely undermined, the efficacy of the state apparatus as the administering mechanism was weakened, and competing groups—notably the military, the students, and youth generally, in the form of the Red Guards—stepped into the vacuum. In spite of Mao's great prestige and continued personal power, the country came close to an-archy, which was ended, at least for the time being, only by a coalition of political groups seeking to restore order to a country in chaos.

The Chinese experience, although unique in Communist history, finds a rough counterpart in certain periods of acute crisis, such as Hungary in 1956, when party and police authority broke down and other groups temporarily acquired greater influence.[14] Although group conflict in China was intense, it was quite unlike the group conflict that occurred in Czechoslovakia. Few of the groups that clashed during the Cultural Revolution were institutionalized, nor were they "legitimate," although they were permitted and even en-couraged by Mao. The methods used were spontaneous and coercive, often violent, and had little in common with the organized processes

[13] See Oksenberg, "Occupational Groups in Chinese Society and the Cultural Revolution," and Vogel, "The Structure of Conflict." Cf. Chalmers Johnson, "China: The Cultural Revolution in Structural Perspective," *Asian Survey*, VIII: 1 (Jan. 1968), 1–15.
[14] One might argue that several regimes were on the verge of such a situation at certain times and averted it only by drastic repression. This was true of Poland in the crisis of 1956, and of the GDR during the revolt of 1953.

of group action in Czechoslovakia or Yugoslavia. As the Cultural Revolution proceeded, the relative position of the main groups shifted radically. Some sections of the military increased greatly in power and influence at the expense of the party organization. The Red Guards escaped the control of those who had incited them to action and became at times a powerful force in their own right. Peasants, workers, and managers successfully defended their own interests against the full impact of the Cultural Revolution. Intellectuals were less successful in protecting themselves against the drive of the revolutionaries, but some, such as the scientists, were less affected than teachers and writers. The main target of the Red Guards, the party and government cadres, although suffering severe setbacks, successfully weathered the storm, and eventually emerged, with the military and the "cultural revolutionaries," as an important element of the "revolutionary committees" established to restore order. In many provinces, however, the military seemed to be the dominant force in the so-called "three-way alliance." Although the system was no longer anarchic, it was quasi-pluralistic in the sense that there was continued conflict among the groups of the ruling coalition. A weakened leadership had at least to consider, and to some extent bargain with, groups such as the workers, the peasants, and the youth.

Political Change under Communism

The death of Stalin and the movement away from Stalinism in the Soviet Union led Western scholars to reevaluate the nature of Communism and among other things to reassess the role of political groups in systems previously regarded as monolithic. During the thaw that followed Stalin's death in the Soviet Union and in some countries of Eastern Europe, group activity became more visible, no doubt as a result of the decline of coercion and the greater freedom of communication. This changing situation clearly did not represent a free play of political groups, but it was something quite remote from the totalitarian model generally regarded as typical of Stalin's era. As differences increasingly manifested themselves between various Communist countries, there was a new appreciation of the mutability of these systems and a growing curiosity concerning the causes of change in these systems. A certain simplified explanation was sometimes offered, which, in the light of what has been said in this chapter, is inadequate to comprehend the complex reality of Communist evolution.

Underlying this explanation was the assumption that political change in the direction of a modernized, or pluralistic, system was the more or less inevitable consequence of economic development, since changes in the economic base inevitably required changes in the political superstructure. It followed that all Communist countries were foreordained to pass through certain common stages of evolution, and eventually to reach a similar destination in the form of an institutionalized pluralistic system. As far as political groups were concerned, this process was presumed to involve a decline in the importance of the police, as coercion became less important; a loss in the power of the party apparatchiki, as ideology became less significant; and a rise in the influence of intellectual and other specialist groups in a complex society requiring accurate information and knowledge.[15]

Even the very rough and imperfect scheme of classification outlined in the preceding pages casts grave doubt on the relevance of this explanation to the real world of Communist politics. It seems clear that political change in the direction of democratic pluralization is not inevitable in the Communist world. In some cases no significant trend toward pluralism has occurred; in others it has been partial and incomplete. Where it has occurred, the evolution has not proceeded stage by stage in a fixed sequence but has pursued a zig-zag course, and has shown itself to be reversible. The path of development is not unilinear, but multilinear, with many options open to individual Communist systems. When change occurs, it may be general or specific, affecting only one sphere; it may be revolutionary, or gradual; it may lead toward greater or less pluralization.

The causes of change, too, are manifold, and are not solely or even predominantly economic. To be sure, economic development is a powerful force that often makes for political pluralization, but it may be counteracted by other pressures moving in the opposite direction. The traditional political culture will be an influential factor that retards or accelerates pluralization. The personality of the leaders, and the distinctive character of Communism in a particular country, will also affect the outcome, perhaps decisively. Any explanation that is persuasive must therefore take into account many factors, the relative weight of which is not easily assessed.

The point from which change originates in Communist societies also varies greatly. In some instances the initiative may come "from above," from leaders whose decisions reflect their own views of the interests of the rest of society, which for its part has little chance to express an opinion except by reacting positively or negatively to the

---

[15] For an interpretation resembling this one, see Ghiţa Ionescu, *The Politics of the European Communist States* (London, 1967).

decisions after they are made. That is, social groups may be mere objects of politics—for instance, the youth or the peasants—and may have no chance to articulate their own interests. Alternatively, the initiative may come "from below," from spontaneous group pressures, either from the elite sectors of the intellectual and the official groups, or less frequently from the broader social groups. In other words, the groups may be a dynamic political force pressing actively for, or against, change. The leaders may react in varying ways, whether by making partial or full concessions to satisfy pressures or by rejecting the interests expressed, forcing the groups to accept the official view. There is also the possibility that they may make no response at all. Group interests may, that is, be articulated, or repressed, or ignored. Thus in most cases, if not all, there will be an intricate interplay between the leadership initiatives and political group pressures, the exact admixture depending on the many distinctive features of the particular political culture. The outcome will vary accordingly.

We must also guard against the assumption that change in the Communist world is inevitably liberal or progressive in the sense of leading to a greater degree of pluralism. Since change in any society involves by definition a modification of the status quo, we customarily classify political groups as liberal or conservative, radical or reactionary, in terms of whether or not they favor change, and of the extent and speed of the change involved. In looking at the Communist world, once viewed as a monolithic system, we tend to think that change must inevitably be toward greater pluralism, and that group activity inevitably contributes to this trend. In fact, whether a given trend is progressive or conservative depends on the nature of the status quo and the character of the changes advocated, and involves a value judgment on the part of the participant or observer. For example, the abolition of censorship in Czechoslovakia in early 1968 was a significant change in the status quo that was considered by many a liberal measure. The post-occupation restoration of censorship, a change in the new status quo, was regarded as a conservative or reactionary measure. Changes in the Communist world, as elsewhere, then, must be judged as progressive or conservative in terms of the character of the status quo in a given country, and on the basis of a precise and defined criterion of evaluation. If we take a greater degree of pluralism as the criterion of progress, we cannot assume that change in the Communist world is necessarily moving in a liberal or progressive direction.

The role of political groups in the evolution of Communist systems

is made more difficult to assess by the fact that groups in general are
not all likely to be moving in the same direction, but almost by definition will be in conflict with each other. Some will favor the status
quo, others will reject it, and their attitudes will shift as the status
quo changes. One *may* take as a hypothesis that certain groups, such
as economists, writers, students, and perhaps managers, favor pluralism because of their desires for greater economic efficiency, for fuller
and more reliable information, or for wider freedom of expression.
One *may* also posit that the central bureaucrats, the police and the
military, the ideologists, and the party apparatchiki resist pluralistic
trends out of adherence to Communist tradition or ideology, the
fear of alien ideas, or a desire to protect their vested interests. Firm
conclusions concerning these hypotheses on the relationship of individual groups to the process of political change must, however, await
much more empirical research on the actions of specific groups, on
specific issues, in specific countries, at specific times.[16]

The External Factor

Finally, in seeking to interpret change in Communist systems, it is
impossible to ignore influences emanating from outside a particular
system, from the international context. Indeed, in the Communist
world, linked as they are by ties of ideology and by close interparty cooperation or control, influences from other members of the group
have special relevance. Hence changes, whether they come "from
above" or "from below," may often be induced "from outside" a given
Communist system. Similarly, there is a significant interaction of political groups across the frontiers of every Communist system. In the
era of Stalin, for example, the impact of certain Soviet bureaucratic
groups, such as the police, the army, and the party, was direct and decisive on their counterparts in Eastern Europe. Moreover, owing to
the policy of imitating the Russian model in all the European Communist countries except Yugoslavia after 1948, the behavior and fate
of various groups in Eastern Europe was more or less determined by

---

[16] Two studies along this line are Carl Beck's "Bureaucratic Conservatism and
Innovation in Eastern Europe," *Comparative Political Studies*, I: 2 (July 1968),
275–94; and Jan Triska's "Party Apparatchiks at Bay," *East Europe*, XVI: 12
(Dec. 1967), 2–8. The state bureaucrats are described by Beck as not playing a
very innovative role in economic reforms. The party functionaries are depicted by
Triska as strongly opposed to economic reforms. Cf. also the analysis of the group
attitudes to economic reform in Andrzej Korbonski, "Bureaucracy and Interest
Groups in Communist Societies: The Case of Czechoslovakia," *Studies in Comparative Communism*, forthcoming.

that of the corresponding ones in the Soviet Union. Likewise, when de-Stalinization was introduced by Khrushchev, this new course had a profound effect on certain former satellites, especially Hungary and Poland, generating similar policy changes by the local leaders and activating certain groups, such as the writers and students.[17] The effect was the opposite in other states, for example China and Czechoslovakia, where the regimes sought to slow down the course of change by taking repressive measures against groups pressing in that direction. In recent years political groups in different Communist systems have had an even more direct impact on each other, owing in no small part to the greater ease and frequency of communication.[18]

A classic illustration of this general phenomenon is the case of Czechoslovakia before and after the invasion of August 1968. The events that occurred in that country after January 1968 had direct repercussions on the leadership and on political groups in the other countries of the bloc, stimulating a desire by some groups to emulate the Czechs and Slovaks, and conversely a determination by other groups to resist such a development. In Poland, for instance, writers and students greeted the Czech reforms with enthusiasm and in March sought to achieve similar objectives at home. By contrast, party apparatchiki and police, and more conservative forces generally, both in Poland and in other bloc countries opposed reform, fearing the consequences for themselves. In the Soviet Union, it may be assumed, powerful groups such as the military and the "Ukrainian" leadership faction strongly opposed the Czechoslovak course, whereas less influential groups such as some intellectuals and more nationalist Ukrainians welcomed it. The invasion itself, reflecting a constellation of conservative and reactionary forces in the Soviet Union and the associated bloc countries, with some limited support from certain Czech and Slovak groups, was designed to block reform and to stifle the active political groups espousing it. At least some small dissident groups in the Soviet Union, the GDR, and elsewhere publicly denounced the invasion and suffered severe penalties. Sympathetic

---

[17] Khrushchev's Secret Speech of 1956, which was published in the West, had an enormous impact in all the Communist countries.

[18] The circulation of "secret," i.e., unpublished, letters and statements across borders, sometimes through the intermediary of Western newspapers and radio broadcasts, has become a significant part of the communications network, for example. A striking instance was the Soviet writer Alexander Solzhenitsyn's letter expressing the opposition of liberal writers to censorship. Although this letter was not discussed at the Soviet Writers Congress in the spring of 1967, it was read and debated at the congress of Czechoslovak writers in the summer.

groups in Yugoslavia, and the leaders of that country and of Rumania, expressed their support of the Czechoslovak reforms.[19]

The ultimate course of change in Communist systems is thus bound up with the interplay of conflicting group pressures within the Communist world as a whole. To the extent that pressures for pluralization make themselves felt, for example in demands for radical economic reform or for freedom of expression in Eastern Europe, they may be met by powerful counterpressures emanating from the Soviet Union, as well as from conservative groups in Eastern Europe itself. Even an independent Communist state such as Yugoslavia cannot entirely escape these external influences. The action of the bloc powers against Czechoslovakia in 1968 suggests, then, that change in the direction of pluralization, far from being inevitable, will in the near future be less likely. The direct impact of China and Chinese political groups, though at present slight in Eastern Europe except in Albania, does exist in a diffuse and primarily negative way, and might in the future become more explicit and positive and affect even the Soviet Union. A reverse movement of ideas and influences from Eastern Europe to the Soviet Union also exists, as the Russian fear of radical Eastern European reforms demonstrates. The post-occupation resistance by Czech and Slovak scholars, journalists, students, and industrial workers aroused widespread sympathy in Yugoslavia and had some immeasurable impact on the people of the invading states, including the Russians. It is impossible at present to judge the relative strength or the ultimate effect of these conflicting tendencies in the long run. In a future crisis, if strong oppositional tendencies crystallized simultaneously in several countries of Eastern Europe, the course of evolution even in the Soviet Union might be decisively affected.

[19] A strong protest was registered by philosophers from East and West, including Hungarians and Yugoslavs, against the invasion of Czechoslovakia (*Književne novine*, Aug. 31, 1968). Earlier, Yugoslav philosophers had protested against the action of Polish authorities in dismissing prominent scholars from their positions in the wake of the March events (*ibid.*, Apr. 13, 1968).

Power and Authority in Eastern Europe

In one of those spasms of chagrin that chronically grip social scientists concerned with Communist systems, James Billington recently tried to explain why students of Communism had failed to predict many crucial events in the Communist world, including the invasion of Czechoslovakia. "There are many reasons for our continuing failure of perception. . . . But two enduring intellectual prejudices are worth pointing out: the tendency to look for political factions rather than underlying forces to explain events; and to make short-term predictions of what national leaders will do rather than seek a strategic perspective on where they stand or an inner understanding of who they are."[1]

Without accepting the premise that prediction of discrete political events is the task of social scientists, one can agree that "failures of perception" about contemporary Communist systems are due in part to a failure to ask the proper questions. In this essay I shall suggest a set of categories—not a model or a theory—which might prove useful in selecting the most relevant data for the study of political change in Eastern Europe, and perhaps in all Communist systems. Thus, this essay is a suggestion for a strategy of research, rather than an attempt at a definitive treatment of political change in Communist societies. And it is a strategy designed for research from a comparative perspective. The categories I use are borrowed from recent writings in political theory and sociology, and I do not try to add to the plethora of categories, terms, and definitions already in the literature. My method is explained by the conviction, first, that the relevance and usefulness for the study of Communist systems of the existing litera-

[1] "Force and Counterforce in Eastern Europe," *Foreign Affairs*, XLVII: 1 (Oct. 1968), p. 26.

ture has not been fully explored and that much might be gained by encasing existing knowledge in its terms; and, second, that whatever refinement of understanding neologisms may contribute is often mitigated by the erection of yet another barrier to communication.

Restating one theory in the language of another does not automatically produce new knowledge. But such a restatement may prompt new insights. . . . Transforming what is already known into different language can yield new insights but not confirmed or verified knowledge. The primary function or the result of restating knowledge is to contribute to scientific discovery. . . . Another result of reformulating what is known is to fit fragmented and seemingly isolated knowledge into generalizations of greater scope.[2]

The central problem to which we address ourselves is political change in post-totalitarian Communist systems. "All utopias from Plato's Republic to George Orwell's brave new world of 1984 have had one element of construction in common: they are all societies from which change is absent. . . . The social fabric of utopias does not, and perhaps cannot, recognize the unending flow of the historical process."[3] The Communist theory of political development is an arrested utopianism, concerned more with revolutionizing society and "system building," in Alfred Meyer's terms, than with "system management" in the postrevolutionary era, or with system readjustment when that becomes necessary. Thus, Communist systems have failed even to evolve a stable leadership succession mechanism or to develop institutions capable of considering and initiating systemic change in routinized, noncataclysmic ways. This does not imply that political change is absent from Communist systems, but it does mean that managing change is often a painful, irregular, unpredictable, and even violent process. This essay argues that there now exist strong pressures for political change in Eastern Europe and examines attempts, even tentative, that are being made to deal with these pressures.

These pressures originate largely in an "authority crisis" confronting some Eastern European polities at present, and others in the foreseeable future. Failure to resolve this crisis, although it may not directly threaten the survival of these systems, will seriously hamper their effectiveness. To resolve this crisis processes of political integration must be undertaken. Political integration establishes authority

[2] Henry Teune, "The Learning of Integrative Habits," in Philip E. Jacob and James V. Toscano, eds., *The Integration of Political Communities* (Philadelphia, 1964), p. 250.

[3] Ralf Dahrendorf, "Out of Utopia: Toward a Reorientation of Sociological Analysis," in N. J. Demerath and Richard A. Peterson, eds., *System, Change and Conflict* (New York, 1967), p. 465.

on the basis of a "political formula." This is part of the process of political development, which optimally leads to the formation of political community. In many systems, Eastern Europe included, the process of political integration is complicated by the need to engage in a parallel process of national integration. Integration processes are nonterminal and ongoing; permanent political integration is never achieved.

These assertions and the terms in which they are made require definition and amplification. Authority "denotes a relationship of inequality between two or more actors measured by unquestioning acceptance of communications or compliance with decisions issued by one actor, a relationship which is perceived as legitimate by all actors involved."[4] In authority relationships, actors hold in abeyance their own critical judgment and accept that of an acknowledged superior.[5] On the societal and political levels authority can be expressed as "the complex of institutionalized rights to control the actions of members of the society with reference to their bearing on the attainment of collective goals. . . . It is the institutionalization of the rights of 'leaders' to expect support from the members of the collectivity."[6] Authority relationships can be established only by agreement; shared values concerning the right to exercise power are the basis of authority. Unwilling compliance, based on coercion rather than shared values or based on the absence of an alternative, is secured by the exercise of power, not authority. Clearly, authority does not exist in pure form in the real world. The threat of the latent exercise of power lies, to some degree, behind many authoritative relationships. Nevertheless, there remains a real, palpable, and significant difference between relationships based on power and those based on authority. Political relationships based largely on authority, with power used to curb only what is commonly agreed to be deviance (crime), are relationships that involve the generation and maintenance of what David Easton calls "diffuse support" for the political system. With the proximate nature of authority in mind, we assert that many Eastern European political actors are seeking to change

4 Alfred G. Meyer, "Authority in Communist Political Systems," in Lewis Edinger, ed., *Political Leadership in Industrialized Societies* (New York, 1967), p. 84.
5 This definition of authority derives from those of Peter Blau, Herbert Simon, Carl J. Friedrich, and Karl Deutsch. For a review of the literature on power and authority in Marxist and non-Marxist political theory, see Alfred G. Meyer, "Autorität," in *Sowjetsystem und demokratische Gesellschaft: Eine vergleichende Enzyklopädie*, I (Freiburg, 1968), 546–64.
6 Talcott Parsons, "Authority, Legitimation and Political Action," in Carl J. Friedrich, ed., *Authority* (Cambridge, Mass., 1961), p. 210.

the relationship of state and society from one based on power to one based on authority, an attribute that at present most Eastern European regimes lack. They are in the grip of an "authority crisis," similar to that plaguing other polities and other bodies, such as the Roman Catholic Church. This crisis occurs when the legitimacy of the hierarchically superior, command-issuing institutions and persons is negated, or at least seriously questioned, and when the cultural and psychological bases of that legitimacy are significantly eroded by processes of social, economic, and political development.

The resolution of an authority crisis can be achieved by a process of political integration on the basis of a new or revised political formula. Political integration involves "the progressive development among members of a political system of a deep and unambiguous sense of identity with the state and other members of the civic body."[7] The loyalty of citizens to the defining values and aspirations of the political system, achieved on the basis of normative consensus governing political behavior, is elicited by the integration process. "In essence the problem of political integration is one of developing a political culture and of inducing commitment to it."[8] If this problem is successfully solved there exists diffuse support sufficient for the stabilization of the political system.[9] The defining values and aspirations that form the normative consensus around which the citizenry is integrated are encapsulated in what Mosca called "the political formula." It is the "legal and moral basis, or principle, on which the power of the political class rests."[10]

A political system that is able to successfully manage the task of political integration, and hence adjustment of the political formula, is one capable of sustained political development. It has the capacity to deal authoritatively with political change and ensure the "persistence" of the system, despite the fact that adjustments have to be made in the detailed workings of the system.

In all political systems, but particularly in those that are former colonies or encompass many nationalities and ethnic groups, national

---

[7] Claude Ake, "Political Integration and Political Stability," *World Politics*, XIX: 3 (Apr. 1967), 487.

[8] Claude Ake, *A Theory of Political Integration* (Homewood, Ill., 1967), p. 1. See also Karl A. Deutsch, *The Nerves of Government* (New York, 1966), p. 150; and Myron Weiner, "Political Integration and Political Development," *Annals of the American Academy of Political and Social Science*, CCCLVIII (Mar. 1965), 52–64.

[9] See David Easton, *A Systems Analysis of Political Life* (New York, 1965), p. 223.

[10] Gaetano Mosca, *The Ruling Class* (New York, 1939). Deutsch (p. 241) uses the term "common spirit" to mean roughly the same thing as "political formula."

integration is a requisite additional to political integration, the establishment of authority, and political development. This is essentially the same process as political integration except that the focus of the normative consensus is not the state but the nation. Not a political identity, but a national identity, is the product of a process of national integration. Again, a variety of formulae may be evolved to guide and define the process of national integration. We shall later examine the links between formulae and strategies of political integration and those used to achieve national integration.

Finally, successful national integration and political integration can result in the creation of a positively evaluated political community. A political community, according to Amitai Etzioni, has three core characteristics: (1) it has effective control over the means of violence; (2) it has a center of decision-making that is able to "affect significantly" the allocation of resources and rewards throughout the community; (3) it is the dominant focus of political identification for the large majority of politically aware citizens.[11] "The sense of political community may be described as a we-feeling among a group of people, not that they are just a group but that they are a political entity that works together and will likely share a common political fate and destiny."[12] By these definitions, citizens of a state in which power, rather than authority, is the integrating force of society are members of a political community. For this reason we add the modifier "positively evaluated" (by the majority of citizens) to connote a community integrated on the basis of authority rather than power.

Having defined our terms, we can proceed to an exposition of the systemic strains that have led to an authority crisis in Eastern Europe and the pressures for dealing with it, and then to an examination of attempts to deal with this crisis.

The strains on the Eastern European systems have both exogenous and endogenous origins. One of the most visible strains on the system has been the failure to maintain as high a rate of economic growth as is desired by the political decision-makers. In fact, some countries have experienced serious economic difficulties. In the 1960's, economic growth in Czechoslovakia slowed to the point where by 1963 Czechoslovakia was the only industrialized country in the world to show a negative rate of growth (–2.2 per cent). Other countries in the area experienced similar trends to a lesser degree, prompting all of them

---

[11] *Political Unification: A Comparative Study of Leaders and Forces* (New York, 1965), p. 4.
[12] Easton, p. 332.

to adopt a series of economic reforms. The details of the economic crises, their root causes, and the reforms adopted to solve them are dealt with in this volume and elsewhere.[13] For our purposes it need only be pointed out that the economic difficulties in Eastern Europe were basically due to the inappropriateness of a "command economy," with all the structural and behavioral consequences flowing from it, to economic systems that had already outgrown the need for mobilization of resources on an enormous scale in order to propel an economy quickly, if inefficiently, from backwardness to "take-off." The socialist economies had reached the point where the mere addition of capital and labor could not produce commensurate growth, because the inefficiencies inherent in the system of planning, administration, and priorities eroded many of the gains that could be achieved by ever greater inputs. Clearly, the era of "extensive" economic development had passed, and a period of "intensive" economic development had to be ushered in.[14] Rather than merely increasing the quantitative expansion of inputs, an emphasis on qualitative development of production factors was indicated. In other words, what was needed was an increase in efficiency, knowledge, skills, information, technological sophistication, specialization, and expertise. As we shall see later on, these characteristics are more easily developed in authority relationships than in power relationships.

The need for intensive economic development seems to us to be paralleled by a need for "intensive political development." The methods of "command politics" become increasingly inefficient and less productive as society, for economic and social reasons, becomes more highly differentiated. Just as the economy stagnates when the command economy is maintained after having outlived its usefulness, so, too, the political system becomes less effective—though it is difficult to measure this—as its political formula becomes increasingly irrelevant. As has been pointed out by people such as Zdenek Mlynář, former head of the Czechoslovak Central Committee's Commission on the New Political Model, the New Economic Model (economic reforms) should be paralleled by the development of a "new political model."

A compelling argument for the development of such a model, or formula, is that the increasing differentiation of society—a new level of social development—requires concomitant political adjustments.

---

[13] Most conveniently in Michael Gamarnikow, *Economic Reforms in Eastern Europe* (Detroit, Mich., 1968).
[14] See Ota Šik, *Plan and Market under Socialism* (White Plains, N.Y., 1967), pp. 49 *et seq.*

Individuals having more education, media exposure, and psychic and physical mobility are more likely to place demands upon and give support to the political system. Therefore, more developed environments can be expected to generate greater quantities of demands and supports for the political system and to be more complex and difficult to manipulate. . . . Development increases the portion of the environment that considers the political system as salient. . . . More individuals move into political statuses in which the lower level needs [i.e., material needs] are no longer pressing. . . . The key to building social and psychological supports to balance increasing demands is meeting the appropriate demands with appropriate action. In order to know the correct action that should be taken in highly developed societies it is helpful to the political elites if an effective feedback network and political brokerage system is allowed to emerge.[15]

As David Apter has pointed out, politics that employ a high degree of coercion, as mobilization systems do, are low information systems.[16] When mobilization no longer is the strategy for both economic and political development, and as that development produces a more differentiated society, the need for information becomes greater and the utility of coercion diminishes.

In addition to these economic and developmental pressures straining the system, generational changes in and of themselves bring about changes in values and orientations. Aspirations and values of Eastern European youth frequently diverge from the defining aspirations and values contained in the political formula. This gap is paralleled by a very pervasive "cognitive dissonance" among Eastern European populations who have had to confront the inconsistencies between the myths of the political formula, or ideology, and objective realities. Adam Wazyk, the Polish poet, expressed this poignantly in his "Poem for Adults" published in 1955.

> Fourier, the dreamer, charmingly foretold
> that lemonade would flow in seas.
> Does it flow?
> They drink sea water,
> crying:
> "lemonade!"
> Returning home secretly to vomit. . . .
> They came and cried:
> "Under Socialism
> a hurt finger does not hurt!"
> They hurt their fingers.
> They felt the pain.

---

[15] Dennis C. Pirages, "Socio-Economic Development and Political Change in the Communist System," Stanford Studies of the Communist System, Research Paper No. 9, Jan. 1966, pp. 11–17.

[16] *The Politics of Modernization* (Chicago, 1965), p. 40.

The apparently universal human need to reduce cognitive dissonance produces a further strain on the stability of the system, its credibility and efficacy, even though this human need is constrained by the knowledge that even more severe deprivations may result as a consequence of attempting to resolve dissonance situations.

In addition to the four endogenously produced pressures for change, two exogenously produced pressures are significant. The first is the abandonment of the use of political terror, for subjective or for more general systemic reasons.[17] Although the relative lack of terror in Poland even during the mobilization phase indicates that at least in that country the employment of terror may have been a matter for indigenous elites to decide, we assume that the decisions to embark on the use of terror and to curtail it were made for Eastern Europe by the Soviet Union. There can be little doubt that in the mobilization era, under Stalinism, terror and other forms of coercion were the "integrating" (as well as selectively disintegrating) forces of the system. The abandonment of the use of terror, therefore, necessitates finding a functional equivalent for it, especially in light of the waning appeals of a dogmatized ideology. The compliance structure of society—authority relationships—must be based on some substitute for terror.

A second exogenous source of strain, related to the first, is the erosion of the essentially imperial organization of the Soviet bloc. Empires are systems "whose coercive base is more integrated than their utilitarian base, and whose utilitarian base is more integrated than their political loyalties."[18] Although the states of Eastern Europe had ideological ties to the Soviet Union, their economic (utilitarian) links were stronger, and their coercive bonds were strongest. The Soviet Union supplied the cohesive force that kept the Eastern European polities stable and integrated. Eastern Europe and the Soviet Union were tied together in a causal or functional integration,[19] so that developments in one had a direct effect on the other. When terror was abandoned and the "new course" was introduced in the Soviet Union,

17 Zbigniew Brzezinski remarks on the abandonment of the use of terror in the Soviet Union after Stalin's death: "While it is likely that terror would have declined anyway, the desperate need to decapitate the secret police, lest it decapitate the various heirs apparent, precipitated a more rapid decline of the secret police than perhaps would have been the case." (*Ideology and Power in Soviet Politics* [New York, 1962], p. 81.)

18 Amitai Etzioni, *The Active Society* (New York, 1968), p. 556.

19 Pitirim Sorokin lists four types of interrelations among various elements of culture. Causal or functional integration describes the relationship between working parts of a car, for example. See "Causal-Functional and Logico-Meaningful Integration," in Demerath and Peterson, *System, Change and Conflict*.

the same happened in Eastern Europe. But the degree of integration between the Soviet Union and Eastern Europe has declined in the last decade, so that not all parts of the system change simultaneously, and there are manifestations of malintegration and even disintegration. One of the consequences of this is that Eastern European polities must now generate cohesive, integrating forces for themselves, the invasion of Czechoslovakia notwithstanding. This is the burden of limited autonomy. Whereas newly independent former colonies must develop integrating capacities in order to survive, the Eastern European states can rely on the Soviet Union to guarantee their survival, but they must develop their own integrating capacities to ensure their effectiveness.

These, then, are some of the motivating forces for the revision of political formulae in Eastern Europe in accord with changing economic and social conditions and in a direction allowing for the establishment, or strengthening, of authority relationships through political integration.

Such relationships, according to Etzioni, can be established on the basis of coercive, utilitarian, or normative power. Although all three are usually involved in integrating relationships, it is the nature of the mix that we are concerned with. Coercive integration, as in prisons, tends to produce alienated behavior. The use of normative appeals for integration tends to generate moral involvement, and utilitarian integrating power generates calculative relationships.[20] David Easton uses "coercion," "outputs," and "stimulation of good will" to mean essentially the same as coercive, utilitarian, and normative power. "Because of the obvious diseconomies in the use of coercion for maintaining a minimal level of support for a system, authorities typically seek to displace it by voluntary and willing attachment based on belief and conviction."[21] Etzioni also claims that "the historical, 'secular' trends seem to be toward less coercion and toward more utilitarian and especially more normative compliance. ... The more active a society ... the more it is expected to rely on normative guidance, for the lower level of resulting alienation makes it more effective."[22] Since normative rather than coercive incentives are the basis of authority, we may say that shifts from power to authority produce less alienated behavior and more effective integration.

[20] These concepts are used in *Political Unification*, e.g., p. 37; *A Comparative Analysis of Complex Organizations* (New York, 1961), e.g., pp. 7–10; and *The Active Society, passim*.
[21] Easton, *A Systems Analysis of Political Life*, p. 275.
[22] *The Active Society*, p. 380.

The generation of normative incentives thrusts values into a position of prime importance. "A value structure symbolically legitimates —that is, makes morally acceptable—the particular pattern of interaction and stratification of the members of a social system."[23] Values are "the general moral and definitional symbols which, when shared, establish the conscious solidarity that characterizes men joined together in a moral community." Values are then given normative expression in specific rules that are designed to aid in the realization of values. "Norms derived from a value structure will provide morally acceptable (i.e., legitimate) rules for performing the roles dictated by a particular division of labor. The efficiency of norms in controlling role behavior is particularly sensitive to the degree of complementarity that exists between the value structure and the environment. . . . The single most generalized characteristic of the disequilibrated system is that values no longer provide an acceptable symbolic definition and explanation of existence."[24] Talcott Parsons and Neil Smelser put it more positively: the integrative subsystem of society "relates the cultural value patterns to the motivational structures of individual actors in order that the larger social system can function without undue internal conflict and other failures of coordination."[25]

Value consensus becomes crucial to integration based essentially on a normative consensus. "Not only is the value system (or Ethos) the deepest and most important source of integration, but it is also the most stable element of socio-cultural systems."[26] In exploring attempts to achieve political integration through normative consensus in Eastern Europe, it will be important to investigate the prevailing value structure in society, the defining values proposed by political elites, and the degree of "fit" or synchronization between them.

Earlier Attempts to Relieve Strain

Strains were felt in European Communist systems long before, but perhaps it was only in the 1960's that various widespread attempts at political integration became visible. Parsons suggests that strains can be relieved by resolution, i.e., "restoring full conformity with normative expectations"; arrestation or isolation, i.e., accommodation so that "less than normal performance by the deficient units is ac-

---

[23] Chalmers Johnson, *Revolutionary Change* (Boston, 1966), p. 13.
[24] *Ibid.*, pp. 42–43, 73.
[25] "The Primary Sub-Systems of Society," in Demerath and Peterson, p. 132.
[26] Pierre L. Van den Berghe, "Dialectic and Functionalism: Toward a Theoretical Synthesis," in Demerath and Peterson, p. 294.

cepted"; and change in the structure itself, i.e., "alteration in the normative culture defining the expectations governing that [strained] relation."[27] Endogenous change is said to occur only when "lower-order mechanisms of control" fail to contain the pressures or strains. In Poland and Hungary in 1956 these mechanisms of control failed to deal successfully with strain, but the relief of strain was not accomplished by alterations in the normative culture, though Gomulka gave the impression that he would preside over such alterations. Instead, the relief tactic adopted was one of arrestation or isolation, with the Polish regime even trying—in fits and starts and with little apparent success—to move toward restoring full conformity. In Hungary a move toward restoration of full conformity was immediately initiated, though it was a conformity to the "new course" system rather than to the norms of Stalinism. By the 1960's, as we shall see, cautious attempts were begun to alter the "normative culture" itself. In Czechoslovakia both the first and the second methods were tried by Novotný, and the third by the Dubček regime. The Soviets have seemingly pressed for the first solution verbally, but have settled for the second type in practice. In Yugoslavia, between 1948 and 1950, the period of "superorthodoxy," the first solution was tried as a means of dealing with exogenously produced strain, but by 1952, when the "Yugoslav model" was elaborated, the third tactic had been adopted.

What is interesting about the current situation is the amount of serious consideration given by individual regimes to the third solution—change in the structure itself. This is the kind of solution that can be subsumed under political integration—or reintegration—and the establishment of authority. Perhaps this attention stems from a recognition that a goal-oriented political system, such as any Communist system must be, has a greater need to revise its political formula than does a means-oriented system, whose authority rests on the perceived legitimacy of its internal processes. The goal-oriented system's authority depends in large part on the achievement of stated goals and the normative fulfillment of defined values. If goals are unattainable, the political formula ought to be revised so that the gap between promise and fulfillment does not undermine authority. In "democratic" societies authority is pluralistic and diffuse because

[27] "A Paradigm for the Analysis of Social Systems and Change," in Demerath and Peterson, p. 197. The oft-repeated criticism of structural-functional analysis for its "conservative" bias, which treats conflict as deviant, does not concern us very much because our assumption is that Eastern European political elites are interested precisely in developing peaceful means of change that are conducive to homeostatic equilibrium.

authoritative communications can be issued by a great variety of authority structures (schools, churches, labor unions, political parties, etc.). In Communist societies authority is centralized, and hence the burden of establishing it weighs that much more heavily on the central political elite.

Conditioning Influences on Integration Strategies

What are some of the conditioning influences and the constraints on the particular strategy of political integration a regime might adopt, on the development of a new or revised political formula? Conditioning influences may be grouped under three headings: historical, situational, and organizational.[28] A fourth type of conditioning influence is the strategy adopted to achieve national integration.

"Historical" conditioning influences on the strategy of political integration would include the history and nature of the Communist party. As the cases of Yugoslavia, Albania, China, North Vietnam, and Cuba demonstrate, Communist regimes that are "authentic" rather than "derivative" enjoy a degree of authority not shared by other regimes, though the Rumanian party seems to have proved that it is possible to become an authentic party-regime. A second consideration is the degree of social mobilization and concomitant malintegration that characterized the mobilization era. How much terror was there, at whom was it directed, how strongly does the memory of it affect current attitudes of elites and masses—these are some relevant considerations. Political culture, used in the sense of "the system of empirical beliefs, expressive symbols and values which defines the situation in which political action takes place,"[29] is relevant, and in the Eastern European context, where there has been an attempt to disrupt and remold the political culture, one must take account of the persistence and subjective evaluation of the pre-Communist political culture; Czechoslovaks regard their pre-Communist political culture favorably, but Hungarians probably do not have such favorable memories of their own political traditions. The predictions and fears that Communist systems would be so effective in political socialization that all traditional values would be subverted have proved to be unfounded. The persistence of traditional values is most visible in Poland, Czechoslovakia, and certain portions of the Soviet Union, but it is a phenomenon common to all Communist systems. Pre-Com-

[28] These categories were suggested to me by Kenneth Jowitt.
[29] Sidney Verba, "Comparative Political Culture," in Lucian W. Pye and Sidney Verba, eds., *Political Culture and Political Development* (Princeton, N.J., 1965), p. 513.

munist value structures cannot be ignored, as was demonstrated in Czechoslovakia in 1967–68. Naturally, political culture is not deterministic, nor can it tell much about an individual participant in a particular political culture. But it can indicate probabilities in group attitudes and behavior.

Situational conditioning influences include the nature of the basic cleavages in society—ethnic, class, generational, social, or religious. Cleavages in Yugoslavia are quite clearly of a different order than those in Hungary; those in Albania are different from those in Poland. In all four countries, ethnic, tribal, religious, and generational cleavages play an important role in politics and must perforce influence any feasible strategy of political integration.

The level of economic and cultural development is crucial. The degree of differentiation in a society will indicate how many and what kinds of interest groups—actual or potential—may exist. It is important to know the level of self-consciousness of these groups and their strategic position in society (e.g., scientists as against musicians). This, too, is only a conditioning influence, for there is no automatic determining relationship between the developmental level of a society and the basis of its integration. Effective political socialization and overlapping group membership may prevent interest groups from developing independent postures on political issues.[30]

A decisive group, especially in Eastern Europe, is the intelligentsia, whose size, mood, strategic situation, scope (e.g., are scientists included?), and historical traditions must be considered. There are significant differences within these dimensions among Eastern European intelligentsias, for example. The extent of the politicization of the population, probably dependent on the level of general development, should be considered in terms of which sectors in the population are the most politicized, sectors being defined in terms not only of class, but of generation, ethnicity, sex, geography, etc.

Finally, perceptions of the outside world and the place of the particular nation-state within it are a central conditioning influence on both foreign and domestic policy. The Soviet Union's conception of itself as a global power as well as a regional and ideological leader compels some predispositions in Soviet behavior in the international area—where it is active in the Middle East, "restores order" in Czechoslovakia, and strives to seize the mantle of ideological author-

---

[30] See Jeremy Azrael, *Managerial Power and Soviet Politics* (Cambridge, Mass., 1966). See also Pirages, "Socio-Economic Development and Political Change," pp. 53–55. Pirages's methods of establishing levels of development are somewhat dubious.

ity from China—as well as at home, where political change is perhaps slowed somewhat by the need to consider its implications for other Communist systems. A public opinion survey in Poland in 1965 showed that the population, including youth, was very much aware of and interested in World War II, that 86.5 per cent of the respondents had close relatives involved in the fighting, and that the respondents rated the Polish contribution to the final victory as third most important after the Soviet Union and the United States.[31] This helps to explain why the "German question" is an effective symbol for mobilization of the population (as in the invasion of Czechoslovakia) and why the "raison d'état" argument remains the firmest prop of the regime.

"Organizational phenomena" central to comparative analysis would include the composition of the party, whether it be mass or elite, old or young, "blue-collar" or "white-collar," proletarian or peasant. That in nearly one-third of basic party organizations in northern Moravia there were no members under 25—in one district there were no members under 25 in nearly half of the party organizations—is an indicator of the prestige and attractiveness to the youth of the Czechoslovak party in the late 1960's.[32] In Bulgaria, whose ratio of students to population is among the highest in the world, only 9 per cent of the party members have a university education, and about 70 per cent do not even have a secondary education. Of the membership 28 per cent is over fifty years old, whereas only 13 per cent is under thirty.[33] It would be important to analyze the composition of the leadership echelons as well as the party as a whole to see if there are significant differences in the nature of these two groups.

The nature, extent, and impact of political socialization varied from country to country even in the Stalinist era, and this undoubtedly has influenced the political attitudes of several generations. Czechoslovak children were never weaned away from family influence as much as Soviet children, and both parents and teachers were able to transmit favorable ideas about Masaryk and the Republic, despite contrary official pressures. In 1959 Bulgaria intensified the ideological aspect of its educational process so that to this day indoctrination

[31] Eugeniusz Olczyk, "Wklad Narodu Polskiego w Zwycięstwo nad Faszyzmem Niemieckim w Swiadomości Wspolczesnych Polaków," *Studia Socjologiczno-Polityczne* (Warsaw), 24 (1967).

[32] V. Mencl and F. Ouřednik, "What Happened in January," *Život Strany*, No. 16 (Aug. 1968); Radio Free Europe, Czechoslovak Press Survey No. 2142 (Munich).

[33] Michael Costello, "Expertise and Partiinost: A Question of Priorities," Radio Free Europe Situation Report (Munich, Nov. 21, 1968).

constitutes a substantial part of education;[34] in the same period Poland de-emphasized the ideological content of education. Public opinion surveys seemed to indicate that in the late 1950's and early 1960's youth in Yugoslavia and the Soviet Union were for the most part unconcerned with religious belief and practice,[35] whereas a recent survey of Polish army recruits showed that nearly 85 per cent considered themselves believers with varying degrees of practice, and nearly 35 per cent explained their faith by citing the influence of their family. "It is difficult for me to say why I believe in God, but from my earliest childhood the family inclined me toward religion and they simply drummed it into me. . . . In my school years I believed in God out of respect for my parents—I didn't want to cause Mom anguish."[36] Perhaps more directly relevant to political change is the fact that the large majority of Polish and Yugoslav youth—and undoubtedly Czechoslovak and Hungarian as well—are not at all interested in a political career.[37]

Finally, it would be necessary to make a comparative analysis of the sources of pressure for change as well as more general strains on the system. Whether pressures for change come from this or that strategic elite, from nonstrategic elites or from other social groups, can indicate the likelihood, the direction, and the scope of political change.

Apart from these kinds of conditioning influences, the strategy of national integration chosen will greatly influence the strategy of political integration. We can postulate three basic strategies of national integration: coercive assimilation, incentive assimilation (acculturation), and cultural pluralism or national-cultural autonomy, with national integration achieved *through* political integration. The strategy to be adopted is influenced of course by the kinds of factors mentioned earlier, and by the particular demographic and social patterns of the country. Eastern European polities have shifted strategies of national integration over time, and these, too, can be seen as shifts

[34] For details see Peter John Georgeoff, *The Social Education of Bulgarian Youth* (Minneapolis, Minn., 1968), esp. pp. 12–13, 32–35, 43, 53–56.

[35] See Stanislaw Skrzypek, "The Political, Cultural and Social Views of Yugoslav Youth," *Public Opinion Quarterly*, XXIX: 1 (Spring 1965), 87–106; and Bohdan Bociurkiw, "Religion and Soviet Society," *Survey*, 60 (July 1966), 62–71.

[36] Czeslaw Staciwa, "Spoleczne Aspekty Religijności Mlodziezy Poborowej," *Studia Socjologiczno-Polityczne*, 24 (1967).

[37] See Skrzypek; also see several surveys of Polish attitudes, including *Some Aspects of the Social-Psychological and Political Climate in Poland*, Audience Research, RFE (mimeo.; Munich, 1961), and *Some Aspects of the Attitudinal and Political Climate in Poland (Attitude Survey II)*, Audience Research, RFE (mimeo.; Munich, 1963).

in the basis of integrating power: coercive assimilation obviously employs coercive power, incentive assimilation is based on utilitarian
appeals, and cultural pluralism, which involves national integration
through political integration, is based on normative appeals. Again,
all polities probably employ all or some of these strategies all or some
of the time, but we are concerned with the general direction and nature of policy. The effects of each basis of integration are no doubt the
same as would occur with political integration: coercive assimilation
is most alienating, cultural pluralism is least alienating, and incentive assimilation falls in between. The Soviet Union has used a mix of
coercive assimilation, incentive assimilation, and cultural pluralism.
The first has been used selectively, and in subtle ways. Cultural pluralism is expressed by the notion of Soviet patriotism. "Our fatherland is multinational . . . but our patriotism is unitary—Soviet. . . .
In each national republic of the USSR Soviet patriotism has its *national distinctiveness* . . . has its *unique characteristics* . . . *but their
patriotism has one socialist content.*"[38] In other words, the nationalities are integrated around common *political* values and aspirations,
but in theory they may express these values through unique cultural
forms. This, of course, is the Stalinist formula of "socialist in content,
national in form." From 1944 to 1953 the Yugoslav party adopted a
strategy of national integration through political integration, but as
the mobilizing force of political values forged in the partisan experience began to wane, the Yugoslavs shifted in theory to an attempt at
incentive assimilation by which national distinctions would give way
to a sense of Yugoslav ethnicity. This having failed, the regime shifted
back to an attempt to define "Yugoslav-ness" in political rather than
ethnic terms. That is, Serbs, Croats, Slovenes, and other groups were
to maintain a distinct *national* identity but to share a Yugoslav *political* identity. This sharing of political values would prevent divisive
nationalist tendencies from hampering the effectiveness of the system.[39] It is possible to trace similar fluctuations in Czechoslovakia
and in Rumania. In Poland, Bulgaria, and Hungary, by now largely
ethnically homogeneous, nationalism rather than national integration is the relevant term. East Germany, of course, is a unique case
and must be treated separately.

[38] I. E. Kravtsev, *Proletarskii Internatsionalizm, Otechestvo i Patriotizm* (Kiev,
1965), p. 45. See also Frederick C. Barghoorn, *Soviet Russian Nationalism* (New
York, 1956), pp. 9–11.
[39] See Paul Shoup, *Communism and the Yugoslav National Question* (New York,
1968). Shoup does not use these categories but we consider this a fair interpretation
of the developments he describes.

It is difficult to fix precisely the relationship between strategies of political and national integration. Can elites pursue a strategy of coercive assimilation or coercive separation simultaneously with a political strategy of authentic participation? Although this may be possible, the logical inconsistency involved will probably activate forces seeking to resolve the cognitive dissonances that inevitably arise in such situations, and there will be pressures on the system to make its strategies more compatible. Certainly, there is a frequent correlation between coercive political integration and coercive national integration. It would be enlightening to trace in parallel fashion the graphs of overall political shifts and change in national integration policy in Eastern Europe in order to try to illuminate the nature of the relationship between national integration and political integration. Perhaps the most enduring aspect of the recent attempt at political integration in Czechoslovakia is the adoption of national-cultural autonomy, resulting in genuine federalization as a strategy of political integration. Similar tandem fluctuations can be traced in Yugoslavia in the past decade, though its nationality problems are very far from being solved and there might be many future fluctuations. Part of the incremental liberalization process in Hungary has been a greater emphasis on the cultural rights of national minorities, the official party daily even going so far as to express its regret at the assimilatory processes taking place among some of the minorities and urging that more attention be paid to the development of national minority cultures. Similarly, along with some very tentative steps toward introducing some authentic political participation, the Rumanian regime has sought to conciliate the Hungarian population in Transylvania and has created nationality councils for Germans and Hungarians, suggesting that councils for others may also be formed. This may have been a short-term attempt to solidify the country in the wake of the Czechoslovak events, but it may also be a harbinger of things to come. In 1968–69 the Rumanian regime has shifted back and forth between liberalization and retrenchment.

In addition to all these conditioning influences on strategies of political integration, there exist influences that can be more narrowly defined as limitations or constraints. Leonard Binder has pointed out that a political formula must fulfill three requirements: "It must conform to the cultural peculiarities of the political community; it must accord with the level of civilization of that community or with the ontological character of its *weltanschauung*; and it must accord with prevailing ideas concerning the ethical bases of political obligation."[40] In the Eastern European context this means that strategies of political integration must be designed with the developmental level and political culture of the country in mind. The political formula must be placed in a "Marxist" context, however defined. The strategy chosen must take into account widely shared values and attitudes. It must also deal with the international position of the nation-state, and calculate the reaction to its formula not only by the Soviet Union and the other socialist countries, but by the West.

The present level of political integration and the degree of authority already enjoyed by the regime also set limits on the maneuverability of the strategists.

In stable systems which have no capacity to transform, the old consensual bases must collapse before new ones can be formed. On the other hand, *transformable* systems fundamentally revise their consensus during the course of their activities [compare Czechoslovakia in 1960–68 with Rumania in 1956–68]. An interesting mechanism by which this revision is accomplished is the broadening of a system by the legitimation of a new alternative and then a gradual shifting of the weight from earlier alternatives to the new one until the center of gravity of the whole system is altered.[41]

Thus, what could not be done in Hungary in 1956 can perhaps be done in the 1970's; what could not be done in Czechoslovakia in 1967 might be done in Rumania.

Strategies of Political Integration

For the reasons elaborated earlier, Eastern European political systems are differentially confronted with authority crises that can be resolved by political integration. For historical, situational, and organizational reasons they have not had some of the advantages that have enabled the Soviet Union to establish greater authority relationships within its system—the very longevity of the system, its highly effective political socialization, and its economic, political, and scientific successes.[42]

Given these disadvantages, in response to the perceived crises two general strategies of integration seem to be emerging in Eastern Europe. A third strategy has been used by systems not yet confronted by authority crises, but there is every reason to believe that in the long run these systems, too, will be confronted by the necessity for reinte-

[40] "National Integration and Political Development," *American Political Science Review*, LVIII: 3 (Sept. 1964), 625.
[41] Etzioni, *The Active Society*, p. 471.
[42] See Meyer, "Authority in Communist Political Systems," pp. 100–101.

gration. This necessity can be ignored by authoritarian systems, but at the cost of lessened effectiveness.

The two emerging strategies can be categorized as authentic participation and national performance. Every system must, of course, manifest satisfactory performance in material and psychic outputs if it is to establish or maintain its authority, but some make performance their main basis of authority while others legitimate themselves with notions of process as well as performance. In other words, there are different emphases on demand inputs and on outputs and feedback.

An authentic participatory system seems to have evolved in Yugoslavia and to have been projected in Czechoslovakia until August 1968. The high level of induced participation in Communist systems, for example in the 99 per cent voter turnouts, is well known, but this is not authentic participation; rather "it provides the appearance of responsiveness while the underlying condition is alienating." Authenticity exists where "the world responds to the actor's efforts, and its dynamics are comprehensible."[43] Authentic participation may be instituted in social and economic spheres to a greater degree than in the political sphere, but in the context of Eastern European political cultures and contemporary values this may be as significant and as desired as direct political participation in the Western sense. Yugoslavia has gradually broadened the scope of participation, beginning in the early 1950's with economic participation in the workers' councils and slowly expanding the notion of "self-management" to the political arena, where there are now contested elections for all levels of government, where interest groups are recognized and their social and political participation is institutionalized, and where a more authentic participation has even pervaded the League of Communists to the extent that republic party congresses are now being held prior to the federal congress. In the view of some Yugoslavs, the republic parties actually function as parts of a multiparty system. To be sure, the question of the scope, nature, and authenticity of economic as well as political participation is by no means settled, and there is a constant debate on these issues. But no one denies that the principle of authentic participation is to be the defining value of the Yugoslav political formula.[44] Process and performance together will maintain

[43] Etzioni, *The Active Society*, pp. 620–21.

[44] For claims that participation is not yet authentic, see, among others, Predrag Vranicki, "L'État et le parti dans le socialisme," *Praxis* (Zagreb), IV: 1–2 (1968), 96–103, and Svetozar Stojanović, "Social Self-Government and Socialist Community," pp. 104–16 in the same issue. See also Zagorka Pesic-Golubovic, "Socialism

the authority of the regime and ensure the continuing political integration of a system that is developing in the direction of a positively evaluated political community.

The development of an authentic participatory formula in Czechoslovakia was arrested by the Soviet invasion. At that point the formula was still in the process of evolution, and it is difficult to say what its eventual content would have been. It is safe to say that electoral reforms, press freedom and other civil liberties, workers' councils, authentically representative trade unions, legitimated interest groups, intra-party democracy and debate, and legal and cultural freedoms would have been at the heart of the formula.

Socialism can only develop if the various interests of the people are allowed to be expressed. . . . This is the main source of the development of free social activity and the development of the socialist system. . . . Political parties in our country cannot exclude common-interest organizations of workers and other working people from directly influencing state policy. . . . The Communist party of Czechoslovakia will use all means to develop forms of political life that will ensure the expression of the direct will of the working class and all working people in political decision-making in our country.[45]

That this was not mere rhetoric and that serious thought was being given to the development of a concrete, wide-ranging, and realistic political formula is proved by the work of the interdisciplinary Commission on the New Political Model concerning the function of interest groups in a socialist society, the role of the party, the nature of participation, and the like. There were even attempts made to develop systems analyses of socialist polities as a guide to correcting "deformations" within them.[46] With the Yugoslav experience as a guide and with a high level of cultural and economic development, the Czechoslovaks might have evolved a sophisticated and effective formula that would have built upon the impressive amount of authority that the Dubček regime had accumulated since January 1968.

National performance strategies de-emphasize demand inputs and emphasize outputs as the main source of support and authority. The

---

and Humanism," *Praxis*, I: 4 (1965), 520–61. For a different but not opposing view, see Vladimir Bakaric, "The Kind of League We Need," *Socialist Thought and Practice*, No. 28 (Oct.-Dec. 1967), 48–67. A very negative evaluation of the authenticity of participation in Yugoslavia is expressed in Nenad D. Popovic, *Yugoslavia: The New Class in Crisis* (Syracuse, N.Y., 1968); a more balanced appraisal may be found in M. George Zaninovich, *The Development of Socialist Yugoslavia* (Baltimore, 1968).

[45] *Akční Program Komunistické Strany Československa* (Prague, 1968), pp. 10, 22.

[46] Jindřich Fibich, "K Systémové Analýze Politicko-Organizačního Modelu Socialismu," *Sociologický Časopis*, IV: 2 (1968), 146–58.

Rumanian regime, starting out with little authority, has in the last five years or so gained a great deal of authority by attributing impressive and visible successes in the economic realm to the political system and the virtuosity of the national character, there being no conflict between the two. The Rumanian party seems to have successfully established itself as an authentic link in the chain of Rumanian national history. It is around these two values—economic development and national pride—that the Rumanian regime seeks to integrate its population. "In the course of establishing a new social regime, a new, superior form of national community has been realized . . . a socialist nation, inheriting and representing in our epoch the most progressive traditions and qualities of the Rumanian people. . . . The Rumanian people know that the transformations that have opened a new era to the socialist nation are due to the direction of the party to which they have entrusted their historic destiny."[47]

It may be that the Rumanian regime is beginning to move to a further reintegration on the basis of more authentic participation. Having established its authority, it is a more "transformable" system that can now rely on diffuse support to help prevent participation from becoming opposition. The achievement of a higher level of economic development may also eventually force such a reintegration, as has happened in some of the countries that have adopted more far-reaching economic reforms than Rumania.[48]

The Polish regime is among the least authoritative in Eastern Europe, with the likely exception of the Husák regime in Czechoslovakia. The Polish political culture—involving Catholicism, a self-image as the "Christ among nations," cultural affinity with the Latin West, hatred of a more powerful but spiritually inferior Asiatic culture to the East—makes it difficult to establish Communism as an authoritative doctrine, especially when many of the bearers of that doctrine are regarded as aliens. "When elites are external [or are perceived as such] (or when some are internal and some external), societal guidance is less effective and the social unit is less active than when all the elites are internal."[49] Whatever authority the regime has

---

[47] Nicolae Corbu and Constantin Mitea, "Le Développement de la nation socialiste et l'internationalisme prolétarien," *Documents, Articles et Informations sur la Roumanie*, XIX: 2 (Feb. 1, 1968). Translated from *Scinteia*, Jan. 24, 1968.

[48] See John Michael Montias, *Economic Development in Rumania* (Cambridge, Mass., 1968), pp. 244–47. For a different view of current Rumanian policy, see J. F. Brown, "Rumania Today: Towards 'Integration,' " *Problems of Communism*, XVIII: 1 (Jan.-Feb. 1969), esp. p. 12.

[49] Etzioni, *The Active Society*, p. 114.

rests on the grudging acceptance of unpleasant realities, *faute de mieux*. The system rests on resignation, not reconciliation, a situation that leads to stagnation without stability.

The "partisan" faction, led by a former Minister of the Interior, Mieczyslaw Moczar, is apparently developing an alternative political formula similar to that which has successfully generated authority in Rumania. There are situational advantages to the development of such a formula. A variety of studies have shown that the majority of Poles regard economic difficulties, not deficiencies in personal freedoms, as the chief failure of the regime. Polish youth are similarly concerned more with economic than with political opportunity.[50] The prewar acceptance of a partially state-controlled economic order, the nationalist-military tradition as embodied in Pilsudski and the "regime of the colonels," and traditional nationalism are other factors making a Rumanian-type strategy feasible. Since the "partisans" are an ill-defined grouping that has not published a systematic political program, it is difficult to say with certainty what their political program really is. But there are obvious attempts made to stress the value of economic efficiency and link up with successful "technocrat" types such as Edward Gierek. The partisan-inspired rewriting of history, particularly concerning the Polish role in World War II, the making of films along these lines, and the stress on the need for patriotism are one aspect of a campaign that strives to make the Polish party representative of the Polish people and its national history. This explains the partisan sponsorship of the effort to make party, state, and intellectual elites *judenrein* and to identify liberal dissenters as alien to the Polish body politic and its ideals. "The creation of a socialist production system, together with a socialist division of labor, does not mean that complete integration has been achieved in the most important area—namely, in the human mind. . . . One of the main elements . . . is the creation in the public of a feeling of co-responsibility for everything which concerns the country. . . . This is the proper meaning of popular patriotism."[51]

Since the youth of worker and peasant origin exhibits less tolerant attitudes than others, and is very much oriented toward economic

---

[50] See the RFE studies cited in note 37 above. See also Zbigniew Sufin and Wlodzimierz Wesolowski, "Work in the Hierarchy of Values," *Polish Sociological Bulletin*, No. 2 (1963).

[51] Andrzej Szczypiorski, "A Feuilleton: Social Integration Under Socialism," Radio Warsaw, Aug. 18, 1968; RFE, Polish Press Survey No. 2148. See also Jot, "Why Are Books by Partisans Selling Well?" *Wspólczesność*, June 19–July 2, 1968; RFE Polish Press Survey No. 2147; and *Polish Perspectives* (Warsaw), Oct. 1968.

efficiency and opportunity, a "partisan" strategy could elicit a positive response not only among various social classes but possibly among large sectors of the youth as well, who, despite the events of 1967–68, are not necessarily crusaders for liberalizing alternatives.[52] In short, an efficiency-oriented, authoritarian, nationalist political formula could gain legitimacy and establish authority for a "partisan" regime—and it may well be that only Soviet support for Gomulka following the "fraternal aid" given to Czechoslovakia prevented a "partisan" accession to power in Poland.

Hungary is just beginning to emerge from its second (post-1956) period of integration on the basis of power, "a long period in which democracy could not be mentioned in Hungary because the party and government were forced to use the language of power."[53] According to Andras Hegedüs, a former premier of Hungary and until his demotion a leading exponent of the need for a new political formula, "The party fighting for power has become a power party, a fact which has had both positive and negative results. . . . The social conditions exist for enabling the Leninist party to change over from a power party into a party fighting for socialist rule over the power of the social special administration."[54] This assertion is by no means widely accepted,[55] and although people such as Gyorgy Lukács argue that the New Economic Model ought to be accompanied by the gradual introduction of a new political formula,[56] important party leaders seemingly disagree.

The official tactic of the Hungarian regime in recent years has been a de-emphasis of politics and of the party, but it is doubtful that this can serve as a long-range strategy of integration. Having a large majority of parliamentary deputies made up of nonparty people while increasing parliament's power, replacing "political managers" by technically trained personnel, and strengthening the independence of the trade unions are all measures that accord well with a popular mood of passivity and indifference to politics. In the last decade the

[52] See Wieslaw Wisniewski, "Postawy Tolerancji—Korelaty i Uwarunkowania," *Studia Socjologiczno-Polityczne*, No. 19 (1965), and Zygmunt Bauman, "Polish Youth and Politics," *Polish Round Table: Yearbook, 1967* (Warsaw, 1967).

[53] L. Rozsa, "The Road of Our Democracy," *Népszabadsag*, Sept. 1, 1968, RFE Hungarian Press Survey No. 1950.

[54] Andras Hegedüs, "On the Alternatives of Social Development," *Kortars*, June 1968; RFE Hungarian Press Survey No. 1947.

[55] See I. Friss, "The Attack on Hegedüs," *Kortars*, Oct. 1968; RFE Hungarian Press Survey No. 1954.

[56] "Interview: At Home with Gyorgy Lukács," *New Hungarian Quarterly*, IX: 29 (Spring 1968), esp. pp. 76–78.

party has failed to reach 65 per cent of its pre-1956 membership, and "there are people who ask: is it worthwhile today to be a member of the party? . . . It would only add to my trouble."[57] Surveys indicate that a large majority of Hungarian youth and even party members are indifferent to party affairs, that the party has become largely an organization of bureaucrats, and that its membership is in many ways demoralized.[58]

Kádár's strategy of "He who is not against us is with us" has been successful in allowing the regime to survive the trauma of 1956; the policy of slow, cautious, incremental change, largely in the direction of "liberalization," has proved suitable to the situational, historical, and organizational constraints imposed on the Hungarians. However, it may well be that economic and social forces will impel the regime to attempt the evolution of a normative consensus. There is a lively debate on nationalism in Hungary today, but owing to external and internal limitations the evolution of a Hungarian strategy might be more in the direction of an authentic participatory one, as Hege-düs has obliquely suggested, than toward national performance. Perhaps a "third road" may be sought.

Bulgaria and Albania remain at levels of economic and social development that enable them to postpone transitions from power to authority. Bulgaria has undertaken reforms to ameliorate the difficulties produced by the "command economy," and there have been indications of discontent among the youth and the intelligentsia, but these strains seem to be so weak that they can be dealt with not by structural change but by "resolution" or "arrestation-isolation." We would expect that in the long run these two polities will also be confronted by the need for some kind of political reintegration.

As noted earlier, the Soviet regime probably enjoys more authority than most Communist regimes owing to such distinctive features as the sheer duration of its rule, which has enabled it to effectively socialize several generations, its position as a global power, and the scientific, economic, and domestic and foreign political successes it has achieved. Nevertheless, the Soviet system is subject to the need for political reintegration common to all polities. It, too, has had to attempt a transition from extensive to intensive economic development. The Stalinist mix of coercive and normative appeals has broken down with the abandonment of coercive appeals and the diminishing ef-

---

[57] *Népszabadsag*, quoted in Tibor Meray, "The Sources of Power," in Tamas Aczel, ed., *Ten Years After* (London, 1966), p. 127.
[58] *Ibid.*, pp. 127-35.

fectiveness of normative appeals. Khrushchev and his successors have tried to substitute utilitarian incentives ("goulash Communism") for coercion. But whereas Khrushchev sought to revive flagging normative commitments by stressing the "state of the whole people" as a scheme of essentially inauthentic participation to generate new commitment, his successors have failed to formulate a revised normative system, according earlier political formulae the kind of lip service one pays to an obsolete deity too venerable to be renounced.

The combination of the ossification and, hence, growing irrelevance of a dogmatized Marxism, a rather mediocre collective leadership that cannot afford political innovation lest the ship of state—and, most important, its helmsmen—be severely upset, and a paralysis of will resulting from the conviction that a defensive conservatism is the least risky course, has led the Soviet Union back to more traditional rhetoric and behavior in which themes of Russian nationalism predominate. World War II demonstrated that the most fundamental integrating force in Soviet society may well be Russian nationalism; and at times when a leadership is faced with internal and external challenges for which appropriate responses are difficult to find, it may be tempted to fall back on this integrating force. There is little doubt that among large parts of the population, and even among some segments of the intelligentsia, nationalistic, authoritarian, and anti-Semitic attitudes are acceptable and even favored. Thus, the Soviet Union may fall into the "national performance" category, perhaps by default rather than by design. Just as the emphasis on nationalism is used as a surefire formula when little else seems to work, so, too, economic reform is adopted, not in the spirit of exhilarating innovation, but in a mood of doing only what is absolutely necessary to keep one's head above water. The same temperament manifests itself in the area of Communist bloc relations: instead of devising a new structure and a new integrating formula for the Communist bloc, the Soviet Union tries merely to ensure the maintenance of the present structure of the group of Communist systems. Thus, while national performance may describe the present ethos of the Soviet regime, it is not really an active strategy. It is more a mood than a program, more a holding operation than a thrust forward. Whether this can provide systemic effectiveness, as against survival, remains to be seen.

The Role of the Party

One of the key issues that must be dealt with by any strategist of political integration in a Communist society is the role of the party.

The Yugoslavs have claimed that "divorcing the party from power" is the logical prospect; the party should perform the function of societal guidance but not of societal management. Rather than concern itself with the administration of the state, the League of Communists should be the guardian of broad ideological principles and the shaper of the population's social and political attitudes. Eventually the party, like the state, is to somehow "wither away." The Czechoslovak party, too, appeared to be abdicating some of its functions and allowing its monopoly of political power to erode with the activation of minor parties, the abolition of party control of the media, and the formation of nonparty political groupings. Such developments were intolerable to the Soviet Union, which correctly judged that they meant the acceptance of a radically new political formula. In Rumania the role of the party has been strengthened along with the development of a national-performance strategy because, in contrast to the Czechoslovak party, the Rumanian party is both "red" and "expert." Since the party was very small when it came to power, it did not need to reward older, politically reliable, but professionally unqualified party members with managerial posts, as the Yugoslav and Czechoslovak parties have had to do.[59] In Rumania, therefore, a greater role for the party and demands for intensive economic development might not be mutually exclusive. The same applies to East Germany, where the national performance strategy has been pursued along with the maintenance of high levels of ideological consciousness. Ulbricht resolved the "red-expert" dilemma in 1963 by initiating a policy of rewarding technical expertise while insisting on a high level of political commitment. In Bulgaria the low level of education among party members may well prove to be a problem in the not-too-distant future. The Polish party is hampered by chronic factionalism; the role of such organizations as ZBOWID (the organization of army veterans), for example, points to internal party weakness that allows other structures a role in the political process, though this does not necessarily mean that the system is deliberately structured as a "hegemonic party system" with political pluralism legitimated.[60]

[59] In 1966 the percentage of engineers and technicians in the Czechoslovak party was 17.3 per cent; scientific workers made up 0.2 per cent. Over 70 per cent of the membership had an elementary education, but only 5.9 per cent had reached the university level. Figures cited in Barbara Jancar, "The Case for a Loyal Opposition under Communism: Czechoslovakia and Yugoslavia," *Orbis*, XII: 2 (Sept. 1968), 424–25.

[60] Jerzy Wiatr has argued that the Polish system is qualitatively different from the Soviet and some other Socialist systems because it institutionalizes and legitimates pluralism. "Elements of Pluralism in the Polish Political System," *Polish*

The larger issue of the role of the party can be conceived as the need to change a "party of solidarity," appropriate to the mobilization era, to a party appropriate to a post-mobilization period. In an authentic-participatory system the party could become a "party of representation," in Apter's sense, appropriate to a "reconciliation system." The problem for a Communist party is that, aside from its natural tendency toward the preservation of its monopoly of power, if it becomes an instrument of representation "the party cannot reflect grievances in the community without weakening the conditions of authority," and it may become a mere "go-between in the dialogue between ruler and ruled."[61] A Leninist party cannot easily accept a role as a mediator between interest groups, a mere reflector of ideas, values, policies, and programs generated elsewhere in society. Nor can all parties easily choose to exercise only ideological functions, as the Yugoslavs claim their party is doing, or to be concerned largely with economic and administrative matters. In the post-mobilization era, in other words, the party is in search of a role.

Whereas some more radical Eastern Europeans suggest that the party simply disappear as a vestigial organ, others recognize that the integration of society requires a guiding mechanism and that the party might well fulfill this need. "The fundamental question of the present historical moment is the transformation of the party from a directing political force . . . into a director of the process of self-management."[62] Clearly, the role of the party is a more delicate issue for systems opting for authentic-participatory strategies, since those opting for national-performance strategies could retain the structure and political position of the party while altering the content of its ideology, thus making it a party of "experts," for example.

Effectiveness and Survival

One may well ask whether, in light of the Soviet intervention in Czechoslovakia, the Soviet constraint on the development of strategies of political integration is so powerful as to overcome all pressures toward the development of such strategies. This may well be the case,

Sociological Bulletin, No. 1 (1966). See also his " 'One-Party' Systems—The Concept and Issue for Comparative Studies," in Erik Allardt and Yrjo Littunen, *Cleavages, Ideologies and Party Systems: Transactions of the Westermarck Society*, X (Helsinki, 1961).

61 Zbigniew K. Brzezinski, "The Soviet Political System: Transformation or Degeneration," *Problems of Communism*, XV: 1 (Jan.-Feb. 1966).

62 Vranicki, "L'État et le parti dans le socialisme," p. 102. See also Stojanovic, "Social Self-Government," p. 108, and Veljko Rus, "Institutionalization of the Revolutionary Movement," *Praxis*, II: 2 (1967), 212–13.

assuming that Soviet behavior itself will not change, but this would seriously reduce the effectiveness of the Eastern European polities. Because of the alienating consequences of coercion it cannot be indefinitely applied to modern societies without crippling their effectiveness. Hungary serves as an example of the long-run need to move from integration by force to integration by authority. There are serious risks involved in trying to assure a system's survival without providing for its effectiveness. "A social system can . . . resist exogenous change and fail to adapt, either by remaining static or by introducing reactionary change. In this case, a cycle of cumulative dysfunction and increasing malintegration is initiated, which beyond a certain point becomes irreversible, and makes revolutionary change inevitable."[63]

The concept of an effective society is an elusive one because the kinds of empirical indicators used to measure the effectiveness of an economy have not yet been developed for measuring political effectiveness. Ted Gurr, Raymond Tanter, and others have developed measures of what might be called *in*effectiveness, and there is a substantial body of literature on organizational effectiveness. Deane Neubauer and Lawrence Kastner offer a way of determining the "level of noncompliance" in a society.[64] Another suggestion is that

governmental effectiveness can be measured uniformly both by objective indices (such as physical survival or increases in the gross national product) and by subjective indices (such as feelings of well-being and belief in an ameliorative future). The problem with objective indicators is that they must be shown to correspond to evaluations of the people. This can be done by comparing what people expect of their government with what they think they are getting.[65]

Seymour Martin Lipset suggests that effectiveness can be defined as the extent to which a political system satisfies the expectations of most members of a society "and the expectations of powerful groups within it that might threaten the system, such as the armed forces."[66]

[63] Van den Berghe, "Dialectic and Functionalism," in Demerath and Peterson, p. 298.

[64] Deane E. Neubauer and Lawrence D. Kastner, "The Study of Compliance Maintenance as a Strategy for Comparative Research," *World Politics*, XXI: 4 (July 1969), 637–40.

[65] Philip E. Jacob and Henry Teune, "The Integrative Process: Guidelines for Analysis of the Bases of Political Community," in Jacob and Toscano, *The Integration of Political Communities*, p. 43. In the same volume Karl Deutsch suggests some other, more general, indicators of "governmental performance" (pp. 143–44).

[66] "Some Social Requisites of Democracy: Economic Development and Political Legitimacy," *American Political Science Review*, LIII: 1 (Mar. 1959), 86.

Whatever the merits of these suggestions, it is certain that Eastern European elites are conscious of the need to develop and maintain what *they* can consider effective polities. Irrespective of the direction of their development there is a growing awareness among Eastern Europeans that if societies are to avoid "entropy," stagnation, and ineffectiveness, they must engage in a continuing, though not continuous, process of political integration and reintegration on the basis of strategies and forces appropriate to their particular developmental level and geopolitical environment. As Hegedüs has written, "There are several possible directions to be followed by our social development, and we cannot even exclude the possibility of a deadlock. But, come what may, we must choose among these possibilities: This is our freedom and at the same time our responsibility."[67]

If, as we have tried to argue, the Communist systems of Eastern Europe are permitted to choose different directions of development and evolve different strategies of political integration, then the systems themselves will become ever more differentiated from each other and the adjective "Communist" will become increasingly imprecise. If, however, they are prevented from evolving individual strategies, their effectiveness may well diminish and the adjective "Communist" will describe stagnant systems, incapable of nonviolent change and hence suffering from arrested political development. Czechoslovakia's development in the next few years may become the paradigmatic case for the more advanced Eastern European polities. The political integration of Czechoslovakia based on a new political formula was interrupted in order to preserve the defining characteristics of an ineffective system. The costs of assuring the survival of the old political formula may become apparent in the near future; the benefits of a more effective system based on authority may not soon be known. It must be admitted that this is a normative rather than a truly descriptive statement, and that the "necessity" for political reintegration is one that can be ignored in the short run. "For most regime-leaders, what [Manfred] Halpern calls 'treading water,' i.e., avoiding repudiation without necessarily increasing support or compliance, may be the most realistic goal. The practice is often made easier by the fact that conscious activities leading to the full repudiation of a regime are also difficult to carry to fruition. A regime can tread water for a long while in a category between full legitimacy and full repudiation."[68]

[67] "On the Alternatives of Social Development."

[68] Richard Rose, "Dynamic Tendencies in the Authority of Regimes," *World Politics*, XXI: 4 (July 1969), 627–28.

Technology and Political Change
in Eastern Europe

R. V. BURKS

Social scientists find it analytically useful to treat Communism in power as a mobilization system. Although the term mobilization is borrowed from military parlance, the aim of Communist mobilization is not, at least in the immediate sense, the prosecution of war, but rather the industrialization and modernization of a backward country under forced draft, through a series of revolutions from above. Soviet Russia under Stalin provides the classic example of this process, all other Communist regimes being variants of the Soviet model. The regimes develop a machinery of mobilization, characterized by central management of the economy; systematic indoctrination of the population; economic, political, and cultural self-isolation combined with xenophobia; forced labor camps; and above all the use of political terror.

Once a fair degree of industrialization and modernization has been achieved, the Communist regime typically enters a post-mobilization stage in which revolutions from above cease to occur, the policies of indoctrination and self-isolation are modified, the use of coercion is played down, and the role of material incentives is increased. Still, the central management of the economy is continued to a greater or lesser degree. Although the machinery of mobilization remains and at least theoretically could be put to its old uses, the requirements of modern industry tend to push Communist leaders toward greater re-

This essay, which first appeared in a slightly altered version as a Memorandum of the RAND Corporation, is based on research made possible by a grant to RAND from the United States Air Force. I wish to thank A. S. Becker, Lilita Dzirkals, F. W. Ermarth, Francis Hoeber, Oleg Hoeffding, Arnold Horelick, F. C. Iklé, Nancy Nimitz, and W. A. Stewart, who individually and collectively played an important part in producing this study. In particular, I would like to thank Gregory Grossman of the University of California, Berkeley, for his helpful insights concerning Soviet-style systems.

liance on the rule of law and improvements in living standards as means of controlling their populations. So far, the Soviet Union and the people's democracies of Eastern Europe are the only Communist regimes of the world to have entered the post-mobilization stage. They did so during the rule of Khrushchev and under the banner of de-Stalinization.[1]

The Problem of Legitimation

In the Stalinist epoch the European Communist regimes were not much concerned with the feelings and attitudes of the masses. The Communists regarded the populations they ruled primarily as a resource to be exploited in much the same way as a material resource; dissent was to be dealt with by terrorism. As they entered the post-mobilization period, however, Communist leaders increasingly solicited the cooperation of their populations in order to avoid relying primarily on coercion. They had found that coercion was not only an inefficient method of operating a modern industrial plant but a method that tended to get out of hand, wreaking havoc among the ruling groups themselves. As for the populations of these countries, they clearly remembered the sacrifices that had been exacted of them, and consequently hated their Communist rulers. This was especially true in countries where Communist regimes had been imposed as a consequence of Soviet military occupation at the close of World War II. In Russia, Yugoslavia, and Albania, where the Communist regimes were largely of indigenous origin, the problem of popular disaffection was not as severe, since the Communists had the active support of important local elements. But even in these three countries the Communist party probably could not have won a majority in a free election.[2]

In addition to undergoing de-Stalinization, Eastern Europe was affected during Khrushchev's rule by the process of "desatellization." This process was dual in nature, involving some reduction in Soviet

[1] For an elegant and perceptive discussion of the Soviet transition to the post-mobilization stage, see Richard Lowenthal, "The Soviet Union in the Post-Revolutionary Era: An Overview," in Alexander Dallin and Thomas B. Larson, eds., *Soviet Politics since Khrushchev* (Englewood Cliffs, N.J., 1968), pp. 1–22. Strictly speaking, Czechoslovakia and Rumania are socialist republics rather than people's democracies.

[2] The currently imprisoned Yugoslav deviationist Mihajlo Mihajlov claims that in a free election the Yugoslav Communist Party would not garner as many votes as it has members. A million persons are inscribed on the party's rolls, as contrasted with an electorate of more than 12.5 million persons. "Unspoken Defence of Mihajlo Mihajlov," *New Leader*, L: 10 (May 8, 1967), 7. The Yugoslav Communist Party probably has a wider spectrum of popular support than most Communist parties.

control and support of the local regimes, on the one hand, and the gradual acquisition by the local regimes of pockets of indigenous support, making them less dependent on Moscow, on the other. The extent of desatellization has been uneven, ranging all the way from independence (forced on the Yugoslav regime, for example, before de-Stalinization began) through various types of client status (e.g., Hungary) to satellite status, complete with the presence of a huge Soviet garrison (e.g., East Germany).[3] Desatellization enhanced the responsiveness of the regimes to popular attitudes by enabling them to be more flexible.

Perhaps the principal problem facing the post-mobilization regimes of Eastern Europe was that of legitimation. The regimes began to search for some modification of their mobilization machinery, together with an appropriate mixture of incentives and rewards, that could gradually convert the hostility of the populations, first into passive acceptance, and ultimately into positive loyalty. The problem varied from regime to regime in urgency, but even the strongest and most stable had a growing need for legitimation. The regime's need was also the population's opportunity: by granting or withholding cooperation, the populations could now exert a certain pressure on their rulers. Thus a slow and usually silent process of bargaining began, in which concessions were traded for cooperation. This became particularly evident after 1956, when events in Hungary and in Poland revealed to the Communists the extent of popular disaffection, and when the West's refusal to intervene convinced the people that the only hope for improvement was piecemeal modification of the existing system.

Generally speaking, the Communist regimes have developed three approaches to the problem of legitimation, all of them interrelated. The first of these is the appeal to national sentiment, an approach best exemplified by Rumanian policy. Not only have Rumanian leaders defied Moscow's wishes by pursuing an across-the-board policy of industrialization (with widespread popular support at home and with extensive financial and technical help from the West), but they have even raised indirectly the Rumanian claim to the Soviet province of Bessarabia.

A second approach is that of attempting to democratize the Com-

[3] For detailed analyses of this transition, see R. V. Burks, "The Rumanian National Deviation: An Accounting," in Kurt London, ed., *Eastern Europe in Transition* (Baltimore, 1966), pp. 93–116; and Burks, "Liberalization of Dictatorship: The East European Experience," paper presented at the 1967 annual meeting of the American Political Science Association (mimeo.).

munist single-party system of government. The outstanding example
here is provided by Yugoslavia, which is working out a system of elections in which the voter will have a choice, not among parties, but
among candidates.[4] By this and other measures, Belgrade has attempted to suggest that in some sense the population has a voice in
major decisions, and that in any case there is a set of rules and a policy
of give-and-take in dealing with conflicts of interest between the rulers
and the ruled.

The third approach to the problem of legitimation, and the one
with which the present essay is concerned, is that of raising living
standards. These have noticeably improved as compared to the bleak
days of Stalinist privation but are still far from being comparable to
the standards of Western Europe. The highest living standard in
Communist Europe is enjoyed by the population of East Germany,
yet the East German living standard is only two-thirds that of the
West German. The political significance of such a disparity is obvious. It is no wonder, then, that economic growth has become a matter of high priority for the Communist regimes in Eastern Europe,
and it is with the problem of growth that we shall begin our discussion.

Stalinist Central Planning and Economic Growth

Between 1951 and 1964 the rate of growth of gross national product
(GNP) in Eastern Europe tended to decline, as Table 1 shows, although it recovered to about 4.5 per cent in 1967–68.[5] There are, to
be sure, immediate reasons for the 1954–61 decline. The high rates
of the early 1950's to some extent reflect postwar recovery, which was
generally delayed in Eastern Europe, and especially in East Germany.
The rates of the later 1950's were again somewhat inflated, this time
by the efforts of East Germany, Czechoslovakia, and Bulgaria to "overtake and surpass" the achievements of the West. The sharp decline of
the early 1960's was in part the result of adjustments made necessary
by this European version of the Great Leap Forward.[6] The improvement in the late 1960's no doubt reflected the Communist regimes'
greater concern for economic efficiency and the consequently greater
role of economists in some regimes. But in addition to the immediate
reasons for these fluctuations in growth rates, there are indications

---

[4] R. V. Burks and S. A. Stanković, "Yugoslawien auf dem Weg zu halbfreien
Wahlen?" *Osteuropa*, XVII: 2–3 (Feb.-Mar. 1967), 131–46.
[5] Letter from Edward Snell to R. V. Burks, Apr. 7, 1969.
[6] *Ibid.*

TABLE 1

Increases in Gross National Product, Eastern and Western Europe,
1951–64

Area	1951–55	1956–60	1961–64
Six Eastern European countries[a]	5.9%[e]	5.2%	3.8%
Nine Western European countries[b]	5.3	4.7	5.2

SOURCE: Data taken from Maurice Ernst, "Postwar Economic Growth in Eastern Europe: A Comparison with Western Europe," in *New Directions in the Soviet Economy: Studies Prepared for the Subcommittee on Foreign Economic Policy of the Joint Economic Committee, Congress of the United States,* Part IV: *The World Outside and a Selected Bibliography of Recent Soviet Monographs and Appendixes* (Washington, D.C., 1966), pp. 875–916, esp. table 4, p. 880.

[a] Albania and Yugoslavia are not included.

[b] Includes Austria, Belgium, Denmark, France, West Germany, Greece, Italy, The Netherlands, and Norway.

[e] All percentages are unweighted averages of annual percentage increases.

that in the longer run, at least by the mid-1970's, the general decline will resume, for Communist economies are increasingly liable to certain kinds of inefficiencies as they advance to industrial maturity.

Before turning to the reasons for these inefficiencies, however, we must place the Communist economies in their world context, since a traditional prime objective of Communist regimes is to catch up with and overtake the West. (The misbegotten "great leap" programs of the 1950's are one consequence of this attitude.) The Communists claim not only that they have created a society that is morally superior to that of the West but also that, in the long run, they will be able to create one that is economically more efficient. Nevertheless, not only the Communist leaders but the populations under their rule take Western Europe, rather than Russia, as their standard of comparison; Eastern Europeans, many of whom tend to look down on the Russians as non-Europeans, assume they are entitled to a reasonable approximation of the Western Europeans' living standard. But the gap between the two standards is sizable. Moreover, the Communist countries are shooting at a moving target, for the West is putting itself through one technological revolution after another. Synthetic fibers, plastics, nuclear energy, transistors, digital computers, xerography, lasers, follow one another in seemingly endless succession. As Western technology becomes more complex, furthermore, the time lag involved in its reproduction by Eastern Europeans becomes greater. The lag now runs anywhere from two to fifteen years, with the odds at least 50–50 that the product will be obsolete in Western terms when it first appears on the Eastern market. In computers, for example, the time lag for Soviet (not to speak of Eastern European) borrowing varies between two and ten years.[7] This is not to suggest that no superior technology is to be found in Eastern Europe. The Rumanians do produce (and market abroad) superior oil-well drilling equipment, for example. But in comparison with Western Europe and the United States, the economies of Eastern Europe are far behind, and thus far from meeting the goals they have set. Why has there been this technological lag?

Having pointed out the political relevance of economic growth in Eastern Europe, we may return to the reasons why the Eastern European economies become increasingly inefficient as they reach maturity. The first reason is that the purpose toward which economic growth in the Communist countries has in the past been directed—the acquisition of power—conflicts with the new concern for living standards, itself a product of economic growth. In Western societies economic growth has from the beginning been mostly consumer-oriented, so that emphasis has been put on light industry and, increasingly in recent times, on services. Some Westerners have come to regard the "military-industrial establishment" in their countries with misgivings, and are reluctant to spend money for military purposes. Communist regimes, by contrast, have historically emphasized the military aspect of economic growth to a greater degree; thus they have concentrated their efforts in the industrial sector, and particularly on heavy industry. They have rigorously limited the amount of foreign help they have been willing to accept, and they have regularly sacrificed the

[7] Presumably the Eastern Europeans would not be more adept at borrowing such complex technology than their Soviet colleagues. As Richard Judy has noted, "Literally all significant technological innovations in computer technology have occurred in the West." For practical purposes every Soviet computer is still custom-made. As of 1968, according to Judy, there were approximately 50,000 computers installed in the United States, whereas in the Soviet Union the number of non-military computers installed was on the order of 2,000; indeed, on the basis of machines installed the Soviet Union lagged behind the United Kingdom, Germany, Japan, and France. See Richard W. Judy, "The Case of Computer Technology," in Stanislaw Wasowski, ed., East-West Trade and the Technology Gap: A Political and Economic Appraisal (New York, 1970), pp. 43–72. In Radovan Richta et al., Civilizdcia na Rázcestí (Bratislava, 1968), table I–2 gives somewhat different figures; for number of installed computers as of 1965 the figures are United States 80,205, Soviet Union 3,500, Japan 1,837, West Germany 2,291, Great Britain 1,600, France 1,500, and Czechoslovakia 36. (Information from tables by Richta has been translated from the Slovak version of his book. Text materials have been translated in Civilization at the Crossroads—Social and Human Implications of the Scientific and Technological Revolution [Prague, 1967], by courtesy of W. E. Griffith.) Wade Holland of the RAND Corporation differs with Richta in estimating the number of installed nonmilitary computers in the Soviet Union in 1968 as somewhere between 5,000 and 6,000.

living standards of their populations, more particularly of the peasantry, in order to acquire necessary investment capital.

When it becomes politically important to keep living standards going up, then, Communist regimes face something of a dilemma. In Eastern Europe entire branches of industry have been developed that can probably never become competitive in the world market because of a lack of raw materials or other structural weaknesses. The huge iron and steel complex at Dunapentele in Hungary, a country that has neither iron nor coal deposits, is a good example. The Dunapentele complex may contribute to the defense of the socialist camp, but it does so inevitably at the expense of the Hungarian consumer. Furthermore, the consumer's desire for a wide range of choice among quality goods and for a variety of services generally goes unsatisfied in Eastern Europe. Stalinist central planning, much like the quartermaster department of an army, is best adapted to the production and distribution of standard wares with a limited range of choice. Stalinist central planners also tend to discourage the development of tertiary or service industries, partly because such industries tend to be exclusively consumer-oriented, and partly because many forms of service are best carried out by small, private enterprises, against which the planners nourish a doctrinal bias.

In addition to this implicit conflict in goal orientation, Stalinist central planning has difficulty coping with the extraordinary complexity and interdependence of a highly specialized industrial society. This situation manifests itself most clearly in a growing informational problem. Under Stalinist planning, of course, most prices are centrally determined, presumably in such a way as to promote rapid industrialization. They do not necessarily reflect the relative scarcity of raw materials or the needs of consumers, as market prices do. As specialization becomes more intense and interdependence greater, price distortion becomes more and more extreme, so that it becomes increasingly difficult to know what anything costs. Thus it is hard to decide, for example, whether retooling in order to introduce a new process is worthwhile. An increasing number of indeterminate variables must enter into each economic decision.

One school of Soviet economists has gone so far as to propose that digital computers be used to produce a set of simulated market prices that could be used for decision-making while the centrally fixed prices continued to govern actual business transactions. But this proposal faces many and perhaps insuperable difficulties. To work out a set of simulated market prices for planning use would require a matrix of some 800 variables times 20,000 products. Aside from the difficulty of transmitting such enormous quantities of information to and from a single center with the necessary speed and accuracy, Soviet industry (let alone that of Eastern Europe) has yet to begin serial production of digital computers.

Another reason for inefficiency, apart from goal conflict and the informational problem resulting from increasing complexity, is that the rate of technological innovation has increased relatively slowly in Eastern Europe. For example, as Table 2 shows, the rate of invention is substantially lower in Eastern than in Western Europe. Another example is provided by the East German metalworking industry. East Germany is probably the most industrially advanced of all the Communist states, including the Soviet Union, and metalworking is of decisive importance for the economy as a whole. And yet we find that two-thirds of the total output of East Germany's centrally managed metalworking industry is produced in traditional workshops and only one-third by assembly line methods (and only 0.5 per cent of assembly line production is automated!). In the shop method, semifinished wares are moved about from one handicraft establishment to the next, each shop making its own specialized contribution to the finished

TABLE 2

Inventions Registered per 100,000 Inhabitants, 1964

Country	Number of Inventions
Belgium	164
Austria	147
Denmark	131
Norway	121
Czechoslovakia	52
Hungary	20
Poland	10
Rumania	7

SOURCES: L. Marinete, "Protection of Original Technical Achievement and the Economic Importance of This Protection," *Invenţii si Inovaţii* (Bucharest), I: 1 (Jan. 1966), 5–7, as translated in Joint Publications Research Service (JPRS) 35,350, No. 567 (May 1966), pp. 61–67, and Statistical Office of the United Nations, *Demographic Yearbook, 1964* (New York, 1965), pp. 126–27. Marinete took his figures from a 1964 publication of the United International Bureaux for the Protection of Industrial Property (Geneva). In R. Richta *et al.*, *Civilizácia na Rázcestí*, table IV–6 shows 56 registrations per 100,000 population in Czechoslovakia rather than the 52 given by Marinete. Richta also shows the United States and the Soviet Union as each having registered 56 inventions per 100,000 in 1964. The Soviet figure is probably accurate, but the United States figure is probably not. Major firms in the United States, such as General Motors, apparently often defend inventions by secrecy. United States patent law requires extremely detailed descriptions of each device and does not always defend the patents against even minor variations. It is, of course, true, for reasons to be given later in the text, that inventors in Eastern Europe have less reason to register their inventions. Nonetheless, the gap between the two sets of countries would probably still be large even if the figures were strictly comparable.

product. Assembly line techniques include what I will call batch production, which involves the movement of teams of workers from one semifinished object to the next, all under a single roof, on the basis of time and motion studies.[8]

This rather surprising state of affairs could presumably be remedied by large-scale imports of Western technology; such a policy has been favored by Communists from the beginning. Unfortunately, the Communist countries have difficulty paying for such imports. It would normally be expected that these countries would begin to replace agricultural exports with machinery as they industrialized. But this has not been the case; machines represent only 2 to 3 per cent of Eastern Europe's exports to the West. Indeed, such exports make up only 20 or 25 per cent of Eastern Europe's total foreign trade. Technologically, the two most advanced countries in the area are East Germany and Czechoslovakia, yet the manufactures of neither of these states are competitive in the West. In the Common Market, Czech and East German manufactures bring only about half the price paid for comparable goods produced by members of the European Free Trade Association.[9]

Since Eastern Europe's manufactures are not competitive, technological imports must be paid for by agricultural products and raw materials; in this sense the Communist economies retain a colonial character. In their haste to build factories, however, the Communist regimes have neglected agriculture so that, in contrast with what happened in the West, the rise in Eastern European agricultural productivity has lagged behind industrial growth. Consequently, the

[8] For percentages of gross industrial production done by the traditional shop method as opposed to the assembly line method, see Ludwig Auerbach, "Industrielle Forschung und Entwicklung in Mitteldeutschland: Die Hintergrunde des Ost-Berliner technologischen Defizits," *Aus Politik und Zeitgeschichte: Beilage zur Wochenzeitung des Parlaments* (Hamburg), Apr. 24, 1968, 3–30.

[9] For actual prices brought by Czechoslovak manufactures in the Common Market in 1964, see "Prices in Czechoslovakia's Trade with the EEC," *Politicka Economie*, 7–8 (July-Aug. 1967), 613–29, as translated in *Foreign Press Digest* (Washington, D.C.), Sept. 28, 1967. The prices quoted may, however, be somewhat misleading, since the items listed may not be comparable in size, weight, design, etc. Joseph Goldmann and Karel Kouba's *Economic Growth in Czechoslovakia: An Introduction to the Theory of Economic Growth under Socialism, Including an Experimental Application of Kalecki's Model to Czechoslovak Statistical Data* (Prague, 1969), pp. 83–91, argues that the low price of Czech manufactured wares in the West can be traced in part to an absolute loss in the efficiency of Czech industry after 1948. The authors note on pp. 88–89: "The fact that Czechoslovak machinery can command on West European markets in general under two-thirds of the per-kilogram prices attained by capitalist competitors, although the factor inputs for the Czechoslovak goods are often higher, is due to a lower technological level, inferior quality in the widest sense, inadequate equipment and servicing, etc."

TABLE 3

Sources of Economic Growth in the USA During the
Years 1839–1957

Period	Average Annual Rate of Growth	Contribution of Extensive Factors	Contribution of Intensive Factors	Share of Intensive Factors in the Total Rate
1839–49	5.2%	5.4%	−0.2%	−3.8%
1849–59	6.2	6.1	0.1	1.6
1859–69	2.3	3.7	−1.4	−60.9
1869–79	6.2	4.2	2.0	32.3
1879–89	6.3	5.1	1.2	19.0
1889–99	4.5	2.9	1.5	33.3
1899–1909	4.3	3.1	1.1	25.6
1909–19	3.8	2.3	1.5	39.5
1919–29	3.1	1.6	1.4	45.2
1929–37	0.2	−0.9	1.1	550.5
1937–48	4.4	2.2	2.2	50.0
1948–53	4.7	2.2	2.4	51.1
1953–57	2.2	0.7	1.5	68.2

SOURCE: R. Richta *et al.*, *Civilizácia na Rázcestí*, table I–12A.

more the regimes industrialize and urbanize, the larger the proportion of their foodstuffs (and raw materials) they require for domestic consumption. To make matters worse, the Common Market has erected tariff barriers that interfere with Eastern Europe's agricultural exports.[10] Thus as the Communist countries industrialize, their ability to import new technology from the West rises more slowly than their import needs. We must, of course, emphasize the fact that the difficulties we are discussing plague only the industrially advanced countries in our group, East Germany and Czechoslovakia. The other countries confront these problems to a lesser degree.

Communist planners have their own explanation of the disadvantages to Stalinist central planning under conditions of advanced industrialization. In the beginning, they assert, growth stems primarily from greatly increased inputs of the factors of production; later growth is the result primarily of improved utilization of inputs. As industrialization proceeds, in other words, growth gradually ceases to be extensive and instead becomes intensive in character. This view of the nature of economic growth is to be found throughout the specialized literature of the Communist regimes and is illustrated by Tables 3 and 4, both of which were prepared by Czech economists.

[10] East Germany is an exception in that interzonal trade, i.e., trade between East and West Germany, is treated by the EEC as internal German trade.

TABLE 4

*Sources of Economic Growth in Czechoslovakia in the
Years 1951–64*

Year	Rate of Growth of National Income	Contribution of Capital	Contribution of Labor	Contribution of Extensive Factors	Contribution of Intensive Factors	Share of Intensive Factors in the Total Rate
1951	9.53%	3.51%	0.00%	3.51%	6.02%	63.17%
1952	10.65	3.55	0.04	3.59	7.06	66.29
1953	6.44	3.35	−0.04	3.31	3.13	48.60
1954	3.54	3.70	0.23	3.93	−0.39	−11.02
1955	10.28	4.17	0.53	4.70	5.58	54.28
1956	5.35	3.79	0.32	4.11	1.24	23.18
1957	7.25	4.77	0.26	5.03	2.22	30.69
1958	8.23	5.01	0.05	5.06	3.17	38.52
1959	6.34	5.93	−0.02	5.91	0.43	6.78
1960	8.08	6.17	−0.26	5.91	2.17	26.86
1961	6.77	5.93	−0.08	5.85	0.92	13.59
1962	1.40	5.69	0.01	5.70	−4.30	−307.14
1963	−2.17	5.15	−0.02	5.13	−7.30	−336.40
1964	0.89	5.23	0.04	5.27	−4.38	−492.13

SOURCE: Richta *et al.*, table I–12C. On the basis of conversations with leading Czech economists, Gregory Grossman has considerable doubt about the calculations on which the first two columns in this table are based. (Conversation with Dr. Grossman at Berkeley, California, June 12, 1969.)

Among Western economists, however, this view of growth is controversial.

Whatever its value to scholars and planners, the extensive-intensive view of economic growth is politically useful to Communist leaders, who can equate the early period of "extensive" growth with the waste and brutality of, for example, the collectivization of agriculture. Similarly, entrance into the period of "intensive" growth, which is identified with technological advances, helps to explain and justify current regime efforts at economic reform. In this connection some recent words of the Soviet First Party Secretary Leonid Brezhnev are worth noting:

I should like to dwell on a feature of our economic development that is assuming ever-growing significance every year. I mean the introduction of the newest achievements of science and technology in all branches of our economy and the scientific-technological progress of all our society. Remember, comrades, what Vladimir Ilich Lenin said: productivity of labor, he stressed, is in the final analysis the most important and main factor in the victory of the new social order. Communism, as opposed to capitalism, means the highest productivity of voluntary labor of conscious and united workers utilizing advanced technology. A scientific-technological revolution, unprecedented in scope and pace, is now taking place in the world. It is causing a real turn-over in one branch of industry after another and opening new prospects for perfecting the control of production and organization of labor. For us Communists, builders of the most advanced society in the history of mankind, scientific-technological progress is one of the main ways of speeding up the rate of construction and the basic ally in the struggle for realizing the great plans of the party regarding the transformation of nature. It can be said without exaggeration that in this particular field, the field of scientific-technological progress, now lies one of the main fronts of the historical competition of the two systems. For our party the further intensive development of science and technology and the wise introduction in production of the latest scientific-technological achievements is not only the central economic task but also an important political task.[11]

"Main front," "central economic task," "important political task," the appeal to Lenin—all these are indications of a deep, if not over-riding, concern with technological and economic growth.

In seeking legitimation through improved living standards, the Communists must substantially improve the efficiency of their econo-mies on a broad front. Since the Communist leaders themselves as well as the populations they rule appear to attach special importance to the problem of technological innovation, however, it will not be amiss if we attempt to isolate this one element in the Communist economy for detailed examination. If we can discern the reasons for the characteristically low rate of innovation we may be able to iden-tify the measures the Communists must take in order to significantly raise the rate of innovation, and indeed, to increase efficiency gen-erally. Once we know what changes in the economy are likely to be required, we may attempt to assess their political consequences. In this way we may learn whether the road to legitimacy through im-proved living standards is really open to the Communist regimes.

Central Planning and the Innovation Process

The Communist system of central planning has acquired an inter-national reputation for being able to industrialize a backward, agrar-ian country quickly. Indeed, the Communist system has used the strategy of acquiring equipment and know-how from the capitalists and then beating them at their own production game. However, although the system may work well enough in the early stages of in-dustrialization, provided the human costs are not counted, it tends to run into trouble in the later stages. To limit the problem to the technological element, why should it be characteristic of Communist

[11] Brezhnev at Minsk, as broadcast by Radio Moscow, Dec. 28, 1968.

central planning that the manufacture of synthetic fibers had to be introduced into the Soviet Union as a consequence of Khrushchev's personal intervention years after such fibers had become basic to Western textile production, and then by importing entire production units from Great Britain?

For one thing, central planners tend to develop biases that aggravate the innovational problem. Since they are interested in economic growth chiefly as an element of state power, and since they are in a hurry, they tend to maximize output at all costs. Thus they emphasize economies of scale. Of any given machine, only a few models will be produced and the production runs will be long by Western standards. In this way central planners reduce the need for costly retooling, with its attendant interruption of the production process. But general purpose machines are less efficient than more specialized types, and the emphasis on economies of scale focuses attention on processes rather than products, although product innovation is at least as important as process innovation in overall economic growth. The relatively low value placed on consumer goods by central planners must also exercise a depressing effect on innovation, since so many of the capitalist technological breakthroughs have come in the consumer field.[12]

There are other obstacles to innovation, much more deeply rooted than the biases of central planners. To understand and evaluate these other obstacles it will be necessary to take a brief look at the innovational process itself as that process is understood in the West, and then to place the process in the institutional context of Eastern Europe.[13] The beginnings of innovation are to be found in pure research, or research conducted without regard to practical application. A recent United States study has shown that on the average something like 90 per cent of the pure, or "nonmission," research necessary to the production of an innovation is completed before the innovation itself is conceived of. As for the separate events that make up the innovative process through the stage of engineering design, but

[12] J. S. Berliner, "Innovation in the Soviet Economy: Preliminary Draft, May 1968, Ten Chapters," ch. 9, pp. 38–45.

[13] For the innovational process per se see Robert A. Charpie *et al.*, *Technological Innovation: Its Environment and Management* (Washington, D.C., 1967), and National Science Foundation, *Technology in Retrospect and Critical Events in Science* (Washington, D.C., 1968). The Charpie report breaks down innovation into five distinct subprocesses. The following percentages are estimates of the distribution of innovation costs among these subprocesses: research and development, 5–10%; product engineering and design, 10–20%; manufacturing engineering and tooling, 40–60%; manufacturing start-up, 5–15%; and market start-up, 10–25%.

not including those of production and marketing, 70 per cent involve nonmission research, 20 per cent mission research, and 10 per cent engineering design.[14]

Since most of the pure research in Western Europe and the United States is carried out in universities, it is reasonably free from political influence. In Eastern Europe and the Soviet Union, by contrast, most pure research is performed by official academies of science whose work is sometimes directly and always indirectly controlled and influenced by the government and the ruling Communist party. During periods of intense coercion this relationship has had some technologically negative results. There have been spurious research plans involving the "rediscovery" of what was already known (at least among scientists) in order to meet planned targets. Some fields of research came to be dominated by incompetent or eccentric scholars, as the field of genetics was presided over by the Soviet academician Trofim Lysenko because his doctrines were politically useful to Stalin. Still other fields were forbidden, notably sociology, psychiatry, input-output analysis, and the theory of relativity. The importation of foreign scientific literature was drastically reduced.[15]

Though these circumstances have undoubtedly discouraged innovation, we should not overestimate their impact in the Communist world at present. The pure research necessary to a given innovation may cover half a century or more. The results of such nonmission research were often available in Stalin's time and are universally available now. Indeed, the twin processes of de-Stalinization and desatellization brought with them a reinstatement of forbidden areas of study and even the introduction of new ones, such as public opinion analysis. The last two or three years have seen the restoration of Czechoslovak and Hungarian universities to the instructional and research autonomy they enjoyed before the Communists seized power. At least in the Czechoslovak case, monies earned by research contract are now placed at the disposal of university authorities.[16]

[14] *Technology in Retrospect*, I, iv–v.

[15] For a noncritical description of pure research in Czechoslovakia—its organization, principal research topics, channels of communication, serial publications, and the like—see Vladimir Slamecka, *Science in Czechoslovakia* (New York, 1963). A comparable but less useful volume by the same author is *Science in East Germany* (New York, 1963).

[16] In East Germany, however, the trend has been in the opposite direction. The various research institutes of given universities are being subordinated for purposes of research programming and direction to specific industrial enterprises. "Colleges Curbed in East Germany," *New York Times*, Jan. 8, 1969.

Research and Development

Mission research and the actual construction of new devices—separate processes often loosely referred to as invention—present a different situation. In the West, much research and development is carried out by private persons tinkering in a basement laboratory in their spare time. Private inventors also exist in Communist countries, and despite the bureaucratic difficulties with which they must contend, their contributions appear to be substantial.[17] Most research and development in the Communist system, however, is done not by private persons but by institutes.

Successful inventors in Communist states receive very limited rewards by Western standards. To be sure, the man employed in the research institute or the development facility has his standard salary supplemented by regular bonuses if the organization he works for is successful. But under Communism few, if any, will get rich on direct returns from their inventions, however important the inventions may be. Patents exist in the form of certificates of authorship, but they are not taken very seriously. Patent lawyers are practically unknown, although larger enterprises in the Soviet Union have recently established departments, staffed for the most part by untrained people, to help inventors fill out the requisite forms.[18] In the Soviet Union patents are granted by a government bureau of secondary standing, i.e., without first priority in the recruitment or payment of its personnel. The wages of patent bureau employees are tied to the number of applications processed, with such results as might be expected.[19]

---

[17] Approximately 40% of all patents issued by the British and American governments since 1900 were issued to private inventors. Over half of all inventions were by persons holding regular jobs and experimenting in their spare time. Half of all inventions were by people without college educations. See Berliner, ch. 7, pp. 10–11. According to E. Zaleski *et al., Science Policy in the USSR* (Paris, 1969), p. 415, 54.1% of all certificates of authorship and patents (awarded only to foreigners) granted in Russia in 1966 were nonsponsored. But the term nonsponsored evidently covers more than individual inventors' groups and clubs of inventors. One indication of this is that of the 96 certificates of authorship in aircraft, aviation, and astronautics, 93 were nonsponsored.

[18] G. Karpunin, "Sonety Tekhniki," *Literaturnaya Gazeta*, 4 (Jan. 24, 1968), 10.

[19] B. Finiasov, "The All-Union Scientific Research Institute of State Patent Review," *Izvestiya*, June 29, 1966, p. 3, as translated in JPRS, *News of Soviet Scientific Organizations*, No. 37,087 (Aug. 18, 1966), pp. 1–6. "A chart hangs on the wall of the department. It contains three graphs: the expert's name, daily norm, and monthly rate. If the expert processes 13 claims in a day, he receives 100 rubles in a month; 15 claims, 110 rubles; 17 claims, 120 rubles; 19 claims, 130 rubles; 21 claims, 140 rubles. There are virtuosos who manage to process 23 claims in a day. This

The successful inventor is given not the right to a royalty but a single payment. The sum he is paid is calculated by a board of experts, on which the Communist party is usually represented, according to a very rough estimate of the economic return. The law in any case stipulates a maximum beyond which the payment may not go regardless of the size of the economic return. In Rumania, this maximum is 100,000 lei, or about $17,000.[20] In the Soviet Union it is normally 20,000 rubles, or approximately $22,000. Successful Soviet inventors may also be awarded honorary academic degrees, or even the title of professor.[21] Such rewards, however, are hardly sufficient to compensate for years of difficult and frustrating labor, and in the case of the private inventor thousands of hours of unpaid-for overtime.[22] Once payment has been made, the invention becomes the property of the state, which in theory makes it freely available to all interested enterprises,[23] and until recently to all member states of the Council for Mutual Economic Aid, Comecon.[24] Until recently, in

---

rate amounts to as high as 150 rubles.... What does it mean to process 23 claims in 7 hours? It means that you must spend 18 minutes per claim.... But if the expert allows himself the luxury of spending not 18 minutes on a claim but, let us say, 32 minutes, his daily norm will immediately fall from 23 to 13 and his monthly pay from 150 to 100 rubles.... It has been known for a long time that to say 'no' is much easier than to say 'yes.' If he overlooks a Copernicus no one will perhaps notice it. But if, God forbid, he again registers the invention of a steam engine, there will be no end to embarrassment." (*Ibid.*, pp. 3–4.)

[20] "Uniform Legislation on Inventions, Innovations and Rationalization," *Viaţa Economica* (Bucharest), 40 (Oct. 6, 1967), 6, 10, as translated in JPRS, *Translations on Economic Organization and Management in Eastern Europe*, 765 (Nov. 22, 1967), 19. This provision held from 1950 to 1967.

[21] Zaleski *et al.*, p. 474; "How to Encourage Innovation," *Ekonomicheskaya Gazeta*, 4 (Jan. 1968), 22, as translated in *Current Abstracts of the Soviet Press*, I: 1 (Apr. 1968), 6.

[22] Czechoslovakia also employs a system of "improvement proposals," which must originate outside the course of assigned duties, bring about an increase in the efficiency of the production process, and be novel to the given enterprise. A committee of experts in the installation examines each improvement proposal to determine its feasibility and usefulness, and the enterprise must test it in practice. The successful originator is given the title of "improver" and a financial reward. His improvement is normally not patentable, but is registered in the Institute of Technical and Economic Information in Prague. Slamecka, *Science in Czechoslovakia*, pp. 61–62.

[23] R. Bakhtanov and P. Volin, "People and Problems in the Reform: Where Do the Conservatives Come From?" *Literaturnaya Gazeta*, 36 (Sept. 6, 1967), 10, as translated in *Current Digest of the Soviet Press*, XIX: 36 (Sept. 27, 1967), 4–6.

[24] Richard Rockingham Gill, "Mercantilism Embodied in Soviet-Czechoslovak Research Agreement," *Radio Free Europe Research: Communist Area*, June 15, 1967; Harry Schwartz, "Soviet Asks East Bloc Members to Pay for the Use of Technology," *New York Times*, Nov. 27, 1966.

other words, inventions produced within the system were treated virtually as free goods.

If the private inventor must persuade a ministry or enterprise to include his device in its formal plan before he can receive his payment, institutional research also has to contend with major bureaucratic obstacles. Perhaps the most important of these is that research and development, on the one hand, and manufacturing, on the other, are administratively independent of each other, and separately financed in the bargain. Thus research and development is carried on in a sort of vacuum without being tested or manufactured in prototype. Only 8.4 per cent of the research institutes and independent design bureaus in Leningrad have experimental factories, and only 16.4 per cent have other experimental production facilities of their own. Nor does an institute assigned a project normally know beforehand which enterprise will eventually be instructed to produce the product or introduce the process; thus even informal cooperation is not possible. Development is also neglected, owing largely to the production bias of the system. Experimental factories frequently end up producing industrially the prototype they have worked out; it is estimated that as much as 50 per cent of the capacity of experimental production facilities is used for that purpose. Experimental factories also suffer from high labor turnover, since their workers are paid on the output basis common to all factories.[25] As we shall see, one effect of neglecting the design bureaus is to shift much of the burden of development to the producing enterprise, which is not equipped for such work and is naturally reluctant to undertake it. In the Communist system, then, the link between research and production is often tenuous.

The typical Soviet or Eastern European research and development institute, furthermore, usually enjoys a monopoly. Thus although research is often duplicated, either intentionally or unintentionally, as a rule this duplication is not competitive, i.e., it is not intended to test alternatives. The value of the completed project is adjudged by a commission of experts, not by the consuming firm. Once it is turned over to the manufacturer, the institute has no responsibility whatever for the innovation. If the project does not stand up to testing, or if there are technical difficulties in production, the enterprise has to handle these problems. The institute has long ago fulfilled its production plan, received its fee from the ministry to which it is sub-

[25] Zaleski *et al.*, pp. 386, 425–26, 433.

ordinate, and distributed the appropriate bonuses to its own employees. In order to collect bonus payments, which are tied to the
volume of documentation for new design and which, with increasing
frequency, are paid out across-the-board, institutes tend to ignore
what has been done elsewhere, giving rise to Khrushchev's complaint
that Soviet engineers were always reinventing the bicycle.[26]

Given these conditions, it is hardly surprising that Soviet and Eastern European research and development does not look promising.
Almost two-thirds of the research institutes and higher educational
institutions in the Soviet Union have never submitted an application
for a certificate of invention. The Soviet special design bureau for
grinding equipment regularly fulfilled its norm during the five-year
plan ending in 1964, but of 47 completed projects, 13 were later abandoned as useless and 20 were later returned by the enterprise because
of structural defects. Not one of the models developed by this 450-
man bureau during this five-year period ever got into regular production. A Soviet decree of October 23, 1968, designed to spur research and development by way of an extensive reorganization of the
institute system, makes a point of warning that "by the time enterprises now being designed go into operation, they should substantially surpass existing enterprises in our country and abroad in terms
of technical-economic indices and technical level of output."[27] What
would almost be a truism in the West appears in the Soviet Union as
an official admonition, carrying with it the implication that many new
Soviet factories are obsolescent by the time they begin production.

In the interest of objectivity this overall picture must be modified
by reference to certain areas—high-speed aviation, rocketry and atomic power, and certain sections of the machine tool and iron and steel
industries—in which the Soviet Union is technologically as advanced,
or almost as advanced, as the West. The West was shaken in 1957
by the sudden appearance of the Soviet Sputnik and more recently
by the fact that the first supersonic transport aircraft to take to the
air was of Soviet manufacture.[28] Moscow has also made important

26 Berliner, *passim*; Zaleski *et al.*, p. 476.

27 "Resolution to Spur Scientific Research and Development," *Current Digest of
the Soviet Press*, XX: 43 (Nov. 13, 1968), 3–6. For an analysis of the decree see Albert Boiter, "Regimentation of Scientists and the Technology Gap," *Radio Liberty
Research*, Oct. 26, 1968.

28 The TU-144, test flown at the end of 1968, contained numerous components—
generators, valves, electronic gear, navigational instruments—of Western origin,
many of them identical to those used in the Anglo-French Concorde. "Technology
in the Soviet Union," *Radio Liberty Research*, Feb. 7, 1969.

advances with hydroturbines and nuclear accelerators.[29] But these are exceptions, directly involving state interests and national pride, on which the Soviet Union concentrates its engineering talent. In a sense, also, these achievements are made possible by deviation from the regular practices of Stalinist central planning. In the aerospace field, for example, an element of competition has been introduced. Various teams of scientists and engineers are set to work on the same problem, but each team is assigned a different approach. The design bureau is given its own experimental factory. And so on. As Zaleski recently noted: "The impression which emerges from both Soviet and Western studies is that the Soviet Union is less technically advanced than the United States in all but a few priority industries, and that in a number of major industries the Soviet Union is technologically behind the industrialized countries of Western Europe."[30]

TABLE 5

Patents Taken Out Abroad in 1965–66 by Four Industrial States

Country	1965		1966	
	Applied For	Granted	Applied For	Granted
USSR	1,675	700	2,268	1,032
France	19,628	12,464	21,090	13,796
United Kingdom	31,729	18,819	31,733	19,388
United States	103,484	70,155	110,897	74,567

SOURCE: Zaleski *et al.*, p. 397. The Soviet Union first adhered to the Paris convention for the protection of international property on July 1, 1965.

Most Eastern European countries naturally lag behind the Soviet Union in technological matters. Even East Germany and Czechoslovakia, which are more advanced industrially than the Soviet Union itself, have special research and development problems of their own as a consequence of their being in the socialist bloc. Because of their industrial capacity East Germany and Czechoslovakia have been called upon to provide their socialist fellows with the broadest possible range of manufactured goods, although in each case a narrow resource base and a limited population would indicate a profound need for specialization.

East Germany, for example, produces about 90 per cent of the items in the international nomenclature in the field of machine con-

[29] Howard Rausch, "Soviet Technology," *The Atlantic*, CCXXIII: 2 (Feb. 1969), 29–35.
[30] Zaleski *et al.*, p. 382.

struction. As a consequence of this kind of overextension, the East German research and development effort is much too thinly spread. Generally, a staff of 100 is considered the minimum for serious work: the Soviet minimum is 250.[31] In East Germany, however, some 70 per cent of the research institutes have no more than 35 employees. In 21 VVB[32] investigated, 65 per cent of the qualified research personnel were performing current production tasks, such as supervision; those engaged in actual research and development had to work with equipment outdated by Western standards and were spending as much as half of their working time doing preparatory chores that in Western countries would be performed by research assistants, secretaries, and aides.[33] Furthermore, too many different research problems were being investigated. In 1964 there were approximately three specialists for each problem in the VVB research centers. Another difficulty is that much research must be undertaken by persons without adequate training. Outside of the traditional East German industries, such as photography and optics, the percentage of engineers and technicians among East German research and development personnel is only 23.3, as compared with 42.9 across-the-board in West German research and development. Moreover, 18.6 per cent of the East German institutes have no university-trained employees, and 67.1 per cent have no more than five.[34]

The East German leadership is well aware that greater specialization in research and development is the key to future economic success. This awareness helps explain the continuing interest of the East German leadership in closer cooperation within Comecon by way of the "socialist" division of labor.[35] Now that Czechoslovakia has been

[31] The journal of the Soviet Ministry of Finance complains if research organizations drop below 250 employees. The Ministry apparently associates bigness with reduced project cost.

[32] Vereinigungen Volkseigener-Betriebe, an intermediate level of economic administration introduced in 1963 and perhaps best translated as trust.

[33] The shortage of secretarial help may in part be accounted for by the Marxist notion of nonproductive labor. The apparatchiki tend to harbor an instinctive feeling that "paper shufflers are up to no good."

[34] Auerbach, "Industrielle Forschung und Entwicklung in Mitteldeutschland." According to an official Czechoslovak report of 1958, only 4.5% of the personnel of research and development institutes were trained scientists. Slamecka, *Science in Czechoslovakia*, pp. 16, 20. In 1957–58, 54 Czechoslovak research and development institutes (out of some 200) were transferred to industrial enterprises or to clusters of plants and enterprises known as "production-economic units." Slamecka, pp. 16–17. This reorganization was subsequently reversed.

[35] For a good statement of the East German point of view see Klaus Stubenrauch, "Problems of the Development of Scientific-Technical Cooperation," *Einheit* (East Berlin), Feb. 2, 1966, 195–204, as translated in JPRS, *Translations on Economic Organization and Management in Eastern Europe*, 557 (Mar. 22, 1966), 1–13.

forcibly forbidden access to West German credits, it is likely that Prague will in due course also press for the right of greater specialization within Comecon.

Manufacture and Marketing

Once a new product or process has been created, either by a private inventor or by a research and development institute, the next step is to find an enterprise manager who will assume the often considerable risks of attempting to manufacture and market it. In the Stalinist planned economy this theoretically presents no problem. The appropriate ministry simply issues instructions to its subordinate enterprises. As we have seen, there are good reasons why the ministry does not always issue such orders. Even when the orders are given they usually encounter resistance at the enterprise level, and sometimes have to be forced on the managers. One of the more interesting bits of evidence to this effect is the difficulty the Soviets encounter in expanding their exports of patents and licenses. Soviet salesmen run into high resistance abroad, in part because much of what they have to offer has not actually been put into production in the Soviet Union. "Therefore," says *Pravda Ukrainy*, "the innovations which we intend to sell under licenses must be introduced into production on a priority basis so that the commodity can be shown to advantage abroad."[36]

One feature of the innovative process that is important in the West but nonexistent in Eastern Europe and the Soviet Union is the small private firm formed precisely to introduce a new product or process. A leading Czech engineer and the technical director for the Ministry of Heavy Industry, Milan Kubát, was sent to the United States in 1967 to study the innovational process in its capitalistic context; he returned to report that 85 per cent of all United States innovation in manufacture and marketing was the work of small private firms, even though four-fifths of them ended in bankruptcy. The percentage of total innovation assigned to small firms by Kubát is no doubt on the high side. It is nonetheless true, as he pointed out, that the major steel concerns in America delayed the adoption of the oxygen converter process for eight or ten years after the introduction of the process by small firms in Austria, Germany, and the United States.

---

[36] "From Invention to Patent License," *Pravda Ukrainy* (Kiev), Dec. 12, 1967, p. 2, as translated in JPRS, *Recent Developments in the Field of Inventions and Patents: USSR*, No. 44,625 (Mar. 8, 1968), pp. 1–3. *Ekonomicheskaya Gazeta* emphasizes the ignorance of Soviet enterprises with respect to the performance of their own products, there being little feedback from consumers.

Engineer Kubát erred in ascribing this delay solely to the evils of bureaucracy, though no doubt red tape played a role. He did not mention the main reason for the delay, namely the huge sums of capital the larger firms had invested in older processes. This flaw, however, does not make Kubát's argument concerning the innovational advantage of the small firm less convincing. Indeed, Kubát proposed that his Communist colleagues develop a socialist counterpart of the small firm by using some form of cooperative.[37] So far, nothing seems to have come of his suggestion.

Thus in the Communist countries with which we are concerned all manufacturing and marketing innovation is necessarily accomplished by large, monopolistic concerns working under ministerial order. What are the obstacles that a manager who receives such an order must face? To begin with, under Stalinist central planning the manager has a physical production target to reach. This target is likely to be set very high in relation to the capacity of the enterprise. The manager's bonuses (not to mention his job) depend on how close he comes to the physical production goal. Innovation frequently requires a change in the manufacturing process, and change causes delay. But the problem is obviously more complicated; otherwise innovation could be promoted by lowering targets and by granting bonuses for innovation as well as for meeting manufacturing targets.

Some of the more basic difficulties have already been discussed, namely, the poor quality of research and development work generally and the inability of the manager, who normally does not command his own research facility, to pressure researchers into providing him with a workable device or process. In practice the innovating manager must do some of the development work on his own, without the benefit of proper facilities or trained personnel. Supply is also a problem. Since innovation changes the manufacturing process, it is likely to require different, possibly unusual, raw materials, in different or even unpredictable quantities. Supplies are centrally allocated, however, and an enterprise must formulate its requirements many months ahead of delivery date. Since central planners are determined to maximize output, they characteristically fail to provide stocks for unexpected demands, delayed delivery schedules, and the like. In these circumstances, even noninnovating managers tend to order more than they really need, or to build up an in-house capacity to

[37] Milan Kubát and Milan Horálek, "Režim tisíce nápadů" ("The regime of a Thousand Ideas"), *Kulturni Tvorba*, 37 (Prague), Sept. 14, 1967, 3–4. Translation courtesy Alexander Vitek.

meet certain needs, by turning out spare parts, for example, or by employing quasi-legal expediters who make a business of locating scarce materials. The unreliability of the supply system naturally presses even more heavily on the innovating manager, for whom an interruption in deliveries can mean shutting down production for an indeterminate period.[38] If the innovation should turn out to be labor-saving, the manager again has a problem on his hands. Unemployment is not tolerated under socialism; by law the manager must find work elsewhere in his enterprise for those displaced. Factories in the Soviet Union and Eastern Europe tend in any case to employ more persons than they need.[39]

Finally, the sale of new products and processes presents a problem. Sales as such are not difficult to make, since command economies tend to be scarcity economies, where demand is likely to be much greater than supply. Nor does the enterprise itself carry the responsibility for sales; it has only to deliver the finished goods to previously assigned warehouses that in turn undertake distribution to consumers. Nonetheless, there is a sales problem because in the Stalinist system innovations are made more often within the chain of fabrication, i.e., with respect to producers' goods, than with respect to finished or consumers' goods. Advances in the construction industry are based on innovations made by the producers of building materials; improvements in textiles are made by chemical plants; and new equipment for the production of automotive vehicles by the machine tool industry. Under capitalism each of the innovating firms and industries has a highly organized and extensive sales system that makes a business of breaking down consumer resistance to the adoption of new products and processes. This sales system promotes the diffusion of new knowledge on an industry-wide basis. Some argue that the technological gap between the United States and Western Europe is in good part due to the more intensive and systematic sales and promotional practices of American producers. At any rate, sales organizations, salesmen, and advertising barely exist under Stalinist central planning, whether we speak of the enterprise or the warehouse; this, in addition to the great risks of innovation in a tightly centralized system, probably contributes to the slow rate at which innovations are put to use under socialism.[40]

[38] Berliner, ch. 6, *passim*. Research and development institutes also have trouble securing appropriate raw materials, since they have to order them many months in advance.
[39] *Ibid.*, ch. 8, *passim*.
[40] *Ibid.*, ch. 10, *passim*.

The Systemic Problem

The material presented so far suggests that both the inadequate importation of foreign technology and the failure to develop an indigenous, self-perpetuating process of innovation are rooted in the same problems. Tight supply lines, low incentives for innovating, the lack of in-house research and development facilities—all serious enough obstacles in their own right—are symptoms rather than causes of malfunction.

The immediate difficulty is that innovation, whether indigenous or borrowed, involves much labor and high risk, for which the rewards that Stalinist central planning offers are inadequate, to say the least. The nature of the system is such that those who should be interested in innovating are deterred from doing so. In fact, the manager who innovates is likely to be penalized. There is no doubt that the capitalist system has failings of its own—such as the nonsense innovation involved in annual changes in automobile models, or the price distortions that come with oligopoly—but by and large the Western market economy not only rewards those who innovate but also penalizes those who fail to innovate. Especially in growth industries, failure to innovate means the loss of markets, and ultimately bankruptcy.

The basic obstacle to innovation in Communist countries is the inability of Stalinist central planning to provide automatic institutional responses to new situations. Indeed, a totalitarian command economy is specifically designed to prevent automatic, self-perpetuating subsystem processes, technological or otherwise. It is a fundamental principle of Stalinist planning that important decisions are to be made from above. Thus in the Communist computer industry everything is held back because the center has not yet got around to providing the necessary services, especially such software as programming techniques. Each computer-owning enterprise must provide its own services, which, of course, it is ill-equipped to do. In the West, by contrast, there has sprung up an entire set of new institutions variously designed to sell, lease, and service computer software. Clearly the need for automatic institutional response becomes greater as the economy becomes larger, more complex, more specialized, and more interdependent.

To continue competing with the West and among other things to raise living standards, the Communist regimes will have to modify their Stalinist system of central planning. This, after considerable hesitation and much factional quarreling, they are now in the process of attempting. Every Communist country in Europe except Albania currently has a reform of its economic system under way. These reforms, of course, are generally directed to the broader problems of inefficiency. They are not concerned with the problem of technological innovation alone, but also seek improved management, more accurate information, better consumer service, and greater responsiveness to demand. All these reforms have in common an effort to introduce some degree of decentralization into the system by assigning authority to lower levels and providing for some degree of spontaneous response to market forces.

Type B Reform

The economic reforms that the regimes have in progress are of two general types.[41] The less radical, though more widespread, we shall call type B. The essence of the type B reform is that the basic mechanism of the central planning system is kept, but the decision-making process is partially decentralized. Much of the machinery of central planning, including many central ministries, is dismantled, and considerable administrative authority is vested in a series of newly organized horizontal trusts. All the enterprises producing a given type of product are subordinated to a trust that takes responsibility for planning and investment decisions throughout its sector. The trust must also provide subsidies for the weak firms in its complex.

Within each trust the individual enterprise is given a measure of autonomy. Its management is no longer assigned physical production targets but is instructed instead to maximize profit by producing the quantity and assortment of its product that will result in the largest possible sales, as measured by value. The marketing of the product is no longer the responsibility of a separate set of warehouses but becomes the responsibility of each producing enterprise, which consults the wholesalers and conducts market research. Management must pay what amounts to interest on its capital; if its capital requirements go beyond what has been allocated by the trust, it may appeal for additional funds to a set of banks operating on commercial terms. Management is also permitted sizable depreciation allowances. Relations between enterprises are placed on a contractual basis, and under cen-

---

[41] The best general account of the economic reforms in Eastern Europe is Michael Gamarnikow's *Economic Reforms in Eastern Europe* (Detroit, Mich., 1968). See also Gregory Grossman's very perceptive analysis "Economic Reforms: A Balance Sheet," *Problems of Communism*, XV: 6 (Nov.-Dec. 1966), 44–45.

tral supervision individual enterprises may enter into contracts with firms in foreign lands. Salaries and bonuses awarded management depend substantially on the amount of profit earned, and managers are permitted to earmark a part of the profit for the housing fund of their working force, for investment, and for research and development.[42] The manager who innovates, either by introducing a less costly method of producing a standard product or by improving the quality of the product, will presumably increase the amount of profit earned by his concern. The added profit will not only help increase his personal income and standing but also improve the position of his firm.

Certain kinds of decisions, however, remain with the center under type B reform. First of all, prices continue to be determined by the central government. They are no longer as arbitrary as they once were: a systematic effort is made under type B reforms to see that prices cover production costs and allow for a margin of profit. But supply and demand play little role in price determination, with the result that the prices of most raw materials remain fixed at levels substantially below those that would obtain under market circumstances. Wages are also centrally determined. Equally important, many raw materials are still allocated by central ministries, though in at least one version of the B reform a network of wholesale houses, also operating on a profit-and-loss basis, is created to handle some kinds of materials. Finally, the auditing of firm accounts, in the East German case, is still done by a central bureau. In short, type B reform attempts to create a somewhat decentralized and much more efficient system of central planning.[43]

Type A Reform

The second kind of reform, type A, is much more radical. In it central planning is not merely modified, but abandoned altogether. Though the state retains ownership of the means of production, the decision-making process devolves from the polity to the economy. Central industrial ministries, in the Stalinist sense of that term, no longer exist; neither does a central planning apparatus. Basic de-

---

[42] Dorothy Miller and H. G. Trend, "Economic Reforms in East Germany," *Problems of Communism*, XV: 2 (Mar.-Apr. 1966), 29–36, provides a good description of a given type B reform. In the Soviet case the bulk of the additional profit is siphoned off by the state.

[43] For the view that the Soviet (type B) reform has so far increased efficiency very little, see Gregory Grossman's comment on Werner Klatt, "The Politics of Economic Reforms," *Survey*, 70–71 (Winter-Spring 1969), 165–68.

cision-making authority is vested in the enterprise itself, although trusts may be retained for some organizational functions. Much as in the West, the government attempts to influence long-range economic development not directly but through such roundabout devices as taxation and fiscal policy.

Under type A reform not only is the manager told to maximize profit but he must also operate in a situation where most prices are determined by supply and demand. In addition to deciding how much he will produce, and in what assortment, he even decides what he will produce. He procures his raw materials not from a ministry or state supply house but from producer firms and wholesalers in a market situation. He has the right to hire and fire labor. He raises much of his own capital, at commercial rates, and in some instances may establish and operate his own research and development facility. In short, the manager has become an entrepreneur. If he operates in the red, he will be removed. If the enterprise remains in the red despite the efforts of a series of appointed entrepreneurs, the enterprise will be closed.

At the same time, moreover, the manager is gradually subjected to competitive pressure; otherwise he could maximize profit simply by raising his prices. Competition can be created by breaking up the huge monopolistic state enterprises of the Stalinist system into sets of competing companies, or by opening the national market to the inroads of capitalist competition, or by some combination of the two. The creation of sets of competing companies would be easier to accomplish, but the second alternative would be more effective, since it is the capitalists who have achieved low production costs and have come up with many new and useful products. To open a Communist market to capitalist competition would require a whole series of drastic changes: the modification of state trading practices, the reduction or elimination of import quotas, and the establishment of at least a semiconvertible currency. At the same time, the opening of the national market would permit an inflow of Western venture capital. This would help relieve the persistent shortages of both hard currency and investment capital. Furthermore, Western venture capital would bring with it the latest in technology and in the bargain would help train the local working force in the use of this technology.

An Evaluation of the Reforms

The weakness of the type B reform lies in the poor quality of the information provided by the price system, which takes into account production costs as well as what can be done in nonmarket conditions but ignores scarcities, i.e., utility to the consumer. Thus it is conceivable, and in some fields of production likely, that under type B reforms enterprises showing a substantial profit would not necessarily be serving the economy well. When thoroughly carried out, however, type B reforms should provide important gains in efficiency over Stalinist central planning; any country, regardless of its stage of development, is probably better off with a type B reform than without it.

The long-term effectiveness of the type B reform, however, probably depends on the stage of development of the country in which it is introduced. Rumania, which began across-the-board industrialization only in the late 1950's, can look forward to high growth rates under Stalinist central planning for years to come. The less radical reform may, however, keep Rumania's innovation and growth rates higher than they otherwise would have been. But for a country like East Germany, type B reform, though promising important gains, will probably be unable to prevent the deterioration of growth rates over a period of five or ten years. Thus the East German regime's outlook for attaining legitimacy by raising living standards is not favorable, particularly since the difference between East and West Germany is so visible. Indeed, the gap between the expectations of the population and the amenities the economy is able to provide may increase.

In this eventuality East Germany (and any other regime in the same position) will probably have to resort to greater repression, although a return to full-blown, systematic terror seems unlikely because of the negative effect such a tactic would have on production. Greater repression might mean instead that goods, ideas, and persons would have greater difficulty crossing the frontier. Police supervision is likely to become more extensive, and socialist legality may be suspended from time to time. Censorship may become severe, and official propaganda would no doubt be given a bigger role in news media and school curricula. Much would be made of the spartan virtues of obedience, discipline, and sacrifice. Though such measures would help cover up an increase in political instability, in the long run they would solve nothing. In fact, they could be taken to signify that the regime had abandoned any real hope of legitimation.[44] Except for

---

[44] When faced with economic difficulties and a sharp decline in living standards (averaging a drop of approximately $5\frac{1}{2}\%$ a year in 1966 and 1967), Fidel Castro responded in 1968 with a campaign of increased moral austerity, greater use of "voluntary" labor, heavier reliance on the army, and reinforced isolation of Cuba from

the most backward countries—Rumania, Bulgaria, and Albania—type B reform promises at best only a temporary gain in efficiency, not a real solution to the problem of economic growth.

Type A reforms, however, also have drawbacks. To begin with, a regime that submits itself to the draconian regimen of market reform has no guarantee that it will end up with a competitive innovation rate and continuous, substantial economic growth. The countries of Eastern Europe are small, limited in natural resources, poorly located, and inhabited by relatively unsophisticated populations.[45] To assert that Stalinist central planning will not provide these countries with competitive efficiency under advanced industrialization is not necessarily to argue that a socialist market will. In the one case we are discussing economic systems, in the other, national endowment. Even with the greater efficiency of market socialism these countries, or some of them, might not develop competitive efficiency. In view of the political risks involved in type A reform, cautious leaders might well opt for some combination of type B reform and political repression to provide the optimum opportunity for the long-term survival of their regimes.

The Risks of Pluralization

Type A reform inevitably involves a certain degree of pluralization. If industrial enterprise is turned over to managers whose mission is to maximize profit in a competitive situation, would it not seem reasonable, especially to socialists, to grant autonomy to the trade unions, or to workers' councils, so that they might protect the interests of labor against the ambitions of management? In this case, would not the workers sooner or later recover the right to strike? Would it be practical to place industry under the rule of the market while keeping agriculture under the rule of the party, with all that party rule en-

---

the outside world. (Professor Edward Gonzalez of the University of California, Los Angeles, at a public lecture on the Irvine campus of the University of California, May 27, 1969. Gonzalez visited Cuba briefly in 1967 and again in 1968. The percentages are his calculations, derived from official Cuban statistics.)

45 The Soviet Union is huge in area, population, and resources, but is also afflicted with a difficult location and an unsophisticated population; in addition, it suffers from an unfavorable climate, a low population density, and an awkward geographic distribution of its natural wealth. The Soviets cannot sell raw materials at world market prices and make a profit. See O. Bogomolov, "Aktualnye Problemy Ekonomicheskogo Sotrudnichestvo Sotsialisticheskikh Stran," *Mirovaya Ekonomika i Mezhdunarodnye Otnosheniya* (Moscow), 5 (May 1966), 15–27; Richard Rockingham Gill, "USSR Exploited by Comecon," *RFE Research: Communist Area*, June 2, 1966; and Harry Schwartz, "Comecon Clouds Hint of a Storm," *New York Times*, Aug. 7, 1966.

tails in the way of subsidizing weak collectives, in unrealistic farm prices, and in the artificial depression of peasant income? Managerial autonomy would also require a much wider availability of reliable economic information—production figures, inventories, unemployment, wage negotiations—still today regarded by Communists as state secrets. Ultimately, some equivalent of the *Wall Street Journal* might come into being. Bond, stock, and money markets would have to be tolerated in order to provide the managerial community with the information it would need.

Equally pervasive insofar as economic change is concerned would be the growing influence of the consumer, whose preferences would have greater and greater impact on the decisions of the managers. Greater consumer influence would mean greater emphasis on the production of consumers' goods and on the development of service industries. One could expect an outburst of apartment house construction and greatly increased availability of passenger automobiles, together with the construction of highway networks, chains of filling stations, and so on.[46] Central authority would undoubtedly seek to limit these developments by means of taxation and interest rates, and in some instances even by tariff barriers and price controls. But if central authority could slow such developments, it could not prevent them, and in any case would face grave difficulty in maintaining its previous policies of high capital investment, preferential treatment of heavy industry, refusal of industrial specialization, and limiting the bulk of the country's trade to Communist countries. Central authority would instead have to deal with a variety of interests—corporate, bureaucratic, local, and individual—and seek to reconcile their diverse requirements. In short, the economy would have recovered a substantial degree of autonomy at the price of becoming pluralized.

The tendency toward pluralization would undoubtedly be reinforced by the abandonment of autarky entailed in opening up the national market to Western competition. To allow a regular inflow of capitalist goods would make it difficult to forbid the entry of capitalist ideas and even of capitalists themselves. If Western businessmen and Western tourists were permitted freedom to move in and out of a country, how could the regime maintain an effective ban on the West-

---

[46] After numerous experiments and a severe crisis of conscience, the Polish government, hardly among the most liberal in economic matters, has resolved to lease all filling stations to private entrepreneurs, who are allowed to profit in proportion to the quantity of gasoline sold. Michael Gamarnikow, "Private Enterprise Redivivus," in a volume on Comecon to be published by Columbia University Press, pp. 38–45.

ern press? Western visitors to Eastern Europe would insist on having their regular newspapers available, and the discarded journals would quickly become the object of a thriving black market. In order to promote basic research, the learned periodicals of the West are already imported in considerable quantity. If there were to be unrestricted publication of economic data to facilitate the semiautomatic functioning of the economy, would not pressures develop for a free press generally? And why should a regime pay the heavy costs of jamming operations directed against Western radio stations if domestic censorship were de facto suspended?

The abandonment of economic autarky would tend to push Communist regimes toward the resumption of normal contacts with the countries of Western Europe. The policy of withdrawal would be put in doubt as well as the xenophobic claim to moral superiority by which withdrawal is justified. Any given regime, moreover, that undertook a type A reform would find itself drawing away from the Communist group for many of the same reasons that it drew toward the West. A socialist market economy could not depend for the bulk of its foreign trade on command economies, even though the command economies were those of ideological affiliates and military partners. Trade between Comecon countries is barter trade, motivated as much by political as by economic considerations. Trade with the West would be multilateral, competitive, and based primarily on economic motives. Heavy dependence on Comecon trade would reduce the meaningfulness of capitalist competition, and to that extent reduce industrial efficiency. Being more efficient, the socialist market regime would tend to sell more to its Communist partners than it would want to buy from them. Since there would be no way to transfer credits so long as the currency of the Communist partner was inconvertible, the socialist market economy might find itself in a position of subsidizing the socialist command economy without any prospect of a reasonable economic return. Apart from any consideration of political independence, the effect of market reform would be to pull the reforming regime out of Comecon and to reintegrate it gradually with the West.

This is not to suggest that the pluralization and the democratization of a polity are necessarily one and the same. On the contrary, I am inclined to the view that the pluralization of a Communist polity may take place without the establishment of either parliamentary government or a multi-party system. To be sure, there is considerable prospect that some of the populations of Eastern Europe would, if given the opportunity, push the process of pluralization rapidly in a democratic direction. A half century of dictatorship—first a local, proto-fascist variety, then the Nazi overlordship, followed almost immediately by Communist totalitarianism—together with the striking economic successes of the Western European states since 1945 have undoubtedly produced among the Eastern Europeans a greater longing for democratic forms than is generally realized in the West.

The Hungarian case is instructive in this regard. For centuries the Magyars dominated such non-Magyar peoples as the Slovaks and the Croats. When the holy kingdom of Saint Stephen was destroyed by the events of World War I, the Magyars first installed a Communist dictatorship under Bela Kun, in the hope of recovering with the help of Soviet Russia the territories they had lost to the Allies;[47] when that failed, they established a proto-fascist dictatorship under Nicholas Horthy that collaborated with the Nazis to the same end. The Horthy dictatorship was followed by a brief interlude of parliamentary democracy, during which the only free and honest election in the whole of Hungarian history (that of November 1945) was held. Shortly thereafter the Soviet army imposed a dictatorship of the proletariat. Nonetheless, or perhaps because of all this, one of the first actions of the Hungarian revolutionary government of 1956 was to announce free elections. No specific date was set. Budapest issued an official statement to the effect that free elections would be held as soon as possible.

Entirely apart from the risk of uncontrolled democratization, the conversion from a command to a market economy threatens to undermine both the discipline and the leading role of the Communist party. Under Stalinist central planning the party apparatus not only makes decisions about rates of growth and areas of industrial concentration but performs a vital interstitial function, especially at the provincial and local levels. If an enterprise has to halt production because a supplier has failed to deliver a critical raw material on schedule, the local secretary uses his party channels to bring pressure on the supplier. When conflicting regulations are issued by different ministries concerning the allocation of enterprise funds, as between the construction of new housing or the building of additional plant capacity, the local secretary is called upon to work out a compromise. If one plant is hoarding machinery that another plant needs, the secretary intervenes again. In a thousand different ways the local party cadres

[47] The only monograph on this subject in English, and a work of high quality, is Rudolph L. Tökés, *Bela Kun and the Hungarian Soviet Republic: The Origins and Role of the Communist Party of Hungary in the Revolutions of 1918–1919* (New York, 1967).

take a hand, even on a daily basis, to keep the ponderous and intricate system of central planning going. The secretary is listened to not only because everyone recognizes the party's leading role but more particularly because he controls his district's *nomenklatura,* a card file of all persons cleared and available for appointment to key positions in industry, in the government bureaucracy, in agriculture, in the school system, and so on. Clearly the role played by the local party secretary and his staff is one of the pillars of the party's power.

In the event, however, of a changeover to a market economy, the party apparatus would largely have to surrender its interstitial function. The expediting responsibilities of the local party secretary would instead be vested in enterprise managers operating within the framework of an autonomous subsystem. Aside from the blow such an arrangement would deal to the prestige of the party, which has made its reputation primarily by its role in industrialization, the party's loss of its economic function would create a major personnel problem. Thousands of faithful apparatchiki would lose their jobs, in addition to other thousands of loyal party members who had served, under the old system, as factory managers or as central planners in the great industrial ministries. Appropriate new jobs for these people would be difficult to find. Theoretically they could staff the boards, commissions, and judicial and elective bodies that the party would have to develop in order to manage and reconcile the conflicting interests of a pluralized society. But apparatchiki have no great personal popularity; many of them have blood on their hands. Nor are these party professionals usually men of exceptional intelligence or bounding imagination; their forte lies rather in dogmatic faith, unswerving loyalty, and unquestioning discipline. As a rule they have little education. In the Bulgarian party at large, for example, some 70 per cent do not have even a secondary education.[48] Data for Czechoslovakia in 1962 showed that only 25 per cent of the managers and leading technicians in industrial enterprises had appropriate university training. The educational level of collective farm chairmen was below the average of that for the population as a whole. Only 29 per cent of the department chiefs in the state bureaucracy and 40 per cent of the leading officials had more than an elementary education.[49] In neither the Bulgarian nor the Czech case are educational data available for the apparatchiki as such, but it would be fair to hazard that party cadres are, on average, less educated than ordinary party members

[48] Michael Costello, "Expertise and Partiinost: A Question of Priorities," *RFE Research: East Europe,* Nov. 21, 1968, p. 3.
[49] Richta *et al., Civilization at the Crossroads,* ch. 4, pp. 36–37.

and government bureaucrats. This is perhaps only another way of saying that the Bulgarian and Czechoslovak regimes are revolutionary.

In all three countries that have attempted to institute type A reforms the personnel problem has proved to be a major obstacle. In Czechoslovakia First Secretary Antonín Novotný tried to compromise by accepting market reform in principle but making none of the personnel changes market reform would ordinarily entail. In the end this tactic contributed to his own undoing. In Hungary First Secretary Janos Kádár has worked out another kind of compromise. The local secretaries continue to maintain a *nomenklatura* and are asked for their opinion whenever a new appointment is to be made in their area, but the final decision is made by the center. The Hungarian apparatchiki have made their opposition to the new system evident in many ways, particularly by ignoring directives from Budapest. Only in Yugoslavia have the old revolutionary cadres largely disappeared from the political scene. The old cadres were made up of veterans of the partisan war, most of whom were semiliterate mountaineers from the backward districts of Montenegro, Bosnia, and Croatia. As the regime moved toward a revisionist economic policy, after 1952, these veterans were gradually pensioned off or transferred to the security police to make room for new and better-educated men. The security police thus came to represent the interests of the partisan veterans; under the leadership of Aleksandar Ranković, they became the principal bastion of orthodoxy and the center of opposition to market reform. In the end it became necessary for the regime to downgrade both Ranković and the police in order to carry out its reform. In compensation, President Tito promised to raise the pensions of retired partisan veterans.[50]

Perhaps the most telling political effect of the shift toward a market economy, however, is ideological erosion, precisely because of the Communist ideology's significance for the self-identity and purposiveness of the Eastern European regimes. I have argued elsewhere that since the death of Stalin and the reforms of Khrushchev, Marxist-Leninist doctrine has come to serve as one of the major bonds holding the regimes to one another.[51] Economic reform of whichever type

[50] R. V. Burks, *The Removal of Ranković: An Early Interpretation of the July 1966 Plenum*, The RAND Corporation, RM-5132-PR, Sept. 1966, *passim*.

[51] R. V. Burks, "The Communist Polities of Eastern Europe," in James N. Rosenau, ed., *Linkage Politics: Essays on the Convergence of National and International Systems* (New York, 1969), pp. 275–303.

runs counter to the orthodox Marxian doctrine of surplus value, according to which profit, rent, and interest are meretricious gadgets concocted by the capitalists in order to steal wealth from the workers. It is all very well to argue along with Kosygin that socialist profit is different from capitalist profit because the former is designed to increase the efficiency of the worker's economy rather than to exploit him; or to imitate the Hungarian practice of referring to interest rates as "capital levies"; or to reintroduce more realistic rentals in public housing gradually as Poland and Yugoslavia have done without ever making reference to the hated term. But in the end the Communist regimes will find it increasingly difficult to disguise from the public, let alone from themselves, that they are in fact borrowing from a system they have denounced as the source of all evil and have viewed as doomed to disappear.[52]

Ideological erosion would be a staggering problem if Communist regimes decided to permit an influx of Western venture capital. Lenin taught that foreign capital was by nature exploitative, bringing to the host nation, among other evils, semicolonial status. Stalin collectivized Soviet agriculture, at the cost of many millions of human lives, in large part on the premise that investment capital would have to be provided by domestic sources if national independence were not to be placed in jeopardy. East European regimes dutifully followed the Soviet example and collectivized, with little loss of life, it is true, but at the cost of great personal hardship. The Communist regimes, then, have accumulated an enormous moral investment both in collectivized agriculture and in the doctrine that foreign venture capital is anathema. Of course it could be argued that the early days of Bolshevik weakness and isolation were now past and that the world community of socialist nations was now powerful enough to deal with capitalist venture capital. But such an argument would be hollow at bottom, thinly disguising a great surrender. The socialist nations' claim to moral superiority would be badly discredited, and the high costs of collectivization would appear to have been exorbitant, arbitrary, and even unnecessary. The value of the dictatorship of the proletariat and even of the Great October Revolution might themselves be placed in doubt.

[52] For a fuller treatment see R. V. Burks, "The Erosion of Ideology," in G. R. Urban, ed., *Talking to Eastern Europe: A Collection of the Best Reading from the Broadcasts and Background Papers of Radio Free Europe* (London, 1964), pp. 199–222.

The Case of Yugoslavia

To date only the Yugoslav regime has been able to decollectivize,[53] and it has done so in the special circumstances of Soviet excommunication and American financial and military support. The immediate reason for decollectivization was the deviant regime's need to broaden its popular base. Many years elapsed before the notion of admitting foreign venture capital was broached, and then it was included in a legislative proposal providing for the organization of joint companies. Under the proposal a foreign firm and a Yugoslav concern would together create a third corporation, with the foreign firm holding up to 49 per cent of the capital stock. The foreigner would provide the equipment and technical know-how; the Yugoslav partner would supply the buildings, the labor force, and the management. Yugoslav sales would be the concern of the Yugoslav partner; the foreigner would look after his own domestic market; and sales to third countries would be the affair of the joint company. In this fashion the Yugoslav revisionists thought to overcome the ideological dangers of foreign venture capital. Yet only the removal of Ranković in July 1966 and a general downgrading of the security police made the passage of the law on joint companies possible. Even so, a solid year of political infighting preceded its final enactment,[54] and the first joint company was formed with an East German concern,[55] as if to demonstrate that the invitation was not limited to capitalist countries. The number of joint ventures formed by the end of 1968 does not suggest a massive inflow of foreign venture capital: five joint corporations, counting the one with the East German concern, and a total foreign investment of $18 million.[56] Westerners were reportedly discouraged by the parochialism of Yugoslav management, which reflected the overriding interests of workers' councils in such local problems as improved hous-

---

[53] Contrary to the general impression, only some 10% of the Polish arable was collectivized (as distinguished from state farms formed from prerevolutionary great estates). At present about 2% of the Polish arable remains in collective farms.

[54] Slobodan Stanković, "Yugoslavia Ready to Receive Foreign Capital," *RFE Research: Communist Area*, Feb. 21, 1967; Harry Trend, "Proposed Principles Regulating Foreign Capital Investments in Yugoslavia Near Enactment," *RFE Research: Communist Area*, Mar. 30, 1967; Zdenko Antić, "Yugoslav Foreign Capital Investment Regulation Enacted," *RFE Research: Communist Area*, Aug. 18, 1967.

[55] Zdenko Antić, "First Contracts for Foreign Capital Investments in Yugoslavia Signed," *RFE Research: Communist Area*, Apr. 25, 1968.

[56] "Joint Investments by Yugoslav and Foreign Economic Organizations," *Yugoslav News Bulletin* (New York), 438 (Dec. 27, 1968), 7.

ing, and by the provision that one-fifth of Western earnings would have to be reinvested in the country.[57]

No other Eastern European regime has so far followed the Yugoslav example. The Rumanian planner Alexander Barladeanu at one point publicly expressed interest in joint enterprises, but he was subsequently demoted amid a number of official Rumanian statements opposing the idea. However, various other, less doctrinally dangerous cooperative arrangements have begun to appear. Under a license with the Swedish firm Ericsson, a Hungarian enterprise is undertaking to manufacture advanced telephone exchange equipment. A British firm has signed an agreement with its Czechoslovak counterpart under which the British will manufacture automatic textile machines, the Czechs will make automated textile finishing equipment, and the two lines will be sold jointly in third markets according to a precisely established distribution pattern; the profits will be shared on a fifty-fifty basis. A German electronics firm, Grundig, sends raw materials to a Polish counterpart, which manufactures parts on a commission basis and then returns the parts to Germany, where they are assembled into finished products. But all of these arrangements stop short of the acceptance of Western venture capital. Only Hungary has laws permitting the establishment of joint enterprises, and these, so far as can be discovered, are limited to selling activities in third countries.[58]

So far Yugoslavia is the only country to have carried out a market-type reform. Czechoslovakia had a type A reform under way at the time of the Soviet occupation in August 1968, but the process of carrying it out had just begun. Hungary also has a market reform under way that is making modest progress, but whether the Soviet Union will permit the transition to be completed remains to be seen. The independent Yugoslav regime, by contrast, began as early as 1952 to move in the direction of market socialism with the introduction of workers' councils, which had the effect of providing ideological

[57] Legislation is now being worked on that will remove this requirement and in addition permit the foreigners' share to go above 49%, should the given workers' council declare such an extension to be in their interest. Interview with Vukašin Dragojević, Deputy Secretary of Economy, Ministry of Economics, and Miroslav Nedelković, Counsellor of the Ministry, Belgrade, May 5, 1969.

[58] "Hungarian Situation Report," *RFE Research: East Europe*, Dec. 1, 1967, Mar. 12, 1968, May 24, 1968, Aug. 8, 1968; "Polish Situation Report," *RFE Research: East Europe*, Oct. 5, 1965 and May 23, 1966; "Rumanian Situation Report," *RFE Research: East Europe*, Sept. 9, 1966, and Apr. 7, 1967; Stanislaw Wasowski to R. V. Burks, Feb. 7, 1969; "Industrial Cooperation with the West," *East Europe* (New York), XVI: 15 (May 1967), 26–28.

camouflage for greater managerial independence from central authority. As already suggested, the battle over market reform was long and hard-fought, and was not decided in favor of the reformers until 1966. And it is no accident that Yugoslavia, among all Communist countries, has moved farthest down the road toward political pluralism.

In Yugoslavia the Communist party has officially abandoned its leading role. With the exception of Tito, who serves as president of the republic, no party official may hold government office. Ministers of the federal cabinet, for example, are party members but may not hold, for example, a secretaryship in the party apparatus as long as they remain ministers. Indeed, the party is not permitted to organize cells in government offices. The apparatus has been substantially reduced in size, and its electoral and agitprop functions have been transferred to a popular front organization called the Socialist Alliance. The security police have been divided into two separate organizations. One is charged with the pursuit of criminals but may not make an arrest without a court order. The other, which deals with foreign spies and saboteurs, presumably enjoys greater leeway. Above the federal and state supreme courts has been established a set of so-called constitutional courts that decide on the constitutionality of legislation and defend the rights guaranteed by the fundamental statute.

The Yugoslav parliament, which meets regularly and for relatively long periods, has virtually replaced the central committee as a national forum for the discussion of policy issues. It rarely votes unanimously and on occasion has forced the cabinet to change or withdraw legislation by a negative vote. Parliament, together with the state legislatures and the Yugoslav counterpart of what we call county councils, is elected under a system in which each nominee must secure the approval of local assemblies of voters, and in which there is increasingly a choice among candidates. At the county level there are almost always twice as many candidates as seats to be filled.[59] The parties of the various republics are autonomous. They control patronage within their jurisdiction, have local militias at their disposal, and even give their opinion in matters of foreign policy. Their influence is considerable and includes the right to a share of foreign service posts. The county councils exercise a wide-ranging authority, managing all schools below the university level and all hospitals, operating all public housing, building and maintaining roads, and levying taxes of their own. Socialist realism has well-nigh disappeared from public life. The press, although censored, is lively and controversial. Tito

[59] Burks and Stanković, "Yugoslawien auf dem Weg zu halbfreien Wahlen?"

and his leading colleagues no longer speak of themselves as Marxist-Leninists, but simply as Marxists.

Thus although economic and political pluralization are not necessarily connected, the evolution of Communist Yugoslavia has probably convinced many Eastern European leaders that the two are very difficult to separate. In Czechoslovakia the revisionists pushed ahead simultaneously with both kinds of pluralization. Not only did the Soviets intervene militarily to slow down and set limits to the pluralization of the Czechoslovak social order, but they also forbade the Eastern European parties to send delegations to the Ninth Congress of the League of Yugoslav Communists, held in March 1969.

On the whole it seems reasonable to believe that the Eastern European regimes cannot achieve legitimation without greatly improving the living standards of the populations they rule. Although appeals to national sentiments and the democratization of the one-party system can to some extent be substituted for improved living standards, in the long run Eastern Europeans are likely to insist on standards more nearly in line with those enjoyed by Western Europeans. Otherwise, the people will withhold the positive cooperation and basic loyalty that will enable the Communist regimes to survive in the post-mobilization period and that will in the end transform them into governments. But in the long run, which essentially means the present in the cases of East Germany and Czechoslovakia and the 1980's in the cases of Rumania and Bulgaria, living standards probably cannot be improved at competitive rates unless the regimes are willing to abandon central planning for market socialism. Yet the shift to market socialism involves major political risks—at best the extensive pluralization of the system, at worst the actual loss of control. In any case the machinery of mobilization would probably undergo drastic modification or even be abandoned.

The alternative to market reform is to improve central planning and retain the machinery of mobilization. Type B reform virtually eliminates the threat of pluralization, but it probably also would lead to declining growth rates sooner or later, a growing gap between the expectations of the population and what the economy could provide, the narrowing of this gap within tolerable limits by means of repressive measures, and thus the indefinite postponement of any genuine reconciliation between regime and population. Of course, if the European Common Market should break up, or if the West should fall victim to another Great Depression, the type B system, and indeed Communism in general, would be vindicated.

Whether a given regime, if left to itself, would choose market reform or type B reform is a function not only of the stage of economic development but also of such factors as the extent of Western influence, the degree of desatellization, and the amount of local support for the regime. Yugoslavia has definitively opted for market reform, after a protracted struggle between her advanced and her retarded provinces. Both Czechoslovakia and Hungary, which share with Yugoslavia the traditions of the Habsburg monarchy, have started to introduce market mechanisms. East Germany, despite her advanced stage of industrialization, together with Poland, has opted for a type B reform, perhaps because the regime is not strong enough domestically to be able to survive any increase in pluralization. Rumania and Bulgaria, as we have already suggested, are still at a stage in economic development where reformed central planning may bring significant gains in efficiency.

The Role of the Soviet Union

Except for Yugoslavia and Albania, however, the Eastern European regimes are not being left to themselves in this matter. Ultimately, the decision on the type of reform they institute appears to rest with Moscow, whose decision depends in the last analysis on whether the Soviet leaders will permit any significant degree of pluralization in Soviet society. Thus the extent of evolution allowed to the Eastern Europeans is in the long run determined by the political situation obtaining inside the Soviet Union. And so we are driven to ask in what circumstances, if any, would Moscow opt for market reform in Eastern Europe, while being prepared to accept the domestic consequences for the Soviet Union? Many disparate elements would play a role in the Soviet decision.

To begin with, the Soviet Union has a vital interest in the legitimation of the regimes it has founded along the land approaches to its vulnerable western frontier. A survey of the checkered history of these regimes will show that Soviet influence in the area reached a high point some time shortly before the death of Stalin and has diminished ever since. Stalin's practice of ruling through the Soviet police helped provoke the Yugoslav defection of 1948. Khrushchev's efforts to govern the area by means of semiautonomous Communist parties contributed to the defection of Albania. His attempt to vitalize Comecon and make it an instrument of economic control was frustrated by opposition from Rumania. Brezhnev and Kosygin have had to invoke the Warsaw Pact to prevent the pluralization of Czechoslovakia. The emergence of a strong and prosperous, if truncated, West Germany and its gradual formulation of a new Eastern policy gives the Eastern European regimes an alternative source of support, and especially of economic assistance and advanced technology. As a consequence of the success of the new West German Ostpolitik, East Germany was threatened with increasing isolation. By the summer of 1968, it must have appeared to the Kremlin leaders that they were faced with the prospect of a Soviet–West German condominium in Eastern Europe, one in which Soviet influence would rest on military and ideological factors, and German influence on economic and technological. Moscow must have an urgent interest in the stabilization of the Eastern European regimes and in a reaffirmation of their pro-Soviet orientation.

If, as the occupation of Czechoslovakia demonstrates, closer economic relations with the West are forbidden, the practicable alternative would appear to be improved and restructured economic relations with the Soviets. The presence of a sizable Soviet garrison in Czechoslovakia is no solution to the grave economic problems that precipitated the Czech crisis in the first place. If not market integration with the West, which is now occurring in Yugoslavia and was threatening to occur in Czechoslovakia, why not market integration with other Communist nations? For any given Eastern European state, the Comecon common market would not offer the best solution, since the greatest degree of specialization and the most advanced technology are to be found in the West. But socialist market integration within the framework of Comecon would create a semimarket of 340 million people, with opportunities for significant gains in specialization and technology. From the standpoint of Soviet and Communist interests, a Comecon common market would seem preferable to declining growth rates and the continued instability and disruption of the Soviet empire in Eastern Europe. Furthermore, such a market would tie the Eastern Europeans to the Soviet Union more effectively than any previous system or tactic.

These speculations are not as far-fetched as they may sound. In fact, they were embodied in proposals put forward by the apparatchik in charge of market reform in Hungary, Rezsö Nyers, in an address delivered to the Political Academy of the Hungarian Central Committee in January 1969.[60] Nyers proposed a Comecon customs union, the

---

[60] Nyers, "Questions of Principle and Practice in Socialist Economic Integration," *Nepszabadsag*, Jan. 23, 1969, as translated in *RFE Research: Hungarian Press Survey*, 1,982 (Feb. 3, 1969).

gradual introduction of a convertible ruble so as to permit multilateral trade within Comecon based on economically meaningful currency exchange rates, and a set of Comecon-wide market prices for key commodities. These changes would bring about the gradual specialization of the member states in lines of production naturally suited to them. Obviously Nyers thinks that the Soviet Union will end up providing Comecon with the bulk of its research and development, assuming that patents are paid for in proportion to their usefulness. Nyers also wants working contacts at the enterprise level, with only broad policy decisions reserved for the central authorities. As for agriculture, he proposes either a coordinated policy of subsidization or "a price system based on proportionate values."[61]

The Hungarian reformer recognizes that some Comecon members, like Rumania, would be unwilling to participate in his scheme, but he sees no reason why his proposal could not be limited to the interested parties as long as the Soviet Union was itself a direct participant rather than merely the organizer of an arrangement involving only the client states. Nyers comprehends the radical nature of his proposal, for he remarks that piecemeal reform of Comecon is not enough and that new foundations must be laid. He envisions a period of transition in the early 1970's and the realization of his regulated common market in the late 1970's. Yugoslav sources report that the Nyers proposal has resulted in divided councils, the Hungarians having the support of the Czechoslovaks "and others," with the opposition being made up of the Soviet Union, East Germany, and Bulgaria. From a Polish publication it would appear that Warsaw may have lined up with Budapest on this issue.[62]

Soviet opposition to the Nyers proposal is understandable. The Soviet Union could not participate directly unless it were willing to introduce a market reform at home. This would mean living with lower growth rates during a relatively long transition period while the long-neglected infrastructure was being restored and renovated, basic distortions in the price structure corrected, and more honest methods of accounting enforced. At the same time power relation-

[61] *Ibid.*, p. 13.

[62] Harry Trend, "Yugoslavia on Comecon's Future," *RFE Research: Communist Area*, Mar. 19, 1969; M. Misiak, "A Blueprint for Closer CMEA Integration," *Polish Perspectives* (Warsaw), Feb. 1969, as reproduced in *RFE Research: Polish Press Survey*, 2,182 (Mar. 12, 1969), 6–16, suggests that Polish economists generally agree with Nyers in such matters as intra-Comecon exchange rates, a convertible Comecon currency, multilateral trade, enterprise-to-enterprise contacts, flexible prices, and domestic economic reform, including the "utilization of the market mechanism."

ships within the regime itself would need to be restructured. The party, the army, and the security police would decline in importance, while the managerial class, the technical intelligentsia, the writers and artists, and the local officials would gain. Decentralization would probably also bring to the surface much of the conflict now submerged by totalitarian practices; literature in particular would tend to become an instrument of political opposition. Regional interests and nationality conflicts would reappear. The Turkic peoples of Central Asia, together with the Ukrainians, would press hardest for genuine autonomy, but the peoples of the Caucasus and the Baltic area would also seek greater independence. The impact that the pluralization of Czechoslovakia was having on the Ukraine, for that matter, was one of the many reasons why Soviet troops were brought to Prague.[63] During the transition period the Communist regimes would run a constant risk of losing control, though I am inclined to believe that this risk would be substantially less in the Soviet Union than in Eastern Europe. With all these changes going on, however, the Soviet leaders would no doubt feel compelled to adopt a more conciliatory foreign policy, especially in their dealings with the West.

It is difficult to conceive of the present Soviet leadership's setting out on such a bold and far-reaching policy as the reorganization of Comecon into a regulated common market, even if the domestic costs were relatively low, or for that matter to imagine the Eastern European conservatives, and especially the East Germans, going quietly along. The party and state apparatuses of Eastern Europe are governed by persons of limited intellectuality and poor education; this is probably also true of the Soviet Union, though perhaps to a lesser degree. Indeed, it may be argued that the ultimate gap between Communist and non-Communist Europe, between East and West, is not technological but analytical. Not only are Communist leaders having to take steps to provide for a wider and more rapid diffusion of Western technology, for example; they are also finding that in order to achieve this result they must relearn their economics or, more properly, refine and sophisticate their Marxist-Leninist intellectual heritage with Western borrowings. The current evolution of Eastern Europe is one vast elite learning process, whether at the technological or the analytical level—a learning process impeded, among other things, by a well-grounded fear of catastrophe and an ingrained suspicion of capitalism. The analytical learning is ultimately the more

[63] R. V. Burks, "The Decline of Communism in Czechoslovakia," *Studies in Comparative Communism*, II: 1 (Jan. 1969), 21–49.

important, since it is in the broad sense prerequisite to the technological. Without a reorganization of the system, rates of innovation, to
use that example once again, will not rise at a sufficiently rapid rate.
To reorganize the system in turn requires an analysis of its failings.

Under the pressure of declining growth rates and increasingly difficult policy choices, the European regimes have developed their own
version of the Chinese struggle between "red" and "expert." A key
question among Eastern European Communists today is how far
economists are to be trusted. In due course, Khrushchev came to understand that Galați, the steel-producing center that the Rumanians
were building on the lower Danube, and Kremikovtsi, the steel combine under construction near Sofia, were white elephants from the
Soviet point of view and that the Stalinist policy of autarky within
the Communist state system was one of the system's major weaknesses.
He therefore attempted to introduce the principle of what he was
pleased to call "the socialist international division of labor." But
Khrushchev's economic policy fell short on several points: he assumed
specialization could be achieved by the long-term coordination of
state plans; he excluded the Soviet Union from participation on the
ground that it was naturally self-sufficient; and he grossly underestimated the strength of the national sentiment underlying the policy of
autarky. Thus his program for the reform of Comecon was never
viable. Meanwhile the Yugoslav Communists, faced with the problem
of creating a viable regime outside the socialist camp, gradually
worked their way into a socialist market, paying the political costs as
they went. The Czechs, faced with the sharp recession of 1962–65, undertook to follow the Yugoslav example. The Hungarian Communists, still trying to live down the events of 1956, took the same line,
but very cautiously. It is perhaps significant that neither Ota Šik, the
formulator of the Czech reform, nor Reszö Nyers, the architect of the
Hungarian, is primarily an economist. Rather, they are party men
who have learned Western economics in an effort to save a political
system in which they believe.

The resistance of orthodox Communists in general, and of Soviet
Communists in particular, to Western economic theory is rooted not
only in their traditional rejection of capitalism but in their adherence
to the notion of a solidary society, which is basic to Communist (or
any other) totalitarianism. For Marxist-Leninists, conflict, enmity,
and falsehood are inseparable, as are the opposite principles, harmony, friendship, and truth. Thus even in a socialist society, which is
for Communists the ideal society in embryo, the interests of the state

are in all cases conceived of as identical with the interests of the party, those of the party with those of the proletariat, those of the proletariat with those of society at large, and so on, in an endless tautology. When citizens act contrary to the official doctrine, as indicated by high rates of labor turnover, or by extensive corruption among bureaucrats, or by internal migration among the intelligentsia, these signs of conflict of interest are either ignored in embarrassed silence, or put down to the survival of "bourgeois" attitudes, or attacked through propaganda campaigns designed to create a new image of the socialist man. Factional conflicts within the party are generally half-suppressed, and only reach the public eye in mysterious outbreaks of purge and counterpurge, in show-trials and in hangings.[64] As long as Soviet and Eastern European Communists continue to conceive of society in these primitive terms, market reform and, beyond that, any form of political pluralization will appear to them as a kind of anarchy in which they cannot survive.

The workings of the world Communist movement, however, tend to push the Soviet center in the direction of internal structural change. Eastern Europe itself has long been recognized as a kind of ideological antechamber to the Soviet Union. In other words, what is permitted in Eastern Europe later becomes politically available inside the Soviet Union. This has been a principal cause of the off-again, on-again character of Soviet-Yugoslav relations. The occupation of Czechoslovakia came in part because Moscow could not tolerate a free press in a client regime and maintain censorship at home. To the unsettling effect of events in Communist Eastern Europe must be added the considerably less substantial influence of the Western European Communist parties. In practice, if not always in theory, Western European Communists now accept the pluralistic character of Western European societies and therefore wish for pluralization in Eastern Europe in order to improve their credibility with their own electorates. The impact of European Communism on Soviet politics has been curiously reinforced by the great schism that now divides Moscow and Peking. Soviet leaders, who have an almost irrational fear of the Chinese, only have their fear confirmed by Peking's pursuit of what now appears to most Russians as extremist foreign and domestic policies designed at best to discredit the Communist movement, at worst to destroy the world in a nuclear holocaust. The Soviet leaders'

[64] For the Communist concept of a solidary society see Gregory Grossman, "Economic Reform: The Interplay of Economics and Politics," in R. V. Burks, ed., *The Future of Communism in Europe* (Detroit, Mich., 1968), pp. 103–40, esp. pp. 122–25.

reaction to Chinese extremism, combined with the instability of the Eastern European regimes and the electoral hopes of the Western European parties (particularly the Italian, the French, and the Finnish), tends to draw the Soviets further along the road of revisionism.

The fate of revisionism in the Soviet Union will ultimately depend on the performance of the Soviet economy. The Soviet gross national product grew at an average annual rate of 7.1 per cent in the 1950–58 period, but fell to 5.3 per cent in the 1958–64 period.[65] Although there has been some recovery since, the Soviet leaders must decide how much longer they can go on sacrificing the interests of the civilian economy to the maintenance of a competitive position in the military and aerospace fields. Admittedly, because of its huge size and natural self-sufficiency the Soviet Union can afford to operate inefficiently for a much longer period than a small, Eastern European economy. Even under a policy of autarky, imports as a percentage of gross national product range from 10 per cent in Poland to 24 per cent in Bulgaria,[66] whereas the corresponding figure for the Soviet Union is 6 per cent. In other words, the hard currency problem will become severe much sooner in the small countries.

Nonetheless, a day of reckoning for even the Soviet Union is not inconceivable. The Soviet Union must struggle to maintain self-sufficiency in foodstuffs with 36 per cent of its labor force still tied up in agriculture, whereas the United States, with 7 per cent of its working force in agriculture, not only feeds itself but has difficulty disposing of its surpluses. A variety of factors help explain the difference in agricultural productivity, but one of the more important is that per acre of sown area Soviet farmers use only 36 per cent as much commercial fertilizer as American farmers.[67] The rate of reduction of manpower in Soviet agriculture is lower than that of any other industrial state. This huge labor force is locked into agriculture, so to speak, by the technological retardation of the civilian economy. It has been estimated that as of 1962 the overall level of Soviet civilian technology lagged behind that of the United States by a quarter of a

[65] Stanley H. Cohn, "Soviet Growth Retardation: Trends in Resource Availability and Efficiency," *New Directions in the Soviet Economy*, Pt. II A (U.S. Congress, Washington, D.C., 1966), pp. 99–132.

[66] Ernst, "Postwar Economic Growth in Eastern Europe," table 18.

[67] "Agriculture in the United States and the USSR: A Statistical Comparison," in *Soviet Economic Performance, 1966–1967: Materials Prepared for the Subcommittee on Foreign Economic Policy of the Joint Economic Committee, Congress of the United States* (Washington, D.C., 1968), pp. 30–35.

century, and that Soviet civilian technology was further behind in 1962 than it had been in 1940.[68]

The Soviets themselves are now introducing a type B reform. It is difficult to foresee whether the gains from this limited, in-system reform will be sufficient to permit the continued postponement of structural change. But it does seem reasonable to believe that if economic inefficiency begins to force drastic alternatives on Soviet policy-makers, such that either the Soviet Union's world stature or the regime's domestic hold seems in danger of being seriously impaired, the Soviet leaders will face up to the costs of market reform. In such an event, the hope of greater productivity and greater stability in Eastern Europe will serve as a powerful additional incentive for change.

[68] Michael Boretsky, "Comparative Progress in Technology, Productivity and Economic Efficiency: USSR versus USA," *New Directions in the Soviet Economy*, pp. 133–256.

Theories of Convergence

ALFRED G. MEYER

During the first decade of intensive studies of Communist systems in the United States after World War II, Communism was generally described as an altogether novel form of government; and the Soviet Union itself tended to be presented as a unique polity. The uniqueness of Russia, of course, is a very old theme that can be traced back to the earliest period of contacts between Russia and the West after the Tatar domination; it was struck with vigor by Slavophiles in Russia and by Western scholars of various schools—Mackenzie Wallace, B. H. Sumner, and John Maynard of the English school, for example, and such contemporaries as Wright Miller and Klaus Mehnert. It can be argued by reference to vague concepts such as national character or culture; and it tends to be promoted by the so-called area studies approach, in which the student steeps himself in the culture he is studying until he becomes thoroughly familiar with its history, geography, social life, political system, economy, language, literature, and art, and related matters. After a decade or two of such exposure, hopefully spiced by travel in the area, he becomes an expert.

The methodological trap concealed behind the assumption of uniqueness is obvious: the truly unique cannot be communicated, except to others who have had similar exposure. The Russian poet Fyodor Tyutchev expresses this with clarity and fervor in this poem:

> Umom Rossiiu ne poniat',
> Arshinom obshchim ne izmerit':
> U nei osobennaia stat'—
> V Rossiiu mozhno tol'ko *verit'*.

I wish to acknowledge the assistance of Janis R. Krohn in the preparation of this essay.

Roughly translated, he says: You cannot understand Russia by applying your intellect; nor can you measure her by a common yardstick.
Her status is unique. You can only *believe* in Russia. Bertram D.
Wolfe has expressed a similar idea very eloquently in a recent article
on the convergence theory. Pointing out that Stalin once accused him
of being an American exceptionalist, he confesses that in fact he was
an exceptionalist for all lands on earth.

I thought for instance of India and China, and wondered how one could
be content to lump them together under the single rubric of "Asian lands"
without losing all sense of differences in their spiritual and intellectual life,
their social structures, literatures, arts, philosophies, faiths, dreams—all the
qualities of life that make these two Asiatic lands more different from each
other than England from France or Germany. During that wide-ranging
debate with Joseph Stalin I became aware of what I had long sensed, that
every land moves towards its future in terms of its own past, its own institutions and traditions. To abstract from these differences, as Marx sought to,
as Lenin did, and as Stalin was trying to persuade me to do, was to miss the
essence of each country's life and history.[1]

If Tyutchev, Wolfe, and other spokesmen for the uniqueness of the
Soviet Union were right, social science would be in a deplorable state.
How can we possibly make generalizations about human behavior in
general if all behavior takes place within unique frameworks? Many
of the alternatives to the pure area-studies approach that were tried
in the first decade or two of postwar "Sovietology" can be better understood if we realize that the scholars sought to express the uniqueness of Soviet Communism in terms of general theories of human
behavior. The system, which remained unique, was now described in
the language of social science, but the chief concepts or approaches
used were applied only to the Soviet Union and Communist systems:
ideological determinism, which made Marxist-Leninist theory responsible for much of what we observed in Communist countries, was not
applied to other polities; the *kto-kogo* approach, in which the deadly
games of a revolutionary mafia in its desperate struggle for control
became the single most important determinant of the entire system,
was recognized as similarly inapplicable to other systems (witness the
round rejection of the writings of Vilfredo Pareto and C. Wright
Mills); finally, the totalitarian model gained currency precisely because it conveyed explicitly and emphatically the novelty, if not the
uniqueness, of Communist systems.

---

[1] "Russia and the USA: A Challenge to the Convergence Theory," in *The Humanist*, Sept.-Oct. 1968, p. 7. His confession of exceptionalism has not, of course,
prevented Wolfe from placing Russia and the United States into highly abstract
classification schemes that contrast totalitarian and free societies.

The implication of all these approaches for the study of Communism was that an understanding of the Soviet Union and its client states was not possible by using the vocabulary, the concepts, the constructs, and the models of Western social science, because the social phenomena from which these conceptual tools were abstracted were absent in the Communist world. One of the most influential essays on the Soviet Union, George Kennan's famous "Mr. X" article, published in 1947, implies, for example, that Soviet Russia does not possess a social structure. Instead, Kennan depicts the Soviet Union as a hard crust of dictatorship on top of a completely atomized society—a shapeless conglomeration of mankind.[2] At the time Kennan wrote, any scholar who would have suggested that there was not only a social structure, but one that might be described in terms of interest groups or of a stratification pattern comparable to that of the United States, would have appeared ridiculous and politically suspect.

The first attempt to break away from this methodological exceptionalism was the refugee interview project launched around 1950 by the Russian Research Center at Harvard University for the United States Air Force. Designed to explore the strengths and weaknesses of Soviet society, the project was given the mandate to apply contemporary survey methods and sociological models. The research revealed, among other things, that the Soviet Union did indeed have a social structure, that some of its social life could be explained by the concept of "informal behavior," and that a wide range of other tools of inquiry, heretofore applied only in the study of Western societies, could fruitfully be employed by students of the Soviet system.

Today, almost two decades since the beginning of that pioneering project, much work on Communist societies is deliberately comparative. This does not necessarily mean that the notion of uniqueness has been abandoned. Comparative work can steer away from this question altogether if it remains on the so-called middle level of theorizing, that is, if instead of developing macro-models of the total system it concentrates on discrete structures or functions. Thus one can study socialization or communication patterns, family life, small-group behavior, decision-making models, elite careers, one-party systems, the functions of ideology, and a host of other phenomena without abandoning the notion that they exist within an essentially

[2] The image of a totally atomized society, and of the Soviet political system as a form of perpetual warfare of the Kremlin against the Soviet people with the principal aim of perpetuating this unstructured state, is elaborated in Bertram D. Wolfe, *Communist Totalitarianism* (Boston, 1956), esp. pp. 259–93; Robert Magidoff, *The Kremlin vs. the People* (Garden City, N.Y., 1953); Zbigniew K. Brzezinski, *The Permanent Purge* (Cambridge, Mass., 1956).

unique framework; or else one can simply disregard the broader framework. Still, the use of a social-science vocabulary that can also apply to Western societies does suggest at least some similarities. Hence some scholars, such as Samuel Huntington and Zbigniew Brzezinski, continue to stress the uniqueness of Communist systems in terms of the use of different words; for example, they differentiate between the term "ideology" in the Soviet Union and the term "belief system" in the United States, between "politicization" in the Soviet Union and "socialization" in the United States. Such contrasting vocabulary, which emphasizes lasting and unbridgeable differences between the two types of systems, was employed also by Lenin and his followers (e.g., nationalism vs. patriotism, competition vs. emulation). Similarly, the Soviet controversies over whether such Marxist concepts as value theory fit both types of society reflect the Communist ideologists' attempt to show the uniqueness of their system.

To discover comparable features in both systems is one step away from the notion of uniqueness. Another step is needed to discover actual similarities or identical traits even if only for discrete features. This step has been taken with increasing frequency in the last two decades. In a recent essay, Alex Inkeles restates the discovery he made some years ago about the similarity of the Soviet and American social structures: "In our examination of the economic systems of the Soviet Union and the United States we stressed that certain similarities should not obscure the basic differences. In assessing the structure of stratification in the two societies we must reverse the emphasis and urge that certain differences between the two systems not be allowed to obscure the basic similarities."[3] There is an observable ideological convergence, which takes many forms. For instance, one could realistically describe both systems as arenas of ideological conflict, with the outcome quite unpredictable, between at least three schools, espousing (1) a doctrine of salvation and damnation stressing the irreconcilable hostility between the two systems; (2) a pragmatic, instrumental orientation seeking to free itself from ideological ties and believing itself to be nonideological; and (3) a humanist alternative to the establishment way of life, sought by congeries of rebels and dissenters. Maurice Duverger has pointed out the similarity between Khrushchev's vision of the Communist future and the widely accepted idealization of the American way of life—affluent, depoliticized, classless, and conflictless.[4] Similarly, Georgy Lukács has visualized a con-

---

[3] *Social Change in Soviet Russia* (Cambridge, Mass., 1968), pp. 408–9.
[4] *Introduction à la politique* (Paris, 1964), pp. 366–67.

vergence of the bourgeois-democratic and proletarian revolutions,[5] and ideological "bridge-builders" in both camps have insisted for quite some time that Marxism and "bourgeois" social science are complementary rather than mutually exclusive.

In this connection, it is remarkable to note how the discovery of similarities by Western scholars has been matched by the Communists in their pronouncements about the profound transformations that have allegedly taken place in the capitalist world. The imperialist camp, according to Soviet theories in the early 1960's, no longer is monolithic; it has become pluralistic. It has ceased being absolutely hostile, and now shares some common interests with socialist countries. It no longer poses an overwhelming threat, because it has been weakened and possibly chastened. The United States, according to the theory of the Khrushchev era, is faced with the problem of adjusting to a world that does not correspond to imperialist dogma or ideology; if it succeeds in making such adjustments, it will be threatened by revolution less and less and its system will acquire some legitimacy. Finally, America's ruling elite has become realistic and reasonable and is in the process of abandoning its ideology of world domination. Much of this sounds like an echo of Western theories of convergence.[6]

Numerous scholars have noted broader similarities in the general quality of life in both societies. The European Communist countries and the societies of Western Europe and North America, they point out, share many of the problems of urban living, from delinquency, alcoholism, and generational conflict to water and air pollution and the rapid exhaustion of natural resources by reckless entrepreneurship. Indeed, it could easily be argued that in both systems the demands of entrepreneurship dominate and even cause such problems as urban sprawl and inadequate city planning, to name only two. There are cultural similarities, too; the products of political art and entertainment in the Soviet Union strikingly resemble the output of commercial mass culture in the United States. Inkeles, who has made similar observations, decries the present cultural sterility of both systems.[7] Moreover, even where there are structural differences, functional similarities between the Soviet and American systems can be

[5] *Realism in Our Time* (New York, 1964), cited in James H. Meisel, *Counter-Revolution* (New York, 1966), p. 111.

[6] See William Zimmerman, "Soviet Perceptions of the United States," in Alexander Dallin and Thomas B. Larson, eds., *Soviet Politics since Khrushchev* (Englewood Cliffs, N.J., 1968), pp. 163–79.

[7] A. G. Meyer, *The Soviet Political System* (New York, 1965), p. 347. Inkeles, pp. 54–55, 60.

described. An example might be the functions served by the Komsomol and Greek-letter fraternities, which I have compared elsewhere.[8]

Some scholars argue that there may be a psychological convergence of the two systems, since both tend to attract people of similar personalities into elite positions. Persons with comparable skills, talents, and attitudes—careerists, conformists, high achievers, people intellectually creative but capable of teamwork—will do well in both societies; David Granick's "red executive," with all his problems and his particular ways of coping with them, is not too different from his American counterpart; and the fate of the dull, the stupid, the deviant, and the unlucky in both societies might also be comparable; even the psychological adjustment that the alienated and the failures make in both systems may be similar. One American sociologist views these various similarities between the Soviet Union and the United States as on the increase:

Most of the important similarities generated by industrialism among modern systems are already in substantial degree present in the Soviet Union. . . . Indeed, if a hypothetical observer from another planet were to view all contemporary societies he would surely be more impressed by the similarities among all industrial societies than by the differences. The question, however, is whether the impact of industrialism will be responsible for *further* similarities between Soviet society and its Western, and especially American, counterparts.

In certain respects, especially those having to do with purely physical appearances—for example, the layout and form of the modern city and the materials and techniques employed in its construction—the answer is certainly, yes. In still other respects, such as the tempo of daily life, fashion, high geographic mobility, access to the pleasures of consumption, and the like, the answer is also yes.[9]

Moreover he points out that the similarities will also be increased because of the expected further reduction of the traditional rural population of the Soviet Union.

It is not only the hypothetical visitor from Mars who would see basic similarities in the two systems, but also, and more significantly, the real observer from the Third World and uncommitted societies. Surely the statement that Inkeles makes about the Soviet Union is pretty much what millions of people think about the United States: "The men in the Kremlin built their country to be ever more awe-

---

[8] Meyer, p. 353.

[9] Allen Kassof, "The Future of Soviet Society," in Kassof, ed., *Prospects for Soviet Society* (New York, 1968), pp. 504–5.

some to some, ever more feared by others, but also to be less and less really admired and ever decreasingly loved."[10]

We started out with some cursory remarks about the view of Soviet Communism as something unique, and then turned to observations about discrete similarities between it and Western society. To proceed from this observation to a statement that the two types of system are *essentially* similar is a significant step, for we would be saying that they belong to the same type or same order of social system. If these similarities are seen to have increased within the framework of historical development, we would be presenting a theory of convergence.

Theories of convergence are as old as the Russian revolution itself, if we think of Waclaw Machajski's wry Saint-Simonian prognosis of the development of a stratified industrial society in which the educated and skilled would emerge as the new ruling class. Machajski was a disillusioned Marxist; and theories of convergence seem to suggest themselves easily to disillusioned Marxists, or at least to Marxists who have become disillusioned about the Soviet Union. Consider the theories of Trotsky, Achminov, Djilas, Mao, and the European and American New Left. In some fashion or other, they all describe the Soviet system as one in which a proletarian revolution gone wrong has resulted in the society reverting to some form of capitalism. Conversely, in the manner of James Burnham, another disillusioned Marxist, theories of the revolution betrayed correspond to assumptions about the end of capitalism and democracy in the West and foretell the emergence of a "managerial" society much like that projected by Saint-Simon, Machajski, and others.

Having mentioned disillusioned Marxists, we ought, perhaps, to mention a contemporary school of writers disappointed with or suspicious of democracy. Political theorists like Jacob Talmon and Giovanni Sartori attribute totalitarian tendencies to democracy, and sociologists like Emil Lederer and William Kornhauser speak of the development of mass society. Although these writers are concerned primarily with an analysis of trends in the West, they see in the Communist world a model or a variant that displays these trends. It is significant that Zamiatin's anti-Communist novel *We* could become the model for Orwell's nightmare, *Nineteen Eighty-Four*, about the future of Britain and indeed the entire civilized world.

When we speak about *the* theory of convergence, however, we usually refer to a prognosis that found adherents beginning in the early

10 Inkeles, p. 60.

1950's—roughly since the death of Josef Stalin. Its chief spokesman was Isaac Deutscher; but his views are echoed in the writings of such a disparate set of scholars as John Kenneth Galbraith, W. W. Rostow, Maurice Duverger, Georgy Lukács, Andrei D. Sakharov, and a host of Eastern European writers.

Deutscher, also a disillusioned Marxist, who has advanced the theory of convergence most forcefully and clearly, predicts the inevitable transformation of both the Soviet and American life styles toward democratic socialism. For the Soviet Union, this means an inevitable trend toward liberalization, though within a socialist framework. He argues that Stalinism has outlived its usefulness.[11] With the modernization of the Soviet Union, Stalinism will now disappear and give way to a democratic political system more functional to the pluralistic social structure that has emerged. Increased affluence and increasing political literacy throughout the population will make it possible for various elites and indeed the masses of consumers and citizens to participate in public life. I have repeatedly maintained that Stalinism was a "system-building" polity which, having accomplished its purpose, must be replaced by a polity geared for "system management." Many economists have similarly argued that the command economy has become dysfunctional and must be replaced by new and more rational planning methods.[12] The party, others have stated, will change its functions from those of unchecked command to those of interest aggregation; in the process it will become more representative by co-opting nonpolitical elites into its top organizations and perhaps evolve, finally, into a multi-party system. Sakharov in addition posits the end of ideology in the Soviet Union, i.e., the emergence of an elite of "realists" victorious over Maoist and Stalinist dogmatists. In short, the convergence theory foresees an erosion of dictatorship and of

[11] Implicit in many of the theories we are discussing is the assumption that, for its time and for the solution of pressing problems facing Soviet Russia, Stalinism was necessary. That question has been debated extensively in the last fifteen years; it seems unnecessary to take a stand on it here.

[12] See, for example, Peter Wiles, "Will Capitalism and Communism Spontaneously Converge?" in Morris Bornstein and Daniel Fusfeld, eds., *The Soviet Economy: A Book of Readings* (Homewood, Ill., 1966), p. 372. Note that Wiles does not accept the notion that such a transformation is inevitable. See also Jan S. Prybyla, "The Convergence of Western and Communist Systems: A Critical Estimate," *Russian Review*, XXIII: 1 (Jan. 1964), 3–17; and Jan Tinbergen, "Do Communist and Free Economies Show a Converging Pattern?" in Morris Bornstein, ed., *Comparative Economic Systems* (Homewood, Ill., 1965), pp. 455–64. For a discussion of Stalinism as a system-building polity, see A. G. Meyer, "Authority in Communist Political Systems," in Lewis J. Edinger, ed., *Political Leadership in Industrialized Societies: Studies in Comparative Analysis* (New York, 1967), pp. 93–100.

ideology. Kassof summarizes much of the Deutscher prognosis after predicting the further homogenization of Soviet society through mass education, mass culture, urbanization, and the like:

At the same time, paradoxically, the very complexity of an increasingly modern and productive society will more and more preclude a return to the relatively primitive totalitarianism of Stalin's day and will also militate against the advent of a more sophisticated latter-day variety. Collecting, ordering—and using—all of the information essential to total control over a society (not to mention how to enforce the policy decisions involved) pose insuperable obstacles even in the era of computer technology. It would be going too far to say that the resulting gaps will simply lead to a pluralistic society, but we probably can count on some increases in individual and group autonomy—a kind of freedom by default. Such a prospect, let it be noted, will be profoundly disturbing to a Communist regime still strongly attached to a utopian ideology of complete social coordination and planning and will lead to repressive episodes during periods of conservative ascendancy. But such efforts are likely to retard rather than stop the erosion. The alternative of enforcing conformity through terror, apart from the political risks entailed, is no longer a realistic answer in a system more than ever dependent upon the rational use of human resources.[13]

For the Western world, and especially the United States, most proponents of the theory of convergence posit a development toward socialism. They assume, and usually say, that socialism is more efficient than the anarchic workings of the market economy, even or especially under monopolistic or oligopolistic conditions. Deutscher argues that technological progress, especially automation, will strengthen the demand for public ownership in large corporate enterprises. Nationalized industries, he asserts, are more efficient in modernizing their equipment and production methods. The inevitable dislocation of labor due to technological change must be cushioned by public measures. In addition, Deutscher assumes that the Soviet Union will present an ever greater ideological challenge, which will convert more and more people to socialism: Soviet Russia will be an increasingly attractive source of foreign aid for developing nations; the Council for Mutual Economic Aid will be more efficient in international economic cooperation than its Western counterparts; and Communist humanism will be more attractive morally, culturally, and ideologically than Western philosophies.[14]

Adding to Deutscher's prognosis, Sakharov postulates a victory of

13 "The Future of Soviet Society," p. 501.

14 Rostow reverses this. He assumes the superiority of the American way of life, foresees the continuing stability of the American system, and projects the development of the Soviet Union in the direction of the American model.

leftist reformists in the capitalist countries leading to a rapprochement with socialism. Duverger maintains that technological development causes the diminution of political conflict and a growth of social and political integration, accompanied by a general growth of government power. Whereas Sakharov ultimately favors world government to solve the problems of poverty and underdevelopment on a global basis, Duverger is a bit more cautious and foresees only the convergence of both major systems in some form of socialism, with residual differences remaining. The Soviet Union will liberalize, the United States will socialize; and "only one thing seems certain, the convergence of the evolutions of East and West toward democratic socialism."[15] In due time, he states, the world will be divided into two major camps, America and Russia in one, and the underdeveloped countries in the other. The major world conflict will be between the affluent and the destitute nations.[16]

The premises and assumptions on which such theories are based can be stated simply. Chief among them is a technological-economic determinism that assumes a given technology causing a functionally corresponding social structure or system of social relations, and similar systems of social relations developing similar political systems. With or without serious reservations, this assumption is widely shared by Western social scientists.[17] Even if a theory of convergence is rejected outright, this deterministic theory is often accepted in considerable measure.

While the Soviet administrative system is ... relatively unique from a structural standpoint, in its functional characteristics it manifests significant similarities to other systems, as reflected in administrative behavior and representation of interest groups. ...

The Soviet party-state system ... performs the function of articulating and aggregating diverse interests, but the means used differ from those in other societies. It has established a hierarchy of interest groups in which heavy industry, science and technology, and the armed forces normally have a privileged status. The perplexities of allocating resources among interest groups are as burdensome in the Soviet Union as in representative systems, and it is probably fair to say that the differences among alternative proposals considered within the Politburo are as great or greater than those

---

[15] Duverger, *Introduction à la politique*, p. 379; for a scathing criticism of this book, see Raymond Aron, *Industrial Society* (New York, 1967), pp. 92–183.

[16] Duverger, pp. 344, 354 *et seq.*

[17] See, for example, Clark Kerr *et al.*, *Industrialism and Industrial Man* (London, 1964), which takes the inevitability of industrialism for granted and asserts that a common technology will have common effects in human relations and in the management of resources.

that divide the Democratic and Republican parties in the United States, the Conservative and Labor parties in the United Kingdom, or the moderate and non-Communist left-wing parties in Western Europe....

The differences between the Soviet and other systems provide one of the best illustrations of the diversity of forms by means of which similar functions can be performed.[18]

In numerous cases, the idea of progress underlying the convergence theory—i.e., that rationality, tolerance, decency, and freedom will inevitably triumph—is supported by an implicit or explicit assumption about the irreversibility of historical developments. A number of those I have quoted here voice this belief, and the same faith is expressed with almost uncanny regularity in comments about the recent manifestations of civil disobedience in the Soviet Union and about the stormy relations between the Communist party and the creative intelligentsia. Alternatively, the convergence theory is a by-product of broad theories of political development, such as that of A. F. K. Organski, who envisages a "stage of abundance" to be reached by developed societies in East and West; this stage is marked by high production and consumption rates, automation, and a decreasing labor force, but also by a highly developed military machine and a political system that gives power to a relatively independent and irresponsible elite who keep the masses of the population in a dependency relationship. In short he forecasts a stratified, authoritarian society, centralized and socialistic, and not necessarily democratic.[19]

A very different concept underlies the theory of convergence offered by Pitirim A. Sorokin toward the end of World War II. Postulating an end result similar to that outlined by Deutscher, Duverger, and others, he presents a theory I shall call cultural determinism, according to which all human societies can be classified according to their principal values. In Sorokin's view, both major systems are committed to gross materialistic goals; both are "sensate" cultures, and he assumes their coalescence.

There is behind the theory of convergence a belief in progress, expressed as theories of development and modernization based on economic determinism. In addition, there is an assumption of functional congruence in a given social system by which any major transformation of parts of the system will be followed by related transformations in all other parts if the system does not disintegrate from excessive

18 Cyril E. Black, "Soviet Society: A Comparative View," in Kassof, *Prospects for Soviet Society*, pp. 25–27.

19 *The Stages of Political Development* (New York, 1965), pp. 186–211.

strain. Such a view would explain the remarkable staying power, if not stability, of the Soviet system and its ability to readjust after major problems of a previous period have been solved.[20] There is implicit in a good deal of Western convergence theory the assumption that Western society, and specifically the United States, is the model toward which all contemporary societies are striving. That seems to me a rather naive assumption and one that confuses "modernization" with Westernization. To be sure, societies as they develop are undoubtedly more modern than before, but there is no reason to assume that they will develop multi-party systems, increased popular participation, freedom of thought and creativity, or a civic culture of mutual accommodation. As Kassof puts it, "the expectation that tensions generated by the incongruency between the Soviet system and the imperatives of industrialism will sooner or later force the Soviet Union to become more 'Western' in some fundamental respect rests, I believe, on an unwarranted assumption."[21] Indeed, the assumption made by Aron, Brzezinski, and Huntington, among others, that the successes won by the Stalinist system, far from leading to its scrapping, will favor a hardening of ideological lines and political institutions, appears as plausible, or at least as conceivable, as the convergence hypothesis.

The theory of convergence that foresees democratic socialism appears to be based on a good deal of pacifist moralizing, wishful thinking, or sheer impatience with the Cold War. Sakharov, among others, quite explicitly sees convergence as the only alternative to mutual annihilation. Similarly, Peter Wiles believes that the one reason far stronger than any deterministic one for the convergence of the two systems is the danger of mutual annihilation.[22] Sorokin fervently desired that relations between the Americans and the Soviets after World War II would be peaceful and cooperative. I have compared the Cold War to the religious wars of the sixteenth and seventeenth centuries and expressed the wish that the present ideological conflict end in a Westphalian peace without a Thirty Years War. But here too a false assumption may be involved. Many theorists of convergence seem to take it for granted that similar systems are more compatible with each other than dissimilar ones.[23] But there is little evidence to

[20] I have attempted an explanation in "The Soviet Political System," in Samuel Hendel and Randolph L. Braham, eds., *The U.S.S.R. after 50 Years* (New York, 1967), pp. 45–54.

[21] "The Future of Soviet Society," p. 505.

[22] Wiles, p. 384.

[23] Pitirim A. Sorokin, *Russia and the United States* (New York, 1944), p. 19; Andrei D. Sakharov, *Progress, Coexistence, and Intellectual Freedom* (New York, 1968).

support such an assumption. It is made so often, I think, because the rhetoric of the Cold War has drummed into our heads the notion that the antagonism between the two systems is a result of the ideological and political differences between them, whereas in fact the causal chain may well have been the reverse.

In short, the prognosis about a meeting of East and West in a happy synthesis of socialist democracy is based on a set of assumptions, premises, and beliefs that are subject to serious doubt.[24] This does not mean that the prognosis might not indeed come true. But to assert this with any kind of assurance, one would have to know far more about the real chances for significant liberalization in the Soviet Union and the real chances for the growth of socialism and the preservation of democracy in the United States. Until such calculations can be made, the Deutscher theory and its many variants remain exercises in wishful thinking.

Quite another, newer, theory of convergence, which has some plausibility, proceeds from the assumption that all industrial societies do indeed share certain salient features; the theory goes on to deny the inevitability of a liberalization and democratization trend, especially since democracy and liberalism in politics, economics, and cultural life, it could be argued, correspond to a phase of modernization that prevailed in Europe and North America many decades ago and is on the decline in these Western societies. Convergence, if it will occur at all, is likely to take place in the form of bureaucratization rather than democratization. The basic assumption underlying this theory is the thesis that industrialism promotes the bureaucratic organization of the total society because of the increasing need for coordination and hierarchy, the need for information management, the irresistible trends toward rationalization, complex organization, and the universal adoption of the merit system, and the related urge to monitor the performance of every individual and every organization. The model for convergence then is not the democratic two-party system or the democratic polyarchic system of government by groups, but the modern bureaucratic organization, either in its corporate form or in the form of huge national governmental bureaucracies, civil or military.

In my recent work on the Soviet political system I have advanced this theory of convergence (without calling it that) by asserting that the Soviet Union can best be understood as a giant bureaucracy, some-

---

[24] It is worth pointing out that the rejection of this prognosis may also be grounded in purely ideological, i.e. nonempirical, assumptions, such as the fear of submergence. See Gregory Grossman, *Economic Systems* (Englewood Cliffs, N.J., 1967), pp. 111–13.

thing like a modern corporation extended over the entire society, or a "General Motors writ large."[25] It is remarkable that the Soviet text-book definition of socialism is almost exactly the same as the Weberian and post-Weberian definition of bureaucracy: both are defined as the imposition of rationality on the affairs of men through complex organization and scientific management.

The Soviet system not only subscribes to the same goals as modern bureaucracy, but is structured in real life very much in accordance with the Weberian model and its indices of rationality. The Soviet Union and the European Communist systems as well stress and insti-tutionalize such principles as hierarchy, staff work, functional differ-entiation of agencies, structured communications, record keeping, the prevalence of rules and regulations, the merit system, and the estab-lishment of measurable performance criteria for the standardized monitoring of performance. In its behavioral aspects, the Soviet sys-tem also replicates Western bureaucracies: we can discover informal organization and informal behavior patterns; we can note that the Soviet system is afflicted with the same typical inefficiencies besetting Western organizations; and we can observe identical psychological types succeeding or not, or adjusting to the bureaucratic life with the same variety of psychological devices.

It is important to note an essential difference here: the trend toward bureaucratization, however universal it may be in the West, can obvi-ously not be identified with the bureaucratization of an entire country under one central controlling hierarchy. Even if the Soviet Union can be described as "General Motors writ large," the fact remains that the real-life General Motors still exists within a larger society, culture, and political system. At the same time, the importance of this differ-ence should not be overestimated either. It may be true that it is eas-ier to quit a large corporation than it is to quit the Soviet Union; but, given the benefits of seniority accumulated by workers and employees, quitting is becoming more and more difficult because too many ac-crued benefits must be sacrificed. Again, it is true that the American citizen is subjected not to one vast multiform bureaucratic empire but to a multiplicity of bureaucracies—his employer; federal, state, and local governments; entertainment monopolies; advertising; insurance companies; car dealers; loan associations or banks; educational bu-reaucracies; welfare agencies; the selective service machinery; and many others. But being subjected to this congeries of bureaucratic

---

[25] *The Soviet Political System,* p. 472.

agencies may not make that much difference to the quality of life of the average man. After all, the centralized machinery of the Soviet system also confronts the citizen with a multiplicity of agencies.

Even on a high elite level the differences may be less than we tend to assume, or they may be lessening as Western systems impose more central regulation and control and as the highest bodies of the ruling party in the Soviet Union become increasingly pluralistic so that the party turns into a hidden multi-party system.

In short, the theory of convergence we are discussing now is based on the assumption that the thorough bureaucratization of life characterizes both Communist and Western societies, and that the resulting similarities of experience and human relations tend more and more to outweigh, neutralize, or even cause the disappearance of the structural and cultural differences in the two types of political systems.

In developing such a theory of convergence, the pattern of evolution of bureaucracy itself might be considered. Modern complex organization and management has gone through a process of development that might suitably be described in terms of some of the following parameters: from simple to complex; from crude to sophisticated; from authoritarian to participatory; from coercive to rewarding; from orthodox to tolerant; from centralized to decentralized; from command to management; from paternalism to fraternalism. Following suggestions made in my book *The Soviet Political System*, which in turn are based on Rensis Likert's proposed typology of administrative organizations, Peter Ludz has suggested that Communist systems may be evolving in four stages, from coercive totalitarianism through welfare totalitarianism and consultative authoritarianism to participatory authoritarianism. I have called the fourth stage "participatory bureaucracy"; and the theory of convergence we are considering here simply assumes that on the basis of current trends some system deserving such a label is likely to develop in both East and West.[26]

The idea of applying organization theory to the study of Communist systems is not novel. Several scholars, among them Gustav Wetter

26 *Ibid.*, p. 243. Rensis Likert, *New Patterns of Management* (New York, 1961). Peter Christian Ludz, *Parteielite im Wandel* (Cologne, 1968), pp. 35–37. One major problem with abstract models of this kind is their tendency to speak in terms of the entire system, as if assuming that all subsystems are structured in analogous fashion. In fact, however, one must be more specific. For instance, it would be necessary to differentiate between various relationships: elite-society, elite-elite, elite-subelite, and the like. But surely, even though the variety of relationships increases as we concentrate on details, it might still be legitimate to classify the entire system by the use of the categories Ludz has suggested.

and Zbigniew Brzezinski, have pointed to similarities in structure and behavior between the Soviet Union or its ruling party and the Roman Catholic Church. But such comparisons are irrelevant to this discussion because my conception of bureaucracy is more limited. I use the term "bureaucracy" to mean the bureaucratic collectivism that has become a major form of social and political organization in the twentieth century, and of which some of the outstanding pioneers are August Bebel and Henry Ford, Alfred Sloan and V. I. Lenin.[27] It is no exaggeration to say that this modern bureaucracy is also a universal ideal—the predominant utopia of contemporary social thought in both the Communist and the non-Communist world, competing primarily with the notion of "development" as the yardstick by which we measure political systems. Bureaucracy as a utopia is founded on the belief that the "administration of things" will spell the end of the "domination of men," a belief quickly shattered for anyone who observes some typical work projects manager in his relations with people, whether that administrator of things be a Lazar Kaganovich or a Mayor Daley. In its most developed, sophisticated, or benign image, the bureaucratic utopia presents itself as a true synthesis of rationality and democracy, of order and freedom, incorporating such disparate values as participation, social justice, stability, and the rule of law. Once this is recognized, the theory of convergence in bureaucracy may appear as optimistic, or at least as neutral and hence perhaps more readily acceptable to empirical scholarship. Its underlying assumptions are similar to those on which the Deutscher-Duverger thesis is based but without the most obvious instances of wishful thinking.

But bureaucracy also represents one of the most persistent nightmares of mid-twentieth-century social thought, partly because some of the irrationalities and dysfunctionalities inherent in it have become obvious. Students of complex organization have become increasingly aware of the informal organization and informal behavior patterns underlying the formal rules and tables of organization, i.e., of the lack of correspondence between theoretical blueprint and actual functions. More important, the post-Weberian student of organization is aware of the waste and inefficiency, the inflexibilities and conservatism, the immunity to feedback, the misdirection of effort and skewing of goals that mark the performance of bureaucracies; and some have concluded that the very aim of imposing total rationality on the af-

[27] Hannah Arendt also views bureaucracy as a novel political system: she calls it the latest form of domination. "Reflections on Violence," *New York Review of Books*, XII: 4 (Feb. 27, 1969), 23.

fairs of men is ludicrous and self-defeating.[28] Crozier ridicules the notion that the "administration of things" might suppress power relationships and inequalities of authority, and a significant proportion of contemporary social psychology deals with the unsettling or disturbing effects bureaucracy has on the personality of the people involved in it. Regardless of how tightly or loosely structured authority may be at the top, regardless of the degree of monolithism or pluralism prevailing, to the people caught in the middle and at the bottom bureaucracy often is a source of alienation and a form of tyranny, a tyranny doubly repressive because it presents itself as the institutionalization of rationality and hence allows no appeal against its decisions. According to Hannah Arendt, in the Aristotelian classification scheme of political systems bureaucracy becomes "rule by Nobody." "Indeed, if we identify tyranny as the government that is not held to give account of itself, rule by Nobody is clearly the most tyrannical of all, since there is no one left who could ever be asked to answer for what is being done."[29] With the consideration of modern bureaucracy as a nightmare, we are touching on theories of convergence that themselves have a nightmarish quality. Social scientists are, perhaps properly, hesitant to consider them; but theories of this kind, which I shall discuss presently, are being proposed with increasing frequency.

A composite version of the apocalyptic theories of convergence I have in mind can be roughly described. Both the Communist world and the highly developed nations of the West are said to be moving toward a social and political system marked by centralization and authoritarianism, with gross political inequalities perpetuated by irresponsible elites wielding unprecedented power. In this world of the future, state and society will have merged into one bureaucratized order. True politics openly and freely pursued by all citizens will have disappeared, and all social life will have become politicized, meaning that it will have become a matter of public concern and political control, regulation, and coordination. Bureaucratic techniques and regulations will have supplanted and replaced law, in the sense of legal principle; in other words, law will have turned into ad hoc regulation, similar to traffic laws, which strip law of its moral legitimation—doubly so since law will still protect old rights and privileges without, however, protecting new ones such as the right to "decent treatment,"

[28] See Alfred G. Meyer, *The Soviet Political System*, pp. 208–9; see also Michel Crozier, *The Bureaucratic Phenomenon* (Chicago, 1964), pp. 156–74, 198.
[29] "Reflections on Violence," p. 23.

to some "inner freedom," or to the refusal to participate in war.[30] The slogan of "law and order" will then have turned into a smoke screen of tyranny. Order, stability, and compliance with rules and regulations will have assumed primacy in the hierarchy of social values; all other values will be relatively incidental by-products.

One of the victims of this triumph of law and order will be the concept of the primacy of the human person. The person, indeed, will disappear in a Kafkaesque administrative world. Persons will be turned into attributes able to be categorized and recorded on punch cards in employment agencies, insurance firms, credit bureaus, and police departments—a trend that Jacques Ellul calls the "technical system of the concentration camp."[31] Helplessly exposed to the manipulations of giant monopolistic bureaucracies and to propaganda, the person loses his autonomy even though he may retain the illusion of freedom. The multiplicity of propaganda messages does not free him to make up his own mind, but creates a psychologically debilitating atmosphere.[32] The elite in this nightmarish projection may permit many diversities and heterogeneities among the people, but only as long as these diversities are irrelevant, according to the motto of Joseph Goebbels: each and every one may seek salvation according to his taste, as long as he does not touch the existing system; or, as Herbert Marcuse puts it, the establishment learns to absorb and castrate all forms of deviance. In the writings of Marcuse, Ellul, and others, modern technological society emerges as a nonterroristic form of totalitarianism, i.e., as a society that because of technological progress has made freedom possible, has rendered repression and domination superfluous, but—supreme irony—has also made it virtually impossible for anyone to recognize these possibilities because the masses are satisfied, the proletariat has disappeared, intellectual dissent is absorbed, and the lonely recalcitrant can be crushed.[33]

In sum, there are some theories direly predicting the convergence of developed systems, Communist and capitalist, within a framework

[30] See Giovanni Sartori, *Democratic Theory* (New York, 1965), pp. 308–11; see also Jacques Ellul, *The Technological Society* (New York, 1964), p. 251.

[31] Virgil Gheorghiu's *The Twenty-Fifth Hour* (Chicago, 1966) is a stirring novel on the theme of depersonalization.

[32] Ellul, p. 276; see also John Kenneth Galbraith, *The New Industrial State* (New York, 1967), ch. 18.

[33] Sakharov (pp. 44–67) explores this theme in some detail, and in some of the theories here being summarized it comes to the surface. These are theories of a coming garrison state or garrison society, or of police states run by intemperate demagogues who keep potential counterelites down by stirring dark fears and thus mobilizing the mob.

of bureaucratic or fascist-like authoritarianism; and these theories, taken together, project the emergence of a totalitarian political system that is very different from the earlier models of totalitarianism, and far more novel. Moreover, it has a very different ideological point. Earlier models of totalitarianism were based on the "we-they" contrast, whereas the theory emerging here is presented in "we also" terms. James Meisel catches the spirit of such theories well when he writes:

The confrontation between Marxists and the bourgeois innovators underwent a subtle change as time went on: it turned into an undeclared convergence. Without officially deserting their camps, some doubting Marxists and some doubting liberals met in the no-man's land between the front lines: theorists of power based on economic class and theorists of the elite that governs by authority were unable to find the line dividing them. Marxist defectors and middle-class rebels jointly happened on the master institution of our time, bureaucratic collectivism, the meeting place of East and West, Bonapartism brought up to date, totalitarian in character even where it can dispense with terrorism.[34]

The arguments supporting such prognoses can only be summarized briefly here. Prominent again is a pronounced technological determinism with Ellul as the chief, though by no means the only, spokesman.[35] The word "technology," however, is misleading in this context. Ellul uses it in the widest possible sense, including administrative and managerial as well as productive techniques. His book argues that modern man has become the slave of his techniques: "The further the technical mechanism develops which allows us to escape natural necessity, the more we are subjected to artificial technical necessities."[36] He asserts that technique dehumanizes and alienates, that it creates diversities totally artificial and devoid of human value,[37] and that this self-enslavement of mankind is beyond human control: "There is no difference at all between technique and its use. The individual is faced with an exclusive choice, either to use the technique as it should be used according to the technical rules, or not to use it at all. It is impossible to use it otherwise than according to the technical rules."[38] In short, we have here, and in a variety of similar works, a

---

[34] Meisel, *Counter-Revolution*, p. 106.
[35] Ellul; Ernst Richert, *Die neue Gesellschaft in Ost und West* (Gütersloh, 1966); Herbert Marcuse, *One Dimensional Man* (Boston, 1964); Alexander Mitscherlich, *Die Unwirtlichkeit unserer Städte* (Frankfurt, 1965); Crozier; Galbraith.
[36] Ellul, p. 429; see also Marcuse, p. 159.
[37] Ellul, pp. 130–31.
[38] *Ibid.*, p. 98.

tragic version of the Marxian dialectic, minus the resolution envisaged by Marx. And a phenomenon that some contemporary scholars have greeted with relief or enthusiasm—the alleged end of ideology— is seen in these theories as a symptom of disaster, as a submergence of humanist culture in technology. If, as Bell, Brzezinski, Huntington, Lipset, and others assert, the humanist intelligentsia has become dysfunctional and will yield to the "pragmatic," "instrumental," or nonideological technician, then the authors here being considered would take this as confirmation of their thesis that technique has triumphed over morality, and the machine over the species. The result is not only the reign of a new ideology that, parading as rationality, is immune to attack, but also the victory of totalitarianism.

Technique cannot be otherwise than totalitarian. It can be truly efficient and scientific only if it absorbs an enormous number of phenomena and brings into play a maximum of data. In order to co-ordinate and exploit synthetically, technique must be brought to bear on the great masses in every area. But the existence of technique in every area leads to monopoly. This is noted by Jacques Driencourt when he declares that the technique of propaganda is totalitarian by its very nature. It is totalitarian in message, methods, field of action, and means.[39]

The tendency of highly developed industrial societies to develop police regimes seems to be based on the assumption that dissent and heterogeneity may be more unsettling and threatening in mature systems than in modernizing ones. Hence, the hypothesis current among students of comparative Communism that terror is functional to modernizing systems as a mobilization device may have to be revised. Terror and repression may have important functions also after the mobilization phase. In the "fully developed" society the need to preserve law and order may become so overwhelming that repression may become routine.[40]

Ellul, in line with his stress on the tyranny of technique, suggests that police techniques will be used in the coming society simply because they are available. We tend to use all newly invented processes and things whether there is a need for them or not, he argues, and he gives the police as an example:

The police have perfected to an unheard of degree technical methods both of research and of action. Everyone is delighted with this development be-

---

[39] *Ibid.*, p. 125.

[40] The current preoccupation with the preservation of order, expressed by public figures as well as social scientists in the Western world, might serve as partial confirmation of such a hypothesis. See, for example, Samuel P. Huntington, *Political Order in Changing Societies* (New Haven, Conn., 1968), esp. ch. 1.

cause it would seem to guarantee an increasingly efficient protection against criminals.... [But] will this apparatus be applied only to criminals? We know that this is not the case.... The instrument tends to be applied *everywhere* it *can* be applied. It functions without discrimination—because it exists without discrimination. The techniques of the police, which are developing at an extremely rapid tempo, have as their necessary end the transformation of the entire nation into a concentration camp.[41]

A further source of these gloomy prognoses of convergence are the theories of totalitarian democracy, mass society, and power elites mentioned earlier. All of them seem to have in common the notion that the *public*, from which both major systems pretend to derive their legitimacy, has in fact disappeared or been put out of action, or become virtually incompetent to participate meaningfully in decision-making.[42]

Prognoses of the growing militarization of life appear to be based, among other things, on an assumption shared by all theories of convergence—the conception of a global society in which the determining structural feature is the difference between affluent and indigent nations. Hence the overriding political problem is that posed by this global class conflict. Until the Malthusian dilemma has been resolved, there are no political solutions to the problem, and recurrent violence practiced by affluent masters and starving subjects alike is inevitable. With the rivalry between the two major affluent powers complicating the situation, mankind faces a prolonged period of international civil war, that "era of world wars and revolutions" Lenin foresaw shortly before his death.[43] Consequently, in both major powers or power blocs, the military establishment will grow in size and power and will penetrate ever more deeply into all phases of civilian life, into education, research, business, labor, and the legislatures. The result will be an increasing resemblance between military and civilian elites and finally the breakdown of the traditional boundaries between civilian and military societies. The nations affected will be ruled by power elites of generals, politicians, and corporate executives devoted to conservatism (system maintenance) at home and counterrevolution abroad.[44] The English sociologist Stanislav Andreski foresees the total

---

[41] Ellul, pp. 100–103; see also p. 272.

[42] For a summary of "democratic elitist" theory based on disillusionment with the common man, see Peter Bachrach, *The Theory of Democratic Elitism: A Critique* (Boston, 1967), pp. 8 and 9, and ch. 3.

[43] The term "international civil war" was first used, to my knowledge, by Sigmund Neumann.

[44] Vernon K. Dibble, "The Garrison Society," *New University Thought*, V: 1, 2 (1966–67), 106–15. Dibble states that his prognosis is an elaboration of Lasswell's

militarization of life and of politics, culminating in the universal so-
vietization of all modern societies: the Soviet Union will be the model
toward which we all will converge, even those systems that "proclaim
that they are fighting to preserve the freedom of the individual."[45]

Finally, the prognosis of convergence in some form of totalitarianism finds support in a variety of psychological theories and hypotheses. Numerous writers, beginning with Freud, have argued that the
industrial way of life produces neuroses on a mass scale.[46] Traditional
or conventional behavior norms, so it is argued, become dysfunctional
more quickly than in previous ages; they may turn into cruel fictions,
and any insistence that they are meaningful reinforces the dysfunctional relation between man and his society. Modern society, with its
complexity, speed, competitiveness, and other demands on the ego,
tends to overtax people, both individually and collectively, according
to Freud; men lose their ability to understand, decide, control, or
orient themselves. Citizenship then becomes as hollow a concept as
freedom or autonomy. As Richert asserts, it is the essence of the modern world that it is out of joint.[47] In the works of Marcuse, the underlying assumption is a lingering unhappiness on the part of all people
that can be manipulated by shrewd political operators and can easily
turn into violence.

An exploration of this psychological theme will turn our attention
to a category of people that modern industrial society seems to produce again and again, a social stratum acting as a political force only
intermittently; when it does act it strongly opposes radicalism, liberalism, heterogeneity, and dissent. These people in Western societies are
prone to join movements classified as the extreme right; in the Communist societies of Soviet Russia and Eastern Europe a similar group
is customarily referred to as the extreme left. In order to avoid misun-
derstanding, I will refer to this political stratum as the backlash.

We are all familiar with the political views of the backlash people:
they are dissatisfied with the current state of the system and place responsibility for the deplorable state of the world on two villains—the

---

famous projection concerning the coming garrison state. Juan Bosch's shrill in-
dictment *Pentagonism: A Substitute for Imperialism* (New York, 1969) is based on
analogous assumptions.

[45] *Military Organization and Society* (Berkeley, Calif., 1968), p. 167.

[46] See Sigmund Freud, *Civilization and Its Discontents*, trans. James Strachey
(Norton, 1962); Alexander Mitscherlich, *Auf dem Weg zur vaterlosen Gesellschaft*
(Munich, 1963); Richert; and Sigmund Neumann, *Permanent Revolution* (New
York, 1947).

[47] Richert, p. 133.

alien conspiracy, whose agents are deep within the fabric of the society, and the soft and cowardly authorities, who do not have the courage to crack down on this criminal conspiracy. The backlash believes in preventive and punitive violence and decries the lack of vigilance in the population as a whole. People of this kind tend to be disciplinarians committed to a work and thrift ethic, pronouncedly puritan, repressive, and indignantly opposed to all forms of hedonism. Post-Freudian students of the authoritarian personality have tended to attribute to broad masses of modern populations a fear of liberation from repressive conventions, a fear masking a desire so strong that it is perceived as threatening the personality of the individual. Both the fear and the desire, the promise and the threat of liberation, are relieved or circumvented by violence, authoritarianism, conformity, and moral indignation. The resulting political tendencies are intense patriotism, xenophobia, nativism, populism, and an ethnocentric hatred of all other minority groups, together with an intense commitment to a crabby religious or political fundamentalism. In its search for conspirators and deviants, the backlash is particularly suspicious of the rich, the educated, and the experts. Heterogeneity and democracy are seen as the cutting edges of subversion; democracy is perceived as loss of control and hence a threat wherever it exists.

There is a good deal of agreement in Western scholarship about the social and psychological genesis of the backlash. These people are generally seen as being caught in a status crisis that may have one of several causes: some of them may have professions that are being squeezed out of the job market by technological advance, and they may be moving down the accepted social scale; others may have become wealthy or powerful so quickly that their own self-estimation has not quite kept up with this change, and hence they feel ill at ease among older elites. In general, the backlash people tend to be relatively undereducated, but they compensate for this by claiming a greater knowledge and wisdom than the formally educated, who are called eggheads and pseudo-experts. Many have recently moved from small communities to cities and have not quite adjusted to the move. In sum, they suffer from modernization; and the underlying aim of their political activity might be said to be that of preventing changes that have already taken place. If this is correct, then it would be at least a partial explanation of the patent irrationality of their politics.

The institutions to which this political force is devoted are the police, the ideological apparat (be it the Communist party or an institution like the House Un-American Activities Committee), vigilante organizations such as the Ku Klux Klan or the Komsomol *druzhiny*, the public prosecutor, and the censor. Indeed, one might measure the success of liberalization in any society by the proportionate weakness of these institutions. The system the backlash people establish when they come to power curiously incorporates all the drawbacks of coercive bureaucratism without any of its benefits. It tends to be coercive but disorderly, elitist but without a well-functioning merit system, hostile to regular procedure, routine, and lawfulness. Its foreign policy, based on a paranoid world image, is likely to be aggressive. Some people would add that the systems established by the backlash similarly incorporate certain democratic and socialistic features but without the mutual forbearance, the tolerance for diversity, and the egalitarianism of democratic and socialist theory.

From the composite picture sketched here, a political system emerges that is similar to fascist and national-socialist regimes. Does this mean that fascism is likely to appear in modern societies? Such a question demands a reexamination of theories of fascism. One thing seems clear: this political order is decidedly a phenomenon of mature systems, systems past the industrialization and mobilization phase of development. Indeed, with further modernization, the forces conducive to its development might increase in strength. At the same time, it does not appear to be an especially viable system, being neither rational nor stable and having established itself on the basis of quickly dissipated popular moods. If these statements are accepted, the most melancholy prognosis one might offer would perhaps be that the future of developed societies, both Communist and anti-Communist, is likely to converge within the framework of bureaucratic totalitarianism. But bureaucratic totalitarianism is unable to prevent the recurrent build-up of serious psychological tensions, which are likely to lead to fascist-like political interludes, followed in their turn by the restoration of bureaucratic routines and orderliness. The business cycle of the nineteenth century having been cured, a psychological cycle can be visualized based on the recurrent eruption and repression of violence. Such a prognosis would be a variant of the model of fascism developed some decades ago by Ernst Fraenkel, which combines the bureaucratic features of the corporate state with the dynamism of a mass movement and charismatic leadership.[48]

Here, then, are three theories of convergence, one that posits the development of both Soviet and American societies within the frame-

---

[48] See Ernst Fraenkel, *The Dual State—A Contribution to the Theory of Dictatorship* (New York, 1941).

work of democratic socialism, a model similar to the Swedish system. The basic assumption here is that a pluralistic society will be able to govern itself only with the help of a democratic, participatory, pluralistic political system based on a civic culture of mutual toleration. A second theory of convergence regards the same social pluralism as the basis for a political order modeled rather on the modern corporation or perhaps on the company town—an order stressing hierarchy, coordination, structured communications, rational elite recruitment, and the like. Hence this is convergence on a bureaucratized polity. Finally, we have an apocalyptic theory of convergence in a new fascist-like totalitarianism engendered by the psychological cost of modernization and the resulting crisis style of political rule. The model here would be the Third Reich. Some would add a fourth theory forecasting the end of both the Soviet Union and the United States in their present forms in a revolution, followed by the thorough restructuring of both polities according to anarcho-syndicalist or socialist ideals. I have not considered this last possibility because it is not, strictly speaking, a theory of convergence, and it is in my view the least likely of all the possible alternatives.[49]

How does one assess the validity or plausibility of such theories as these or of counter-theories, whether they stress the uniqueness or the opposing positions of Russia and the United States?

Convergence theories as variants of development or modernization theory share with it one methodological weakness: theories of modernization have a tendency to be explicitly or implicitly teleological because they must make some assumptions about the end product of development. The meaning of "modern" must be defined. If theories of modernization seek to avoid this trap (assuming that we agree that teleology is a "trap"), they easily fall into another—ethnocentrism, which may take the form of assuming that modernization will be achieved only under conditions or in a sequence the writer's favorite system (not necessarily his own) has experienced. With reversed values, these caveats apply as well to theories of reverse progress, decay, or impending disaster, including the apocalyptic theories of convergence we have described.

Some scholars would warn about yet another trap—determinism—but I am not sure whether that deserves to be taken seriously. All science, including that dealing with man and society, is deterministic in

---

[49] For an interesting recent statement agreeing with this assessment, see Barrington Moore, Jr., "Revolution in America?" *New York Review of Books*, XII: 2 (Jan. 30, 1969), 6–12. Moore is very convincing in his assertion that any serious attempt at revolution-making in the United States would hasten the coming of a fascist-like regime.

the sense that it seeks to uncover and explain correlations between discrete phenomena with the aim of forecasting future events. The trap is not the assumption that explanations are possible—presumably on the basis of some "deterministic" relationship—but the assumption that simple explanations can be provided. It is the great simplifiers against whom one must be on one's guard, just as we must guard against those who would not want us to make any generalizations whatever.

Either to accept or to reject any of the theories of convergence discussed above would be unwarranted. These theories, in their present form, are no more than hypothetical projections. It would require an elaborate effort to make the many hypotheses on which they are based operational and then to verify or falsify them. In their present state, therefore, theories of convergence are no more than heuristic devices, alerting the scholar to various possibilities of development. They are dreams and nightmares based on a selective perception of reality and put together with the aid of that highly important ingredient of scholarship—imagination. As heuristic devices, or models, they must not be taken too literally, for real life is always more complex and confusing than even the most sophisticated models. This becomes apparent as soon as we seek to match empirical data with the models, for instance by placing individual elite members in the Communist world within the classification scheme suggested in this article. Should Shelepin, Moczar, Ceauşescu, or Husák be classified as bureaucratic authoritarians or representatives of the backlash, or do they fit neither category? And if, as we would doubtless find, they cannot be classified with certainty, how can they be compared to the Kádárs, Dubčeks, and Gomulkas, except by breaking through the facile generalizations offered here?[50]

One can apply these imaginative projections by using them to propose or speculate about the trends in structure or behavior that are likely to promote or prevent one or the other type of convergence—to say nothing about possible subtypes of development. The task is formidable. It involves no less than a comprehensive theory about the mechanics of social and political change, together with an equally comprehensive gathering of aggregate data on all relevant phenom-

[50] See Jerry Hough, "The Soviet Elite: Groups and Individuals," *Problems of Communism*, XVI: 1 (1967); also see Jerry Hough, "The Soviet Elite: In Whose Hands the Future?" *ibid.*, XVI: 2 (1967), for pertinent ideas on how to classify the so-called neo-Stalinists. See also Radio Liberty Research Paper No. 17, "The Political Credo of N..G. Yegorychev" (1967), which demonstrates the difficulty of classifying members of the Soviet elite.

ena in the contemporary world. With a generally accepted theory of social change plus adequate data, one might conceivably assess various salient trends realistically. But in order to determine whether or not these trends spell convergence in any of the meanings used here, these results would still have to be weighted; especially one would have to balance the importance of converging phenomena against those aspects of the systems that predictably will not converge.

There are some differences that, even convergence theorists tend to agree, will not disappear even when the systems of the United States and the Soviet Union may have converged. One might begin a list of "residual" differences with ideology, assuming that even if the systems become more and more like each other, they will cling to their rhetoric, their symbols, their holy political writings, just as after the Westphalian Peace the warring Christian denominations maintained their separate doctrines and places of worship. Yet in time these "ideological" differences between Catholics and Protestants became politically irrelevant, or of the most marginal relevance. To ideologists in both camps, they may continue to appear fundamental; but not so to the average citizen, to the various elites, or to the social scientist observing actual behavior in the two polities.

Not likely to disappear also is the difference between the two property systems. Strangely, little is made of this point by proponents or even by detractors of convergence theories. Perhaps critics have not made this a central point because they do not wish to be accused of Marxist views or because, like Burnham, they consider property law to be an irrelevant variable. I, for one, believe that it is not irrelevant or incidental at all, but is in fact a crucial variable in determining the goals and functions of the economy and in structuring the social stratification pattern and with it one of the bases of the political system and the priorities to which it is geared. Nor would it be easy to assume that there will be convergence in this respect. Can any scholar today seriously visualize a return to private property in the means of production in the Soviet Union or a meaningful inroad into the economic powers of corporate business in the United States?[51]

In addition to the property system there are other areas of social life that are likely to remain different. I have in mind national culture patterns, ranging from trivial matters such as food preferences to more

[51] A recent textbook on comparative economic systems states this as follows: "Once we are fully aware of the basic differences in the structures of the private enterprise and the centrally planned economies, we cannot count on a convergence of the two systems unless we expect a fundamental change in economic philos-

profound and politically salient differences. Of special interest here must be the political cultures, particularly the notable contrast between the individualism ingrained in Americans and the collectivism to which a vast majority of the Soviet people seem to subscribe quite genuinely. Political structures or forms have also become so traditional that they are likely to be retained even if overall convergence is to take place—the Soviet system, the presidency, the party systems, the entire political career ladder that leads to high office in the respective countries. Cyril Black sums up this view: "The United States and the Soviet Union, or Japan and Italy, will converge in the sense that their bureaucratic efficiency, occupational structure, level of education, and per capita consumption of raw materials and energy will become more alike—but their political values, their means of reconciling conflicting interest groups, and their authority patterns in family and social organizations, for example, are likely to remain significantly different."[52]

It is these projected differences that could serve as points of departure for critics of all convergence theories. Exceptionalists, regarding national culture as the essential determinant of any society, must reject the possibility of convergence as long as they can demonstrate that national culture still prevails. Indeed, authors like Brzezinski and Huntington find it easy to concede many points made by convergence theorists; they themselves foresee the growth of centralization in the United States (or, as a gloomy alternative, the rise of fascist-like mass movements) and the reduction of the tension between state and society in the Soviet Union (barring some less desirable alternatives). But they particularly stress historical and cultural patterns, especially the process by which modernization is achieved, and hence they cannot admit that the convergence concept is meaningful. For Bertram Wolfe, the difference between a totalitarian polity and one that provides freedom of opinion and control over public authorities outweighs all similarities. Similarly, Raymond Aron dismisses the similarities of industrial societies as irrelevant, because industry, he writes, is a means rather than an end, and hence its forms do not define or identify a society. The essence of a society is contained in the

---

ophies in either East or West. For both will have to develop policies that are in harmony with their basic character, and maintaining consistency within two fundamentally different philosophies cannot lead to convergence." George N. Halm, *Economic Systems* (New York, 1968), p. 401.

[52] "Soviet Society: A Comparative View," in Kassof, *Prospects for Soviet Society* (New York, 1968), pp. 48–49.

goals it posits for itself; and in this respect the two societies remain diametrically opposed—Soviet Russia manages its production for the purpose of maintaining or increasing its power, whereas America does so for the purpose of providing prosperity for its people.[53] Most critics of convergence theories would add that one other difference is perhaps most crucial, and that is the procedural difference. Contemporary democratic theory in the West generally defines democracy in procedural terms. The important problem then is not who rules and how, but how authorities are chosen, tamed, and controlled. And the critics of convergence theory seem to take it for granted that America is successful in this, whereas the Soviet Union is not, and that this distinction is likely to prevail. This is sometimes expressed by saying that the United States political system, in contrast to the Soviet system, has an effective public, which retains and may indeed cultivate the power to organize and agitate against specific targets and thus to deprive institutions or policies of legitimacy they have heretofore enjoyed. Examples of the use of public power might be the California grape boycott, Ralph Nader's campaigns, the indignation caused by the Santa Barbara oil leakage, or the controversy over the proposed deployment of anti-ballistic missiles. The critics of convergence theories assume that the ability of the public to see through the ideological masks of public and private bureaucracies is likely to increase. The spokesmen for convergence theories of the gloomier kind assume the opposite.

Given the primitive state of social science, a choice between these various theories and counter-theories can be made only on ideological, moral, or political grounds. To become convinced that convergence is or is not likely, the scholar must make a political choice between essential and incidental elements of the social system. That choice is subjective.

The choice is also inescapable. Developmental trends in both societies are there, can be observed, and present the problem of projecting them into the future. The question of whether the Soviet Union and the United States are likely to become more similar to each other, and to what degree, is a question posed by reality. Thus, however speculative these theories and a discussion of them may be, such speculations are a legitimate undertaking for the student of Communist and non-Communist societies.

[53] Zbigniew K. Brzezinski and Samuel P. Huntington, *Political Power: USA/USSR* (New York, 1964); Wolfe, "Russia and the USA: A Challenge to the Convergence Theory," pp. 3–8; Raymond Aron, *Industrial Society*, pp. 92–183.

Communism and Change

DANKWART A. RUSTOW

Change is the central theme of Communist theory from Marx to Mao, and change is a striking feature of Communism as a political movement from the formation of the Communist League in the 1840's to the varieties of Communist regimes of our own day. Yet social scientists have had difficulty fitting the changes in Communist systems into any convincing theoretical perspective.

Change was at the very heart of the Marxian system—a pervasive emphasis that sets it apart from previous social philosophies. Dialectical materialism claimed to provide the scientific explanation for historic change in "all hitherto existing societies." On that basis, Marxian theory ventured to predict, and Marxism as a movement undertook to hasten, the social changes of the future, including the final cataclysm that would once and for all sweep away the very principles of change that had determined the course of all previous history.

But as Communist movements came to power in Russia, Eastern Europe, China, and elsewhere, they did not make history stop; rather, they released new forces of change. Lenin's coup of 1917 and the following years of civil war made the members of a small conspiracy the rulers of a vast bureaucratic empire. Stalin after World War II managed to push Russian power far beyond the old imperial limits. Mao, at the head of a large peasant army, claimed the heritage of the Manchus. Khrushchev announced plans to transform Russia into the world's most affluent consumer society, and Mao's colleague Lin Piao unveiled a strategy for outflanking capitalism in a worldwide revolution of poor countries. All the while Communists in Russia, in China, and elsewhere were claiming to transform not only the political and economic structure of society but the very nature of man.

Not all the changes, however, conformed to Communist prescriptions. Lenin's New Economic Policy already was a thinly disguised admission of at least temporary failure. A generation later, Stalin's death set off a protracted struggle between liberalizing and repressive forces. Within various Communist countries this struggle manifested itself—in the unrest in East Germany and Poland in the early 1950's, in the Hungarian Revolution of 1956, and in the Czechoslovak crisis of 1968. Among Communist countries Tito's defiance of Stalin and the prolonged contest between Moscow and Peking clearly posed the question of monolithic versus polycentric Communism.

Where change has been so pervasive and sweeping, why have social scientists found it so hard to explain?

Communist theorists, committed to the truth of Marxism, have quarreled endlessly about the correct interpretation of a doctrine held to be unchanging. The doctrine itself recognized that circumstances might call for varying applications, but all Marxists, no matter how bitter their quarrels, were agreed that only one application could be correct in any one set of circumstances. From Communist theory there could be deviation; in Communist practice there could be correct or incorrect adaptation; in neither could there be basic change. Arguing within the Marxist framework, Communists have been unlikely to formulate an independent point of view from which to perceive or account for transformations in Communism. For any governing Communist party to admit the reality of basic change in Marxism would have been to undermine the legitimacy of its own dictatorship.

But non-Communist social scientists, free from such theoretical blinders or political exigencies, did little better in developing any general theory of social change, into which Communism could be fitted, perhaps, as a special case. This failure is all the more remarkable in view of the potent stimulus that the founders of modern social science received from Marx himself. Max Weber, it has been said, "became a sociologist in a long and intense dialogue with the ghost of Karl Marx."[1] Much the same may be said of his major contemporaries, notably Vilfredo Pareto, Emile Durkheim, Ferdinand Toennies, Thorstein Veblen, and Robert Michels. Weber described the impact of Calvinism and other religions on economic attitudes, and thus he neatly inverted Marx's notion of religion as part of an ideological superstructure based on economic foundations. Durkheim, in another

[1] Albert Salomon, "German Sociology," in Georges Gurvitch and Wilbert E. Moore, eds., *Twentieth Century Sociology* (New York, 1945), p. 596.

attack on the materialist interpretation of history, demonstrated that people committed suicide at times of mounting prosperity. Pareto found that ruling elites derived their power from many sources other than economic control, and Michels concluded that the most egalitarian movements were likely to give rise to tight new oligarchies; both therefore curtly dismissed Marx's vision of a classless, ungoverned society of the future. These and other social scientists of the early twentieth century shared Marx's desire to search out the forces of historic change; but they distrusted Marx's grand system and were eager to diversify, break down, or disprove his particular account of those forces.

One of Weber's major preoccupations was the process of institutionalization in modern bureaucracy. His most influential American disciple, Talcott Parsons, concentrated instead on identifying the universal functions that were the prerequisites of any society. By definition, such functions were timeless and hence not themselves subject to change. Insofar as Parsons, David Easton, and their contemporaries retained an interest in social processes, it was the process of equilibrium rather than of basic change that attracted them. As modern sociologists retreated from grand historical theory into small-scale empiricism or into scholastic definition-mongering, change tended to recede from their view.

Political science as a separate discipline developed mainly in Britain and the United States and hence felt the Marxian impact more remotely. Men like James Bryce and A. Lawrence Lowell were confident that democracy was universally applicable, and its rise and spread therefore supplied one common evolutionary theme to their researches. But this confidence by the 1930's had yielded to considerable skepticism, and the solid antecedents of political science in constitutional law did little to alert the discipline to other sorts of change.

A glance at any American textbook on foreign or comparative politics of the 1930's, 1940's, or 1950's shows how ill equipped the authors were to deal with political change. If France moved on from the Third to the Fourth Republic, the text material was simply updated by deleting the chapter on the one and adding a chapter on the next; if the Fourth Republic gave way to the Fifth, the same procedure was repeated. Just as Léon Blum and Daladier would join Dreyfus, Thiers, and Napoleon I in a perfunctory section on historical background, they were in turn joined by Vincent Auriol and Henri Queuille on the textbook writer's rubbish heap. The mechanism that might lead to the collapse of one republic, the alternative symbols of authority that might furnish the basis for the next—these were not considered a proper part of the traditional course in foreign political institutions. Furthermore, even though most of the major European countries were governed on a wartime emergency basis for about one out of every three years in the early twentieth century, and though each world war contributed markedly to expanding the economic power and other functions of government and to mobilizing the mass electorate, the professors in their ivory towers continued to write their texts on the comforting assumption of perpetual peacetime normalcy.

This legal-institutional approach succumbed to the "behavioral revolt" of the 1950's. But behaviorism in political science meant an emphasis mainly on clearer concepts (and hence, by an ironic reversal, on more confusing neologisms) and on exact, quantifiable observations, chiefly survey data. The most abundant reservoir for such survey data was contemporary American society—contemporary because corpses cannot profitably be interviewed, and American because many foreign societies turned out to be dictatorships where the public expression of most political opinions was a criminal, if not a capital, offense. Behaviorism thus reinforced at first the provincial and unhistorical outlook of many political scientists in the United States.

The study of political development and political modernization as it has evolved in the last decade marks a liberation from such earlier limitations. The concept of modernization itself shows strong Marxian and Weberian influences. When applied to social and political developments over a number of generations or centuries (as, for instance, in the work of Cyril Black, Barrington Moore, and Samuel Huntington),[2] it can go far toward supplying a general theory of social change. For example, if modernization is defined as "widening control over nature through closer cooperation among men,"[3] it is relatively easy to demonstrate that Britain and Russia have modernized since the days of Henry VIII and Peter I.

The concept of modernization has an obvious relevance to the Communist regimes of the twentieth century, preoccupied as they are with problems of industrialization, of elaborating governmental institutions, and of transforming the social structure. Yet most of them have been in power for too brief a period to allow for any firm

[2] Cyril E. Black, *The Dynamics of Modernization* (New York, 1966); Barrington Moore, Jr., *Social Origins of Dictatorship and Democracy* (Boston, 1966); Samuel P. Huntington, *Political Order in Changing Societies* (New Haven, Conn., 1969).
[3] See Dankwart A. Rustow, *A World of Nations: Problems of Political Modernization* (Washington, D.C., 1967), p. 3.

judgments about their pace of modernization. Even the estimates of Russia's industrial progress differ sharply depending on whether it is measured against a 1913 or a 1921 base.

The shorter the time span, the less helpful the perspective of modernization. In assessing the shifts of policy from Macmillan's government to Wilson's or from Khrushchev's to Kosygin's, modernization may well be kept a constant. There still remains a need, only partially fulfilled in the current literature, to devise a number of intermediate concepts that would connect the broad theory of modernization with the data of day-to-day empirical research.[4]

The study of Communism by non-Communist scholars developed in relative isolation from these trends in twentieth-century sociology and political science. Moreover, the scholars who established the field cannot be accused of ignoring change as they traced the evolution of doctrine from Saint-Simon and Marx to Stalin and Guevara, or the vicissitudes of policy from the New Economic Policy to the Great Cultural Revolution. A remarkable proportion of them had been Marxists in their youth, and they tended to accept a number of basic Marxist assumptions, even (or especially) when they deplored the betrayal or the withering of the original ideas. It seems fair to say that well into the 1930's the Western literature on Communism remained exegetic, polemical, or descriptive and at a relatively low level of abstraction. The scarcity of empirical data on Russia (at least until the 1950's), the intricacies of "Kremlinology," and the linguistic difficulties involved in mastering Chinese sources tended to preserve the somewhat esoteric and cliquish character of the specialty.

The large body of writings on totalitarianism marked a new departure. The concept itself was developed by a group of brilliant scholars, mainly German socialist or liberal refugees in the United States, to celebrate (before or after the event) the Nazi-Soviet alliance of 1939.[5]

[4] See Dankwart A. Rustow, "Modernization and Comparative Politics," *Comparative Politics*, I: 1 (Oct. 1968), 37–51.

[5] The word totalitarianism was first introduced into English usage in the late 1920's as a description of the ideological pretensions of Mussolini's regime (see "Totalitarianism" in *International Encyclopedia of the Social Sciences*). Wider currency for the term began a decade later. See especially Franz Borkenau, *The Totalitarian Enemy* (London, 1940), p. 20: "Nazidom is *Brown Bolshevism*, as Bolshevism could be described as 'Red Fascism.'" (Borkenau's preface is dated 1 December 1939.) See also Eduard Heimann, *Communism, Fascism, or Democracy?* (New York, 1938); Franz Neumann, *Behemoth: The Structure and Practice of National Socialism* (New York, 1942; 2d ed. 1944); Sigmund Neumann, *Permanent Revolution: Totalitarianism in the Age of International Civil War* (New

Communism no longer was viewed as a unique phenomenon. Its roots were traced in Western intellectual history as far back as Rousseau and even Plato. The political organization of Stalinism, as well as Nazism, was seen as a perverted outgrowth of tendencies toward mass behavior present in all of modern industrial and democratic society. All in all, the concept of totalitarianism served to raise the field of Communist studies to an unprecedented level of theoretical generality.

Whatever its virtues, the theory of totalitarianism remained ill equipped to support detailed and diversified comparisons between Communism (or its Nazi twin) and the democratic societies that constituted the major empirical reservoir for the broad stream of sociological and political science theory. Whereas Communism and Nazism could be compared to each other, and perhaps even to Fascism, Peronism, or Japanese militarism, totalitarianism taken as a whole remained "historically unique and *sui generis*."[6] The theory was equipped even less to account for basic changes under Communism, let alone toward or beyond Communism. Any system that fulfilled the essential criteria of totalitarianism, such as the well-known sixfold list of Friedrich and Brzezinski,[7] was held to be driven by its own dynamism in an unalterable direction, immune to basic change except by unconditional military defeat. (And, of course, the disappearance of Nazism in the defeat of 1945 deprived the study of totalitarianism of much of its comparative breadth.)

The very term totalitarianism, moreover, provided a set of blinders to the perception of change. Total control of society cannot, by definition, be expanded. Nor can it, again by definition, leave room for contrary forces that might effect any fundamental transformation. Empirical support for this view came not so much from available data about Russian realities under Stalin as from the very scantiness of such data. Press censorship and the ban on travel across the Soviet frontier were among the most undeniably total aspects of totalitarianism.

It is instructive at this point to reflect briefly on the verbal analogy between the concepts of absolutism and totalitarianism. Louis XIV

York, 1942); Hannah Arendt, *The Origins of Totalitarianism* (New York, 1951); Carl J. Friedrich, ed., *Totalitarianism* (Cambridge, Mass., 1954); Carl J. Friedrich and Zbigniew K. Brzezinski, *Totalitarian Dictatorship and Autocracy* (Cambridge, Mass., 1956; rev. ed. 1965); and Jacob L. Talmon, *The Origins of Totalitarian Democracy* (New York, 1960).

6 Friedrich and Brzezinski (1956), p. 5.

7 *Ibid.*, pp. 9–10.

might boast that it was he who was the state, that his powers therefore were unlimited. We know today that the persistence of regional organization inherited from the feudal past, the lack of transport and communication, the strong grip of custom on human thought, and the exigencies of the huge subsistence sector of the economy provided constraints far more inexorable than any that might have been imposed by mere constitutional theory. The "mighty Bourbon monarchy," a leading historian reminds us, "lacked the flexibility in raising the rate [of taxation] that the smallest American municipality enjoys" in our own day.[8] But taxation at least was a device well known to Louis XIV and his ministers. What of public education, of conscription, of economic controls through central discount rates, currency devaluation, or nationalized management? What of the power of the press, of radio, of television? Poor Louis! Three centuries of political evolution have exposed his boast as a paranoid fantasy.

Totalitarianism is that same fantasy updated and refurbished. Each concept assumes that there is some finite set of political functions, that these are all presently known, and that one organization headed by a single individual controls them all. Each therefore concludes that the power wielded by the despot through his agents is absolute, is total. But political power depends on human capabilities and needs. "The power of a man," according to Hobbes, "is his present means to obtain some future apparent good."[9] To appraise it, we must know something about the range of means at his disposal and about the ends that to him appear good. Power, that is to say, varies with changes in human knowledge, in technology, in social organization. The theory of totalitarianism is too pessimistic, for it underestimates the difficulties of controlling a far-flung organization and of perpetuating such control beyond the life of a mortal individual. It similarly underestimates the forces of resistance that subjects can bring to bear against even the most oppressive rulers. And the theory is wildly optimistic, for it ignores the rapid growth of modern technology and organization and hence the ever-new cruelties that man can yet inflict on man.

Students of Communism began their rapprochement with sociologists and political scientists when these social scientists were still largely in their static mood of imperceptiveness to change. The functional conception of sociology, much like the theory of totalitarian-

---

[8] R. R. Palmer, *The Age of the Democratic Revolution* (Princeton, N.J., 1959–64), I, 90.

[9] *Leviathan* (1651), Book 1, ch. 10 (Everyman edn., New York, 1950), p. 69.

ism, assumed that all social functions were finite in number and known—even though Robert Merton, Parsons, and others might quibble about the definitive list. And just as Parsons and Easton were concerned to trace the self-equilibrating mechanisms of social systems, it was plausible to assume that institutions and groups in Soviet politics provided the dictator with his opportunity to play each off against the other. Totalitarianism was an equilibrium system with a Hitler or a Stalin as its master-balancer.

Other approaches did equally little to develop a theory of Communist change. Even the psychological-cultural interpretation of Communism could lend support to the notion that Communists, by the very nature of their mental processes, were bound to apply the same "operational code" in the Cuban crisis of 1962 as they had at Brest Litovsk in 1917. The recent "convergence theory," although it explicitly hypothesized about change in Communist systems, was too imbued with ideological elements, even wishful thinking, to furnish any promising new basis. The theory of modernization (as we have seen) measured change by generations or centuries, and could not without the help of much intermediate conceptualization be applied to regimes that originated as recently as 1917 or 1949.

Most past approaches, then, do not readily seem to yield a convincing theoretical perspective on change in Communist systems. What is required, therefore, is perhaps the development of a general theory of political change, of which changes in Communist ideas and practice would be so many particular applications. This, frankly, is a plea for taking "the long road to theory."[10] But it may well be the only way that leads to the goal. Not having stumbled along into every previous cul-de-sac of social theory, it may well be that Communist specialists can help their confreres in political science and sociology avoid some of the detours ahead.

The contributors to this volume have taken several important steps on this road toward a theory of Communist change. They do not, of course, agree in all their interpretations any more than they are at one in their terminological tastes or methodological tenets. There is no unanimity among them; at best there is convergence.

In the following pages I shall single out some themes in the preceding chapters that seem to me particularly fruitful—as well as one or two that I find insufficiently represented. I shall then proceed to dis-

[10] See Stanley Hoffmann, "International Relations: The Long Road to Theory," *World Politics*, XI: 3 (Apr. 1959), 376–77.

cuss how some of these might be fitted into a broader theory of political change.

Most of the authors (with the conspicuous exception of Richard Lowenthal) reject the term totalitarianism as inadequate to an understanding of Communist realities. John Michael Montias, in his discussion of economics, adds an interesting argument for this shift. The totalitarian model, he points out, may serve to emphasize the distinction between Communist and Western systems, but it is hardly adequate for a comparison *among* Communist systems. Several of the contributors, most emphatically Chalmers Johnson and Jeremy Azrael, propose instead to classify the Communist regimes as "mobilization systems." This sounds like an improvement, since "mobilization" is by definition a process, an instance of change. Such a perspective, presumably, can envisage far-reaching changes as Communist systems launch upon mobilization, as they proceed with it, and as they accomplish (or perhaps decisively fail to accomplish) it. Whereas different Communist systems may be compared according to their rates of mobilization and the means employed, the term "mobilization system" can also permit comparison between Communist and certain non-Communist countries, such as the single-party states of Africa.[11] Finally, mobilization in the present context has the advantage that, in contrast to modernization, it may be measured in decades instead of in centuries.

Against all this there stands a single disadvantage. The phrase "mobilization system" is one of the many neologisms recently bestowed upon the language with such selfless abandon by my colleagues in sociology and comparative politics. Its usage therefore is perforce unsettled, and today's authors are not in full control of the meaning that the term will convey to their readers some years hence. Or, as a neologist might put it, there is a high probability that its use will correlate negatively with the functional requirements of diachronic interpersonal communication. Still, there is no need to quarrel about words as long as we agree on concepts and perspectives—as I hope my comments on Lowenthal will make clear.

Gordon Skilling departs even further from the totalitarian model in restating, with useful caveats and elucidations, his group perspec-

---

[11] The phrase originated with a leading student of African politics, David Apter, who considers totalitarianism a limiting case—and one empirically not possible—of the mobilization system; see his *Politics of Modernization* (Chicago, 1965), p. 388. Robert C. Tucker, who uses the term movement regimes, also makes clear the African comparison; see his article "Towards a Comparative Politics of Movement-Regimes," *American Political Science Review*, LV: 2 (June 1961), 281–89.

tive on Communist politics. As Alfred Meyer reminds us, the assumption made by some of the theorists of totalitarianism that the Soviet population was an atomized mass rather than a structured society did not stand up to a first examination of the empirical data, notably those supplied by the Harvard refugee interview program. The years of de-Stalinization added further evidence, since that process enhanced both the importance of various organizational or occupational groups and their visibility to the observer. The group approach, aside from its better fit to the Communist facts, can serve to link the study of Communist countries to one of the major bodies of empirical political theory as developed on the basis of American and other Western data.

In the recent literature on comparative politics, the group approach has often yielded to a variety of functional schemes. The well-known study edited by Gabriel Almond and James Coleman, *The Politics of the Developing Areas*, still combined both elements, with each regional chapter offering a section on political groups and political functions.[12] Yet it was the functional part of the treatment that attracted the greater attention.

One may hope, however, that groups as a tool of analysis in comparative politics will have an early revival. Functional categories, such as aggregation, articulation, and mobilization, require a great deal of definition, quibbling, and "operationalization" before they can be applied to the data. Only a subtle and well-trained observer will know a function when he sees it. By contrast, anyone can identify a government official, a soldier, a farmer, a journalist, or a member of a religious or linguistic minority. Hence the group approach saves time by allowing us to get into the empirical data for any one country and hence to proceed to comparisons among countries.

In Skilling's particular group scheme, however, there is one point that requires close attention. He refers to groups such as those just listed as "interest groups," and he distinguishes them from "opinion groups." But actually his interest groups are occupational and demographic categories. Whether the farmers, or trolley-car conductors, or women, or Kalmyks, or Uniates share any political interests is a question that must be settled by empirical research rather than prejudged by analytical categories. It is important, in this context, to keep in mind David Truman's basic distinction between "categoric groups,"

---

[12] This twofold approach represented a compromise among the six authors arrived at in the course of the book's preparation. Almond's emphasis on a "probabilistic theory of the polity" in the introductory chapter represented a subsequent evolution of his thinking.

which are "collections of people with some common characteristic" singled out by the observer, and "groups in the proper sense," which "interact with some frequency on the basis of their shared characteristics."[13]

Just as most of the contributors to this volume have rejected the concept of totalitarianism, so they reject a widespread simplistic notion of social change. Some of the more popular theories of economic development assume that the pattern of economic evolution is unilinear, that there is a single standard sequence of "stages of growth." The metaphor of growth encourages this assumption, and so does the Hegelian and Marxian legacy of philosophic history. But the notion is remarkably widespread even among American social scientists who proudly flaunt their anti-Marxism. To such unilinearism American political scientists and sociologists writing on "political development" have added a second questionable assumption—that political evolution is a surface reflection of underlying economic and social changes. This second notion, too, is part of the Marxist heritage. Yet many of our American colleagues in political sociology cling to it much more tenaciously than do the Marxists—who, since Lenin, have grown fully conscious of the primacy of politics—or, for that matter, the economists, such as Simon Kuznets, Joseph Spengler, Albert Hirschman, and W. Arthur Lewis, who are fully aware of the political basis of economic development.

The contributors to this study are to be commended for avoiding both fallacies, that of unilinearism and that of economicism. Chalmers Johnson in his introduction insists that "although political characteristics can properly be reduced to social or economic characteristics for some purposes, such a procedure would dissolve rather than elucidate the peculiarly political problems of Communist policy-making." (Or as Reinhard Bendix and Seymour Martin Lipset once put it, such reductionism may easily "explain away the very facts of political life.")[14] Azrael rejects explanations that ascribe de-Stalinization to the effect of social and economic pressures. Skilling insists that evolution is multilinear, and his formulation in turn is close to the conception that underlies Lowenthal's masterly comparison of the dynamics of the Communist systems in Russia, Yugoslavia, and China. That conception does not assert—as do some of the totalitarian theorists—that all Communist regimes are alike; nor does it go to the opposite and intellectually sterile extreme of viewing each of them as

---

[13] *The Governmental Process* (New York, 1958), p. 24.
[14] "Political Sociology," *Current Sociology*, VI: 3 (1957), 85, as cited in Dwaine Marvick, ed., *Political Decision-Makers* (New York, 1961), p. 14.

unique. Rather it presents Communist societies as facing a number of similar challenges and responding to them in a number of different ways.

Lowenthal retains the term totalitarianism, but interprets it in a dynamic way. Marxism as reinterpreted and applied by Lenin, Tito, and Mao was a program for transforming the entire society, and the instrument of transformation was to be the party's centralized control over all organized social effort. The challenge that confronted the three experiments consisted in a multiple set of tensions. One basic tension stemmed from the utopian elements in the Marxist vision, which are in conflict with some universal human and social realities. A second tension stemmed from the change of locale: whereas Marx had formulated his diagnosis and his program of action for the most advanced industrial societies, Lenin, Mao, and Tito applied them to countries in the early stages of industrialization. A third tension arose precisely as this gap of industrialization was bridged: the party dictatorship had been developed as an instrument for forcing the economic pace, but now (in Lowenthal's words) the "political system has to respond to the pressures generated by an increasingly advanced society" and therefore grope for some new form of legitimation.

Lowenthal concentrates on the three major countries where Communism developed indigenously. In the countries where Communist regimes were imposed by outside conquest all other tensions are periodically overshadowed by a fourth, that between revolution from outside and the need for indigenous legitimation.

A very similar perspective underlies Alexander Dallin and George Breslauer's more detailed analysis of terror as the most characteristic instrument of the totalitarian attempt at political transformation of the society. Up to a point terror serves the dictatorship's stated goals, but beyond this point there is a clash of means and ends. Furthermore, the ends themselves are in conflict with underlying realities. The Communist claim to reshape human nature and human society at will rests on an unwarranted assumption of man's indefinite malleability. And the correlate of that assumption becomes a Faustian delusion of omnipotence on the part of the Communist leaders.

What several of the contributors here have done is to restore purpose to a central place in their analysis of Communism. This renewed emphasis on purpose is remarkable in two respects: it meets Marxism more nearly on its own philosophic ground, and it overcomes a severe limitation of the behaviorist analysis of society. Each of these points deserves brief elaboration.

It is hard to imagine how a movement as self-consciously purposeful as Marxism could be analyzed without regard to purpose. Yet Western non-Marxist critics all too often have dealt with Communist aims only under the somewhat misleading heading of ideology. Now it is worth remembering that "ideologue" originated as an epithet, applied by Napoleon to Madame de Staël's circle, and that Marx and Engels themselves continued to use "ideology" in that same derogatory sense, most notably in their tract against the Hegelian Left entitled *The German Ideology*. The gravest reproach that Marx brought against the ideologues of his own day was precisely that they ignored the fundamental relationship between thought and action. "The philosophers have only interpreted the world in various ways," Marx sneered; "the point is to change it." His own ambition was to change the world not on the basis of just another arbitrary, metaphysical, and subjective interpretation. Rather it was the scientific interpretation of society, grounded in logical concept and empirical observation, that was to furnish the first valid guide to social action. Some years ago, Alfred Meyer made this point succinctly by entitling his book *Marxism: The Unity of Theory and Practice*. To apply the ideological label to Marxism itself not only amounts to a subtle insult. It also generally reveals the critics' deep-seated skepticism about the possibility of scientific understanding of society and of rational action based upon it. All that remains therefore are subjective values, personal attitudes, irrational beliefs, and arbitrary moods—in short, ideology. Starting from such a prejudice, American authors have often been unable to appreciate the deep seriousness with which Marxian views are held by Communists—a seriousness not contradicted but rather confirmed by the intensity of their doctrinal and exegetic quarrels.

What seems to me implicit in the chapters by Lowenthal and others is a broader view: that a scientific understanding of society, and a critique of social action based on it, are indeed possible; that Marx made some of the first major contributions to such an endeavor; and that a century later we can more readily see some of the fatal limitations in his scheme, such as his rigid determinism and his utopianism with regard to the sequel of revolution.

Implicit also in such reasoning is a view of empirical evidence that goes beyond that common in "behavioral science." Under the influence of John B. Watson's behavioral psychology, American social science as a whole has for some time now been hostile to the notion of purpose as a central element in social and political reality. Science, it is widely held, must be based on replicable and quantifiable observations of overt behavior. Watson himself developed his theory on the basis of his observation of starving rats, whose purpose to keep alive was constant and single-minded and hence could be factored out of the equation. Since then human purposes have been readmitted to the behaviorist scheme through the back door of "verbal behavior," ascertained in attitude surveys that readily can be quantified although their replicability remains dubious. Moreover, as Robert Dahl has suggested, social scientists of the behaviorist persuasion have abandoned some of their militant zeal just because their insistence on empirical evidence, clear definition, and quantitative measurement has been so widely accepted.[15] Perhaps it is time, therefore, to readmit human purposes through the front door of social science analysis. Indeed, if Hobbes's definition is accurate (and I cannot think of any contemporary one that improves on it) the political actor's purpose— his "future apparent good"—must be taken into account in assessing power itself, the most fundamental of political concepts.

Once we have restored the actor's purpose to political science discourse, we have several ready clues for the analysis of political change. Most political actions are deliberately aimed at change. The initiative in politics is typically taken by those who are dissatisfied with the current state of affairs. They impose a newly written constitution on a hereditary monarch to curtail his autocratic powers. They establish a new party in order to represent interests that have so far been neglected within the political process. They form pressure groups in order to secure legislation more favorable to various business interests. They organize trade unions so as to secure for the workers a larger share of the economic returns of society. They propose a parliamentary motion of censure or plan a conspiratorial coup to bring down the government.

There are two possible sequels of political action aimed at change. It either succeeds or fails. The nature of the original political activity is transformed in either case. The transformation of a successful political action or movement is almost automatic: a goal attained need no longer be pursued, an innovation repeated is no longer new. The successful organization therefore must either disband or find a new purpose.

Take the opposite case of a political action or movement that fails.

[15] "The Behavioral Approach in Political Science: Epitaph for a Monument to a Successful Protest," *American Political Science Review*, LV: 4 (Dec. 1961), 753–72.

It too may dissolve because it gives up the attempt, or else it may persist in talking about the same aims without being able actively to pursue them. Once again the choice is between death and survival through change—in this case change from a meaningful political plan to an empty political incantation. The revolutionary phraseology of Marxist parties, whether under the Hohenzollern empire or under the present French and Italian republics, provides a perfect illustration.

One kind of intentional political change of major importance is accession to power, and here again success itself automatically and necessarily transforms the nature of the enterprise. Once the seizure of power has succeeded, the task is no longer to seize power but to retain it. The contrast between the forces that bring a given form of government into existence and the forces that maintain that same form is sharp and clear whatever the particular regime. For example, postcolonial states originate in militant anticolonial nationalism but survive through careful management of their economic and foreign policy programs. Military regimes typically result from secret plotting and armed revolt but endure as they obtain a wider basis of support and alliance with civilian bureaucrats or a political party. Charismatic leaders, according to Weber, establish their credentials by performing seeming miracles but preserve their legitimacy through routinization and bureaucratization. An absolute monarchy is best sustained by unquestioned acceptance of tradition and heredity but evidently cannot be newly founded on the same principle. Democracy arises through conflict and compromise but survives by virtue of growing consensus. Similarly, Communist regimes, which have been installed by revolutionary elites or by conquest from abroad, consolidate their rule through the growth of a domestic mass party and of its bureaucracy.

There is a similar and often rather abrupt change in the careers of individual political leaders, setting firm limits to the possibilities of a purely psychological interpretation of the leader's performance. An American politician, for example, must obey very different tactical imperatives in winning his party's presidential nomination, in getting himself elected to the presidency, and finally in exercising executive power from the White House. A Communist leader, similarly, must behave differently as a party subaltern rising through the ranks, as one of the contenders in a succession struggle, and as the dictator who has finally made it to the top.

Succession struggles, of course, are a vivid reminder of a change that is greater than politics, rooted as it is ultimately in man's mortality. In streamlined and centralized dictatorships, such as those set up by the Communists, this type of change becomes a factor of prime importance. The Communist world still has not found any new balance after the upheavals that accompanied and followed Stalin's death, and surely the disappearance of veteran leaders such as Tito and Mao is likely to inject a highly dynamic factor into the Yugoslav and Chinese situations.[16]

One of the many memoranda that the contributors to this volume considered during their meeting in the summer of 1968 dealt with the situation in Czechoslovakia as of mid-August. The Czech developments, the author held, had proved conclusively that all Communist systems are subject to inexorable changes toward liberalization and pluralism. Similar memoranda probably were circulating at that very time in the Kremlin—although where our colleague spoke of liberalization and pluralism these documents more likely spoke of counterrevolution and reaction. But terminology aside, there must have been two other crucial differences. The American memorandum was making a single, unilinear generalization and hence implying a flat prediction. The Kremlin presumably thought in terms of contingent predictions, that is of alternatives and choices. Unless such and such steps are taken, the Russian memoranda must have said, there will be an even faster drift toward counterrevolution. And whereas the American analysis was concerned chiefly with the parallel evolution of Communist regimes considered as domestic political and social systems, the men in the Kremlin were sure to be keenly aware of the ties between international and domestic realities. Unless the Czechs are forcibly restrained, the Kremlin hawks must have asked, how can we control our own restless intelligentsia?

One may hope that some of the perspectives on political change implicit in this volume will be elaborated with regard to Communist and non-Communist countries. But in proceeding with this elaboration we must remember that political change is not just multilinear. Much of it is fashioned by men who can exercise a choice between these multiple cases of evolution. It is the social scientist's function to ascertain the margin of human choice and to clarify the choices in that margin.[17]

---

[16] See Dankwart A. Rustow, "Succession in the Twentieth Century," *Journal of International Affairs*, XVIII: 1 (Winter 1964).
[17] Rustow, *A World of Nations*, p. 17.

Index

Index